Managing Conflict through Communication

2 → 8q

3 → 3q

4 → 5q

5 → 7q

6 → 4q

7 → 5q

8 → 6q

10 → 5q

12 → 12q

Spousal Abuse
CH4
5q

60 total
Questroo

THIRD EDITION

Managing Conflict through Communication

Dudley D. Cahn

State University of New York, New Paltz

Ruth Anna Abigail

Azusa Pacific University

Boston ■ New York ■ San Francisco
Mexico City ■ Montreal ■ Toronto ■ London ■ Madrid ■ Munich ■ Paris
Hong Kong ■ Singapore ■ Tokyo ■ Cape Town ■ Sydney

Editor-in-Chief: *Karon Bowers*
Series Editor: *Brian Wheel*
Editorial Assistant: *Jenny Lupica*
Marketing Manager: *Suzan Czajkowski*
Senior Production Administrator: *Donna Simons*
Cover Administrator: *Elena Sidorova*
Composition Buyer: *Linda Cox*
Manufacturing Buyer: *JoAnne Sweeney*
Editorial-Production Service: *Omegatype Typography, Inc.*
Electronic Composition: *Omegatype Typography, Inc.*

For related titles and support materials, visit our online catalog at www.ablongman.com.

Between the time website information is gathered and then published, it is not unusual for some sites to have closed. Also, the transcription of URLs can result in typographical errors. The publisher would appreciate notification where these errors occur so that they may be corrected in subsequent editions.

Library of Congress Cataloging-in-Publication Data

Cahn, Dudley D.
    Managing conflict through communication / Dudley D. Cahn, Ruth Anna Abigail. — 3rd ed.
        p.   cm.
    Rev. ed. of: Conflict / Roxane S. Lulofs, Dudley D. Cahn. 2nd ed. c2000.
    Includes bibliographical references and index.
    ISBN 0-205-45880-7 (pbk.)
        1. Conflict (Psychology)—Textbooks.   2. Interpersonal conflict—Textbooks.   3. Conflict management—Textbooks.   I. Abigail, Ruth Anna.   II. Lulofs, Roxane Salyer. Conflict.   III. Title.

    BF637.I48L85   2007
    303.6—dc22

                                                                    2005056117

Printed in the United States of America

10 9 8 7 6 5 4 3 2 1   10 09 08 07 06

Photo Credits: p. 29 © Larry Fleming/Pearson Education/PH College; p. 51 © Marc Anderson/ Pearson Education/PH College; p. 82 © Shirley Zeiberg/Pearson Education/PH College; and p. 263 courtesy of Gordon A. Jorgenson III; all other photos are courtesy of Ruth Anna Abigail.

CONTENTS

Preface   xiii

P A R T I   **Understanding and Responding to Conflict**   1

1 Introduction to the Study of Conflict   1

Defining Interpersonal Conflict   2

Negative View of Conflict   6

The Inevitability of Conflict   9
Conflict Is a Fact of Life   9
Interpersonal Violence Is Not a Fact of Life   11

Defining Conflict Management   12

Conflict Communication as Productive or Destructive   14

Manage It   17

2 Types of Conflicts   22

Unreal Conflicts   23
False Conflicts   23
Displaced Conflicts   25
Misplaced Conflicts   25

Real Conflicts   26
Competitive Situations   29
Interpersonal Violence   31
Issues in Conflicts   32

Manage It   36

3 Responding to Conflict: The S-TLC System   40

The S-TLC System   41

Stopping: Taking Time Out 42

Thinking about the Conflict: Analyzing Conflict Situations 42
Thinking about Changing the Other Person, Situation, or Self 43
Thinking about Your Goals 46
Trained Incapacities 46
Mind-Mapping Approach 48

Listening in Conflict Situations 50

Communicating in Conflict Situations 52
The "Linear" Model: Message Senders and Receivers 52
The "Transactional" Model: People Communicating Together 53

Manage It 55

4 Communication Options in Conflict Situations 58

Nonassertive Communication Behavior as an Option 60

Aggressive Communication Behavior as an Option 61
Verbal Aggression 63
Nonverbal Aggression (Physical Violence) 63

Passive-Aggressive Communication as an Option 65

Assertive Communication Behavior as an Option 66

Communication Considerations: Which Conflict Communication Option Is Best? 70
The Occasion (Including Time and Location) 71
The Other Person 71
Your Needs 71

Manage It 72

5 Conflict Styles, Strategies, and Tactics 77

Conflict Styles versus Strategies 78

Conflict Strategies and Tactics 80

Collaboration: The Preferred Conflict Strategy 83
Low Personal and Relationship Stress 84

High Personal and Relationship Growth and Satisfaction   86

Phases of Collaboration   87

Manage It   91

6 **Effectively Confronting Others   95**

Confrontation as a Conflict Communication Skill   96

**The Confrontation Ritual: Six Steps to Successful
Interpersonal Conflict Resolution   97**

Preparation: Identify Your Problem/Needs/Issues   98

Tell the Person "We Need to Talk"   99

Interpersonal Confrontation: Talk to the Other about Your Problem   99

Consider Your Partner's Point of View   102

Resolve the Problem: Come to a Mutual Understanding and Reach an
Agreement   104

Follow Up on the Solution: Set a Time Limit for Re-Evaluation   104

Doing Conflict Messages   104

General Tips on Being Assertive   104

Using I-Statements   105

Components of I-Statements   108

Advantages of Using I-Statements   110

Challenges Associated with I-Statements   110

Manage It   111

7 **Cooperative Negotiation in Win–Lose Conflicts   116**

Negotiation Basics   117

Competitive Negotiation   118

Cooperative Negotiation   119

Some Research on Tactics and Strategies in Negotiation   119

Concessions   119

Threats   120

Principled Negotiation   121

Separate People from the Problem   121

Focus on Interests Rather Than Positions   122

Generate More Options   122
Base Decisions on Objective Criteria   127

Converting Competitive Negotiation into Cooperation   127
Seeking Commonalities   127
Talking Cooperation   128
Consulting before Acting   128
Communicating Frequently   128
Controlling the Process, Not the Outcome   128
Thinking Positively   128
Considering Your BATNA   129
Engaging in Fractionation   129

Manage It   129

P A R T I I   Theoretical Perspectives on Managing Conflicts   134

8   Social-Psychological Perspectives of Conflict   134

Intrapersonal Theories of Conflict   135
Psychodynamic Theory   135
Attribution Theory   138
Uncertainty Theory   141

Relationship Theories of Conflict   143
Social Exchange Theory   143
Systems Theory   147

Manage It   149

9   A Process View of Conflict: Phases, Stages, and Cycles   152

Phase Theories of Conflict   153

Patterns and Cycles in Constructive Conflict Processes   155
Prelude to Conflict   155
The Triggering Event   158
The Initiation Phase   159
The Differentiation Phase   159
The Resolution Phase   161

Patterns and Cycles in Destructive Conflict Processes   163
  The Confrontation Avoidance Cycle   164
  The "Chilling Effect": A Diminished Communication Cycle   167
  The Competitive Conflict Escalation Cycle   169

Manage It   172

10   Conflict Climate: Power, Distrust, and Defensiveness   177

Power Imbalance versus Equality   178
  Giving the Less Powerful More Power   180
  Combining Forces to Manage the Conflict   183
  Giving Power to the Relationship Itself   184

Distrust versus Trust   184

Supportive Behavior versus Defensive Behavior   188

Manage It   191

11   The Escalation of Conflict: Stress and Anger   196

Stress and the Escalation of Conflict   197
  Sources of Stress   199
  Responses to Stress   199
  The Impact of Stress on Conflict   203

The Process of Anger   205
  Dealing with Our Own Anger: Three Processes   205
  Before Expressing Anger   207
  Expressing Anger Effectively   208
  Anger as a Secondary Emotion   210
  Responding to Another's Anger   211

Manage It   211

12   Impression Management in Conflict Situations   215

Understanding the Demands of Face   216
  Defining Face   216
  Positive and Autonomous Face   217

Preventive Facework   218

Supportive Facework 220

Corrective Facework 221
  Repair Rituals 222
  Responding to Others 224

Manage It 225

13 After the Conflict: Forgiveness and Reconciliation 229

Relational Transgressions 230

The Role of Forgiveness and Reconciliation in Conflicts 232

Dimensions of Forgiveness 232
  Forgiveness Is Not a New Concept 234
  Why Don't People Forgive? 234
  Advantages of Forgiveness 235
  Moving beyond Victimization 237

Past Forgiveness: Reconciliation 239
  Steps to Reconciliation 239

Manage It 245

14 Mediation as Third-Party Intervention 250

Alternatives to Dispute Resolution 251

Formal versus Informal Mediation 252

The Role of the Mediator 253

Mediators as Communication Rules Enforcers 255

The Mediation Process: Step by Step 256
  The Intake Process 256
  Opening Statement 257
  Describing the Dispute 259
  Common Ground 260
  Final Agreement 261
  Ending the Mediation 263

Manage It 264

Afterword:　The Ideal Conflict Manager　268

　　Conflict Proneness　268

　　　　Developing a Playful Spirit　270

　　Conflict Management Principles　271

Answers　283

Glossary　285

References　297

Index　315

PREFACE

Although many people may not admit it, most people encounter conflict quite frequently. These conflicts typically occur between friends, spouses, dating partners, colleagues at work, and family members. Yet people tend to feel negatively about conflict and do not handle confrontations well. We believe that the common mismanagement of conflict explains the bad name given to the subject. We intend to help you learn more constructive attitudes and positive conflict management and resolution skills so that you feel less apprehensive about engaging in interpersonal conflict and better able to manage and resolve it.

Conflict is one of the grand challenges of our time. It occurs because there are deep divisions in our society that carry over into our interpersonal relationships. There are cultural divides between ethnic, racial, and religious groups. There are political and value barriers that separate conservatives and liberals. There are gender gaps between the sexes. There are economic and power divides between upper and lower economic and social classes. There are age barriers between younger and older citizens. Although these divides carry over into interpersonal relations, people of similar backgrounds also find differences difficult to overcome.

Where there is a divide, we must look for bridges. A common bridge for barriers in interpersonal relations is communication. As a first step in communicating, the conflicting parties must meet to deal with the issues that divide them. They must take time out of their busy schedules, spend money and allocate often limited resources, pay attention to matters they consider unimportant, and listen to people they would like to ignore. In so doing the conflicting parties create or repair channels of communication that lay a foundation for bridging the gap that separates them. Sometimes it takes outside intervention to bring the conflicting parties together.

Meeting together and paying attention to the issues and to each other is an important first step, but more is needed. In the next step, the conflicting parties must communicate. How do they communicate? What do they say? How do they say it? Communication scholars have thoroughly researched the communication processes in conflict situations, and thus have a great deal to offer students interested in studying conflict.

First, communication as a discipline offers a wide variety of pedagogical tools for successfully managing conflict situations. Communication textbooks provide general principles and skills that are applicable to conflict situations. Many, like this one, analyze specific common problems and issues to teach you how to manage conflicts in your everyday life. Our goal is to add to your communication competence. After learning what is effective, students are often amazed at how a change in behavior can produce such dramatic results. They are pleased to discover that they can learn something useful and desirable in a communication course that studies conflict management.

Second, communication scholars are sensitive to ethical concerns as they create solutions to challenges such as conflict. They are not only interested in what works in conflict situations, but what is appropriate. They want everyone to have input, to have an equal say in the decisions that affect them, and to create mutually satisfying solutions to their problems—nonviolent solutions that they can live with and continue to support. This may require a moral change in addition to behavioral changes, so that conflicting parties learn to respect each other and work together in ethical ways to produce morally sound agreements.

Third, many communication scholars view communication, conflict, anger, mediation, and negotiation as processes. A process is dynamic, ongoing, and ever-changing. It evolves through steps or stages. Taking a process view of conflict helps students like you to better understand the way conflict changes over time—often escalating or getting out of hand—so that you can take concrete steps to change the direction of your own conflicts and intervene in the conflicts of others.

Fourth, communication researchers study the role of stress and negative attitudes as key contributors to conflict, anger as an escalator of conflict, and emotional residues as barriers to reconciliation. These psychological factors are as important as the social and physical behavior of the conflicting parties.

Taking into consideration the communication discipline's contributions, the purpose of this textbook is to apply a communication approach to the study of conflict. Although the challenge of conflict initially appears enormous, the subject is divisible into manageable parts or learning modules. Moreover, as a discipline, communication has identified many principles and techniques that prevent conflicts from resulting in serious damage to the parties involved. Some of these principles and techniques are preventive in nature; others repair channels of communication and restore relations. To this end, we offer *Managing Conflict through Communication,* the third edition of Lulofs and Cahn's earlier work, *Conflict: From Theory to Action* (Second Edition, 2000), as a primary text for undergraduate college courses in interpersonal communication and conflict management.

This new edition is updated to reflect advances in the communication study of conflict. As college teachers we are sensitive to the assessment movement taking place in higher education. Although we do not want to reduce the subject of conflict to mere behavior techniques, we do wish to change the underlying logic of previous editions of this textbook by placing greater emphasis in this edition on the practical applications of our ideas for effective management of conflict. We view each chapter as a learning module, beginning with specific objectives, followed by instruction containing a summary clearly tied to the opening objectives, and finally ending with rubrics, or practical exercises, that capture the key ideas in the chapter. Our thinking is that successfully completing the rubrics is an indication that our students have mastered the content.

In addition, after using this text in our own classes, we have made many changes in the content to increase readability, clarity, and reader interest. Students like you want to know exactly how to confront someone they know personally and how to better manage their present conflicts. They want to know specifically what to say and exactly how to say it. Part I responds to students' need to learn immediately how to effectively deal with problems and issues by introducing the S-TLC (stop, think, listen, and communicate) system for responding to conflict and six steps to successful confrontation. Part I presents an elementary theory of conflict that enables students to identify different types of conflict situations that require different ways of responding, depending on the situation.

Although Part I describes preferred ways to manage conflicts, a number of factors may escalate the conflict and require more advanced management techniques. Part II explains advanced concepts and techniques that further your skills at managing and resolving interpersonal conflicts in light of potential escalating factors. In addition to introducing you to the process nature of conflict and the role emotion plays in escalating conflict, this part of the textbook tackles more difficult management skills and techniques, like stress and anger management, face saving, conflict climate, forgiveness/reconciliation, and mediation. In Part II, a more advanced theory of conflict builds on the earlier chapters to better enable you to identify different processes that escalate or de-escalate conflict. The textbook concludes with an afterword on the Ideal Conflict Manager, which summarizes the key techniques and principles described in earlier chapters.

As you use this book, remember that conflict often results in personal change. Expect to question thoughts, feelings, and behaviors that you have taken for granted in the past and to add new ideas and actions to your ways of thinking and behaving.

Acknowledgments

The most important people for us to thank are the students who have used the first two editions of the book and have given us great feedback about its utility. We also want to thank all the students who permitted us to use their stories in illustrating the concepts in this book.

We would like to thank the reviewers of the third edition: Mary L. Mohan, State University of New York at Geneseo and Gerald L. Wilson, University of South Alabama.

I (Lee) have my students to thank for the new edition of this textbook. This is probably due to the fact that I teach this course entirely online at SUNY New Paltz, which is quite a different experience from teaching face to face. Students seem more open to express themselves online, revealing what they don't know as much as what they do. From their comments, I was able to determine their needs and problems in reading the assignments and discussing the key ideas. I found myself explaining more and revising parts of our early textbook on conflict to respond to these discoveries. In addition, students offered insights and supplied the class with numerous examples of conflicts in their lives, which broadened my perspective along with the class. Finally, some students did not hesitate to make suggestions directly to me. Thanks to my many students' input and encouragement, the end result is a clearer work with a broader perspective than our earlier textbook.

Although students encouraged us to create a new and clear edition of a conflict textbook, there are those who work at SUNY New Paltz, where I teach, who encouraged my scholarly pursuits, especially my previous department chairs Rob Miraldi and Lynn Spangler as well as my colleagues Janice Anderson and Mary Kuhl. I hasten to express my appreciation to my current department chair, Patricia Sullivan, and our Dean, Jerry Benjamin, for their support of my travel requests and a sabbatical leave.

As I have done in earlier works, I would like to express my appreciation to the many scholars who have shared with me their ideas, criticisms, and suggestions on the books I have written on conflict. Among them (in alphabetical order) are William Benoit, Charles Brown, Nancy Burrell, Daniel Canary, Donald Cushman, Clare Danielsson, Steve Duck, Sally Lloyd, Michael Roloff, Stella Ting-Toomey, Dolf Zillmann, and my co-author Ruth Anna Abigail. I have been most fortunate to know them all and work with them on the subject of conflict.

Like many other authors, I have my spouse to thank for her patience, understanding, and willingness to put up with my mood swings and the occasional fuzziness she could see in my eyes as I would swing from attention to inattention, which occurred as I reflected on what I had recently written or realized what I should have written instead. Sharon has strongly encouraged my writing efforts and allowed me a lot of time and the necessary space to accomplish this project like she did for the ones before. I appreciate the fact that, while we have learned how to collaborate as our marriage evolved, she did not see this project as an issue for a family conflict.

First and foremost, I (Ruth Anna, formerly Roxane S. Lulofs) wish to thank Lee for getting this project started. If not for his efforts, this edition would still be a figment of our imaginations. He has labored hard to rethink the chapter structures and incorporate new ideas into this text.

I would like to thank the members of my department, the Center for Adult and Professional Studies at Azusa Pacific University, who have all been a great support to me in my scholarly endeavors, particularly Fred Garlett, CAPS director. Cathy Heffernan and Stephanie Fenwick, my departmental colleagues/friends/partners-in-subversion, have especially been a great support to me as I have juggled my CAPS and general faculty duties with the production of this textbook, as well as becoming as close to me as sisters. Likewise, Murray Flagg and Doug Campbell have been the best two brothers I have ever had—I could vent, discuss, question, or cry with them, dump a class on them that I couldn't teach, and escape for a cup of coffee with them. The emails I receive from Helen Sterk from Calvin College have also served to motivate me when I didn't want to work, and lunch with Ginny Carter always came just at the right time.

In addition, I would like to acknowledge my intellectual debt to several great teachers I have encountered in my quest for lifelong learning: Thomas Frentz, W. Barnett Pearce, Stephen Littlejohn, Lawrence Frey, and Marsha Fowler. The classes and seminars I took with these scholars have impacted my thinking immensely.

I thank the many students who used previous editions of this text and made suggestions for improvement, as well as those who shared their conflict stories and art with us.

On a personal note, I thank my husband, Bogdan Mulka, for rekindling my belief in "happily-ever-afters," his family for welcoming me with open hearts, and my children, Kathy and David Lulofs, and my sister, Vicki Salyer McGuire, for reminding me about what is important in life.

1

Introduction to the Study of Conflict

OBJECTIVES

At the end of this chapter, you should be able to:

- Define interpersonal conflict and give examples of conflict situations.
- Explain why many people view conflict negatively.
- Explain why conflict is a fact of life.

- Explain why violence is not a fact of life.
- Define conflict management and give examples.
- Explain how conflict management has the potential to convert potentially destructive interpersonal conflicts into productive ones.

KEY TERMS

adverse effects
conflict management
conflict metaphor
conflict resolution
destructive conflict
equifinality
incompatible goals

incompatible means
inevitability of conflict principle
interdependence
interpersonal conflicts
interpersonal violence
meta-conflict perspective
negative view of conflict

outcomes
perception
positive view of conflict
problematic situation
process view of conflict
productive conflict
sense of urgency

For the longest time, I thought conflict was like having a big wave come at me on the beach. If I moved fast enough, I might be able to dive under it. Sometimes I could just stand my ground against it. And other times, it knocked me on my rear. But until recently, I didn't really think I could ride that wave, to turn it into something useful. I'm not sure I can do that with all my conflicts—I am better off diving under some, but they don't knock me down as often as they used to.

If you are like most people, you probably would rather not have conflict knock you down or cause you to go diving to avoid it. On the contrary, you probably want to know exactly how to confront someone you know personally and how to better handle your present conflicts. You want to know specifically what you can say and exactly how you can say it. To meet this need, we designed Part I to teach you how to use effective communication behavior to manage your everyday conflicts. We believe that if you learn how to apply basic conflict management principles in conflicts while in college, you may continue to use these ideas and techniques after you graduate in your future partnerships, family, work, and other important interpersonal relationships.

In this first chapter of Part I, we introduce you to the study of a subject that is as common as getting up in the morning: dealing with conflict in our everyday lives. Most of us are able to recognize when we are in a conflict. If a friend says, "We need to talk," we know a different situation exists than "I need to talk to you." If a friend needs to talk to us, we can act as a sounding board or a source of advice, but when a friend says, "we need to talk," we usually know there's a problem, and the problem includes us.

In this chapter we define interpersonal conflict and discuss some of the different ways people view it. We believe that conflict is not simply a part of life, *conflict is life as usual.* People regularly experience times when their wants and desires are contradictory to the wants and desires of people important to them. Just as important, we can see no reason for conflicts to ever evolve into violent behavior. Conflicts exist as a fact of life, but we believe violence does not. In addition to defining interpersonal conflict, we also define conflict management and explain how to convert destructive conflicts into productive ones. These ideas make it worth your time and effort to learn how to more effectively manage your interpersonal conflicts.

1.1 Think about It

Author Hilaire Belloc said in *The Silence of the Sea* that "All men have an instinct for conflict: at least, all healthy men."[1] Why do you suppose he claims this? How can an instinct for conflict be healthy?

Defining Interpersonal Conflict

First, we need to separate interpersonal conflict from the other kinds of conflict often studied in college level communication courses. Some conflict situations involve people with whom we have some sort of important relationship (friends, romantic partners, family members, and colleagues at work), so we call these **interpersonal conflicts.** These conflicts are over more personal matters and involve people we care about. Other kinds of conflicts exist, too. There are cases where several people, who may or may not have prior relationships, attempt to resolve an issue, make a decision, or solve some problem (group, departmental, and organizational conflicts), so we call these intragroup conflicts or just group conflicts. These conflicts typically involve a group or organizational culture that may facilitate or hinder the resolution of conflicts. Finally, other cases occur where one group of people attempts to resolve an issue or solve some problem with another group of people (racial, ethnic, cultural, and international conflict), so we call these intergroup conflicts. Such conflicts may involve the intervention of third parties such as translators, mediators, arbitrators, or conciliators and a thorough understanding of two or more unique cultures. In this text we focus on interpersonal conflicts because they are common to all of us and our approach to handling them may have far reaching consequences for us.

Second, we should note that English-speaking people use many different terms as synonyms for interpersonal conflict or their experience of it: confrontation, verbal argument, disagreement, differences of opinion, avoidance of confrontation, avoiding others, changing the topic, problem-solving discussion, interpersonal violence, physical abuse, sexual abuse, verbal abuse, silent treatment, stonewalling, glaring at one another, making obscene gestures, expressions of anger, hostile reactions, ignoring the other, unhappy relationships, simply giving in, accommodating, going along reluctantly, not making waves, competition, negotiation, bargaining, mediation, disputing, quarreling, threatening, and insulting. Even though this is a long list, you can probably add to it. Because there are so many events people refer to as conflict, we think it is important that we have a common reference point as we begin this text in the form of a definition for interpersonal conflict.

Finally, we spell out our definition. Unlike many other textbooks on conflict, we prefer to define interpersonal conflict as a **problematic situation** with the following four unique characteristics:

1. the conflicting parties are interdependent,
2. they have the perception that they seek incompatible goals or outcomes or they favor incompatible means to the same ends,
3. the perceived incompatibility has the potential to adversely affect the relationship if not addressed, and
4. there is a sense of urgency about the need to resolve the difference.

If you are like a lot of us, when you first read a definition of a key term, you don't realize all that the definition entails. So, let's consider what is interesting, unique, and useful about the way we define interpersonal conflict. First, our definition focuses on problematic situations. A *situation* exists where there are people who play out particular roles in a given context that consists of a familiar setting at a particular time. Many situations tend to recur, so we experience a déjà vu feeling like "we were here before." Buying lunch at a fast food restaurant is a situation on a small scale; interviewing for a job is a situation on a larger scale. Conflicts are situations that generally exist somewhere between these two examples. Situations become *problematic* when partners perceive that they seek different outcomes or they favor different means to the same ends. Experts often view conflict as two or more competing responses to a single event, differences between and among individuals, mutual hostility between them, or a problem needing resolution.[2]

Instead of focusing on the situation, many other conflict textbook authors define interpersonal conflict as an "expressed struggle"[3] or "conflict interaction,"[4] suggesting that it consists of visible interaction, a communication pattern, or a verbal exchange, but we recognize that some conflicts are not overt, apparent, or open. Just as one can claim that "we cannot not communicate," a conflict may exist even when people are not arguing or even talking to each other. We can recognize that we are experiencing a conflict long before we actually say or do anything about it. By emphasizing the notion of a conflict situation, we can include people who are not speaking to each other, purposively avoiding contact, giving each other the silent treatment, using nonverbal displays to indicate conflict, or who are sending mixed messages to each other. For example, one study found that when people experienced negative emotions, they became more evasive and equivocal. Thus, it is likely that when people are first thinking about a conflict, they may not even say anything about it; rather, they may evade the topic or communicate about it in ambivalent terms.[5] A related study also found that women who have a hard time expressing emotion tend to display more negative facial expressions while displaying fewer positive facial expressions that endured for short periods. These expressions in turn increased men's negative feelings and anxiety levels.[6]

Recognizing these conflict situations should help you understand the many avoidance strategies people often use when in a conflict situation. Moreover, our definition reveals that many different types of conflict situations exist rather than just one. In Chapter 2, we describe those different types of conflict situations. Recognizing conflict types should help you understand your interpersonal conflicts so that you can choose strategies and tactics that are most appropriate for dealing with the conflict.

1.2 Think about It

Overall, would you say you are a person who deals with conflict fairly easily or one who finds conflict difficult? What makes it difficult or easy? What prompted you to take a class in conflict management?

Second, by emphasizing the interdependence between or among the conflicting parties, we focus on conflict in interpersonal relationships. **Interdependence** occurs when those involved in a relationship characterize it as important and worth the effort to maintain. We underscore the fact that interpersonal conflicts occur with people who are important to us. Not only are we in an important relationship with the other person, but we want to maintain that important relationship. We may argue with a stranger, have a difficult time returning a defective product to a store, or endure the bad driving habits of another on the road, but these are not examples of interpersonal conflict because the conflicting parties are not interdependent; they have no interpersonal relationship. Some of the skills involved with arguments with strangers overlap the skills taught in this book. If you have to return a product to a store, for example, and you expect resistance or difficulty, explaining the situation carefully using the skills outlined in later chapters should boost your chances of success. However, we don't befriend, love, or intend to live with everyone we meet. While this doesn't give us permission to act irresponsibly, it frees us from thinking that we have to worry about our relationship with a person we don't know, as this narrative illustrates:

> I accidentally locked my baby in the car. It was so stupid—I realized just as the door latched that my purse was on the seat and my keys were in the purse. I panicked, but a kind person called the fire department, which will come and open a car under those conditions. A crowd gathered round the car while they were trying to find the "Slim Jim" to unlock it, and this couple parked nearby. They approached the crowd, looked in my car, and said "There's a

baby in there!" Then the woman looked up at me and said, "Someone ought to kick you in the ass!" and walked away. I was dumbfounded. All I could say was, "That was unnecessary." The fireman working on my car patted me on the shoulder and told me to ignore them—that everyone made mistakes. But it still hurt to have someone attack me like that.

Because the above writer is unlikely to have anything to do with the other woman in the future, there is an option to ignore her comments and walk away. But imagine if a good friend had told her something similar. She probably would feel a need to address the other's judgment.

Most conflict definitions emphasize the role of perception in conflict. **Perception** is the process in which we make sense of what we see and hear. Conflicts arise when people think there is an incompatibility or "divergence of interest . . . a belief that [their] current aspirations cannot be achieved simultaneously,"[7] or that their activities or goals are incompatible with those of the other party. This often encompasses a feeling on the part of one person that another has violated expectations for the relationship but has failed to account for that violation. The idea of incompatible goals or means is central to definitions of conflict. **Incompatible goals** occur when we are seeking different outcomes; for example, we each want to buy a different car but we can only afford to buy one. **Incompatible means** occur when we want to achieve the same goal but differ in how we should do so; for example, we agree on the same car, but not on whether to finance it or pay cash. Incompatible goals and means can create the perception that the other is frustrating one's attempts to achieve something, or they may create a perception of relationship violation. Simons argued that conflicts are more serious than simple disagreements or differences of opinions because in conflict people believe another threatens their interests.[8] What we want to emphasize is this: Whether or not people's perceptions of the conflict situation are accurate, until they are able to confirm or change those perceptions, they act as though they are real. Our perceptions drive our view of reality, and, sometimes, they drive us quite poorly! Thus, it is vital that we learn to assess our perceptions for their truthfulness, checking them against the facts and then choosing our actions wisely.

Third, the conflicts that interest us most are those that could have adverse effects on the relationship if we do not manage the situation effectively. **Adverse effects** are like stains on the relationship—they are noticeable and make people uncomfortable and dissatisfied with the relationship. If people dominate their partners and always win their arguments, the partners may feel unhappy and look for more satisfying relationships elsewhere. If conflicts leave people feeling dissatisfied, they may refuse to forgive, seek revenge, and become abusive. If people feel helpless in a relationship, they may grow apathetic, uncaring, or lose interest in it. If people avoid dealing with issues, their relationship may lack positive outcomes because problems are not getting resolved. The point is that our relationships generally deteriorate when we manage them poorly. Most people in a relationship would rather look for opportunities to make their partners feel better and cause the relationship to grow. But if they perceive that they cannot do that, they may look elsewhere for relational satisfaction.

Conflicts between relational partners may or may not adversely affect their relationship. They may engage in a difference of opinion over some "public issue," such as healthcare, a war overseas, or welfare, or they may argue over more "personal issues" that are tied directly to their relationship, such as trust, jealousy, or time spent together or apart.[9] Obviously, the latter have more potential adverse effects for their relationship than the former. Although some problems or issues need resolution for the sake of a relationship, how partners handle the conflict almost always has consequences for them. "Winning or losing a conflict may be relatively inconsequential compared to how we communicate during the conflict."[10] We can choose to handle a conflict in a way that improves our relationship or resort to verbal and nonverbal ways to undermine it.

Fourth, our definition emphasizes that the issue or problem has reached a point where it needs effective management sooner rather than later. Although letting problems mount up is usually not a good idea, people often let unresolved issues fester and grow until they can't take it any longer and explode. The interpersonal conflicts that interest us most are those that have this **sense of urgency** because they are approaching the point where they must receive attention or else. We can relate this idea to the previous one where we draw attention to the potential for adverse effects on the relationship, if the issues are not addressed.

In the next section, we address a topic that greatly affects our ability to learn how to better manage our conflicts: the common negative view of conflict. If we are to become effective conflict managers, we must overcome this bias that limits our competence.

Negative View of Conflict

The difficulty of discussing conflict is that people often don't even like to use the word "conflict" to describe their experiences, as this narrative demonstrates:

> I don't have conflicts, because to me, a conflict is when you have no place left to go. I'm right; you're wrong, so let's forget it. Up to that point, I bargain or argue, but I don't have conflicts.

Even when we are able to recognize one when we are in the middle of it does not mean we have begun to think about conflict as something that is potentially helpful.

How or what do most people generally think of conflict? What comes to mind when you think of interpersonal conflict? How would you complete this sentence: *To me, conflict is like . . .*

1.1 Apply It

Imagine representing your attitudes toward conflict visually rather than through language. What would your conflict art look like? What materials would you use? What kinds of colors would you use? What kinds of images would best represent your feelings about conflict? Write down a description of what you would do, or better yet, take some time to actually make your conflict art.

Would you describe conflict as like a war, battle, or fight? Would you say conflict is more like a struggle, uphill climb, or contest of wills? Is it explosive, violent, an exploding

*This pastel piece by John Montejano depicts conflict as a storm looming
over a peaceful pasture.*

bomb? Do you think of conflict as like being on trial, a day in court? Perhaps you see it as
a game, match, or sport? Or, would you describe it more as a communication breakdown, a
barrier between you and another? Perhaps you see it as a storm on the horizon.

Conflict is associated with negative feelings.[11] We know that many people do not feel
confident about handling a conflict.[12] In a study, researchers asked people to describe past
interpersonal conflicts and found that they overwhelmingly used negative terms to describe
their conflicts: "It is like being in a sinking ship with no lifeboat, like a checkbook that
won't balance, like being in a rowboat in a hurricane."[13] The participants in the study reported that the conflicts were uniformly destructive or negative, suggesting that when they
effectively managed an interpersonal conflict, respondents did not think it was a conflict at
all.[14] This is typical of a **negative view of conflict:** the idea that conflicts are painful occurrences that are personally threatening and best avoided or quickly contained.

To say what conflict is like is an exercise in creating a **conflict metaphor,** where you are
asked to compare one term (conflict) with something else (struggle, exploding bombs, being on
trial). Metaphors are not only figures of speech but also a reflection of how we think.[15]

How we think about something like conflict creates an expectation as to what can,
will, or should happen, and the sort of emotions and actions that might occur.[16] Because
thoughts, feelings, and actions are intertwined, we need to examine our attitudes, beliefs,
emotional reactions, and behavior in conflict situations. If people describe conflict in negative terms and remember conflicts as unpleasant events, such thinking limits their actions in
new situations. The actions people choose are a result of the way they interpret situations.
How they think about conflict in general terms affects how they see their current situation,
how they see the conflict issue, what choices they think are available to them, and how they
view the other person's actions. As people choose their responses, they affect the outcome

of the conflict situation, and how they view the outcome of a conflict depends largely on their choices and their responses to the others involved.

1.2 Apply It

Ask your friends to describe their feelings about conflict to you. What kinds of words do they use? Do they tend to think of conflict as negative or positive?

What do we learn from a collection of metaphors people give when asked what conflict is like to them? First, interestingly, we find that not everyone uses a metaphor to describe a conflict unless they are prompted to do so.[17] However, those who do so often use metaphors that are associated with the strategy used to respond to conflict—people who use negative strategies use more negative metaphors. Others who are more passive use metaphors that reflect powerless feelings.

Second, we learn that not all people choose the same adjectives when describing what conflict means to them. Apparently people vary in which adjectives they choose to describe their perception of interpersonal conflict. These words reflect somewhat different views, which are themselves in conflict. Quite often a person who sees conflict as a "battlefield with relationships being the casualties" does not compare it to being on trial or a day in court, as another might. Probably, neither person thinks of conflict as like a basketball game, a tennis match, or some other sport. Although people may vary in their perceptions of conflict, most seem to reject the idea that interpersonal conflict is a positive, healthy, and fortunate event—one they should welcome. This common but negative attitude toward conflict hinders us from learning how to better manage our conflicts. Although people often think that they can learn new communication skills to improve the way they handle interpersonal conflicts, they do not realize that their attitudes, beliefs, and emotional reactions may have to undergo change as well.

What does a negative view have to do with conflict management? We wish to make the point that part of the reason why many people dislike conflict is because they do not handle conflicts at all well.

Simons wrote almost 20 years ago that at one end, conflict is seen as a disruption of the normal workings of a system; at the other, conflict is seen as a part of all relationships.[18] Conflicting parties often experience a dialectical tension; that is, they expect (logically and intellectually) to experience conflict but want to settle it as soon as possible so that their lives can return to "normal." Interestingly, the various Chinese characters used to symbolize conflict reflect this tension between the positive and negative dimensions of conflict. As other writers about conflict have noted, the standard character consists of the characters representing "opportunity" and "danger." People use additional characters to represent conflict situations consisting of such combinations as "to fight–to discuss," "to stand for–to stand against," and "collision–point."

Just as one can view a glass of water as half empty but another sees it as half full, so can we switch from a negative view of interpersonal conflict where we see it as threatening to a positive view where we see it as an opportunity to resolve problems and improve our relationships with the people who mean the most to us. This is a **positive view of conflict.**

It is helpful to take a more positive view of conflict because the fact of the matter is that conflict is here to stay. The omnipresence of conflict is the topic discussed in the next section.

The Inevitability of Conflict

Conflict Is a Fact of Life

Whether we change our attitudes about it or not, conflict is a fact of life. We encounter it at home, at school, and at work.

> I never thought that I would have "roommate" problems at my age. Actually, the problems are with my new husband, but they remind me of stuff I went through in college—when to do the dishes, how to sort the mail, who should take messages, when does the trash go out, who picks up after his(!) dog, who does the housework. I am amazed at the number of issues that arise when living with another person that I simply took for granted in marrying again, and the fact that all of them seem to require a major discussion to resolve frustrates me.

Think over years past and recall the conflicts, complaints, or grievances you had with these three types of people: (1) neighbors living a few houses a way, (2) next-door neighbors, and (3) family members (or teammate, close friend, roommate, or romantic partner). With the more distant neighbors, the appearance of their home and yard, noise, or their pets and children trespassing on your property may have upset you. As for your next-door neighbors, a number of serious problems are common. Many of the same conflicts occur that happened with the distant neighbors and more—like disagreements over property lines, dropping in on you too often, borrowing tools and not returning them, unsightly fences, invasions of privacy, making noises far into the night, blinding lights, talking to you every time you go out into your yard (especially when sunbathing). What about your family members? Here you could probably write a book. You may have had disagreements over study habits, sleeping habits, smoking, snoring, messiness, household chores, use of a car, friends who are noisy or sleep over, paying bills, buying furniture, TV, tools, and borrowing clothes. If you substitute teammate, close friend, or romantic partner, you have likely accumulated a list of disagreements.

1.3 Think about It

Do you believe that if you have the right partner you will live conflict free? Is it possible to find someone who presents no problems? Do you expect others to respect your property and privacy? What do you do when they don't?

Undoubtedly, you can add many examples to these lists. The question is this: What happens to conflicts as relationships become closer, more personal, and more interdependent?

If you compare the lists you created for the three types of relationships above, you probably found that as the relationship becomes closer and more interdependent (from a distant neighbor to a next-door neighbor and from a next-door neighbor to a roommate, teammate, close friend, or romantic partner),

- the more conflicts occur,
- the more trivial (minor) complaints become significant ones, and
- the more intense your feelings are.

> Before I started keeping track of my conflicts, I didn't think that I was involved in many conflicts. Now, I see that I have a lot of conflicts, and that I could have handled them differently. Acquaintances, outsiders, and strangers make me angry, but I choose not to get into a verbal conflict with them. It just isn't worth the time or effort. Basically, I just walk away or change the topic.
>
> I also noted that I deal with my conflicts differently with people closest to me. I have the greatest difficulty reaching an agreement usually with the people that I care most about. It frustrates me when the people closest to me cannot understand how I feel. Such is the case with my father. He is home alone all day and does nothing to keep himself busy. In my opinion I think he enjoys getting into conflicts with me just to have something to do and to make me communicate with him.

Communication researchers recognize that a number of studies show that conflict is a "common and inevitable feature" in close social relationships.[19] As we go from our relationship with a distant neighbor to that of a roommate, we are not only physically closer, but we also feel emotionally closer. In addition, the behavior of someone close to us usually has more consequences for us than the behavior of those more physically and emotionally distant. This interdependence means that the individuals involved can "potentially aid or interfere with each other. In interpersonal relationships, parties depend on each other for a wide range of emotional, psychological, and material resources."[20]

Building on an idea that Foa and Foa originally devised, Rettig and Bubolz identified seven types of emotional, psychological, and material resources that produce satisfaction in long-term romantic relationships.[21] As you might have guessed, those aspects that provide satisfaction in relationships have the potential to create conflict when people perceive they are lacking. In order of importance, they are:

- love—nonverbal expressions of positive regard, warmth, or comfort
- status—verbal expressions of high or low prestige or esteem
- service—labor of one for another
- information—advice, opinions, instructions, or enlightenment
- goods—contributions of material goods
- money—financial contributions
- shared time—time spent together

The authors claim that in the best kind of long-term romantic relationship, partners believe that they get what they deserve. Although their research focuses on romantic partners, many of these seven resources are relevant to other types of interpersonal relationships, including roommates, neighbors, friends, co-workers, and family.

When we cooperate in the conflicts we experience, we may think that we and the other person get what we deserve. However, we often compete instead because we fear that cooperation may not yield the results we desire. Even when we intend to cooperate, our words and actions often reflect only our own needs rather than the needs of our relationship, which may make our partners think that they have to stick up for their own interests. As we think more in terms of ourselves than as friends, partners, or members of a family, the relationship is threatened, perhaps arousing strong feelings. So, conflicts usually include incentives to compete and cooperate.

Because we do become closer to and more interdependent with some people than with others, we can expect more conflict. No wonder Stamp found that conflict plays a role in the creation and maintenance of interpersonal relationships.[22] The **inevitability of conflict principle** runs contrary to the idea that, if we look long and hard, we can find people with whom we can share conflict-free lives. It means that we should cease our efforts to find perfect people and learn how to manage the conflicts we are sure to have with those closest to us. We need to learn how to deal with minor as well as major conflicts, how to maintain our objectivity when engaged in conflict, and how to keep our self-control.

Although conflict is inevitable, we argue that it need not always turn violent. Unfortunately, too many people see violence as a necessary way to deal with conflict, but other options exist.

Interpersonal Violence Is Not a Fact of Life

Because of its ubiquitous nature, violence in interpersonal conflict has received a significant amount of attention from social scientists in communication and other disciplines.[23] **Interpersonal violence** is not difficult to recognize; it occurs when one person imposes his or her will on another through verbal or physical intimidation. The term *violence* refers to medium to severe acts, such as physical violence and severe verbal abuse.[24] Interpersonal violence occurs where one person inflicts pain on a partner; it is a violation of what many people consider to be socially acceptable. Abusive behavior ranges from less intense, such as verbal attack, to more intense, such as physical attack. People may plan their attacks, or they may think they act spontaneously with violence or abuse.[25] According to our view, interpersonal violence, physical aggression, and abusive relationships are a type of interpersonal conflict, albeit an extreme and unhealthy type.

1.4 Think about It

What are the real-world implications of saying "interpersonal violence is not a fact of life"? Under what conditions would you see interpersonal violence as acceptable? Why?

We take this opportunity to introduce the concept of interpersonal violence because every interpersonal conflict carries with it the seeds of abuse. Not only is this so, but frequently people expect their conflicts to turn violent. Violence is becoming increasingly prevalent in American social life, making interpersonal conflict management an essential social skill. By teaching nonviolent solutions to problems, setting an example in our daily lives, and raising our children to resolve interpersonal conflicts peacefully, we are helping to reduce a serious social problem. Thus, learning to avoid escalation (i.e., learning de-escalation) is an important goal of this textbook.

The idea that conflicts need not turn violent implies that we have options when handling our differences with others. Speakers turn to violence when they lack knowledge and verbal skills.[26] This is where interpersonal ethics enters in. Folger and Poole note that a person is acting unethically communicatively when his or her messages force another person "(1) to make choices he or she would not normally make, or (2) to decline to make choices he or she would normally make, or both."[27]

The notion of choice applies to interpersonal violence in two ways. First, when we turn violent or others use violence against us, people are using force to prevent others' freedom of choice. Second, the notion of choice should help us realize that we need not turn violent in the first place. We always have choices in conflict situations, we are all responsible for our own actions, and we can make a difference in our lives and others. Although conflict is inevitable, it need not, and should not, harm our relationships with others, get out of hand, and turn violent. Having defined interpersonal conflict, discussed the implications of our definition, and addressed the negative bias that affects our perceptions of conflict and the way we respond in conflict situations, we next turn our attention to the idea of managing our conflicts.

Defining Conflict Management

Everyday language reflects the variety of ways in which we regard conflict: We talk about handling conflict, dealing with it, avoiding it, or resolving it. We define **conflict management** as the behavior a person employs based on his or her analysis of a conflict situation. Another concept, **conflict resolution,** refers to only one alternative in which parties solve a problem or issue. Conflict management refers to alternative ways of dealing with conflict, including resolution or avoiding it altogether.[28] Folger and colleagues consider effective conflict management as "the type of interaction that will create productive conflict."[29] Teaching you to satisfactorily manage your conflicts using effective and ethical interpersonal communication behavior is the goal of this textbook. How we effectively manage our conflicts involves a system that we describe in detail in Chapter 3 along with negotiation techniques presented in Chapter 7.

Again, the implications of this definition need emphasis. First, our definition implies that you have choices to make when in a conflict situation. You can choose among various options to deal with conflicts. You may avoid or confront conflicts. You may react peacefully or violently. You may treat others with respect and civility or verbally abuse others. You may simply give in or insist on "having everything your way." We describe options that lead to effective conflict management in detail in Chapter 4 and present confrontation techniques in Chapter 6. The point we want to make here is that your choices can turn a destructive conflict into a productive one or vice versa.

Second, our view suggests that, in order to effectively manage conflict, you must analyze it by taking a meta-conflict perspective. You may recall that one of the fundamentals of interpersonal communication is the idea of *meta-communication,* where one tries to objectively look at interaction between people and talk about it intelligently. We might sit back, observe a couple of friends interact, and then describe their interaction pattern to them. Perhaps we observe that one person dominated the conversation, that is, talked the most and controlled the topic of discussion. In conflict, the ability to take a **meta-conflict perspective** means that you can look back on the conflicts you have experienced, analyze what you did well and what you did poorly, and learn from your mistakes. Eventually, you may even monitor your present interpersonal conflicts, realize what is going on, alter your behavior, and better manage the conflicts.

Third, our view suggests that in order to effectively manage conflict you must take a process view of conflict, because processes are what people manage in social situations. Although some conflicts may escalate and get out of hand, other conflicts may de-escalate and leave partners feeling better about their relationship. We intend to discuss the process view in much greater detail later in Part II, but we may briefly describe it as follows: A **process view of conflict** recognizes that a conflict is ongoing, dynamic, changeable, and not necessarily predictable. From such a view, conflict unfolds and proceeds through stages that may branch off in a variety of directions. In addition, processes have ingredients that affect one another.

In basic communication courses, you probably learned that the communication process involves one person sending a message to another person (receiver) through some channel. Such a communication model also contains a provision for noise (interference) and for receiver feedback, so that the receiver can indicate to the message sender that she or he received the message as intended. We can apply this communication process model as managers of conflict. One conflicting party (the message sender) may send any of the following messages to the other party of the conflict (the message receiver):

> I am not speaking to you.
> I don't want to talk about that.
> I disagree with you.
> I want to fight.
> I don't like you.
> I don't like what you said.
> I don't want to see you anymore.
> I want something to change.

The sender of such messages may use any of the following channels:

> Face-to-face
> Synchronous via some medium like the phone or instant messaging
> Asynchronous via the mail, email, or another person as the message carrier

Noise may consist of distractions in the face-to-face environment (such as TV, other people, or loud sounds) or technical difficulties that delete messages via the Internet or cut off contact on a cell phone.

In a conflict, feedback from others may consist of nonverbal reactions, such as facial cues (anger, hurt, sadness), body movements (standing up or walking out), gestures (making a fist, becoming more dynamic and lively), tone of voice (screaming, yelling), or verbal responses (name-calling or swearing).

Most important, though, conflict processes are characterized by **equifinality.** The formal definition of equifinality is that one cannot necessarily predict how something will turn out based on the way it started, nor can we infer what the beginning stages of a process were based only on our observation of its ending. That is, although we know that the conflict process "starts" with some sort of message (or non-message) from the sender, continues with some sort of response (or non-response) from the receiver, and is conducted through media subject to noise, we cannot always predict the trajectory of a conflict situation. The same behaviors that contain a destructive conflict sequence with one person may, on occasion, exacerbate a conflict with a different person. This warning is not meant to contradict all the productive means of conflict management presented to you; rather, it is a caution that no particular message or behavior is a type of magic guaranteed to resolve a conflict.

While the above description of conflict and communication processes may sound familiar to many of us, we would hope to create and manage a more productive conflict process—one that might begin with the words, "We need to talk," and end when people reach an agreement. We specifically describe how to do this in the following chapters.

Conflict Communication as Productive or Destructive

Effective conflict management consists of acting and reacting in problematic situations in such a way as to convert potentially destructive interpersonal conflicts into productive ones. When conflict exists, you must take action to deal with the problem, either through open confrontation or through less direct, more tacit methods. Earlier, we discussed the generally held negative view of conflict and recommended that you take a more positive view. People who hold the negative view tend to see conflict as destructive, while those who hold the positive view see it as productive. This is an important observation because how people think and feel about conflict affects the way they make choices in conflict situations. If one approaches conflict as a problem in need of resolution or an opportunity to persuade, more constructive choices are likely than if one views conflict as frightening. One woman reports her change in attitude toward conflict.

> The most valuable lesson I have learned is that conflict is not necessarily bad. I no longer see conflicts as a danger to relationships. My acceptance of conflicts as the result of relationships has helped minimize the discomfort I feel in conflict situations.

Conflict is destructive or dysfunctional when it leaves the participants dissatisfied. On the other hand, conflict is productive or it serves a useful purpose when the participants are all satisfied and think that they have gained as a result of the conflict.[30] However, feelings about the outcome are not enough to determine the productivity of a conflict. Some conflicts, although uncomfortable in the short run, may serve the needs of those in the relationship in the long run, or may even serve others outside the parties' relationship or society at large.[31]

This makes sense, particularly for people who are uncomfortable engaging in conflict at the outset. If, for example, you have a new roommate, and you find almost immediately that your personal habits are diametrically opposed, you might feel uncomfortable as you initiate a conflict with your roommate in order to find some point of agreement on your habits. Because you do not know the other well, the conflict episode may seem strained and awkward. Afterward, you may think you did not respond verbally in the best way possible. However, if you see improved changes in behavior over time, then we can conclude that it was a productive conflict. It pays to enlarge your view of a conflict to include not only the outcomes or results but also you and your partner's actual behavior within the conflict itself as measures of successful conflict management.

1.3 Apply It

Take a piece of paper and draw two columns on it. On one side, describe an unproductive conflict. On the other, describe a productive conflict. What are the differences between the two conflicts? How can you apply your learning to the next conflict you face?

How can we see conflict as negative and destructive? A conflict is destructive when it harms the relationship because the partners do not manage it in a way that is mutually satisfactory. Moreover, when participants in the conflict lose sight of their original goals, when hostility becomes the norm, when mismanaged conflict becomes a regular part of the interaction between people, it is destructive. Finally, we characterize **destructive conflict** as a tendency to expand and escalate the conflict to the point where it often becomes separated from the initial cause and takes on a life of its own.[32] Consider this person's account of poorly handled conflicts.

> When in conflict with those closest to me, I experience a lot of frustration, anger, anxiety, irritation, and resentment, and I handle conflicts badly. I tend to "fly off the handle" a lot, not thinking first. Because I get upset, I yell, accuse, or become sarcastic. I usually don't look at the other person's point of view because I am too busy yelling or stomping around the room. For example, I gave one friend, Jason, an incorrect reason why another friend, Tim, was not going to have a drink. I told Jason that Tim had a problem with alcohol, which wasn't really true. When Tim found out what I told Jason, he got upset (understandably) with me, and we had a nasty argument, which continued to the following night. I remember yelling, swearing, flaying my arms in the air, kicking a chair, and accusing him of being from an alcoholic family (which wasn't true). I know Tim must have thought I sounded ridiculous. But I cannot reverse communication. I find it is difficult to work out a solution to a problem after saying hurtful words to the other person. When I think back on my past conflicts, the majority were over trivial matters and I could have handled them differently.

According to our view, destructive conflict occurs when there is an increase in the issues, number of people involved, costs to the participants, and intensity of negative feelings. It includes a desire to hurt the other person and to get even for past wrongs. Destructive conflict occurs when there is escalation and parties fail to consider their options. Lastly, destructive conflict places heavy reliance on overt power and manipulative techniques.

We believe that **productive conflict** occurs when a conflict is kept to the issue and to those involved. It reduces the costs to the participants and the intensity of negative feelings. It includes helping the other person and letting go of past feelings. Productive conflict occurs when there is no escalation and no interpersonal violence. It features an awareness of options in conflict situations. Productive conflict does not rely on overt power and manipulative techniques. Along with these characteristics, we think that a productive view of conflict situations includes flexibility and a belief that all conflicting parties can achieve their important goals.[33]

We have distinguished productive conflict from destructive on the basis of mutually favorable or unfavorable outcomes. We need to say more about the idea of **outcomes,** or the results people are seeking to achieve when they engage in conflict. Sometimes, these goals are clear at the outset, and at other times they develop as the conflict continues. We realize that the term *outcomes* may suggest the resolution of some issue or solution of some problem. However, many people are satisfied even when these goals are not achieved. All they want from the conflict situation is for the other party to show interest in the problem, show concern for their feelings, and pay attention to their wants, needs, or interests, even if their wishes are not fulfilled. These are more personal, emotional outcomes that are associated with perceived fairness, acceptance as a person, and justice. There is a common understanding that complaints need attention by those responsible. Grievances deserve their "day in court." In conflicts, both parties are anxious to tell their side of the story and want others to hear them out. If you take the time and make an effort to meet with me and show interest in my concerns, I may leave a conflict situation at least somewhat satisfied or feeling better than if you continue to ignore me or treat me badly. Better yet, you may make future decisions based on my recent input.

Everyone has a preferred way of behaving in particular situations. Routines and rituals are useful because repetitive tasks are performed without really thinking about them. But falling into a routine or resorting to comfortable behavior in a conflict is not necessarily the most adaptive response in a particular conflict situation. For example, if your routine is to withdraw in conflict situations, which is a useful strategy sometimes, you may lose your input on a problematic situation because you were not willing to become involved and now must live with undesirable results. If you fail to fight for what you want now, are your hands tied in the future? On the other hand, if you dominate the conflict situation and have your way in this conflict, does it affect your ability to negotiate with this particular person in the future? Does your behavior adversely affect your relationship?

1.5 Think about It

Before reading this chapter, how did you feel about confronting others when a conflict arises? Did you feel positive or negative about it? How did that affect the way you handled past conflicts? Do you think you would be more successful if you felt more positively about conflict?

Although people in interpersonal relationships typically plan and engage in negative and destructive communication practices, they can choose to learn conflict communication patterns that reduce stress and produce greater understanding of each other's perspectives, more satisfying outcomes, and more frequent resolution of problems. The benefits of a more constructive approach, especially in cases where the interpersonal relationship is of importance, are obvious. How you convert potentially destructive conflicts into productive ones is the subject of the following chapters.

Manage It

Our goal in this first chapter was to help you understand the nature of interpersonal conflict, its place in our lives, and some of the variables intrinsic to its management or resolution. Conflict occurs between interdependent people who seek different goals or who wish to engage in different activities. Two important characteristics of conflict are that the perceived differences have the potential to adversely affect the relationship if not addressed and that there is a sense of urgency about the need to resolve the difference. As we noted, however, conflicts do not have to be verbally expressed to affect the relationship.

Conflict is inevitable—as relationships become closer, more personal, and more interdependent, more conflicts occur, trivial (minor) complaints become more significant, and feelings become more intense. Conflict is inevitable, and so it holds a kind of dread for us—because we know we have often mishandled it in the past. This negative view of conflict may lead us to make poor decisions in our present situations; thus, we urge our students to adopt a more positive view of conflict.

Although conflict is inevitable, interpersonal violence is not. We need not choose violence when other options are available. The rise of violence in interpersonal relationships makes interpersonal conflict management an essential social skill.

Conflict management is the behavior we employ based on our analysis of a conflict situation, using both effective and ethical interpersonal communication skills. In addition, we must realize that we make choices, and these choices have consequences. Effective conflict management can change potentially destructive conflict into productive conflict, minimizing expansion of the issues, number of people involved, costs to the participants, and intensity of negative feelings. Effective conflict management can attenuate the desire to hurt the other person and to get even for past wrongs and can move us away from reliance on overt power and manipulative techniques. It features an awareness of options in conflict situations. Along with these characteristics, a productive view of conflict situations includes flexibility and the belief that all conflicting parties can achieve their important goals. The following chapters address the means by which we can use effective conflict management techniques to change destructive conflict into more productive conflict.

The title of this book, *Managing Conflict through Communication,* reflects the view that a positive view of interpersonal conflict underlies competent communication behavior. The first step in managing conflict is to adopt a mindset that embraces conflict as an opportunity while recognizing the risks involved. This mindset recognizes the importance of personal responsibility and encourages flexibility in oneself and in others within the conflict situation. The mindset also recognizes that although communication may not work miracles, it usually helps when managing conflicts. Most important, this mindset rejects easy solutions and recognizes the complexity of conflict situations and their outcomes. Adopting these new attitudes toward conflict is not an overnight process. It takes time and work. The important idea is that we become aware of our behavior in conflict situations and start to identify the way our thinking about conflict situations affects the outcomes we obtain. Self-awareness is the first step toward more effective conflict behavior.

1.1 **Work with It**

Read the following conflict narrative and answer the questions following it.

> There are three of us presently living together. The conflict is with a roommate who lived with two of us (I just transferred in) last semester. She moved out with a friend because it was free room and board. Sometimes she decides she doesn't feel like driving the twelve miles home, so she stays the night with us. This went on just about every night last week. When here, she wore my clothes every day (without asking first), slept on our couch (which gave us no place to study), ate our food, and used our personal items like shampoo and makeup. I finally had enough when she walked by me after class wearing my brand new wool coat with the sleeves rolled up and said, "Hi! I'm wearing your coat!" As I looked over my shoulder to see her continue by I noticed she also had on my shoes, pants (that were too small for her), and a sweater of mine. She is a wonderful, sweet person and there never was any problem with her other than this. I don't mind if people borrow my clothes, but I prefer that they ask first and that I get them back in the condition I lent them. I also think I should wear my clothes more often than other people do. Also, I'd like it if she would plan when she is spending the night so she could bring her own clothes, makeup, and food. As the saying goes, "I love her but I can't afford to keep her!" I've asked her in the past not to stretch out my clothes and have made comments about the food being eaten, but she seems oblivious to the situation. After a week of this I finally had it with her and really blew up! I screamed and yelled at her and she burst into tears, packed up, and left. It felt good letting off all that pent-up anger, but I somehow wish it hadn't worked out this way.

1. How would you apply the authors' definition of interpersonal conflict to this narrative?
2. What do you think the friends' view of conflict is (positive or negative) and why?
3. Are conflicts like these expected among friends?
4. Was there potential for violence here? Why or why not?
5. How would you apply the authors' definition of conflict management to this narrative? Was it managed or mismanaged, and why?
6. How could the friends have converted this interpersonal conflict into a more productive one?

1.1 **Remember It**

Write an essay in which you apply the ideas presented in Chapter 1 to your life situation. Be sure to address the following topics.

1. Define interpersonal conflict, and give an example of your own recent conflicts.
2. Explain your view of conflict (ranging from negative to positive) before taking this course.
3. Explain why conflict is a fact of life for you personally.
4. Explain why violence is not a fact of life for you personally.
5. Define conflict management, and give an example of your own recently managed conflict.
6. Explain how more effective conflict management might make the above example of a conflict more productive.

Work with It

This exercise asks you to write an essay describing the conflicts you encounter over at least a two-week period. Before writing, you need to keep track of your conflicts for a couple of weeks or more (see conflict records that follow). You may include recent conflicts that occurred prior to this assignment if you remember them in detail.

When preparing to write this essay, keep in mind our definition of a conflict situation. Some students say they cannot do the papers in this class because they have no conflicts. This means that they do not understand Chapter 1. Remember that unexpressed conflicts do exist. For example, according to the way conflict is defined in this textbook, a conflict exists any time we would prefer to do something but give in to others and do something else, or we may simply avoid confronting others, which is a type of conflict. So, we actually may have more conflicts than we may think.

In your essay, address the following topics:

- What do you think of the authors' definition of interpersonal conflict? (For example, you might start out giving the authors' definition and explain how well it fits with the conflicts you are presently observing in your life.)
- Would you say that it is inevitable to experience conflict with these individuals?
- In what ways were the conflicts *productive* and in what ways *destructive?*
- Conclude with a paragraph on *how satisfied* you are with the way you and the others handled these conflicts and any *problems* you have when attempting to manage your interpersonal conflicts.

Conflict Records

Instructions: Make ten copies of this record. Over the next two weeks or so, observe your conflicts and fill out a record for each one. After you accumulate ten or more, you should be ready to write your paper.

Interpersonal Conflict Record

Date: _____ Time: _____ (AM/PM) Length of argument (time): _____

Topic/Issue of conflict: _____

How often has this issue come up in the past?

     Rarely   1   2   3   4   5   6   7   8   9   Very Often

What actually started/triggered the conflict? _____

_____

_____

_____

_____

Description of the conflict: verbal argument, physical abuse, silent treatment/stonewalling, changed subject/made light of conflict, etc.: _____

_____

_____

Emotions you experienced: _____

_____

How did it end?_____

_____

Intensity of disagreement:

     Low   1   2   3   4   5   6   7   8   9   High

Degree of resolution:

     Resolved   1   2   3   4   5   6   7   8   9   Unresolved

NOTES

1. Hilaire Belloc, *The Silence of the Sea,* retrieved May 17, 2005 from www.quoteland.com/topic. asp?CATEGORY_ID=32
2. These definitions come from (in the order presented): (1) H. Wayland Cummings, Larry W. Long, and Michael Lewis, *Managing Communication in Organizations,* 2nd Ed. (Scottsdale, AZ: Gorsuch Scarisbrick Publishers, 1987), p. 150; see also Clyde H. Coombs and George S. Avrunin, *The Structure of Conflict* (Hillsdale, NJ: Lawrence Erlbaum Associates, 1988), who define conflict as "the opposition of response (behavioral) tendencies, which may be within an individual or in different individuals" (p. 1). (2) Gary P. Cross, Jean H. Names, and Darrell Beck, *Conflict and Human Interaction* (Dubuque, IA: Kendall Hunt Publishing, 1979), p. v. (3) R. D. Nye, *Conflict among Humans* (New York: Spring Publishing, 1973). (4) Lynn Sandra Kahn, *Peacemaking: A Systems Approach to Conflict Management* (Lanham, MD: University Press of America, 1988), p. 3.
3. William W. Wilmot and Joyce L. Hocker, *Interpersonal Conflict,* 6th Ed. (New York: McGraw Hill, 2001), p. 41.
4. Joseph Folger, Marshall Scott Poole, and Randall Stutman, *Working through Conflict,* 4th Ed. (Boston: Allyn & Bacon, 2001, p. 5.)
5. Joseph P. Forgas and Michelle Cromer, "On Being Sad and Evasive: Affective Influences on Verbal Communication Strategies in Conflict Situations," *Journal of Experimental Social Psychology* 40 (2004), 511–518.
6. Marnin J. Heisel and Myrian Mongrain, "Facial Expressions and Ambivalence: Looking for Conflict in All the Right Faces," *Journal of Nonverbal Behavior* 28 (2004), 35–52.
7. Dean G. Pruitt and Jeffrey Z. Rubin, *Social Conflict: Escalation, Stalemate, and Settlement* (New York, Random House, 1986), p. 4.
8. Herbert W. Simons, "The Carrot and the Stick as Handmaidens of Persuasion in Conflict Situations," in Gerald R. Miller and Herbert W. Simons, *Perspectives in Communication in Social Conflicts* (Englewood Cliffs, NJ: Prentice Hall, 1974), pp. 172–205.
9. Amy Janan Johnson, "Beliefs about Arguing: A Comparison of Public Issue and Personal Issue Arguments," *Communication Reports* 15 (2002), 99–112.
10. Amy S. Ebesu Hubbard, "Conflict between Relationally Uncertain Romantic Partners: The Influence of Relational Responsiveness and Empathy," *Communication Monographs* 68 (2001), p. 400.
11. Amy M. Bippus and Emma Rollin, "Attachment Style Differences in Relational Maintenance and Conflict Behaviors: Friends' Perceptions," *Communication Reports* 16 (2003), p. 113.
12. There is also a line of research that suggests that not all families prepare their children equally well for conflict later in life. Ascan F. Koerner and Mary Anne Fitzpatrick, "You Never Leave Your Family in a Fight: The Impact of Family of Origin on Conflict-Behavior in Romantic Relationships," *Communication Studies* 53 (2002), 234–252.
13. Suzanne McCorkle and Janet L. Mills, "Rowboat in a Hurricane: Metaphors of Interpersonal Conflict Management," *Communication Reports* 5 (1992), 57–66.
14. Ibid., p. 63; see also Jacqueline S. Weinstock and Lynne A. Bond, "Conceptions of Conflict in Close Friendships and Ways of Knowing among Young College Women: A Developmental Framework," *Journal of Social and Personal Relationships* 17 (2000), 687–696.
15. S. I. Hayakawa, *Language in Thought and Action,* 4th Ed. (New York: Harcourt Brace Jovanovich, 1978).
16. McCorkle and Mills, 57–66.
17. Suzanne McCorkle and Barbara Mae Gayle, "Conflict Management Metaphors: Assessing Everyday Problem Communication," *The Social Science Journal* 40 (2003), 137–142.
18. Herbert W. Simons, "Persuasion in Social Conflicts: A Critique of Prevailing Conceptions and a Framework for Future Research," *Speech Monographs* 39 (1972), 227–247.
19. Fran C. Dickson, Patrick C. Hughes, Linda D. Manning, Kandi L. Walker, Tamara Bollis-Pecci, and Scott Gratson, "Conflict in Later-Life, Long-Term Marriages," *Southern Communication Journal* 67 (2002), 110–121.
20. Joseph Folger, Marshall Scott Poole, and Randall K. Stutman, *Working through Conflict,* 2nd Ed. (New York: HarperCollins, 1993), pp. 5–7.
21. Uriel G. Foa and Edna G. Foa, *Societal Structures of the Mind* (Springfield, IL: Thomas, 1974); Katherine D. Rettig and Margaret D. Bubolz, "Interpersonal Resource Exchanges as Indicators of Quality of Marriage," *Journal of Marriage and the Family,* 45 (1983), 497–509.
22. Glen H. Stamp, "A Qualitatively Constructed Interpersonal Communication Model: A Grounded Theory Analysis," *Human Communication Research,* 25 (1999), p. 543.
23. Loreen N. Olson and Dawn O. Braithwaite. "'If You Hit Me Again, I'll Hit You Back': Conflict

Management Strategies Of Individuals Experiencing Aggression during Conflicts," *Communication Studies* 55 (2004), 271–286.

24. Loreen N. Olson, "Exploring 'Common Couple Violence' in Heterosexual Romantic Relationships," *Western Journal of Communication* 66 (2002), p. 104.

25. Dudley Cahn and Sally Lloyd (Eds.), *Family Violence from a Communication Perspective* (Thousand Oaks, CA: Sage, 1996), p. 6.

26. Janet R. Meyer, "The Effect of Verbal Aggressiveness on the Perceived Importance of Secondary Goals in Messages," *Communication Studies* 55 (2004), 168–185.

27. Joseph DeVito, *The Interpersonal Communication Book,* 6th Ed. (New York: HarperCollins, 1992), p. 77.

28. Dudley D. Cahn, *Intimates in Conflict* (Hillsdale, NJ: Erlbaum, 1990), p. 16.

29. Folger et al., 2001, p. 17.

30. Morton Deutsch, "Conflicts: Productive or Destructive," *Journal of Social Issues* 25 (1969), 7–41.

31. Brent Ruben, "Communication and Conflict: A Systems Perspective," *Quarterly Journal of Speech* 64 (1978), 202–210.

32. Deutsch, 1969.

33. Folger et al., 2001, pp. 6–7.

2 Types of Conflicts

OBJECTIVES

At the end of this chapter, you should be able to:

- Compare and contrast different types of unreal conflicts.

- Compare and contrast real conflicts based on the degree of importance.

- Compare and contrast real conflicts based on their degree of competition.

- Compare and contrast real conflicts based on their degree of violence.

- Differentiate between tangible and intangible issues.

- Differentiate between behavioral, normative, and personality conflicts.

KEY TERMS

arguments
behavioral issue conflicts
competition
conflict game
conflict issues
displaced conflict
false conflicts

intangible issue conflicts
mere disagreements
misplaced conflicts
overblown conflict
personality issue conflicts
physical aggression
real conflicts

relationship/normative issue
  conflicts
tangible issue conflicts
unimportant conflict
unreal conflicts
verbal aggression/abuse

> Something that I've found very helpful is learning about different conflict types. I used to think that conflict was all the same—it was hard and it took all my energy to deal with it. Knowing that there are different kinds of conflicts has helped me realize that I don't need to deal with all conflict in the same way. Knowing what I am faced with makes it a lot easier to choose to deal with it.

Although we may think of conflict as only productive or destructive, conflicts come in many different shapes and sizes. As researchers have explored the concept of conflict, they have identified different types of conflict situations that require different ways of dealing with them; as such, you enhance your effectiveness as a conflict manager by learning these different types.

We need to understand what kind of conflict we are engaged in, because different types of conflicts call for different methods of management. In the last chapter, we emphasized the role of choice in conflict management. Conflict managers choose among behavioral options based on their analysis of the conflict situation. As a first step in this analysis, conflict managers must determine the type of conflict. The purpose of this chapter is to describe different ways of classifying conflicts, based on whether or not they meet the conditions for interpersonal conflict as listed in our definition. In addition, we describe the different kinds of issues that typically arise in conflict situations. Through your understanding of different types of conflicts, you can learn to choose more wisely among the options of confrontation or avoidance. Further, we expect that you understand that even when a conflict is "real," you may choose to avoid the issue. Some conflicts are worth the time and energy of engagement. Many are not. Those who manage conflict well have learned to make this choice based on the kind of conflict they are encountering.

Of greatest concern to anyone studying conflict is the ability to determine a real conflict: a conflict that is both perceived and verifiably occurring, which requires some kind of response. To help you do this, in this chapter we distinguish real from unreal conflicts and explain how they range from minor, noncompetitive, and nonviolent to significant, competitive, and violent conflict situations. We also differentiate tangible from intangible conflicts. Figure 2.1 provides a visual representation of the way the types of conflicts relate to one another. As you read about the different types of conflicts, keep in mind that there is some overlap between the types. The categories we have created are meant as tools to clarify our thoughts and help us decide which conflicts really should be addressed.

Unreal Conflicts

Conflicts are either real, or they are unreal. There is nothing in between. **Unreal conflicts** either don't exist in reality but are thought to exist in someone's mind, or do exist in reality but are misperceived. The problem for conflict managers in dealing with unreal conflicts is that we act as though they are real because we have not judged the situation accurately. Treating an unreal conflict as though it is real may cost us unnecessary time and energy. Even though some may think that discussion of this topic is not warranted, because unreal conflicts do not exist anyway, the simple fact is that we encounter them frequently and expend unnecessary energy worrying about them. Understanding that unreal conflicts exist may help us to stop, step back, and consider whether we are indeed experiencing a conflict before attempting to analyze our situation. Three common types of unreal conflicts are false conflict, displaced conflict, and misplaced conflict.

False Conflicts

False conflicts occur when at least one person in an interdependent relationship thinks that there is a conflict but after talking to the other(s) involved, finds there is no conflict.[1] This narrative demonstrates a false conflict.

> I was hanging curtains in my daughter's room, and it was pulling at the material, so I picked the kitten up and put it behind me without looking. I should have known better—there were objects all over the floor and apparently it landed on something the wrong way. I heard a meow-spit-hiss, and turned around to see it favoring one leg. Horrified, I picked it up and rushed it to the vet to find that its leg was broken.

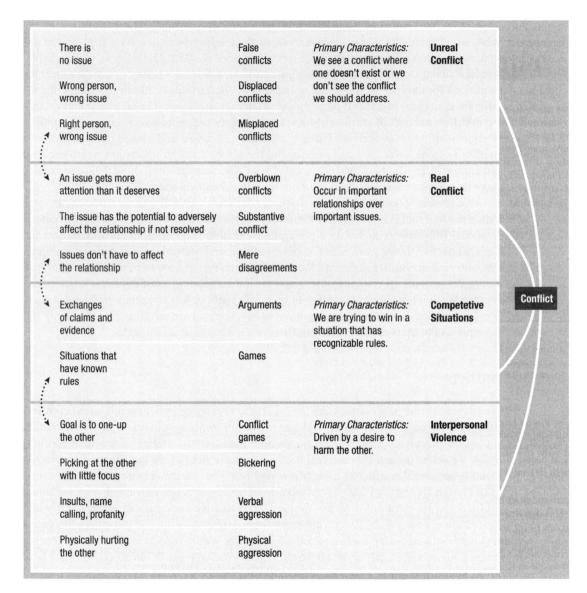

There is no issue	False conflicts	*Primary Characteristics:* We see a conflict where one doesn't exist or we don't see the conflict we should address.	**Unreal Conflict**
Wrong person, wrong issue	Displaced conflicts		
Right person, wrong issue	Misplaced conflicts		
An issue gets more attention than it deserves	Overblown conflicts	*Primary Characteristics:* Occur in important relationships over important issues.	**Real Conflict**
The issue has the potential to adversely affect the relationship if not resolved	Substantive conflict		
Issues don't have to affect the relationship	Mere disagreements		
Exchanges of claims and evidence	Arguments	*Primary Characteristics:* We are trying to win in a situation that has recognizable rules.	**Competetive Situations**
Situations that have known rules	Games		
Goal is to one-up the other	Conflict games	*Primary Characteristics:* Driven by a desire to harm the other.	**Interpersonal Violence**
Picking at the other with little focus	Bickering		
Insults, name calling, profanity	Verbal aggression		
Physically hurting the other	Physical aggression		

Conflict

FIGURE 2.1   The Relationship of Four Types of Conflict. This figure displays the four main categories of conflicts. The lines connecting conflicts from one category to the next indicate conflicts that often resemble one another. Careful analysis is needed to determine the kind of conflict being experienced.

When I picked my daughter up from school, I tried to find some way to explain gently that it was my fault her kitten was injured. She simply looked at me and asked, "Is Sheba okay?" I replied that she was, although she would wear a cast for four weeks. My daughter said, "Well, accidents happen, Mom. You didn't mean to hurt her." I thought I would drive the car onto the sidewalk in amazement. I expected fireworks, and all that happened was a fizzle.

Because we may assume that we are in a conflict due to the limited knowledge we have, false conflicts are generally resolved with sufficient information. Asking, and being told, leads to resolution fairly easily. Other false conflicts have to do with what people think that the other person might have done before they get their facts straight. Conflicts concerning beliefs, facts, or perceptions generally arise from a lack of information or distorted information. Imagine thinking you are in conflict with someone only to find that you are not. This is one reason why we need to talk to the other party. Otherwise, we may fret for nothing.

Displaced Conflicts

A second kind of unreal conflict related to interpersonal conflicts is **displaced conflict,** which occurs when people direct a conflict toward the wrong person, avoiding a confrontation with the appropriate person. They almost always happen with people with whom we have an interpersonal relationship, whom we think of as a "safe target" for our frustration. The person we avoid is someone we do not want to offend or provoke because that person has greater power (rank, physical strength, or nasty reputation). The common example of displaced conflict is Dan, who is angry at his boss but doesn't say anything to him, then comes home to his loving wife or children, whom he abuses with his anger.

2.1 Think about It

How do you make amends after you have engaged in a displaced conflict with someone close to you? What can you do to avoid such displaced conflicts in the future?

Misplaced Conflicts

Misplaced conflicts occur when people argue about issues other than the ones at the heart of the conflict.[2] We engage in conflict with the right person, but the conflict occurs over the wrong issue. The following story, told by a wife about her marriage, is an example of misplaced conflict with serious implications for the relationship:

> We've been seeing the marriage counselor for several weeks now, and we deal with all sorts of issues like my husband's problem with the way I do the housework (even though I work full-time) and my concern that he doesn't put enough time and energy into his business. But I get the impression that we're just putting out little brush fires when the forest is burning down. The heat of the real conflict is so intense we keep going around it. I think the real problem is that he treats me more coldly and cruelly than he would treat a stranger. He never touches me or shows me any kind of affection.

Whereas displaced conflicts involve directing frustration toward a "safe" *person,* misplaced conflicts involve "safe" *issues* that people are more willing to talk about than the issues that underlie them.

In the preceding example, his concern over the housework and her concern about the effort put into the business are legitimate issues. The real issues, however, are masked by these "safer" issues. The wife uses the housework as a weapon against a husband who emotionally abuses her: It bothers him to have the house messy, so she just cannot seem to get around to doing it. It helps that she works outside the home. She can say, with some legitimacy, that there is not enough time to do everything. She does not really want to deal with his lack of respect, so talking about his lack of business efforts is a safer issue. Because they keep dealing with the small, visible conflicts instead of looking at the pattern of their conflict behavior, the small conflicts continue to multiply until one or the other leaves or until they learn how to deal with the conflicts. Deutsch argued that manifest or overt conflict is difficult, if not impossible, to resolve unless the underlying conflict has been dealt with in some way or unless the overt conflict is separated from the underlying conflict and treated in isolation.[3]

Because misplaced conflicts revolve around "safe" rather than "real" issues, they are often difficult to diagnose. A conflict issue that comes up repeatedly may mask a deeper issue between those involved. However, you need to understand that, where conflicts are managed rather than resolved, the same issues may arise frequently with no other underlying meaning. For example, if you are a person of tidy habits rooming with a messy person, the issue of cleanliness is likely to arise often, but it probably does not mask a deeper issue other than the fact that you have different habits. Misplaced conflicts concern relational issues such as power sharing, expectations for behavior, respect, means of showing affection, and so on. Because these issues are central to the way people relate to one another, people often find it easier to focus on visible issues, such as money or work habits, where any difference in action is observable.

False conflicts, displaced conflicts, and misplaced conflicts have the seeds of relational harm within them. Usually they require that we apologize for the way we reacted in the situation, explain our misunderstanding and outside stresses, and confront the real issue if there is one.

2.1 Apply It

Take a sheet of paper and make three columns on it. Label the columns false conflict, displaced conflict, and misplaced conflict. In each column, identify a conflict you experienced or witnessed that took one of these forms. Your description should answer:

- What was the conflict about?
- Why did you think there was a conflict?
- How did you resolve the conflict?

Real Conflicts

Real conflicts actually exist in fact, are perceived accurately, and range from minor issues to those that are serious enough to hurt the relationship if they are left unattended. Although some people often become quite agitated and excited when they find themselves disagreeing with another person, **mere disagreements,** while real conflicts, may occur over issues that are peripheral to a relationship, as when relational partners hold different political views or find themselves disagreeing over the worth of a movie. Recognizing when an issue is not central to the relationship helps us to know that we are in a mere disagreement that does not require a great deal of energy on our part. Because it does not threaten the relationship, we devote only this limited discussion to the topic of mere disagreements. Simply put, partners resolve mere disagreements when one person decides to agree with the other, or when both "agree to disagree" because the relationship is more important than the issue. The key question in determining whether you are in a mere disagreement is to ask yourself if you must resolve the issue.

2.2 Think about It

Have there been times when you paid more attention to a critical comment from someone than you needed to? How did you free yourself of the negative feelings it aroused? Did you feel competent in the way you dealt with the situation?

Perhaps the opposite of a mere disagreement is an **overblown conflict,** which occurs when people exaggerate a conflict, generally using a relatively unimportant issue as a focal point. Unlike a misplaced conflict, where people are using a safe issue as a means of masking a deeper issue, these issues constitute a real conflict. However, the conflict is overblown by one or more of the parties who attributes far more significance to it than the conflict deserves. This narrative illustrates an overblown conflict.

> I had been having a really bad day. I was so stressed out and overburdened by homework and job responsibilities, and to top it off, I had a huge paper I was working on that was due in two days, which I had barely even started. Mary chose this particular time to enter the room and discuss the positioning of our bathroom towels on the rack. She seemed frustrated that the four of us, who were sharing the bathroom, had taken to haphazardly pushing and stuffing our towels through the narrow metal rods, thus having them all scrunched up together, which did not allow them to dry properly. I felt that this was such an inane discussion, I suddenly overreacted and really told her off.

Although the towels represent a conflict issue the roommates should discuss rationally at some point, in this overblown conflict they have served the person trying to study as a way to release her frustration about her lack of progress. Overblown conflicts are often resolved when the person who has done the ranting and raving apologizes, usually making some excuse for the untoward behavior (e.g., "I was stressed out") that the target of the conflict accepts as a reasonable excuse. Later in Chapter 9, we suggest how to better manage stress so we can prevent overblown conflicts.

Whether overblown or not, real conflicts that are more important than mere disagreements are the primary focus of this book. In Chapter 1, we defined interpersonal conflict as a problematic situation in which the conflicting parties are interdependent, perceive that they are experiencing incompatible goals or the means to those goals, or perceive that one of the people in the relationship has acted in ways that violate expectations without sufficiently explaining why. Further, the perceived incompatibility or violation of expectations has the potential to adversely affect the relationship if not addressed, and there is a sense of urgency about the need to resolve the difference. Consider the following example.

> After working as a nurse all week, I usually end up also cleaning the house, taking care of the kids, and doing the laundry on the weekends. Meanwhile, my husband plays golf most of the time. Would you believe that when he gets home, he often arrives in a bad mood because he lost or had a bad day? What does he have to complain about? He is playing a sport, while I am working on the weekends, too.

What makes this problematic situation a real conflict? First, we cannot accuse the wife of seeing a problem where none exists. It's clear that there is a disparity between what she expects should happen in her relationship and what really is happening, and the average onlooker would agree that the disparity creates a problem. Second, this conflict is the kind that grows worse over time. Even if the wife doesn't say anything now, she is likely to resent her husband's golfing more and more, particularly as it does not seem to result in a more pleasant person returning from the golf course. There are really two conflicts presented here: One is that the husband is playing golf instead of helping with the housework, and the second is his moodiness due to how poorly he plays the game. Most of this textbook includes principles and techniques designed to help you deal with real conflicts.

To determine whether an interpersonal conflict is real and important enough to manage, we suggest that the first questions you ask of yourself when faced with a problematic situation are these:

- Is this really a conflict?
- Is the other person important to me? Do I have a relationship with that person? If I have a relationship, do I want it to continue?
- Is this person really interfering with goals I consider important? Are we engaged in incompatible activities?
- Did this person just do something I consider unacceptable without explaining him/herself?
- If I don't do anything about this, is it going to affect the way I feel about the other person?

The last question has to do with determining the importance of the conflict to the person with the complaint. Sometimes, you can have a real conflict—a problematic situation in which one person interferes with another's goals, engages in incompatible activities, or fails to account for untoward behavior—but that **unimportant conflict** is not likely to continue to create problems in the future because it is insignificant or a one-time event. Depending on their effect on at least one of the conflicting parties, real conflicts are located on a scale from more to less important. Consider Larry's story.

> I came home from work and my wife was sitting near the door waiting for me. She said she had to talk to me about something she got in the mail. I realized that she had opened the credit card bill and I knew we were going to have a *big* problem. I hadn't told her the truth about how much money I had been spending, and she's a person who thinks we shouldn't even have credit cards. It's no wonder when I can't seem to control myself.

Competitive games are those in which the rules are known and generally agreed on, although people sometimes take issue with their application.

Suppose we asked you to explain why this situation is important to Larry and his wife. First, you might say that this issue has considerable potential of having serious consequences even though they may love each other a great deal. Second, you should point out that the narrated incident has all the elements of an important conflict. One of the parties has broken important rules of the relationship: Purchases have been made that were unknown to the other person, and those purchases are apparently too large. An apparent disagreement over the way Larry spends money cries out for resolution. Because Larry's spending habits could adversely affect his marriage, this behavior pattern represents an important issue.

Competitive Situations

Although we differentiated among real conflicts that ranged from minor to overblown, we can also differentiate among them based on their degree of competition. They range from noncompetitive to competitive.

> Competition . . . involves striving for scarce objects (a prize or resource usually "awarded" by a third party) according to established rules which strictly limit what the competitors can do to each other in the course of striving; the chief objective is the scarce object, not the injury or destruction of an opponent per se.[4]

Competition is a situation in which we have a desire to win, either by topping the other in an argument, a game, or some kind of larger rivalry. Americans often watch or participate in competitive events. Perhaps this is because we view competition as "a challenge to develop our resources and ourselves."[5]

Sometimes competition is healthy and fun when approached as a game. The danger to competitive situations is that we tend to see them as having only win–lose outcomes. If we don't walk away as winners, then we are walking away as losers. The difficulties arise when we take our losses in competition as reflections of our personal competence.

In less formal circumstances, interpersonal behavior resembles a competitive game. Nicole's account of her desire to do well in a class explains the idea of competition.

> My roommate, Jen, and I decided to take the same class together. Every time I saw her studying for a class, I'd anxiously ask her what class she was studying for, and if it was our class, I'd soon be studying my notes too. My goal with Jen was not an intent to "beat her" to get a better grade than she would get; I simply wanted her to think of me as a good student and not an "incompetent dimwit."

In extreme cases, competition has the potential to affect the relationship, if either person finds the competition upsetting. But a competition may make a relationship interesting and may not do damage to it. It depends on whether or not those involved find the competition fun and harmless. In this narrative, for example, competition does not seem to fit well in the relationship.

> I like to play Ping-Pong, and I often win. One friend keeps challenging me to see if eventually he will win (no conflict), but the other was offended after a couple of games (conflict). He said, "It's no use playing against you, you always win." So, if he and I are to preserve a friendship, we shouldn't play Ping-Pong, or I'll have to take it easy and (not too obviously) lose sometimes.

Arguments, or the exchange of claims about some idea, are a staple of everyday life as a form of competition that ranges from mild to severe. We argue about politicians, politics, whether a movie is worth seeing, whether being a vegetarian is reasonable—in short, life gives us many opportunities to express our opinions by stating claims and offering reasons for making those claims. Many of us find people who are reluctant to express an opinion to be boring. An argument turns into a serious real conflict, however, when one person's desire to express an opinion becomes a need to win an argument without space for anyone else's opinion to receive equal consideration. When only one viewpoint is legitimate, conflict arises from the argument.

2.3 Think about It

When does the urge to compete affect your relationships? How do you make sure that both you and the other person understand that the competition is "friendly" rather than something more serious?

2.2 Apply It

Take a sheet of paper and make six columns on it. Label the columns mere disagreements, overblown conflicts, unimportant conflicts, real conflicts, arguments, and competition. In each column, identify a conflict you experienced or witnessed that took one of these forms. Your description should answer:

- What was the conflict about?
- Why did you think there was a conflict?
- How did you resolve the conflict?

Interpersonal Violence

Another way to differentiate among real conflicts is based on their degree of violence. Unlike the types of conflict discussed so far, interpersonal violence involves harming another person physically, emotionally, or mentally. For example, a couple may start by disagreeing over where to place fruits and vegetables in the refrigerator ("they should go over here"; "no they should go there"), but escalate into **verbal aggression/abuse** (insults, name calling, and the like),[6] and may even wind up screaming and throwing objects. We have more to say about verbal abuse in Chapter 4, but for now we want to say that, in some cases, verbal abuse may escalate into **physical aggression,** when one or both parties physically attack the other. Later, when asked what they were fighting about or what started the argument, the two may not even remember, which is a sure sign that the conflict itself is unimportant. Bickering, verbal abuse, and physical abuse are all forms of interpersonal violence that people tend to see as conflicts.[7] We should point out that communication scholars are quite concerned about such interpersonal behavior. Bickering, verbal abuse, and physical aggression are not recommended and often characterize problematic relationships in need of help, although the partners may not think so.

2.4 Think about It

How has an important conflict turned into verbal abuse in your past? Did verbal aggression resolve the issue? How did it affect your relationship with the other person?

Conflict Games.   You may wonder why we think conflict games are a form of interpersonal violence. Conflict games are a way people try to keep others off balance so they can maintain a sense of superiority. Their purpose is to harm the other person.

Conflict games are not oriented toward addressing a particular issue in the relationship. A **conflict game** follows a series of steps toward a well-defined payoff (usually a "snare") that may hurt, embarrass, anger, or offend the other person.[8] One person's description of her relationship with her mother resembles a conflict game.

> I always feel like part of a chess game when doing conflict with Mother. She moves carefully, then sits back waiting for you to fall into her trap. Sometimes I see the bad move, sometimes I don't, but it seems as though she is happiest when someone falls into the trap.

Some examples of often-played conflict games include:

- "If It Weren't for You," which is used to blame others for one's own problems;
- "I'm Only Trying to Help," in which the initiator brings up some problem of the listener so that the other sees the initiator as a savior;
- "NIGYSOB," in which the initiator maneuvers the other into a position of vulnerability to punish the other;
- "Yes, but," in which a person asks for advice and then rejects all suggestions as not useful (proving that his or her problem is more serious than anything anyone could imagine); and

- "Wooden Leg," in which people respond to the conflict concerns of others by using a variety of excuses to show that the responder cannot meet the expectations or requests of the person making the request.

The problem with such game-playing in conflict is that the game-player does not seek or work toward a mutually satisfactory outcome. Rather, game-players' goals are to attain the payoffs that allow them to remain in control of the other person, and not to resolve an issue. When choices are limited or when players cannot leave the situation, the game can become destructive to the relationship.

The solution to game-playing is easy to state but hard to perform: Refuse to provide the payoff. Consider the following "If It Weren't for You" game between two roommates:

DANA: You cashed my rent check too soon! I told you not to cash it until Monday. Now three of my checks have bounced, I got charged $30.00, and I can't pay my part of the phone bill!

CHRIS: You didn't say anything about holding the check.

DANA: Why do I have to tell you everything! You always do this to me. I can't believe how much my bank account gets screwed up because you don't wait to cash my checks until I tell you to.

CHRIS: We both have to pay the same amount of rent, at the same time, every month. It's your responsibility to make sure you have enough money to cover your share. It's not my responsibility to make sure it's okay to cash your check before I go to the bank.

The important move in this exchange is for Chris to assert himself and call attention to the fact that the other is playing a game. You can note such phrases as "You always do this to me . . . because you . . ." as being indicative of the "If It Weren't for You" game. By doing so, you refuse to play. If Chris becomes defensive about cashing Dana's check, Dana can continue to play the "If It Weren't for You" game and find even more problems for which Chris is responsible. It is important to realize when we are subjected to game-playing and to make it clear to game-players that we do not play their games.

Issues in Conflicts

One more way to discriminate among real conflicts is to categorize them according to the type of issue involved in the conflict. **Conflict issues** are the focal point of the conflict, the "trigger" that people point to when they are asked what the conflict was about.[9] Interestingly, whether an issue is major or minor does not affect the relational satisfaction of those experiencing it; rather, it is the way people handle their conflicts that affects their satisfaction with their relationship.[10] Table 2.1 lists the two types of conflict issues and gives examples of the way we might address them in a conflict situation.

Tangible Issues.   There are two broad classes of conflict issues: those that concern tangible issues, and those that concern intangible issues. **Tangible issue conflicts** involve one's personal property, money, land, grades, promotions, water/food/air supply, natural resources (oil, timber, precious metals), awards/rewards, jobs, and so on. When tangible

TABLE 2.1 **Issues in Conflicts**

Tangible Issues	Intangible Issues		
Concern material resources that are divisible in some way, such as money, time, etc.	Involve immaterial resources that we value, such as esteem, power, love, etc.		
"I think we need new windows this year, even if we have to borrow the money to get them."	Personality Issues	Relationship/ normative Issues	Behavioral Issues
	"I don't like the selfish way you act"	"I expect you to call me if you're late"	"Why did you buy a new stereo without talking to me about it?"

resources are scarce, conflicts involving them take more than interpersonal communication to resolve; they require more advanced problem solving techniques. Some examples of conflicts involving scarce resources include:

- Another person asks to move in with you and your roommate in an apartment or room designed for only two occupants.
- You and another must share only one car.
- There is not enough money for both of you to buy what you each want.
- Both parents want full custody of the children.
- An ex-spouse believes that she or he cannot maintain the current standard of living and at the same time pay alimony to the ex-partner.

Tangible, resource, or interest-based issues generally are conflicts that are countable and divisible, such as how we behave in regard to handling money, time, and space. Tangible issues are most susceptible to win–lose thinking and present a challenge for those who would create win–win outcomes. In the case of a married couple discussing how to spend their vacation, let us say that she likes the fact that they "always go to the East Coast to visit her parents," but this time her husband wants to go to Hawaii. They do not have enough money to do both. A solution that would seem like "winning" to both of them might consist of a vacation package in the Caribbean that would allow them a stop on the East Coast. People in conflicts over tangible resources often have a difficult time seeing the other person's perspective, and the production of win–win outcomes is often time consuming. This narrative describes a behavioral conflict based on tangible issues.

> My parents wanted me to come back and attend school near them next year. My mom said she missed me and wanted me to go to school nearby so that I could commute from my parents' house. They're having a hard time letting me go. They tell me they can't afford this college. I work 30 hours a week and would pay for school on my own if I could take out more loans, but they are against that idea. There is so much tension in my family over this. I grew up in this state—my parents are the ones who moved. There's nothing for me there and I don't want to leave here.

Tangible, resource-based issue conflicts are almost always real and important conflicts: They occur between interdependent people arguing over issues and possible solutions that could potentially affect their relationship. We return to the subject of conflicts based on tangible issues and how to resolve them in Chapter 7, where we discuss negotiation.

Intangible Issues.   Another kind of conflict issue revolves around intangible issues. **Intangible issue conflicts** are not over hard, physical, or observable assets. They involve love, attention, cooperative and beneficial behaviors, respect, power, self-esteem, and caring. Although these resources are often initially perceived as being scarce, this is a misperception, because conflicting parties can share them.

Some intangible conflicts involve **personality issue conflicts,** which focus on a whole constellation of behaviors such as being dominating, introverted, selfish, or achievement oriented. "Alanna always does this." A lazy person presents problems for a highly productive, motivated individual. A shy person may make social life difficult for an outgoing, extroverted person. Behaviors are involved, but there is more going on. The conflicting parties differ on a way of life or values. Individuals need to make deep-seated changes, which are possible, but difficult and unlikely. Often personality conflicts do not result in mutually satisfying outcomes.

Relationship/normative issue conflicts involve rules, norms, and boundaries that partners have tacitly or overtly agreed on. Sometimes one friend decides to change the nature of the relationship to a romantic one, but the other person is caught completely off guard and finds the other's advances offensive or inappropriate because she wants them to remain "just friends."

Still other intangible conflicts are **behavioral issue conflicts,** which concern specific and individual behaviors we can observe such as the way we handle money, time, space, and so on. The issue concerns *how* we have done something more than what we have done. We should not confuse these with personality and relationship issues, which also consist of behaviors. These behaviors are simple, one-time occurrences. When Mike is late to meet Sara, she might object because she was worried about him. If Mike is always late, this is more of a personality issue because Sara may think that he is disrespectful of her and forgetful.

2.3 Apply It

Take a sheet of paper and make four columns on it. Label the columns tangible issue conflicts, personality issue conflicts, relationship/normative issue conflicts, and behavioral conflicts. In each column, identify a conflict you experienced or witnessed that took one of these forms. Your description should answer:

- What was the conflict about?
- Why did you think there was a conflict?
- How did you resolve the conflict?

When resources are not scarce, people do not have to gain at the other person's expense. Conflicts involving resources that are not scarce are often resolved through interpersonal communication (as discussed in Chapters 3–6). Sometimes, though, people perceive that the conflict is over scarce resources when in fact it is not. This conflict, for example, initially looks like a conflict over scarce resources.

> A conflict started when my friend and I both changed our majors to the same one and began having classes together. She would expect me to give her my answers to study guides for tests. When I did not, the conflict began. She is just lazy, and she procrastinates. She would wait until the last moment and then expect me to help her. I do not think I should give her the work that I spent hours doing. It was not like she had been working on it all weekend and needed help. She just wanted the answers so that she did not have to do the work herself.

Information, and the work required to attain it, is considered a scarce resource. Even more significant, however, is the question of relational boundaries in this situation. The issue that really drives the conflict is intangible and concerns the apparent lack of respect the asker has for the narrator. The narrator admits that the conflict has been three years in the making. Her friend has been taking advantage of her ability to stay on top of assignments for quite a while. The information at stake here seems like a scarce resource, but anyone can attain it if he or she is willing to look for it. On the other hand, the narrator believes that her work efforts are appropriated by another without any kind of compensation. In a real sense, her friend is "stealing" from her—time, effort, and information—because she is not giving anything in return (in addition to the fact that cheating is wrong). In this situation, if the use of competent communication and conflict skills cannot help the narrator to establish boundaries, we could conclude that the relationship is not worth preserving. At the very least, the narrator has the right to say, "I will no longer feed you the answers, even if that costs us our friendship."

Conflicts over issues that are intangible, and, thus, not truly scarce resources (even though conflicting parties may think otherwise), include situations like these:

- One partner has not been paying enough attention to the other partner (ignoring her or him).
- One person offends another by using sexist, racist, stereotyped, or otherwise offensive language.
- One person's behaviors, habits, or actions annoy or upset another person.
- One partner needs time alone or time out with friends.

Note that the common feature of these examples is that they all involve nonmaterial issues. Usually, we do not lose in situations where we are asked to spend more time with a partner. So in situations like this, being aware of the effects of one's behavior on others is not a win–lose situation. Asking one's relational partner to allow time for other friends or to leave one alone should not threaten the partner or take away from the relationship. When one is involved in situations like these, careful diagnosis of the conflict should allow the implementation of the interpersonal communication and conflict skills discussed in Chapters 3–6.

Manage It

This chapter focuses on the skills associated with recognizing different types of conflicts so as to select the appropriate response. Recognizing that we are seeing a conflict where none exists, or that we are having a conflict with the wrong person or over the wrong issue helps us to focus on the conflicts that really do require our attention.

Real conflicts are important to us. They involve issues that cannot be reduced to a simple disagreement or explained away, like an overblown conflict. Real conflicts revolve around issues that have the potential to end the relationship if they are not addressed. We know that we're not experiencing a real conflict when it becomes clear that the issue is one on which we can agree to disagree, or when we realize that we are giving far too much attention to an issue that doesn't deserve it. It also helps to recognize when we are turning a competitive situation into a conflict situation that can harm the relationship by expecting a win–lose outcome. Moreover, although it is realistic to expect that conflicts will sometimes involve verbal or even physical aggression, the judicious use of conflict management strategies may keep conflicts from escalating that far.

Real conflicts may involve both tangible and intangible resources. Tangible resources are often considered scarce because people believe there are not enough of them to be distributed equitably. Tangible issues involve one's personal property, money, land, grades, promotions, water/food/air supply, natural resources (oil, timber, precious metals), awards/rewards, jobs, and so on. Intangible resources are not physical or observable assets, and include love, attention, cooperative and beneficial behaviors, respect, power, self-esteem, and caring. Although these latter resources are perceived as scarce, this is a misperception, because we can share them. Where resources are not scarce, people do not have to gain at the other person's expense.

Conflicts over intangible resources can be classified into one of three types—personality, relationship/normative, and behavioral issues. Personality issues focus on a whole constellation of behaviors such as being dominating, introverted, achievement oriented, and so forth. Relationship/normative issues involve rules, norms, and boundaries that partners tacitly or overtly agree upon. Behavioral issues concern specific and observable individual behaviors such as the way we handle money, time, space, and so on. As we use the term here, behavioral issues do not reflect one's personality, nor do they reflect a norm expected in a relationship. All these become issues when one does something upsetting to another or does not do what was expected.

Although we need to learn how to manage our real conflicts over important matters, we often resolve unreal conflicts by apology. Later in this textbook, we learn how to confront others in noncompetitive and nonviolent ways. Moreover, we learn negotiation techniques that apply to tangible conflicts as well as other confrontation skills for dealing with conflicts over intangible issues.

2.1 Work with It

Read the following narrative and answer the questions that follow.

> My husband often has too much to drink, but usually it makes him more cheerful. He always hands over the keys to the car, and I drive home. At this one party, though, he was exceptionally rude to me. He told me to get out of his way and mind my own business. When we left he insisted on driving home, scaring me to death. For three days I didn't say anything more to him than I had to: breakfast is ready; dinner is ready—you know. Finally, he said, "I don't know what I said or did at that party, but you haven't talked to me since then. I was really drunk. What did I do?" I told him he insulted me and scared me to death driving home. He was shocked. He denied behaving that way. Then he launched into calling me names. I dropped the subject because I didn't want him getting more upset.

1. Is this narrative an example of a real or an unreal conflict? Why?
2. Is competition involved here? Why or why not?
3. Is this an example of a tangible or intangible type of conflict?
4. Based on the nature of the issue involved, is this also a behavioral, normative, or personality conflict?

2.2 Work with It

Identify whether the following narratives describe tangible or intangible conflicts. Justify your answers based on the definition of tangible and intangible conflicts. Check your answers on page 283.

1. Crumbling Walls: Tangible or Intangible?

   We were given a small amount of money by my husband's parents. When they sent it, they indicated that they intended for us to use it for improvements around the house. They knew we needed to replace a crumbling wall and that our windows weren't much good on bad weather days. However, they made the check out to my husband, and he thinks that because it came from his parents, he should have the largest say in how the money is spent. That wouldn't bother me too much, except that he wants to buy an expensive "toy" with it that only he will use. Any kind of work we do on the house benefits both of us—we improve its value, we lower utility bills, and all that. This seems really unfair to me, but I don't know how to talk to him about it without both of us getting angry.

2. The House: Tangible or Intangible?

   My wife has been unemployed for several months. She's had a couple leads on jobs, but they haven't gotten anywhere. She doesn't seem to be trying very hard. In the meantime, I've been working overtime to try to keep us from going into debt. And then she expects me to do her "honey-dos" around the house on the weekends. If we were both working, I wouldn't mind as much, but it hardly seems as though she does anything all day while I am gone. The house is barely clean and when I ask her what she did all day she just shrugs and says she doesn't know. I'm really frustrated.

2.3 Work with It

After doing this exercise, check your answers on page 283. If you have trouble with the answers, re-read the relevant part of Chapter 2.

Type of Issue

Identify the correct <u>type of issue</u> (behavioral, relationship/normative, or personality—not the type of conflict) involved in the following interpersonal conflicts.

1. I was brought up in the same house as my sister, but we are so different. I have worked since I was 12 years old. I am a neat person, and I do housework when it must be done. I could never imagine stealing from anyone, let alone my mother and sister. Meanwhile, my sister has always been a constant partier and is perhaps the sloppiest and laziest girl I have ever met. She was never able to hold on to a job because she did not want to get up for work. When I was about 13, I used to babysit and I tried to save some of my money. Even then, my sister would steal my money because she was too lazy to earn it herself.

2. Here is an example from my own family that happens constantly. We decide to have dinner out in the evening. My husband gives our children the choice of going to restaurant A or B. The kids pick A, which serves fast food. He really isn't in the mood for fast food, so he argues for B, which is a restaurant with seating and waitresses. It then becomes absolutely ridiculous as he tries to campaign for his choice over theirs. Why give them a choice at all if he is going to argue? If he expected or wished them to say restaurant B in the first place, why not just state that from the get-go?

3. My boyfriend and I are both divorced, and we have been together for ten years now. The problem is that I have been very patient in the hope that he will decide to get married someday. The past couple of years, I have tried to bring up the subject but he acts like he doesn't hear me. He changes the subject, or doesn't respond. When he does respond, he simply says that he isn't ready for that yet. He acts like he likes living together, but he just won't make the commitment.

Type of Conflict

Identify the <u>type of conflict</u> (false, real, misplaced, displaced, mere disagreement—not type of issue) involved in the following interpersonal conflicts.

4. My mother and I are constantly fighting about things like money, cars, school, values, and morals. I think the real issues are her controlling me, me wanting my independence and feeling that she hasn't taken correct responsibility for me as her child, financially or emotionally. She'll criticize me for not doing something "right," but I know she is really upset because she was unable to control my decision.

5. Very often I do this to both my family and my friends. If I am having a bad day, I definitely take out the frustration on a friend or my brother. I snap at them for no apparent reason and yell at them. I know that this isn't the way to deal with everyday life, but it is just something that I do.

6. There are many times when my boyfriend and I think that we have a problem but then after talking realize that we are both being silly. Things pop up in our mind, we get all upset, we start arguing, and then we calmly work things out. Many times it is over things that don't even exist.

7. I have no major disagreements. In my family or among my friends when we fight we say how we feel and then go on with whatever we are doing. I try and accept other people's views and not hold it against them, and I expect the same respect. We agree to disagree.

8. I work with other people and we have to agree on how to proceed or we wouldn't get anything done. Every decision has an affect on everyone at work. We are always dealing with issues that affect all of us.

2.1   **Remember It**

Write an essay in which you apply the ideas presented in Chapter 2 to your life situation. Make sure to address the following topics.

1. Give your own example of a real conflict you encountered or witnessed.
2. Give your own example for each of the different types of unreal conflicts.
3. Give your own example of a real conflict involving competition or violence.
4. Give your own example of a tangible conflict.
5. Give your own example of an intangible conflict that is primarily a behavioral, relationship/normative, or personality conflict.

N O T E S

1. Morton Deutsch, *The Resolution of Conflict* (New Haven, CT: Yale University Press, 1973).
2. Ibid.
3. Morton Deutsch, "Conflicts: Productive or Destructive?" *Journal of Social Issues* 25 (1969), 7–41.
4. Raymond W. Mack and Richard C. Snyder, "The Analysis of Social Conflict: Toward an Overview and Synthesis," in Fred E. Jandt (Ed.), *Conflict Resolution through Communication* (New York: Harper and Row, 1973), p. 34.
5. Laura Tracy, *The Secret among Us: Competition among Women* (Boston: Little Brown, 1991), p. 4.
6. Dominic Infante and C. J. Wigley, "Verbal Aggressiveness: An Interpersonal Model and Measure," *Communication Monographs* 53 (1986), 61–69.
7. Shinobu Suzuki and Andrew S. Rancer, "Argumentativeness and Verbal Aggressiveness: Testing for Conceptual and Measurement Equivalence Across Four Cultures," *Communication Monographs* 61 (1994), 256–279.

8. Eric Berne, *Games People Play* (New York: Ballantine Books, 1964).
9. See, for example, Deutsch, *The Resolution of Conflict*, op. cit.; Harriet Braiker and Harold Kelley, "Conflict in the Development of Close Relationships," in Robert L. Burgess and Ted L. Huston (Eds.), *Social Exchange in Developing Relationships* (New York: Academic Press, 1979), pp. 135–168; Paul Wehr, *Conflict Regulation* (Boulder, CO: Westview Press, 1979); and Thomas R. Harvey and Bonita Drolet, *Building Teams, Building People: Expanding the Fifth Resource* (La Verne, CA: University of La Verne, 1992).
10. Duncan Cramer, "Relationship Satisfaction and Conflict over Minor and Major Issues in Romantic Relationships," *Journal of Psychology* 136 (2002), 75–81; see also Duncan Cramer, "Linking Conflict Management Behaviors and Relational Satisfaction: The Intervening Role of Conflict Outcome Satisfaction," *Journal of Social and Personal Relationships* 19 (2002), 425–432.

3 Responding to Conflict

The S-TLC System

OBJECTIVES

At the end of this chapter, you should be able to:

- Briefly explain the S-TLC system for dealing with conflict situations.

- Briefly explain how to "stop" and not respond habitually when in a conflict situation.

- Explain in depth different ways to "think" about a conflict.

- Offer constructive advice to someone who doesn't "listen" well.

- Briefly explain why the transactional model of communication is preferable to the linear model for managing conflict situations.

KEY TERMS

analysis	listening	thinking
communication	mind-mapping	trained incapacity
identity goals	relational goals	transactional model of
instrumental goals	S-TLC	communication
linear model of communication	stopping	

In previous chapters, we define conflict and discuss many different types that have implications for how one should handle a conflict. Of particular importance are real, important conflicts that concern intangible issues. To manage them effectively, you need specific communication skills. A communication skill is "the successful performance of a communicative behavior . . . [and] the ability to repeat such a behavior."[1] You need to identify different types of conflicts and know how to fit the communication skills to the appropriate situation. The purpose of this chapter is to describe a set of communication skills that are most useful for managing conflict situations in which the issues are intangible. After reading this chapter, you can apply the following system to create a mutual understanding in a conflict situation.

3.1 Apply It

Before reading the rest of this chapter, ask a good friend to evaluate you on your communication skills. How do their answers compare to yours?

excellent listener ⊢——┼——┼——┼——┤ poor listener

understands others easily ⊢——┼——┼——┼——┤ doesn't understand easily

easy to understand ⊢——┼——┼——┼——┤ hard to understand

Where could you make the most improvement in your communication skills?

The S-TLC System

The **S-TLC** system is an acronym for Stop, Think, Listen, and Communicate. We use the hyphen in *S-TLC* to help you recall the system because we all need a little TLC in our lives; so we thought you could easily remember S-TLC. Note, however, that our TLC stands for something different from Tender, Loving Care. By following these four steps, you can often resolve interpersonal conflicts through basic communication skills.

■ *Step 1: Stop.* When you realize that a conflict exists, begin by saying: "Stop!" Don't become so upset that you start to lose control of yourself. Instead, try to calm down and cool off. Try to control your mental faculties.

■ *Step 2: Think.* Think before you act! At an elementary level, try not to take the conflict personally. At a more advanced level, think about your goals, wants, and needs and those of your partner.

■ *Step 3: Listen.* Listen before you say anything! The tendency of most people is to justify themselves the moment they hear criticism, rather than really listening to what the other person is saying. We believe that as important as what we say in a conflict is the ability to truly hear what the other person is saying.

■ *Step 4: Communicate.* Decide how to communicate and do it! You could react with violence or not. What are the outcomes if you react violently? What would happen if you don't? You could respond by communicating in a destructive way such as aggressive speech. You could respond by avoiding the conflict altogether or by simply giving in. You could sit down and discuss the problem with the other person. In this chapter, we describe a transactional approach to viewing communication that avoids some of the pitfalls committed by those who take a linear approach to communication. Further, throughout this textbook, numerous additional communication techniques are discussed.

3.1 Think about It

As you consider the S-TLC approach to conflict, which step gives you the biggest problem? Do you want to change what you do at that step? When you are taught new ways of responding, do you try to use them? If not, why not?

This chapter focuses in depth on the S-T-L-C parts of the acronym, and provides specific means for stopping, thinking, listening, and communicating to others in conflict. Let us begin with "stopping" at the onset of conflict.

Stopping: Taking Time Out

Stopping is like taking a time out. For many people this is not too difficult. For others acquiring skills for slowing down the conflict is imperative. Some suggestions are these:

1. Exit temporarily to calm yourself.
2. Get a glass of water or some other beverage and take sips of the beverage before you respond to the other person.
3. Counting backward from 100 can also help calm you down.
4. Change the problematic topic for a while to allow time for the air to clear.

3.2 Think about It

How hard is it for you to stop a conflict? If you find it easy to not respond automatically, what advice can you give others who have trouble with this step? Whether you find this step difficult or not, what ways do you prefer if you try to take a "time out"?

It would help at this point for us to ask you to list as many ways as you can for stopping and taking time out in a conflict situation. Then we ask you to compare your list with others, perhaps your classmates. You can add their suggestions to your list. Try to compare your list with as many people as you can (if possible, the entire class). We now turn your attention to thinking about the conflict.

Thinking about the Conflict: Analyzing Conflict Situations

Thinking is a way of analyzing a situation. Thinking about a conflict is likely to result in more satisfying outcomes than if one goes into a conflict without thinking about it ahead of time.[2] The purpose of this section, then, is to increase your ability to understand and analyze

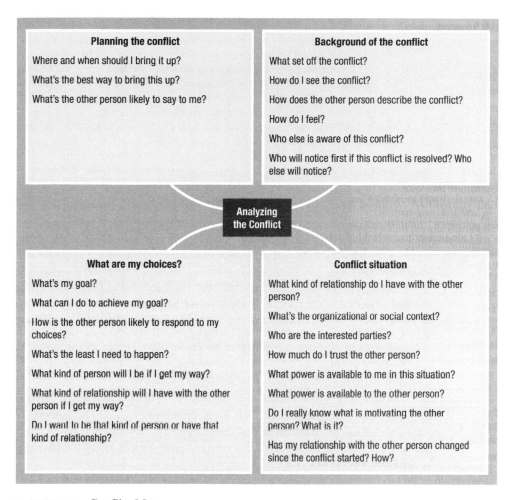

FIGURE 3.1 Conflict Map

conflict situations, so that you can choose the most effective conflict behavior. An important step in thinking about the conflict situation is to look at it as a whole, as depicted in Figure 3.1. It is helpful to keep these questions in mind as you examine a conflict.

Thinking about Changing the Other Person, Situation, or Self

The first step in thinking about a conflict is to understand that we have three options to contemplate: We can try to change the other person, we can try to change the situation, or we can try to change ourselves.[3] If you were this person, how might you have handled the conflict she describes?

> Both of our cars are old, and we definitely need to replace one of them. We really ought to replace both, but we can't afford to right now. We've been looking at different vehicles. My husband wants a truck because he goes camping a lot, but that means I'd be left with a barely

functional car much of the time. I have to drive to work, which isn't far, but I have to ferry our teenagers around quite a bit to get to their various activities. And my car isn't that roomy, which means it's hard for me to negotiate with other moms to trade off driving places. I think we need a minivan or a station wagon. It seems to me that one of those would benefit the whole family more, but all he can talk about is the fact that his truck is old and doesn't have air conditioning. Except for driving to his various campsites, he doesn't drive—he walks to school and doesn't spend much time driving the kids anywhere. I could go trade in my car by myself, but I sure don't want to live with that kind of decision—I'll hear about it for years, assuming it doesn't cause a divorce.

What are the various options open to this couple?

How can one person change another? Can or should we persuade the other to change his or her wants or needs? Perhaps the wife can convince her husband that buying the truck is selfish and immature in light of the family needs for a car that all can benefit from and enjoy. Maybe she can convince him that his idea is unfair to her or the family. She could argue that spending family money should benefit the family as a whole rather than one person in particular.

How can people change the situation? The couple could decide to purchase two less expensive vehicles than either a new truck or a new station wagon, purchasing used vehicles in better condition than the ones they have. She and her husband could take out an auto loan for one of the new vehicles. She could purchase the car she wanted by herself and live with the consequences. Finally, she could choose to leave the relationship because she is not getting what she wants out of it. All of these options would require greater effort and are more complicated than changing the other or oneself.

How can people try to change themselves? Can or should they change their wants or needs? The wife could decide that the husband really needs and deserves his truck. She may decide she can live with her car for a couple more years. She could agree to purchase his new truck on the condition that he take on more responsibility for driving their children to different places.

3.2 # Apply It

Take a sheet of paper and make three columns. In each column, describe a conflict in which

- you thought the other person should change,
- you were able to change the conditions of the conflict, and
- you thought you should change yourself.

Which of the changes was easiest to implement? Why?

In established relationships, patterns of conflict become part of the way in which people relate to one another. Because of these established interaction patterns, people may think they do not need to analyze conflicts with the other person: They think they understand how the other person expresses desires and know automatically how to respond. An excerpt from *Because It Is Bitter, and Because It Is My Heart* by Joyce Carol Oates illustrates this tacit knowledge people develop about others:

> Under Dr. Savage's guidance she is becoming more career-minded. Under Mrs. Savage's guidance she is becoming more self-effacing, more feminine. Occasionally Iris will challenge a dogmatic remark of Dr. Savage's and the two of them will talk together animatedly, with a heady intellectual passion. Less frequently, Iris will challenge a remark of Mrs. Savage's but the two of them never precisely disagree . . . such head-on confrontations are not Mrs. Savage's style. (When the subject of Martin Luther King comes up, in connection with King's proposed civil rights rally in Washington, D.C., in late August of 1963, Mrs. Savage says, "I do admire Reverend King, it's a blessing from God that [African Americans] have such a saintly leader. If it weren't for him there'd be such anger everywhere," and Iris says impulsively, "But not to be angry, for some people, is hypocritical," and Mrs. Savage says, "Oh!" in a small, still, quizzical hurt voice . . . and changes the subject.)[4]

Iris knows that her responses to Dr. and Mrs. Savage must differ because of their varying approaches to conflict: Dr. Savage expects confrontation and argument, while Mrs. Savage does not. Iris's impulsive disagreement with Mrs. Savage is out of character; throughout most of the novel she mirrors to the Savages so that they see themselves in her. Because Iris understands the demands of the situation so well, she is highly regarded by the Savages and, as she is an orphan, is "adopted" by them and made to feel part of their family.

The situational knowledge that Iris demonstrates is a foundational skill for acting effectively in conflict situations. In the introduction to their test of a three-component model of competent conflict behavior (consisting of motivation, knowledge, and skills), Spitzberg and Hecht claimed:

> The more knowledgeable a person is about the specific context, specific other, and specific topics discussed, the more likely this person is to possess the requisite information, experience, and repertoire to act competently in this situation.[5]

The authors studied naturally occurring conversations, in malls, at the beach, waiting in lines, and so on, which were interrupted to request completion of the questionnaire. Their study demonstrated strong relationships between communication motivation and skills and outcomes such as communication satisfaction and perceptions of competence. However, they failed to demonstrate any strong effect of knowledge on conversational outcomes. Knowledge was assessed with questions such as, "I knew the other person well," "The conversation was similar to other conversations I have had before," and "I was (un)familiar with the topic of the conversation." The authors concluded that, because the majority of the conversations they studied occurred between people who knew each other well, the knowledge component was not as important. Perhaps the knowledge the people had of one another had become more implicit than explicit, guiding behavior in covert rather than overt ways. "Knowledge of conversational forms, other, and topic may increase in importance in novel situations that tax a person's creativity in assimilating information from prior communicative experience."[6]

Thinking about Your Goals

A key factor to think about prior to confronting another person is your goal. What are the possible goals when a conflict presents itself? If you wish to reflect on your and others' goals in a conflict, you need to understand the three types of goals that are relevant. Put-nam and Wilson argued that people pursue instrumental, relational, and identity goals in negotiation, some of which are generated ahead of time and some of which arise during the course of interaction. These goals are sometimes ill-defined, may emerge during interaction, or may change as interaction progresses. Understanding the dynamic nature of goals can increase your options in conflict situations.

Instrumental goals are those that require the opponent to "remove a specific obstacle blocking completion of a task."[7] If you want a professor to change a grade, for instance, your instrumental goal is the actual changing of the grade as a result of your interaction with the professor. **Relational goals** involve attempts to gain power and to establish trust as the relationship between the bargainers is established. Relational goals would include establishing your right to question the grade you received while not infringing on the professor's power. **Identity goals** concern how bargainers view each other in the situation. Not only are people motivated to maintain and support each other's facework, but they sometimes desire to attack the face of the other in a conflict situation. In questioning a grade, for example, you would want to make sure that you do not attack the professor's face; comments such as "your grades are unfair" or "you never give consideration to what I say" are face-attacks. A more face-supportive comment is "I believe I met the requirements because I . . . "

3.3   Apply It

Take a sheet of paper and make three columns on it. Label the columns instrumental goal, relationship goal, and identity goal. In each column, describe a conflict you experienced or observed with that goal. What made it a conflict? How did you resolve the conflict?.

Trained Incapacities

We could more easily think about our problematic situations if it were not for our trained incapacities. What are they? A **trained incapacity** occurs when a person's abilities and talents actually limit the person's thinking.[8] Because the behavior has become generally beneficial (in nonconflict situations), the person expects it to work in conflict situations where it is inappropriate. Four such trained incapacities are goal-centeredness, destructive redefinition, evaluative tendency, and using standards.

On the one hand, goal-centeredness is generally positive: People identify the end point they hope to reach and then take the necessary steps to get there. It can function as a trained incapacity, however, when people are so eager to achieve the end point that they do not adequately think about all the dynamics of a situation. The narrative below illustrates this desire to resolve a conflict too quickly without examining all the options one could take.

An interesting situation is occurring with another tenant and my roommate and me in our apartment building. We have assigned parking spaces, and the tenant that parks next to my roommate has a tendency to pull his car in and park it in half of her space. She has asked him to pull over because she has trouble opening her door. He becomes upset because his car is soaked by the sprinklers located on the other side of it. Two nights ago when we came home, he was over his line and into our space. My roommate parked very close to his car because she thought it might make him realize how close he was parking. However, he got angry and left a nasty note on her car. Both parties are not happy. I see the situation as petty, and I think that the neighbors need to work out some kind of agreement instead of exchanging unpleasant words or notes.

Redefinition is the ability to adapt to situations as they change: As new elements enter a situation, people change their thinking to accommodate them. Redefinition can help move a conflict to resolution if participants stop defining the conflict in their own terms and start defining it in terms of mutuality. Destructive redefinition may occur, however, when participants decide that winning the issue or beating the other person is their major goal. Consider how one person shifted from making a pass to being obnoxious about it.

My friends and I went out for a beer after a football game. One of the customers became belligerent. Nothing new. Except that he turned his affections toward Kate, one of my friends. As I have said before, one way to gain my attention is to show disrespect to one of my friends. Well, I couldn't allow this boy to do this without a talking to. Which is all that I wanted to do, just talk to the guy and let him know that his actions and words were not appreciated nor tolerated. Well, as I walked away, he used colorful words and imagery to tell me how he felt, which I don't mind. But, he insisted on continuing and again approached my friend. Well, I went over to him again and asked him to show his respect to the lady. At this point he took a swing at me. I have learned self-defense over the years and reacted instinctively to his punch, which landed him on the floor. I didn't worry about him after that, because his friends came over and dragged him away.

Have you ever gotten so mad at someone that you could only think about getting even or seeking revenge? We hope you now realize that this is no way to resolve a conflict.

Evaluative ability is beneficial when it generates critical thinking about a topic and allows for more complete discussion of an issue. However, one relies on it too much when no solution seems feasible and the flaws overwhelm their usefulness. Evaluation can also stifle the introduction of issues, leading to situations in which conformity is more important than the examination of issues. Sometimes this trained incapacity is seen when people think they have "talked a problem to death" without really coming up with any kind of solution for it. An instance of a person's evaluative ability keeping them from solving a problem is found in this narrative.

We have a $31,000 piece of equipment that is not functioning properly. Because of some serious budget problems a year ago, we had to let the person go who maintained this equipment as part of her lab chores. There was a big pall over the lab because of this money crunch, and a lot was being asked of everyone since the boss had asked me to come up with a solution to the budget problem. I began implementing a proactive budget recovery program that required everyone's serious participation. I didn't have the heart to ask anyone to accept the additional chore of maintaining the equipment, so I took it on myself, although my skills weren't really up to it. I wanted to straighten out a few organizational aspects of this chore, and organize the facility before I asked anyone to do it. We hired a new person, but I didn't want to dump it on her immediately. Because the equipment is down so much, we got permission to use an identical piece in another lab, and now our equipment has become an expensive paperweight. This is hard on lab relations, but I cannot seem to find a plan that I think is workable.

A final kind of trained incapacity is the use of *objective standards* or expectations for behavior. Established standards are often useful as guidelines for decision making and interaction but are a problem when parties in the conflict believe there is one right answer and refuse to compromise that position. In the following example, the husband's standards for good restaurant service were inflexibly applied in a demanding manner.

My husband and I went out for an early dinner at a nice restaurant. The restaurant was practically empty, but we were seated next to a table that had a recently stained cover. The table had been cleared but had not been re-set for dinner. My husband, who once worked as a server in a 5-star restaurant, was horrified that the cloth was there—he felt that it should have been removed immediately even if the table wasn't set. He told the person who seated us that is was disgraceful, he told our server, and when the manager came over to ask if she could be of help, he told her. He was not appeased by their report that the busboy had not come in and it would be taken care of when he arrived. And no one was taking his "hint," if you could call it that, that the cloth simply be removed regardless of whether the table would be immediately re-set. The manager finally took it off but I could tell she was completely exasperated by his disgust at the tablecloth. Even after it was removed he kept saying that being forceful was the only way to get things done, and he was convinced he was right because everyone gave in to his demand. I was so embarrassed by his behavior that I left the waitress a *very* good tip.

People do not always realize that in spite of participating in an emotionally draining situation, there are payoffs to continuing a conflict. One such gain is that the relationship with the other person continues, even if stressful and upsetting to one or more of the individuals involved. Another gain is the delight people feel when they can prove how wrong the other person is and how right they are about the issue. In the narrative above, the husband is convinced he is right and everyone else is wrong—clearly his payoff in the conflict is in getting his way. In addition, the opportunity to exert power over the other person through conflict interaction may perpetuate a conflict situation. Let us now turn our attention to a method for analyzing conflict situations.

Mind-Mapping Approach

When thinking about a conflict becomes difficult, a "right-brain" approach to analysis, called mind-mapping, might work.[9] **Mind-mapping** is a method for making your ideas visible. By looking at them together and linking them, you can often think of a better way to deal with a problem than you would have by simply thinking about it in an analytical way. This method has become a great tool for encouraging creativity, brainstorming, and learning.

To make a mind-map, you should have a large piece of unlined paper, a pen, and some highlighters. You can make your map smaller and without color, but colors help you

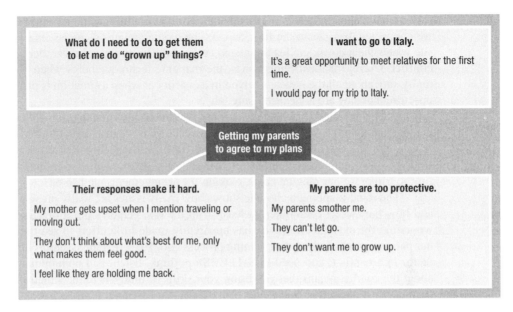

FIGURE 3.2   Specific Conflict Map

start to see relationships between concepts. Start in the middle of the paper with your pen and write down what you think the conflict is about. Now, write down everything about the conflict that comes to your mind. Write quickly and don't restrict your thinking. The first step is getting everything on paper.

Once you have your thoughts down, start making connections. Draw colored lines between concepts that seem related. Use those colors to help make sense of the conflict. identify ideas that are related. There is no "right" way to draw a mind-map because it reflects what you are thinking about the conflict.

For example, suppose you put yourself in the following situation.

> This conflict has been ongoing with my mother and father for two months now. My parents are too protective of me and they tend to smother me at times. They don't think of what is best for my life and me, only what would make them feel better. For example, I want to go to Italy this summer, but my parents don't want me to go because it's too far. I would completely pay for the trip, but instead of them realizing how great an opportunity this is for me to visit relatives I've never met, they don't want me to go because they can't let go and let me grow up. I love to travel anywhere that's new, and they keep holding me back. Another example is the fact that I want to move out and live on my own. But then when the idea comes up, my mother starts crying and becomes most upset.

Figure 3.2 illustrates a mind-mapping approach to the problem and shows a finished map. The woman describing the conflict might start with the idea that her parents are overly protective. She would write this down on the paper and circle it. Related to being protective is her parent's lack of enthusiasm for travel to Italy or moving out of the house. These ideas are written down, circled, and connected to the central idea of protectiveness. An issue related to traveling to Italy is the fact that the woman is willing to pay for the trip herself, so we connected that idea to the Italy trip. As the woman relates some issues to other issues, she writes them down, circles them, and connects them to the various other aspects of the conflict. Useful for identifying issues, the mapping technique helps when people are not really sure about all the issues involved in a conflict or when a situation is problematic and upsetting but they are not exactly sure why.

Once you have identified the conflict issues, you can begin to prioritize them: What is the most important issue here? What issues exceed your control? In the preceding example, the parents' feelings about her moving out or traveling alone are outside the control of the student. However, she can demonstrate her ability to do these challenges by saving money for the trip or for her moving costs, making the arrangements, and so on.

The mind-mapping technique shows how many issues are really present in a conflict and how they affect each other, at least from the one person's point of view. The young woman in the example, however, has apparently made little effort to see the matter from her parents' point of view; the chaining process could describe the issues as her parents see them. In a conflict, you need to S-TLC: Stop, think, listen, and communicate. Thinking about the conflict means that you bring your skills of **analysis** to the situation. In the next section, we discuss some means for improving your listening.

Listening in Conflict Situations

Most popular advice on conflict emphasizes speaking skills: Say it this way, at this time; assert yourself. But communication is the interaction of two or more people, and conflict occurs because the people have unmet needs and goals. No one likes to hear "I can't believe you feel that way," or "You're wrong," when he or she is trying to explain feelings.

Listening is a desire to pay attention to the other person, characterized by openness to the other person's views, willingness to suspend judgment during the discussion, patience to hear the other out, an empathic response to the other person, and a commitment to listen to all the other person has to say.[10] Listening does not come naturally. Rogers noted the following:

> Our first reaction to most of the statements, which we hear from other people, is an immediate evaluation or judgment, rather than an understanding of it. When someone expresses some feeling or attitude or belief, our tendency is, almost immediately, to feel, "That's right"; or "That's stupid"; "That's not nice." Rarely do we permit ourselves to understand precisely what the meaning of his statement is to him. I believe this is because understanding is risky. If I let myself really understand another person, that understanding might change me. And we all fear change.[11]

We typically feel defensive when others have something critical to say about us. We do not want to know that we are not doing well or not doing all we should do. We want to think everything is fine. Defensiveness is "a somewhat hostile, emotional state which causes people to either partially or totally reject incoming messages and other stimuli which they perceive as being incorrect or contradictory to their point of view. . . . [It] affects both our perception and our subsequent behavior."[12]

Listening is reflected in how we orient ourselves to each other physically as well as mentally.

Defensiveness arises from the interaction of people in a situation and occurs when people have a perceived flaw that they do not want to admit and they are sensitive to that flaw. When sensitive people believe that another has attacked their flaw, they respond to defend themselves. Certain behaviors do foster defensiveness, but they do so because people tend to react defensively with regard to certain topics.[13]

> My friend and I both struggle with a lot of psychological and emotional problems. Lately, we have both worked on areas in our lives. She is trying to assert herself more, and I am to the point where I cannot take any more advice on how to run my life. I need to start thinking about what I want to be, not what everyone else tells me I should be. Unfortunately, these two areas have run into each other. She feels she needs to tell me how she feels about everything, including how I act. For example, she told me the other day that I should just say, "I can't go with you today," instead of giving a long explanation. She told me when I give a long explanation it seems that I am trying to make up an excuse and that I just don't want to go with her. I told her I really couldn't handle that kind of criticism right now, and she said "no problem." Two days later, we got into it again when she got mad at me for something that wasn't my fault. She still believes she should assert herself and tell me exactly what is on her mind, and I still cannot handle it right now. It's a stalemate.

Effective listening consists of several skills, some of which may seem obvious to you, and others that may seem new. This list, while not exhaustive, can help to make you a better listener in conflict situations.

First, stop whatever you are doing and give your attention to the other person. Others feel frustrated when you do not give them your full attention. One student, for example, reported that whenever she has a meeting with her boss, he continues to read and answer his e-mail as she is talking to him in the office about issues that need resolution. She rarely walks out feeling as though he knows what is happening in the office and what she is doing about it.

Second, look at the other person. It's harder to let your mind wander when you are making eye contact. Third, engage in positive nonverbal feedback. Head nods, vocalizations such as "uh-huh," and forward lean toward the other all indicate interest. Make an effort not to engage in what are called adaptive behaviors like chewing on your nails or examining your skin or clothing carefully. These tell the other person you are not listening, even when you may be.

Fourth, work on understanding the other person's feelings, not on arguing with the other person. Indicate that you are following the other person's train of thought or not, but avoid making comments that diminish the importance of the other person's feelings or assert that the feelings are invalid.

3.3 Think about It

What are you thinking about when others talk? Do you concentrate on what they are saying or do you think about your own ideas instead? After listing to someone, can you write down most of what that person told you? If not, why not?

To concentrate only on one's own goals is to misunderstand the nature of conflict. More importantly, though, listening is a way to affirm the value and worth of others. One author wrote that the feeling of being truly heard is so close to the feeling of being loved that most people cannot tell the difference.[14] Next, we turn to the topic of communicating.

Communicating in Conflict Situations

Typically, the field of communication has embraced a wide variety of perspectives of communication. In this chapter, we'll introduce you to two of those perspectives and demonstrate how looking at communication in that manner affects the way we define and perceive conflict.

The "Linear" Model: Message Senders and Receivers

A way in which communication researchers have traditionally viewed communication is to define it as a process of sending and receiving messages. Some communication studies have focused primarily on the sending or encoding of messages and how people in certain situations tend to engage in certain kinds of message production behaviors. These studies raised questions related to goals, purposes, and intentions of message senders. Other communication studies have examined the receiving or decoding of messages and how people are likely to respond to messages. These latter studies raised questions related to the effects of messages on receivers.

Focusing on message senders or message receivers is a way of studying communication. This orientation to communication has been called the **linear model of communication,** because it focuses on the sequential production of messages with either the senders as the starting point or the receivers as the end point. For the most part, it has focused on issues of fidelity—is what was "received" the same meaning as what was "sent"? A visual metaphor for the linear model of communication is a conveyor belt that runs back and forth between two people. The "sender" puts a message on the belt, sends it to the "receiver," who then does something to the message and sends it back to the sender. Along the way, the message is sent via one channel or another and is distorted by external sources, or "noise."

When applied to communication, the linear model suggests that interpersonal conflict is something we do to someone. We take a position and try to convince the other of our view. We are right and the other is wrong, so we argue. We would view the conflict as a misunderstanding because the other does not agree with us. Taking a defensive position, we would not bend, we would not really listen, or we may not even let the other person talk, because we want to convince the other (and not let the other convince us). Our focus is on the end result, which means getting the other to change his or her mind or behavior. In addition, using a linear model to explain conflict often results in trying to fix the "blame" of the conflict situation on one person or another, not recognizing that both people in a conflict situation contribute to the emergence of the conflict. In the extreme, this mode of thinking might lead us to point the finger of blame at the other and accuse the other of stupidity, making a wrong decision, or doing something wrong behaviorally. We may yell and scream until the conflict tilts in our favor. There are other ways to manage conflicts. Our need for an alternative approach leads us to the "transactional" model of communication.

The "Transactional" Model: People Communicating Together

Although researchers have commonly referred to senders and receivers of messages in the past, it is more common today to talk about **communication** as a process by which people make or create meaning together. This is commonly called the **transactional model of communication.** While the linear view emphasized the end product of communicating (convincing, persuading, controlling, or dominating the other), the transactional view emphasizes the process of communicating. Such an approach recognizes that communication (and by extension, conflict) isn't something we do "to" one another, but something we do "with" one another (like teamwork). A conflict is not seen as something that happens when one person "sends" a message to another indicating that he or she is unhappy with some behavior performed by the other. Rather, conflict is seen as the behaviors of each person, in response to one another, exchanging messages, hearing each other out, trying to cooperate, conjointly creating an understanding in which both people perceive themselves as being in conflict with one another, mutually sharing responsibility for the conflict situation, and working together to better deal with it. Conflict is viewed as giving and taking, working together for a solution to a problem, discussing, and arriving at mutual understandings, consensus, agreement, and resolution. Both conflicting parties have a responsibility toward empathizing with each other, avoiding judgment, keeping an open mind, welcoming feedback, and realizing that both may have to adapt to resolve the conflict situation. It is no accident that the transactional approach to communication consists of many concepts and skills taught in basic interpersonal communication courses. Some other differences between the linear and transactional views of communication are:

1. The linear view focuses on how an individual's behaviors are followed by another's responses to them, while the transactional view emphasizes what people do together. Thus, the transactional view highlights the "inter" in interpersonal communication and conflict: how people collaborate, cooperate, and work together to negotiate and re-negotiate an understanding, agreement, or consensus.

2. Whereas the linear view treated people as though they have set identities before, during, and after communication or conflict, the transactional view includes the idea that whenever we are in communication with others, we are negotiating and re-negotiating who we are—our definitions of ourselves and the impressions we make on others.

3. While the linear view also treats relationships as fixed entities that do not change (once friends, always friends; once enemies, always enemies), the transactional view acknowledges that, whenever we are in communication with others, we are negotiating and re-negotiating our understanding of our relationship.

The advantage of the transactional view is that we begin to recognize the importance of both people's behavior in the conflict situation. One person acting "competently" in a conflict situation, using good communication skills, usually cannot bring the conflict to some resolution. It takes two people to make the conflict, and it takes two people to manage or resolve it. The way people talk about the conflict together, the way they express messages in response to one another, and the way they "read" each other's nonverbal messages as the conflict is being enacted all create the conflict situation as well as manage it or move it to resolution. The primary difference between the linear and transactional focus in communication is seen in the visual metaphors we might use to explain each. While the primary visual metaphor for the linear model is a conveyor belt, in the transactional model, communication (and hence conflict as a type of communication) is seen more as a dance that two people do together.

3.4 Think about It

How can you understand conflict better by explaining it from a linear model or a transactional model? Which one makes more sense to you? Why?

We have a great deal more to say in the next chapter about communicating, where we describe how to choose the appropriate communication option for managing a particular conflict. We hope you choose to react nonviolently unless in self-defense and when violence is the only option. Remember that some people believe that violence is never an option. They claim that if you put your mind to it you can always find a nonviolent solution to any problematic situation. We strongly encourage you to try communication first. The next chapter explores your communication options in detail.

3.5 Think about It

How do you normally communicate with others in a conflict situation? What do you usually say and how do you usually say it? How did these conflicts usually turn out? Were you satisfied with the outcomes?

Manage It

This chapter introduces you to one of the most important tools in conflict management—the S-TLC system. The S-TLC system teaches us to stop, think, listen, and then communicate with the other person. By following these four steps, we can often resolve interpersonal conflicts through basic communication skills.

"Stop" means not reacting blindly and responding habitually to the other person. When we take time out, we can then consider our options and try to exercise them rationally. After we have stopped, we need to think, or analyze the situation to try to know what is really happening within it and the range of possibilities it presents. Rather than taking the conflict personally, we need to think about changing the other person, the situation, or ourselves. What are the goals, wants, and needs of those in the conflict? When thinking about a conflict becomes difficult, a "right-brain" approach to analysis, called mind-mapping, often helps. In thinking about the conflict, however, we need to be aware of interference from trained incapacities. Because the behavior has become generally beneficial (in nonconflict situations), we expect it to work in conflict situations where it is inappropriate.

After stopping and thinking, it is important to listen to the other person. Listening well can prevent our turning an unreal conflict into a real one. Listening to the other does not mean we agree. It simply means that we consider the other person's opinion important, and that we try to hear and understand it before we make a point of saying what's on our mind. Although our tendency is to become defensive when we hear a critical remark, listening without immediately defending oneself can make the difference between a productive and a destructive conflict.

Finally, we need to recognize that communication is not simply saying what's on one's mind. Communication (and, by extension, conflict) isn't something we do *to* the other person, but something we do *with* one another (like teamwork or like a dance). We communicate in conflict situations by stopping, thinking, and listening before communicating.

The advantage of the transactional model is that we recognize the importance of both people's behavior in the conflict situation. One person acting competently in a conflict situation and using good communication skills usually cannot bring the conflict to a resolution. It takes two people to make the conflict, and it takes two people to manage or resolve it. By taking both parties' behavior into consideration, we can better determine what communication option we should exercise in a given conflict situation. We can respond by avoiding the conflict, sitting down and discussing it with the other person, or reacting with aggressive speech or violent behavior. The best of these options is communicating about the conflict. The various ways to approach a conflict are discussed in the next chapter.

3.1   Work with It

Read the following case study and answer the questions that follow it.

> When engaged in conflict with my brother, Carl, we usually begin with a period of silence where we both contemplate our reasons for feeling as we do. We usually think the problem over thoroughly before we say anything. Then comes the verbal argument (I prefer to call it a discussion). We try to be compromising and focus on the problem. We are supportive, encouraging, direct, and honest. We express positive feelings for each other to let each other know that we care and want things to work out. We are careful about letting the other express himself while trying to understand his point of view. If you asked either of us, we could summarize the other's concerns quite accurately. I would say we believe in equal power. Finally after we get everything off our chests and get the matter resolved, we poke fun at each other and feel like a weight has been lifted off our shoulders.

1. Did the parties use the S-TLC system for dealing with this conflict situation? How so?
2. What do you think the parties probably did to "stop"?
3. What do you think the parties probably did during the "thinking" step?
4. What techniques do you think the parties probably used during the "listening" step?
5. Did the parties take a transactional view of communication? Why or why not?

3.2   Work with It

Read the following case study and answer the questions that follow it.

> I had just bought a new computer and was in the process of setting it all up. Space is a precious commodity in university housing. My roommate has had a laptop computer for over a year that obviously requires less space to operate than does a full-sized computer like mine. He also has a printer that takes about half the space of mine. He located a new desk, and together we moved it in. The new desk was half again as big as the one already in the room, and he started using it first.
>
> Once I got my computer and started to set it up, I realized that it was a tight fit to squeeze all the equipment into the available space, and I asked my roommate if we could switch desks. He quickly and firmly replied "no way, Jim." I asked why not, since my computer took up so much more space, and it was already cramped in the corner where my desk is, without even having all the equipment set up. He replied that he simply liked the bigger desk so that he could spread out more. It was clear that he meant to keep it.

1. In what ways could the narrator change the roommate? Should he try to do that?
2. In what ways could the narrator change the situation?
3. In what ways could the narrator try to change himself?

NOTES

1. Brian H. Spitzberg and Michael L. Hecht, "A Component Model of Relational Competence," *Human Communication Research* 10 (1984), 577.
2. Rory Remer and Paul de Mesquita, "Teaching and Learning the Skills of Interpersonal Confrontation," in D. Cahn (Ed.), *Intimates in Conflict: A Communication Perspective* (Hillsdale, NJ: Lawrence Erlbaum Associates, 1990).
3. William W. Wilmot and Joyce L. Hocker, *Interpersonal Conflict,* 7th Ed. (New York: McGraw Hill, 2007), p. 239.

3.3 Work with It

A skill that is useful in conflict situations is the ability to think about the conflict and its various implications. One way to analyze conflict is to create a "conflict map" that identifies the elements in the conflict's structure and process. To create a conflict map, it helps to first create a narrative that describes the conflict as thoroughly as possible. Write out the conflict as though you were telling someone else about it. As you do so, try to recall everything that has happened up to this time. Using a mapping process can help you see the entire conflict at a glance and may help you to see relationships among concepts that you might not see if you simply answered the questions in a linear fashion.

3.1 Remember It

Write an essay in which you apply the ideas presented in Chapter 3 to your life situation. Make sure to address the following topics.

1. Briefly explain how you can use the S-TLC system for dealing with conflict situations in your life.
2. Briefly explain how you personally can *stop* and not respond habitually when in a conflict situation.
3. Explain in depth different ways you learned from the text to *think* about a conflict.
4. What constructive advice (based on the chapter) could you offer to someone who doesn't *listen* well?
5. Briefly explain how you would view *communication* in a conflict situation from a transactional point of view.

4. From *Because It Is Bitter, and Because It Is My Heart* by Joyce Carol Oates. Copyright © 1990 by the Ontario Review, Inc. Used by permission of the publisher, Dutton, an imprint of New American Library, a division of Penguin Books USA Inc.
5. Spitzberg and Hecht, 1984, p. 577.
6. Meira Likerman, "The Function of Anger in Human Conflict," *International Review of Psychoanalysis* 14 (1987), p. 152.
7. Steven R. Wilson and Linda L. Putnam, "Interaction Goals in Negotiation," in James A. Anderson (Ed.), *Communication Yearbook 13* (Newbury Park, CA: Sage, 1990), p. 381.
8. The idea of trained incapacities was generated by Kenneth Burke, *Permanence and Change* (Indianapolis: Bobbs Merrill, 1954) and developed by Folger and Poole.
9. See, for example, Tony Buzan, *The Mind Map Book* (New York: Penguin, 1991); and Nancy Margulies, *Mapping Inner Space: Learning and Teaching Visual Mapping,* 2nd Ed. (Zephyr Press, 2001).
10. William H. Baker, "Defensiveness in Communication: Its Causes, Effects and Cures," *Journal of Business Communication* 17 (1980), 33–43.
11. Carl R. Rogers, *On Becoming a Person* (Cambridge, MA: The Riverside Press, 1961), p. 18.
12. Baker, pp. 33, 35.
13. Glen H. Stamp, Anita L. Vengelisti, and John A. Daly, "The Creation of Defensiveness in Social Interaction," *Communication Quarterly* 40 (1992), 177–190.
14. David Augsburger, *Caring Enough to Hear and Be Heard* (Ventura, CA: Regal Books, 1982).

4 Communication Options in Conflict Situations

OBJECTIVES

At the end of this chapter, you should be able to:

- Compare and contrast the four communication options for dealing with conflicts.

- Explain the three factors you should consider when choosing among the four conflict communication options.

- Describe the primary communication considerations that should influence your choice of a conflict communication option.

KEY TERMS

accommodating
aggressive communication
assertive communication
avoiding
basic communication rights
collaborating
communication apprehension
communication considerations

competing
compromising
conflict communication options
gunny-sacking
nonassertive communication
nonverbally aggressive
    communication

passive-aggressive
    communication
verbally aggressive
    communication

I've been learning to stop, think, and listen in conflict situations. Sometimes I think that's the easiest part, because I'm still tempted, even after doing those things, to let the other person know exactly what I think, and I'm still tempted to do it in a way that "gets" them. So now I'm trying to remember that there's more than one way to let someone know what I think.

Stop, think, listen, and *communicate!* But what are your communication options in conflict situations? Researchers have identified five different conflict strategies that people use in problematic situations:[1]

- **Avoiding** occurs in a conflict situation when one or both parties do not address the issue at all.
- **Accommodating** occurs when at least one smoothes over a conflict, gives in to the other, or doesn't make waves.
- **Competing** occurs when at least one dominates or tries to force his or her decision on the other.
- **Compromising** occurs when no one totally wins or loses, each getting something (perhaps) of what she or he wanted.
- **Collaborating** occurs when both parties develop a mutually satisfying outcome or agreement.

In this chapter we identify and explain the communication behaviors that are associated with these commonly accepted conflict strategies in the hopes that you consider the conflict situation and choose the most appropriate communication behavior option: nonassertive, aggressive, passive-aggressive, or assertive behavior. We want to emphasize that (1) we can choose how to respond in a conflict situation, and (2) the choices we end up making have consequences. We hope this reinforces the idea of individual responsibility for one's actions. When involved in a conflict situation, refraining from actions you would not like to receive and developing a sense of fair play are useful guidelines. The following sections explore some of the implications and factors that are relevant when considering each of these conflict options, based on the assumption that with some instruction and practice many people are able to modify their behavior to better adapt to their circumstances.

This is not intended as an exercise in labeling people as personality types such as nonassertive or aggressive. Nor is this a psychological approach that digs for deep emotional problems that account for personality disorders. Our goal is to identify certain conflict communication behaviors that are viewed as good or bad habits or behaviors learned from good or poor models and apply them in problematic situations where the issues are intangible. Quite often we engage in destructive behaviors without realizing the harm they do to others. The important point about this approach to conflict is that if we have learned how to behave poorly, then we can unlearn it. The change is sometimes difficult, but it is possible. At the end of this chapter, you can apply four different conflict strategies and their associated communication behaviors and know when it is appropriate to use them. Let us begin by describing the **conflict communication options** in greater detail.

4.1   Apply It

Take a piece of paper and write a description of a conflict you recently experienced or observed. Below your description, draw four columns and label them nonassertive, aggressive, passive-aggressive, and assertive. After reading the section on each type of communication behavior, describe how you could respond to your described conflict with that particular behavior. How effective would it be? Why?

Nonassertive Communication Behavior as an Option

I notice that when I am physically and emotionally close to someone like my boyfriend, I am nonassertive. Sometimes I don't want to say anything because I don't want to hurt him. I feel the need to protect him, so I try to ignore the problem or talk to a third person about it. Although it seems unproductive, it is the only way I know to try to keep him from suffering. At other times, I start out being nonassertive, but I don't always stay that way. I have avoided confronting some conflicts until I am so upset that I become furious and can no longer hold back. Then I explode!

We define **nonassertive communication** as the ability to avoid a conflict altogether or accommodate to the desires of the other person through the use of verbal or nonverbal acts that conceal one's opinions and feelings. When people decide to use nonassertive communication, they fail to speak up for their interests, concerns, or rights. People may fail to speak up for their interests in a number of different ways:

- They may do it in only one situation for a particular reason. Perhaps they let someone choose a movie to see that does not interest them because on that occasion it is their friend's birthday.
- People may also choose to avoid conflict in certain types of situations or relationships. In this case, they may think that they should never argue with their father, boss, or aging grandparent.
- Finally, some may choose to avoid conflict altogether regardless of the situation. This happens when individuals do not think that others would or should take their needs into consideration.

Nonassertive communication comes in two forms: conflict avoidance, where one avoids the other person, doesn't speak to him or her, or won't discuss a problematic topic, and accommodation, where one simply gives in or goes along without giving a contrary opinion or agrees without voicing any complaint. Nonassertive communicators tend to allow others to interrupt them, subordinate them, and "walk all over them like a doormat." They often have poor eye contact, poor posture, and a defeated air about them. We may recognize the nonassertive communicator by her or his indecisiveness. People complain that when they confront someone who responds in a nonassertive way, the other often apologizes too quickly, refuses to take the conflict seriously, becomes evasive, stonewalls (avoids or ignores them), or walks out. A nonassertive communicator may sound sarcastic, but when confronted the person denies any wrongdoing. We would classify as nonassertive statements like these:

"I don't dare say anything."
"I want to avoid creating unpleasantness for myself."
"What good would it do to speak up?"
"I went along because I didn't want to offend anybody."
"I don't want to make waves."
"It's okay for you to take advantage of me. I don't mind."
"I don't want to say anything that will make you uncomfortable, upset, or angry."
"Whatever you decide is okay with me."

The concept of nonassertiveness is similar to **communication apprehension,**[2] or the level of anxiety a person feels in response to interpersonal, group, or public communication situations. Both terms describe people's failure to engage in conflict with others. For example, people who describe themselves as high in communication apprehension in interpersonal relationships prefer accommodation as a conflict style. However, in a group of people, they tend to prefer conflict avoidance, but if a conflict is unavoidable, they prefer to compete in an effort to end the conflict quickly. In any case, people high in communication apprehension find it difficult to use the assertive style when in conflict.[3]

When they avoid dealing with the problems that plague them, both the people who choose nonassertive communication behavior and their partners lose. If they accommodate by giving in, their partners may win the fight, but the accommodators lose it. A person who gives in time after time may eventually believe that he or she has "had enough" and leave the relationship, so both end up losing in the long run.

4.1 Think about It

In what kinds of situations has nonassertive communication behavior been called for? Were there disadvantages for you? Under what conditions, if any, might this behavior produce an advantage?

Aggressive Communication Behavior as an Option

> My father was a person who hit first and asked questions later when he was angry. I learned early in my life how to appease him so that I wouldn't get punished as frequently. But it took me a long time to realize that my husband wouldn't hit me because he was angry. I guess I just kept waiting for him to act like my father.

From a communication perspective, we define **aggressive communication** as the ability to force one's will (i.e., wants, needs, or desires) on another person through the use of verbal or nonverbal acts done in a way that violates socially acceptable standards, carried out with the intention or the perceived intention of inflicting physical or psychological pain, injury, or suffering. While people may engage in "friendly competition," they may also partake in many other competitive events that intend physical harm or unwanted domination of others. When people decide to force others to give them what they demand, they advance their interests, concerns, or rights in a way that interferes with the interests or infringes on the rights of others. Their communication behavior reminds us of bullies when we were in grade school.

Aggressive communication behaviors range from mild forms of verbal intimidation to more severe beatings to extremely violent rapes and homicides. Aggression ranges from carefully planned attacks to sudden emotional outbursts that injure others. People use aggressive communication to get what they want at the expense of others in many different ways. They may choose aggressive behavior in only one situation for a particular reason, in certain types of situations or relationships, or regardless of the situation.

Verbally aggressive people often use their bodies to emphasize their point. Standing over another person while bringing up a conflict will be seen as aggressive.

What communication behaviors does an aggressive communicator give off? Aggressive communication may take two forms: physical and verbal aggression. Aggressive communicators tend to interrupt, subordinate, and stereotype others. They engage in intense, glaring eye contact, put forward an invading posture as they bear down on others, and emit an arrogant air about them. They try to dominate others by being loud, abrasive, blaming, intimidating, and sarcastic. We would call the following statements aggressive:

"I have never lost an argument."
"His stereo was so loud, I had to go over and pull the plug out of the wall. Then, he got the message."
"I try to make others look bad, so that I look good. I try to get my way at all costs."
"I am the boss. I know what's best."
"I don't care what you think."

If they don't start a fight by getting physical, they react with violence the instant the other party "provokes them." Aggressive communicators often get nasty in an argument by "hitting below the belt" (using intimate knowledge against the other), bringing up unrelated issues, making promises they don't intend to keep, using other people (attack through friends or family), and demanding more.

People who resort to aggressive communication often win conflicts at the expense of their partners, because they care less about relational goals than their own.[4] Over time the losing partner may eventually "get fed up" and leave a relationship with one who is aggressive, so both end up losing in the long run.

4.2   **Think about It**

When have you engaged in friendly competition? When has competition involved bodily harm, domination, or sore feelings? Under what conditions, if any, might aggressive behavior result in an advantage to you?

Verbal Aggression

The realization that communication plays a role in violence has resulted in a new field of study focusing on "interpersonal violence" that studies both verbal and nonverbal aggression.[5] In communication research, **verbally aggressive communication** is defined as a person's predisposition to attack the self-concept of another person in order to cause psychological pain for the other.[6] Verbal aggression takes the form of character attacks, insults, ridicule, profanity, and threats. Verbal aggression can also include stereotypes and prejudice.[7]

A large body of research in a variety of settings demonstrates the importance of avoiding verbal aggression. Students are less likely to attend college classes taught by verbally aggressive professors.[8] A study of health workers found that incidents of verbal aggression caused as much or more stress on the job as incidents of physical aggression.[9] Parental verbal aggression is linked to adolescent dissociative experiences.[10] College students describing patterns of aggression in their homes demonstrate the link between verbal and physical aggression. As the frequency of the verbal aggression between their parents increases, so does the incidence of physical aggression. Parents who attempt to solve conflicts through "rational" means (i.e., talking it over) are much less likely to engage in physical aggression during conflict episodes.[11] Verbal aggression is also a part of a pattern of escalation that frequently leads to episodes of physical violence in dysfunctional marriage couples.[12] Men who are exposed to family-of-origin violence are more likely to be verbally aggressive, domineering, and negative with their dating partners, showing potential for physical aggression.[13]

Verbal aggression often plays a role in conflicts that get out of hand. In actuality, physical (nonverbal) and verbal abuse often occur together, sequentially or simultaneously. While not all verbal aggression leads to violence, nearly all violent episodes begin with verbal aggression. Next we discuss **nonverbally aggressive communication.**

4.3   **Think about It**

Does it strike you as strange to refer to swearing or name calling as a form of aggressive behavior? What do you think of the old saying, "Sticks and stones will break my bones but words will never hurt me"? Under what conditions, if any, might you gain advantages by using this communication behavior?

Nonverbal Aggression (Physical Violence)

Physical aggression is often linked to initial verbal aggression. Infante and colleagues' work established that abusive husbands are more verbally aggressive than nonabusive spouses.

They are also less argumentative, in that they are less able to verbally defend their position and refute the positions that others take.[14] Further research has linked verbal aggression in marriages to domestic violence.[15]

Research shows that men are more likely to resort to physical violence toward their female partners. Bograd reports that "wives suffer significantly more physical injuries than do husbands."[16] According to Marshall, males are more likely to hit or kick a wall, door, or furniture; drive dangerously; act like a bully; hold and pin; shake or roughly handle; grab; and twist an arm, whereas more females receive these acts.[17] As Dobash and Dobash state, "Certainly, there is a vast body of evidence confirming the existence of persistent, systematic, severe, and intimidating force men use against their wives . . . [that] does warrant the use of terms such as wife beating or battered woman."[18] Former or current boyfriends or husbands kill more than half of all women homicide victims, usually after they are separated.[19] Research also shows that male partners and fathers are more likely to physically harm their women and children than vice versa.[20]

One of the biggest difficulties in examining physical violence is the effect that social expectations have on violent behavior. In many cases, people see violent behavior as necessary and appropriate; indeed, sometimes it is the only acceptable solution to them.[21] In addition, the presence of bystanders to the conflict may escalate it into violence or reduce its likelihood.[22] Feld and Robinson found that the presence of bystanders decreased the use of violence by men toward women, but increased the use of violence of women toward men.[23]

Noting that abusers are more likely to use violence in the home where they expect the rewards to outweigh the costs of abuse, Margolin argues that women suffer greater penalties than do men for domestic violence.[24] If abusive behavior is more "costly" to women, men are more likely than women to beat or abuse their partners and children who love them. Further, if violence committed by men is more likely to avoid sanctions such as police intervention, loss of status, and public humiliation, men's violence toward family members is less subject to social control. Finally, due to their greater size and socioeconomic status, men may abuse family members "with less fear of reprisal." When one combines the privacy of the home with the lack of stigma, lack of social sanctions, and lack of social control, getting his way whenever he wants it may outweigh the cost of a man's being violent.

Given the link between verbal aggression and physical aggression and the deleterious effects of physical aggression upon people and relationships,[25] we would argue that neither behavior is an appropriate first move in a conflict situation. Under extreme pressure, it is understandable that people may become verbally aggressive. When attacked, people may resort to physical aggression in self-defense. However, we maintain that initiating the use of either of these behaviors in a conflict situation is, at best, unwise and, at worst, destructive to the relationship.

4.4   Think about It

Sometimes abusive parents say they merely teach strict discipline. What do you think is the difference between punishing and disciplining a child? When do people overstep their parental authority to punish their children?

Passive-Aggressive Communication as an Option

> When I didn't like the way my team at work felt about something, I would go directly to the boss and win her over to my position. That way, it would look like the boss didn't like the group's idea. Admittedly, I did get nasty sometimes when I would tell her what was going on behind her back. She was always interested and would probe me whenever I was in her office. I know that members of my team suspected what I was up to. None of us much liked each other.

At first glance, passive-aggressive communication behavior appears to be a type of aggressive behavior. However, the passive-aggressive communicator (seemingly like the conflict avoider or accommodator) does not openly and directly stand up for her or his interests, concerns, or rights. Instead, one might argue that passive-aggressive communication behavior is a type of nonassertive behavior. The problem with that claim is that this individual tries to get her or his way but does it "behind the other's back." The passive-aggressive communication behavior is a type of its own with some characteristics from both the nonassertive and the aggressive types.

We define **passive-aggressive communication** as the ability to impose one's will on others through the use of verbal or nonverbal acts that appear to avoid an open conflict or accommodate to the desires of others, but in actuality are carried out with the intention (or perceived intention) of inflicting physical or psychological pain, injury, or suffering. When people engage in passive-aggressive communication, they do not openly and directly stand up for their interests, concerns, or rights, but attempt to get what they want by underhanded means. For example, one may go behind a co-worker's back to undermine his or her project at work, but in the meantime tell the co-worker how pleased one is with it. Meanwhile, when displeased, the co-worker does not engage in threatening or abusive behavior.

What communication behaviors do passive-aggressive communicators give off?

- They may spy on others to get information to use against them.
- They may withhold something the other person wants, such as approval, affection, or sex, in order to get what they want.
- They may operate behind the scenes in an attempt to undermine others or to motivate outsiders to act against their adversaries.
- They may spread lies behind their adversary's back and engage in back stabbing.
- They may disclose some personal information to people they shouldn't after it was told to them in confidence.
- They might encourage attacks from outsiders.
- They may simply refuse to defend the adversary when others are attacking her or him.
- They may give away to others something of value to their adversary to make them think that they are perceived as friends when they are not.
- They may deny to one's face that a problem exists while at the same time fail to cooperate.

Scholars have compiled the following list of passive-aggressive behaviors,[26] to which we have added a few of our own:

- forgetting promises, agreements, and appointments
- making unkind statements, and then quickly apologizing
- playing a stereo too loudly, slamming doors, banging objects
- not doing chores
- taking more time than usual to get ready
- getting confused, sarcastic, helpless, or tearful without saying why
- getting sick when one has promised to do something
- scheduling too much at once
- evading meetings so that others are inconvenienced

On occasion, we all get sick, make noises, fail to do a chore, or overschedule activities, but the passive-aggressive communication behavior is done with malicious intent.

Initially, passive-aggressive communication behavior is of the win–lose variety. It may result in one getting what he or she wants while "doing in" the other. Eventually, however, the situation may turn into the lose–lose type, because when the victimized individual discovers the truth, he or she may end the relationship and have nothing more to do with the abuser.

While it might seem that passive-aggressive communication behavior is not recommended, we might need it on rare occasions. In situations when the other represents a serious threat if openly confronted, sometimes we have to go behind the person's back. For example, we might turn a criminal in to the police by going directly to them without the criminal knowing what we are up to. Unique occasions such as this warrant passive-aggressive behavior.

4.5   Think about It

Do you think one is engaging in aggressive behavior when she or he reports another to the police or takes someone to court? Under what conditions, if any, might this form of communication behavior result in an advantage to you?

Assertive Communication Behavior as an Option

Using the preceding discussion of verbal aggressiveness makes identifying assertiveness easier. Assertiveness is a concept that became popular in the 1970s through programs such as EST and others, which trained people how to say "no" to others in interpersonal confrontations.

> I am assertive with my daughter. When the issues are important (dating, car rides, new boundaries), I am an active and empathic listener. I allow her to focus her thoughts and views so I can understand and address them. Our arguments aren't loud or upsetting. I am calm and never raise my voice. I always try to use reason to try to find a solution. Resolutions to conflicts come about through compromise and collaboration.

A way of confronting others in conflict situations, **assertive communication** is defined as the ability to speak up for one's interests, concerns, or rights in a way that does not interfere with the interests or infringes on the rights of others.[27] It also means being able to "communicate your own feelings, beliefs, and desires honestly and directly while allowing others to communicate their own feelings, beliefs, and desires."[28] Assertiveness is seen as a middle ground between nonassertiveness, which is failing to stand up for your personal rights or doing so in a dysfunctional way, and aggressiveness, which is standing up for your personal rights without regard for others.

Although we may see unusual situations where nonassertiveness, aggressiveness, and passive-aggressiveness may serve a purpose, generally communication scholars advocate assertive communication behavior as a preferred means for managing a great many conflict situations because it combines a regard for the other with a regard for one's own personal goals. Because it tries to satisfy everyone, leaving no hard feelings, assertiveness is a concept linked to communication competence.

Asserting yourself appropriately means taking seriously your **basic communication rights,** which derive from those rights, concerns, or interests common to all communicators. You have the right to:

1. be listened to and taken seriously,
2. say no, refuse requests, and turn down invitations without feeling guilty or being accused of selfishness,
3. be treated as an adult with respect and consideration,
4. expect that others will not talk to you in a condescending way,
5. not feel what others want you to feel, to not see the world as they would have you perceive it, and to not adopt their values as your own,
6. your own feelings and opinions as long as you express them in a way that doesn't violate the rights of others,
7. have and express your interests, needs, and concerns as long as you do so in a responsible manner,
8. change your opinions, feelings, needs, and behaviors,
9. meet other people and talk to them,
10. privacy—to keep confidential or personal matters to yourself,
11. have others leave you alone if you wish,
12. ask others to listen to your ideas,
13. ask for help or information from experts and professionals, especially when you are paying for it,
14. not assert yourself, confront someone, or resolve a conflict, and
15. ask others to change their behavior when it continues to violate your rights.

You can add to this list. Do some of these items surprise you? Are you violating the rights of others? With these rights comes responsibility. For example, in the next section, we present some communication considerations that may cause you to choose nonassertive communication behavior when it is appropriate. Moreover, to expect fair treatment from others, you must also respect the communication rights of others and treat them "as you yourself would like to be treated." Viscott argues that a person's rights in any relationship are not something to be questioned. Our communication rights are the same both in and out of relationships. But as we enter into relationships, it becomes our task to help all involved to recognize and protect those rights.[29] This is why we tend to favor collaboration over compromise, which may not protect all of the rights for both parties.

Assertiveness is the appropriate expression of one's point of view. Such messages reflect the premise that all persons should communicate in a manner that does not violate self-worth; the needs and goals of both persons have equal value. The outcomes of assertive behavior may include the accomplishment of goals, reinforcement of the self-concept, and perhaps relational development or maintenance.[30]

Four defining features set assertive people off from other types. They are:

1. open in that they do not withhold information, opinions, and feelings,
2. contentious in that they take positions and define issues clearly,
3. not anxious in that they are not afraid to initiate relationships or conversations, and
4. not intimidated in that they choose to confront others rather than avoid them or simply give in to avoid "making waves." .

One study comparing communication behaviors and assertiveness found that assertive people see themselves as talkative, precise, not easily persuadable, and contentious. They also experience low anxiety about communication situations and are likely to impress others.[31]

Behaviorally, assertiveness is contrasted with aggressiveness, in which one's own needs are preeminent, and passivity, in which one's needs are underemphasized. Writers in the area of assertiveness claim that it promotes more caring and honest relationships with others,[32] and they associate the concept with flexibility of response, arguing that assertiveness includes the ability to determine when not communicating one's rights is the best course.[33] Although most early writers associated assertiveness with flexibility of response,[34] we now associate it more with saying what one thinks in order to achieve one's own goals, although not at the expense of the other person. Lane described an assertive individual as one who "emphasizes his/her ideas by a change in tone of voice, exhibits dominant statements, makes statements more often than asks questions, and lets others know of his/her needs and wants."[35] Is Amanda being assertive in the following interchange?

> The three of us have our own houses and families, and so my sisters and I have tried to take the burden of holiday dinners off our mom, because it tires her out so. Audrey and I really enjoy the cooking and entertaining, even though it's a lot of work, but Amanda doesn't. We were planning the year, figuring out who would take what holidays, when Amanda said, "I really don't care to cook any more holiday dinners. I'd rather visit with people and enjoy myself." Audrey and I were really irritated by that. I mean, who doesn't want to sit and visit with people on holidays rather than cook? But we got to thinking about it—frankly, Amanda's dinners aren't all that great anyway. The food isn't burnt, but she just doesn't take the time to make tasty meals. If she doesn't enjoy it, why put a burden on her when Audrey and I like to do it? We decided that her keeping the kids from running wild and keeping the outer room under control is a fair exchange.

Amanda is being assertive in stating her dislike for holiday dinner preparation. However, the fact that the other two sisters have to work out the meaning of the message and decide on a way to resolve the conflict means that they could have handled the conflict better. An assertive message would take into account not only personal wants ("I don't want to cook anymore") but also the needs of others who have to do the cooking. If Amanda had also said, "I'll keep the kids in line and help set up or clean up if you two do the cooking," it would have reflected assertive and collaborative behavior. On the other hand, Audrey and her sister were also not assertive, because they did not respond immediately to Amanda's statement. Instead, they worked out the problem by themselves. To better manage the conflict, Amanda should offer something in place of cooking. In the absence of such an offer, Audrey and her sister should have immediately asked Amanda why she felt it was fair simply to exclude herself from the holiday work.

As an assertive person, you must show respect for both yourself and others. You are encouraged to use the first-person singular pronoun (I, me, my) because you are a fellow human being and your needs are as important to you as others' needs are to them. You should have self-confidence and manifest it in the way you talk, walk, and carry yourself generally. It should not bother you when others talk in the first person because you recognize that their needs are as important to them as yours are to you. You do not need to like or agree with the ideas of others, but you need to respect how they feel and their right to say what's on their mind as long as they respect your rights, too.

What communication behaviors does an assertive person give off? Of course, assertive communication does not include the behaviors described above as nonassertive, aggressive, or passive-aggressive. Instead, assertive communicators tend to state their feelings, wants, and needs directly and in a responsible manner. Assertive communication includes good eye contact, straight posture, and an air of competence. People are assertive when they are able to disclose their feelings (both positive and negative), offer their opinions, and provide information as needed. Assertive communications consist of spontaneous expressions of warmth, humor, caring, and cooperation. Assertive people are also effective listeners, which requires that they determine how deeply the other feels about an issue and restate the other's feelings in their own words. We would consider the following statements as assertive:

"I try to satisfy the other person and myself."
"I like to consult others before I act."
"I try to get everything immediately out in the open."
"I'll tell you what I think, and I want you tell me your ideas."
"I am concerned about everyone. I don't want anyone left out."

When people chose not to engage in nonassertive or aggressive communication, and instead speak up about their concerns, interests, and needs, they and their partners may both win. Assertive communication behavior gives others a chance, which is a good idea when a relationship is important to you. She or he says what the problem is so that the other may choose to do something about it. The other person may not respond in a manner that the assertive person would prefer, but at least the other is given a chance to do so.

Moreover, by asserting themselves, people may avoid **gunny-sacking,** or storing up hurts and anger until it they explode. Bach and Wyden call this harmful strategy gunny-sacking because "when . . . complaints are toted along quietly in a gunny sack for any length of time they make a dreadful mess when the sack finally bursts."[36] By not gunny-sacking, assertiveness may prevent a relationship from turning sour. All too often, people say, "If only he (or she) had said something. I never knew there was a problem." We shouldn't wait until it is too late or lose our self-control. It isn't fair to our partners or us. By getting troubles off our chests, we can monitor one another, adapt as needed, and avoid little problems turning into bigger ones. The relationship between assertive partners has the most opportunity for mutual satisfaction and growth.

4.6 **Think about It**

In what kinds of situations are you most likely to be assertive? Were there disadvantages for you? Under what conditions will being assertive produce an advantage?

The degree to which a person's behavior is labeled aggressive or assertive often depends on the observer. It also depends on who is performing the behavior. Generally speaking, a man and a woman can behave the same way in conflict and yet others may perceive each differently. For example, given the same behavior he is seen as assertive, but she is called aggressive. Despite sex differences in the way people are perceived, we can differentiate, at least on a general level, between aggressiveness and assertiveness in conflict situations. Both seek satisfaction of one's own interests, but assertiveness takes the other into consideration while aggressiveness does not or even violates the other. In the next chapter, specific conflict messages that reflect assertiveness are discussed. However, at this time, we need to present some **communication considerations** that favor one conflict communication option over the others.

Communication Considerations: Which Conflict Communication Option Is Best?

4.2 **Apply It**

Respond to each of the following statements according to this scale:

A = Always true
B = May or may not be true (it depends)
C = Never True

1. The first thought that comes to mind is the best to say. _____
2. You should do what your boss or supervisor tells you to do. _____
3. You should treat those who love you nicely. _____
4. When you're sure you're right, you should press your point until you win the argument. _____
5. You should keep quiet rather than say something that will alienate others. _____

Look over the questions in Apply It 4.2 and answer them. As you do so, keep in mind the basic principle, "It depends." For each question, what is called for in one situation is inappropriate in another. This implies that flexibility is key. Hart and colleagues stress the importance of flexibility in interpersonal encounters by identifying "B" as the preferred answer to all such statements.[37]

Although many advocates of nonviolence claim that physical aggression is never an appropriate response, it would seem that it is justified in a few specific cases (involving self-defense). However, we are unable to imagine a situation in which a verbally aggressive or a passive-aggressive response is appropriate. Effective communicators are assertive when it is appropriate and nonassertive when the situation justifies it. When is it appropriate for us to engage in assertive or nonassertive communication behavior? Three communication considerations are the occasion, the other person, and your needs.

The Occasion (Including Time and Location)

In many respects, an occasion is like a situation. Recall from Chapter 1 that we said a "situation" exists when people play out particular roles in a given context that consists of a familiar setting at a particular time. You can think of a situation as being like a type of book—novel, nonfiction, collection of short stories, mystery, and so on. Just as there are many mysteries, novels, and nonfiction books, an occasion would be the equivalent of a particular book—this mystery, this romance, this thriller, where the time and place create unique expectations that guide our behavior. Like situations, occasions tend to recur—one mystery may seem similar to another. But just as different books call for different readings, so do different occasions call for different behavior. What might call for an assertive, aggressive, or nonassertive response on one occasion may not in another.

The Other Person

Although the people involved and affected by your behavior are part of any situation, we want to call special attention to these elements because they must be taken into account in a conflict. We treat our parents, grandparents, significant others, siblings, children, employers, employees, and friends differently simply because of who they are and what they mean to us. We may find it more appropriate to be more assertive in one type of interpersonal relationship than another. Moreover, if we choose to be assertive, we need to consider the needs of the other person.

Your Needs

You are an important element in every conflict situation. You should consider your own needs and how you have prioritized them. Not all our needs constitute a life or death situation. We must satisfy at least some of our needs if we want to live a life worth living, but some needs are better put off at least temporarily or reduced to a less prominent position. Generally, we are more assertive on matters that make an important difference in our lives, requiring collaboration. In some instances, we can let go of less important concerns, such that we might end up in a compromise.

Consider the collaborative conflict style and assertive communication behavior:

- when a conflict is over something that is important to you
- if you will "hate yourself" later for not letting your feelings, ideas, or opinions be known
- when a long-term relationship between you and the other person is important

- when the other person can handle your assertiveness without responding with aggression or passive-aggression
- when the other person is cooperative
- when a win–win solution to a problem is possible

Consider the avoiding or accommodating styles and nonassertive communication behavior:

- when you think you are wrong or have a poor idea
- when the emotional hurt offsets any benefits that might result
- when something has occurred that is more important to the others than it is to you
- when a long-term relationship between you and the other person is important

Consider the competing style and aggressive communication behavior:

- When you have exhausted the other options, and you are in a physically threatening situation in which you must defend yourself to avoid being seriously injured or killed. Even then, use the minimum force necessary to overcome the threat. Let the police and the courts take the matter further.
- When a physically threatening situation exists for others and you choose to intervene on their behalf.

Consider the competing style and passive-aggressive communication behavior:

- When you are in a physically threatening situation. You may have to go behind the other person's back and secretly report him or her in order to avoid direct confrontation where the other might seriously harm you.

4.3 Apply It

Take a piece of paper and write a description of a conflict you recently experienced or observed. Below your description, draw three columns and label them the occasion, the other person, and my needs. How does each aspect of the conflict impact the way you should react to the conflict you've described?

Manage It

This chapter identifies the choices we can make in conflict situations. Just as there are many different types of conflicts and kinds of conflict issues, so there are different ways that we can respond to conflicts. Many people do not realize that they have options and can freely choose among them, with differing results.

A person may choose to respond to a conflict nonassertively by avoiding the conflict altogether or by accommodating the other person's goals. When the conflict is not important to us, avoiding and accommodating can be appropriate responses. However, we run the risk of ignoring important issues until they grow so large that it is difficult to address them effectively.

On the other hand, a person may respond to the conflict behavior of another competitively by responding with overt aggression or by responding in a passive-aggressive manner. We maintain that physical aggression is seldom warranted except in situations of self-defense. Passive-aggressive behavior is warranted when there is implied danger in confronting the other, but it is not a good response over the long term.

Sometimes we choose to split the difference and compromise with the other person. In important conflicts, though, our best option is to choose collaboration by assertively speaking up for our interests, concerns, or rights in a way that does not interfere with the interests or basic communication rights of others.

Effective communicators are frequently assertive, sometimes nonassertive, and rarely aggressive. How does one determine when to choose one option over another? Three factors everyone should consider when choosing among the four conflict communication options are the occasion/time/location, the other person, and one's own needs. The communication considerations described in this chapter can help us decide when it is appropriate to use one type of conflict communication behavior or another.

Our first response in a conflict situation is not necessarily the best one. We need to slow down, think about the situation, and then respond to the other, using the skills discussed in this chapter. The only way to develop conflict skills is to use them in conflict situations.

In addition to learning about the communication options that exist in conflict situations, we need to identify the primary ways that people deal with conflicts. We present these in the next chapter.

4.1 Work with It

Read the following case study and answer the questions that follow it.

> I was trying to teach a class when a student came in to remove some audiovisual equipment. He didn't explain why he was there. I had to ask him. I then asked him if it could wait until the end of the class. He said no. I said "Okay," rather reluctantly. He left, and then came back about five minutes later. I said nothing. When he came back the third time (all the while making noise and making it difficult for me to continue the class discussion), I finally said (in a level voice), "You are disturbing my class and I must ask you to stop coming in. This really bothers me." He replied, "I'm having a bad day." My female students thought the student should have initially apologized for the disruption, explaining his actions to begin with, and should have responded more adequately at the last. My male students said that I "went nuclear" on the student!

1. What conflict styles associated with which of the four communication options for dealing with conflicts are illustrated in this narrative?
2. What changes in communication behavior by the participants would result in different conflict styles and outcomes?
3. What communication behavior option is preferable in the above narrative?

4.2 Work with It

Identify the correct communication option associated with the statement: aggressive, passive-aggressive, nonassertive, or assertive. After doing this exercise, check your answers on p. 283. If you have trouble with the answers, re-read the relevant part of Chapter 4.

1. I not only have a high regard for the other, I also have a high regard for myself and my own personal goals.
2. I allow the other persons to interrupt me as much as they want. I believe that I am sensitive and subordinate to them. I am extremely indecisive and need time to think before settling a conflict. I often accommodate to the other person's view.
3. I find that I use this behavior a lot at work and with the people with whom I work. I find myself forgetting promises, appointments, and agreements; making unkind statements about others when they are not around; scheduling too many tasks to do at once; gossiping about the people I am in a conflict with. I continuously deny that something is wrong, but then fail to cooperate.
4. I don't let a lot bother me up to a certain point. Because of this, I do think I am letting other people get what they want and accommodating them. I know that I avoid serious conflicts in this manner. But when I am pushed past my limit my automatic system takes over and I shake like a leaf. It scares me into a sweat.
5. I always seem to try to impose my will onto others. I know that I need to chill out at times but sometimes my anger takes over when I am in a heated argument. I bring up topics that the other person wasn't expecting. I use this style in situations where I need to win. I am highly competitive.
6. I resort to swearing and other forms of verbal intimidation.
7. Conflict can just be unproductive. I just save my breath rather than trying to explain my point of view.
8. I make sure that my opinion is known and do the best I can to make sure my interests are known. But I also do not like anyone else to feel left out in a conflict situation. I am clear and concise in telling others what I believe the problem to be and possible ways to remedy it. Another behavior I have in a conflict situation is to be listened to and taken seriously. I believe everyone should be taken seriously, especially in a conflict situation.
9. I try to be careful not to hurt anyone else's feelings with anything I say. I like to express myself in a responsible manner so as to not offend others.

4.1 Remember It

Write an essay in which you apply the ideas presented in Chapter 4 to your life situation. Be sure to address the following topics:

1. What conflict styles are associated with which of the four communication options for dealing with conflicts?
2. Describe four different conflict situations in which you have used or could appropriately use each of the four communication options for dealing with conflicts.
3. Explain why that option is preferable for managing each of the four conflict communication options, using the three key factors described in the chapter.

NOTES

1. Robert R. Blake and Jane Srygley Mouton, *The Managerial Grid* (Houston: Gulf, 1964); Robert H. Kilmann and Kenneth W. Thomas, "Developing a Forced-Choice Measure of Conflict-Handling Behavior: The Mode Instrument," *Educational and Psychological Measurement* 37 (1977), 309–325; M. Afzalur Rahim, "A Measure of Styles of Handling Interpersonal Conflict," *Academy of Management Journal* 26 (1983), 368–376.

2. James C. McCroskey, "Oral Communication Apprehension: A Summary of Recent Theory and Research," *Human Communication Research* 4, (1977), 78–96.

3. Pamela S. Shockley-Zalabak and Donald Dean Morley, "An Exploratory Study of Relationships between Preferences for Conflict Styles and Communication Apprehension," *Journal of Language and Social Psychology* 3 (1984), 213–218.

4. Randall C. Rogan and Betty H. La France, "An Examination of the Relationship between Verbal Aggressiveness, Conflict Management Strategies, and Conflict Interaction Goals," *Communication Quarterly* 51 (2003), 458–469.

5. Sally Floyd and Beth Emery, "Physically Aggressive Conflict in Romantic Relationships," in Dudley D. Cahn (Ed.), *Conflict in Personal Relationships* (Hillsdale, NJ: Lawrence Erlbaum Associates, 1994), pp. 27–46. For more information on the relationship of verbal to nonverbal aggression, see Michael E. Roloff, "The Catalyst Hypothesis: Conditions under Which Coercive Communication Leads to Physical Aggression," and Colleen M. Carey and Paul A. Mongeau, "Communication and Violence in Courtship Relationships," both in Dudley D. Cahn and Sally A. Lloyd (Eds.), *Family Violence from a Communication Perspective* (Thousand Oaks, CA: Sage Publications, 1996), pp. 20–36 and 127–150.

6. Dominic A. Infante and C. J. Wigley, "Verbal Aggressiveness: An Interpersonal Model and Measure," *Communication Monographs* 53 (1986), 61–69.

7. Roxane S. Lulofs and Dudley D. Cahn, *Conflict: From Theory to Action,* 2nd Ed. (Boston: Allyn & Bacon, 2000), pp. 211–212.

8. Kelly A. Rocca, "College Student Attendance: Impact of Instructor Immediacy and Verbal Aggression," *Communication Education* 53 (2004), 185–195.

9. Belinda R. Walsh and Emma Clarke, "Post-Trauma Symptoms in Health Workers Following Physical and Verbal Aggression," *Work & Stress* 17 (2003), 170–181.

10. Carolee Rada Verdeur, "Parental Verbal Aggression: Attachment and Dissociation in Adolescents," *Dissertation Abstracts International: Section B: The Sciences & Engineering,* Vol 63(3-B), Sep 2002, pp. 1571.

11. Murray A. Strauss, "A General Systems Theory Approach to a Theory of Violence between Family Members," *Social Science Information* 12 (1973), 103–123.

12. Sonia Miner Salari and Bret M. Baldwin, "Verbal, Physical, and Injurious Aggression among Intimate Couples over Time," *Journal of Family Issues* 23 (2002), 523–550.

13. Kathy Skuja and W. Kim Halford, "Repeating the Errors of Our Parents? Parental Violence in Men's Family of Origin and Conflict Management in Dating Couples," *Journal of Interpersonal Violence* 19 (2004), 623–638.

14. Dominic A. Infante, Teresa A. Chandler, and Jill E. Rudd, "Test of an Argumentative Skill Deficiency Model of Interspousal Violence," *Communication Monographs* 56 (1989), 163–177.

15. Clyde M. Feldman and Carl A. Ridley, "The Role of Conflict-Based Communication Responses and Outcomes in Male Domestic Violence toward Female Partners," *Journal of Social and Personal Relationships* 17 (2000), 552–573; see also George Ronan, Laura E. Dreer, Katherine Dollard, and Donna W. Ronan, "Violent Couples: Coping and Communication Skills," *Journal of Family Violence* 19 (2004), 131–137.

16. Michele Bograd, "Why We Need Gender to Understand Human Violence," *Journal of Interpersonal Violence* 5 (1990), p. 133.

17. Linda L. Marshall, "Physical and Psychological Abuse," in William R. Cupach and Brian H. Spitzberg (Eds.), *The Dark Side of Interpersonal Communication* (Hillsdale, NJ: Erlbaum, 1994), pp. 281–311.

18. R. Emerson Dobash and Russell P. Dobash, "Research as Social Action: The Struggle for Battered Women," in Kersti Yllo and Michele Bograd (Eds.), *Feminist Perspectives on Wife Abuse* (Newbury Park, CA: Sage, 1988), p. 60.

19. Lenore A. Walker, "Psychology and Violence against Women," *American Psychologist* 44 (1989), 695–702.

20. Marshall, op. cit.

21. Loreen N. Olson, "'As Ugly and Painful as It Was, It Was Effective': Individuals' Unique Assessment of Communication Competence during Aggressive Conflict Episodes," *Communication Studies* 53 (2002), 171–188; Loreen N. Olson and Tamara D. Golish, "Topics of Conflict and Patterns of

Aggression in Romantic Relationships," *Southern Communication Journal* 67 (2002), 180–200.

22. Marie S. Tisak and John Tisak, "Expectations and Judgments Regarding Bystanders' and Victims' Responses to Peer Aggression among Early Adolescents," *Journal of Adolescence* 19 (1996), 383–392.

23. Scott L. Feld and Dawn T. Robinson, "Secondary Bystander Effects on Intimate Violence: When Norms of Restraint Reduce Deterrence," *Journal of Social and Personal Relationships* 15 (1998), 277–285.

24. Leslie Margolin, "Beyond Maternal Blame: Physical Child Abuse as a Phenomenon of Gender," *Journal of Family Issues,* 13 (1992), 410–423.

25. See, for example, Sandra A. Graham-Berman, Susan E. Cutler, Brian W. Litzenberger, and Wendy E. Schwartz, "Perceived Conflict and Violence in Childhood Sibling Relationships and Later Emotional Adjustment," *Journal of Family Psychology* 8 (1994), 85–97, who argue that both witnessing parental violence and experiencing violence with siblings results in the use of physically aggressive behaviors later in life. See also Hendrie Weisinger, *Anger at Work* (New York: William Morrow & Company, 1995), pp. 161–164; and Suzanne M. Retzinger, *Violent Emotions: Shame and Rage in Marital Quarrels* (Newbury Park: Sage Publications, 1991).

26. Joyce L. Hocker and William W. Wilmot, *Interpersonal Conflict,* 4th Ed. (Dubuque, IA: William C. Brown, 1995); George Robert Bach and Herb Goldberg, *Creative Aggression: The Art of Assertive Living* (New York: Avon Books, 1974).

27. Robert E. Alberti and Michael L. Emmons, *Your Perfect Right: A Guide to Assertive Behavior* (San Luis Obispo, CA: Impact, 1970).

28. Judy C. Pearson, *Interpersonal Communication: Clarity, Confidence, Concern* (Glenview, IL: Scott Foresman, 1983), p. 130.

29. David Viscott, *Risking* (New York: Pocket Books, 1977).

30. Mary Jane Collier, "Culture and Gender: Effects on Assertive Behavior and Communication Competence," in Margaret L. McLaughlin (Ed.), *Communication Yearbook 9* (Beverly Hills, CA: Sage, 1986), p. 578.

31. Robert Norton and Barbara Warnick, "Assertiveness as a Communication Construct," *Human Communication Research* 3 (1976), 62–66.

32. Patricia Jakubowski and Arthur J. Lange, *The Assertive Option: Your Rights and Responsibilities* (Champaign, IL: Research Press, 1978).

33. Alberti and Emmons, op. cit.

34. See, for example, Ronald B. Adler, *Confidence in Communication: A Guide to Assertive and Social Skills* (New York: Holt, Rinehart & Winston, 1977).

35. Shelley D. Lane, "Empathy and Assertive Communication," paper presented at the Western Speech Communication Association Convention, San Jose, CA, February 1981, p. 10.

36. George R. Bach and Peter Wyden, *The Intimate Enemy: How to Fight Fair in Love and Marriage* (New York: Avon, 1969), p. 19.

37. Roderick P. Hart and Donald M. Burks, "Rhetorical Sensitivity and Social Interaction," *Speech Monographs* 39 (1972), 75–91; Roderick P. Hart, Robert E. Carlson, and William F. Eadie, "Attitudes toward Communication and the Assessment of Rhetorical Sensitivity," *Communication Monographs* 47 (1980), 1–22.

5 Conflict Styles, Strategies, and Tactics

OBJECTIVES

At the end of this chapter, you should be able to:

- Explain the disadvantages of viewing overall plans for dealing with conflict situations as styles rather than strategies.

- Identify five conflict strategies and their two underlying factors.

- List and explain the phases of collaboration.

- Discuss the advantages of collaboration.

KEY TERMS

accommodation	conflict styles	relationship stress
avoidance	exit strategy	strategy
collaboration	loyalty strategy	tactic
competition	neglect strategy	voice strategy
compromise	personal stress	
conflict strategies	relationship strategy	

In Chapter 5, we discuss the idea of conflict styles and strategies consisting of behaviors that escalate or de-escalate conflicts. In the last chapter, we introduced you to the five commonly accepted conflict strategies—avoiding, accommodating, competing, compromising, and collaborating.[1] In that chapter, we described these conflict strategies in the hopes that you analyze the conflict situation and choose the most appropriate communication behavior: nonassertiveness, aggressiveness, passive-aggressiveness, or assertiveness.

Here, we discuss conflict strategies and tactics in detail. You are expected to learn to identify the appropriate strategies to use and describe the advantages and phases of a particularly useful conflict strategy known as collaboration. But first, we need to explain why we prefer the use of the term *strategies* rather than *styles* even though conflict theorists who take a styles approach have made contributions to our understanding of conflict management.

5.1 Think about It

Consider a recent activity you engaged in. Were you actively engaged or did you play a more passive role as an overall style? What strategy did you enact as you participated in the activity? What specific behaviors you engaged in, or tactics, were consistent with your strategy and style?

Conflict Styles versus Strategies

Originally, researchers defined **conflict styles** as a preferred set of behaviors for dealing with conflict situations and used whenever possible. Similarly, Folger, Poole, and Stutman define a conflict style as "a consistent, specific orientation toward the conflict, an orientation that unifies specific tactics into a coherent whole."[2] Researchers, so inclined, treated style like an attitude, a general tendency to behave a certain way regardless of the situation. In conflict situations, people supposedly tend to respond to conflict situations based on their conflict style, or their preferred way of dealing with conflicts. When enacting a conflict style, people also employ both strategies and tactics. Styles are similar to strategies in that both are overall plans for dealing with conflicts.[3] Styles differ from strategies in that one selects a **strategy** as an overall plan for one situation only, but if a person has a tendency to select the same strategy again and again, we call it a conflict style. A **tactic** is a specific observable behavior that moves a conflict in a particular direction in line with the strategy. Therefore, each style or strategy is associated with a particular set of related behaviors.

Researchers have found that some individuals are quite consistent in their conflict styles across different types of conflict situations, and the researchers found that they could predict the conflict style quite well from knowledge of certain intellectual and personality characteristics.[4] Further, some evidence exists that conflict behaviors are learned at a fairly young age and, at least when interacting with parents, consistent styles persist into young adulthood.[5] The type of conflict style people develop appears to have more to do with the way they perceive themselves as an individual than with ethnicity or sex.[6]

In everyday interaction, conflict styles are sometimes associated with particular behaviors. Early on, researchers identified only two conflict strategies or sets of related behaviors, cooperation and competition, but more types were added over the years.[7]

Although we intend in this chapter to switch from a styles approach to a strategy approach, we do want to point out two useful outcomes that have resulted from the identification of preferred conflict strategy. First, the idea of using one style for all occasions highlights the disadvantages associated with reliance on a single conflict style. For example, it is the case that a person might succeed at work with one conflict strategy that would fail at home.

My husband, Peter, is a doctor who works in a hospital emergency room. He is used to making the decisions and giving orders. When he becomes impatient, he turns red and yells at the nurses and orderlies. So much of what goes on there is life and death where seconds really matter. The problem is that he can't leave his "dominant personality" at work when he comes home. He'll snap at me and the kids and even yells at us when he loses his patience. I tell him that we are not an emergency medical unit, just a family. He didn't always act like this, but years at the hospital have turned him into a tyrant.

Second, the notion that styles exist calls attention to the fact that styles may themselves cause conflict at the process level. In other words, the behaviors people use may themselves contribute to a conflict between persons. Suppose that we combine individuals with the same or different conflict strategies. What might we expect? If a competitor is paired with an avoider or accommodator, he or she wins at the expense of the other. If a collaborator or compromiser sticks to his or her conflict strategy and tries to work with a competitor, the conflict may end in a stalemate. If two avoiders or accommodators (or one of each) are paired with one another, we might predict that they would accomplish little. Lori would say, "Jane, you decide." Jane would say, "No Lori, you decide." And so on it would go. If two competitors are paired, they "may become stuck in a destructive win–lose pattern of interaction," where the conflict could escalate and turn violent.[8] If two compromisers work together, they may quite easily resolve the problem, but not to their satisfaction. However, if two collaborators are matched, they would both take a problem solving approach, use integrative behaviors, and work toward the goal of finding a mutually satisfying solution. Of course, this sounds ideal.

At this point we need to explain our discomfort with the conflict styles approach and elaborate on the disagreement that exits between communication scholars regarding conflict styles versus strategies. Some researchers define conflict styles as "a preferred set of behaviors" or "a consistent, specific orientation toward the conflict," which means that they view conflict styles as "relatively stable aspects of the individual's personality."[9] This suggests that people are quite predictable, inflexible, and unable to adapt to different situations or changing circumstances—that their behavior is stereotypical. It also implies that people can't change, which also means that we "may not be motivated to change in order to break out of destructive patterns."[10] This view is problematic in the face of reality. While these conflict styles theorists believe that individuals maintain a particular style of communication throughout a conflict situation, actual research shows that individuals switch from one strategy to another as a conflict progresses, suggesting that not everyone has a single preferred style.[11]

Moreover, little association was found between preferences for particular styles and actual observed conflict behavior.[12] When people are asked to choose styles from a list, they tend to indicate the use of different styles than when they are asked to write out the way they would do a conflict. This is because people are generally able to recognize what is good to use in a conflict when the list is in front of them, but when actually faced with a conflict, apprehension tends to constrain their range of choices.[13] In addition, Conrad found only a moderate relationship between a person's reported style preference and his or her actual behavior.[14] Regardless of their reported conflict style, supervisors reported the use of collaborative-type styles more often than any other approach, but their behavior showed a consistent preference for the use of coercive tactics with noncompliant subordinates. Collaborative behaviors are seen as socially desirable and are therefore reflected in what people say they do. When compliance is vital, however, most people use stronger tactics.

An alterative view avoids labeling people as "avoiders," "competitors," or "collaborators," and focuses instead on specific types or constellations of behavior. Along these lines,

Wilmot and Hocker emphasize the need to focus on "patterned responses, or clusters of behavior, that people use in a conflict situation."[15] This approach does not imply that we are stuck in a rut. We are capable of change and adaptation. Although a style may dominate a person's actions for a while, she or he may abandon it and replace it with another. This is where strategies (and their related tactics) come into play. If we learn the alternative strategies available for managing conflict situations, we may improve our outcomes. This way of viewing conflict behaviors has the advantage of offering us options that we can compare and contrast.

Therefore, in the remainder of this chapter we refer to **conflict strategies** as overall plans consisting of a cluster of behaviors that people use in a specific conflict situation. We use the term *strategies* to refer to categories of tactics, not types of people, as the term *style* suggests. Although a behavior may occur in more than one of the clusters of behaviors, when the behaviors occur together they are interpreted as one strategy or another. Postponing, for example, may indicate that a party is trying to collaborate "because it gives both sides a 'cooling off' period, but it can also be an avoidance tactic."[16] However, when combined with other behaviors associated with working together or not, it becomes clear when a party is collaborating or avoiding the conflict. Moreover, keep in mind that we are talking about the set of behaviors and not labeling the individuals involved. Finally, note that these strategies may apply only in one conflict situation, so one is free to switch strategies as the need permits.

5.2   **Think about It**

In dealing with conflicts, do you find that you tend to characterize just one style? Do you tend to avoid, compete, accommodate, compromise, or collaborate? Are you satisfied with the outcome of conflicts when you use this style? Do you use the style all the time or are there exceptions?

Conflict Strategies and Tactics

There is research support suggesting that these conflict strategies exist across cultures, although cultures vary in their preference for particular strategies over others.[17] Table 5.1 lists conflict strategies derived originally from research conducted by Blake and Mouton and renamed by Kilmann and Thomas as well as Rahim.[18]

Perhaps due to the usefulness of a conflict strategy assessment tool developed by Kilmann and Thomas, we find that their set of terms are often used in the research literature, so we tend to prefer to use them most often ourselves: avoiding or avoidance, accommodating or accommodation, competing or competition, compromising or compromise, and collaborating or collaboration.

Originally, the five strategies were identified on the basis of how much concern a person had for the relationship with the other person and for attaining his or her personal goal. One can have little concern for either of these, or a high concern for both of them,

TABLE 5.1   **Five Common Conflict Strategies**

Blake & Mouton	Kilmann & Thomas	Rahim
Avoiding	Avoiding	Avoiding
Smoothing	Accommodating	Obliging
Forcing	Competing	Dominating
Compromising	Compromising	Compromising
Confronting	Collaborating	Integrating

or some other combination in between. Rahim later labeled these two basic dimensions underlying the five strategies as concern for self (or for one's personal goal) and concern for others (or for the relationship).[19] As shown in Table 5.2, the five strategies differ in the way they maximize or minimize one's own or the other's outcomes (winning versus losing). While we briefly introduced these terms in Chapter 4, in this chapter we explore them in greater depth.

Avoidance means not addressing a conflict at all. Generally, people who avoid confrontation do so because they have a bad history of dealing with conflict in general. They may also think that the problem may simply go away on its own. We can add that they are not sufficiently concerned about solving a problem to risk confrontation or do not care enough about their relationship to use confrontation to improve or clarify the situation. Behaviors indicative of this strategy include choosing to withdraw, leave the scene, avoid discussing issues, or remain silent.[20]

Accommodation means smoothing over conflicts, obliging others, and not making waves. Those who simply give in try to maintain the illusion of harmony. As a result, they suppress the conflict issue in this situation because they do not want to risk ill feelings. By accommodating, one gives up personal gains for the benefit of one's partner. Perhaps one is so concerned about the relationship and the other person that he or she suppresses personal needs, interests, and goals, and thus does not make waves. While the partner of the one who

TABLE 5.2   **Five Conflict Strategies, Their Definitions, Objectives, and Behaviors**

Conflict Strategy	Definition	Objective	Behavior/Tactic
Avoidance	withdrawal	lose–lose	phyically absent or silent
Accommodation	acquiesce	lose–win	give in; don't make waves
Competition	aggression	win–lose	selfish, argumentative
Compromise	trade-offs	win and lose	wheeler-dealer
Collaboration	mutual satisfaction	win–win	supportive of self and other

Source: Reprinted from *Letting Go,* by Dudley D. Cahn, by permission of the State University of New York Press. © 1987, State University of New York. All rights reserved.

A competitive strategy often results in conflicts that are more angry and stressful than they need to be.

is accommodating may derive considerable personal growth and satisfaction, the one who accommodates is not deriving similar benefits.

Competition means dominating, controlling, and forcing one's decision on others. Those who use a competitive strategy in a given conflict situation are not necessarily un-caring about the other, but they favor their own self-interests or task accomplishment more than they favor other people's interests or feelings about that situation. Since the objective is "win–lose" in favor of one's self, one gains at the other's expense. As defined here, those who choose the strategy of competition appear to others as argumentative, aggressive, con-trolling, and selfish in this conflict situation.

A middle-of-the-road approach is **compromise,** which means making sure that no one totally wins or loses. People who compromise in a conflict situation are interested in finding a workable rather than an optimal solution. There are occasions where compromise can contribute positively to the outcomes in a conflict situation, especially in situations in which all parties cannot have what they want. However, compromise can also contribute negatively to the outcomes if all parties exchange offers and make concessions, and walk away from the conflict feeling unsatisfied with the outcome. As a strategy favoring trade-offs involving "give and take," it is designed as a realistic attempt to seek an acceptable (but not necessarily preferred) solution of gains and losses for everyone involved. This strategy is not ideal because regardless of the initial objective, in the end neither party may win using it, as they both lose at least some of what they had hoped to achieve.

Collaboration means using integrative behaviors and developing mutually satisfying agreements to solve the problem once and for all. Collaboration, then, has two essential ingredients. First, it consists of integrative behaviors such as cooperation, collective action, and mutual assistance. When people collaborate, they work together toward the same ends in compatible roles. We call this teamwork. To an observer, the collaborators appear to work side by side and hand in hand. This approach is in direct contrast to opposing or competing individuals who counteract, antagonize, and work against one another.

Secondly, collaboration means that the partners have in mind the same goal, which is to strive for a mutually satisfying solution to the conflict. Mutually satisfying solutions are win–win outcomes. Collaboration emphasizes one's own self interests but also respects the other's interests, needs, and goals. While collaboration may involve confronting differences, it requires a focusing on the problem and includes sharing information about everyone's needs, goals, and interests. In fact, Folger and his colleagues refer to the collaboration approach as the "problem solving orientation." [21]

All too often, conflicting parties are too quick to compromise, when greater effort would produce a solution that completely satisfies both of them. For example, conflicting parties might settle for the following:

Examples of Compromise	Examples of Collaboration
Alternate driving the car	Go together to events
Split driving 50:50	Take a bus/train
Split housecleaning chores	Hire a housecleaning service
Alternate watching TV programs	Watch one and tape the other
Alternate holidays with family	Combine families for the holidays
Divide the money between them	Increase the amount so that both get what they want

5.1 Apply It

Write out a description of a conflict you recently experienced or observed. How would you have handled it using each of the five conflict strategies (avoiding, accommodating, compromising, competing, and collaborating)?

Collaboration: The Preferred Conflict Strategy

Why study conflict styles or strategies? In previous chapters, we have offered options and even suggested that, although we favored a tendency toward assertiveness, there are times when aggressive, nonassertive, and passive-aggressive communication behavior is called for. The idea we would like to foster is that, while flexibility, openness to alternatives, and adaptability are important interpersonal communication skills, we also favor a tendency toward the collaborative conflict strategy, which is proactive in nature and incorporates cooperative, integrative, and assertive behavior.[22] In theory, Blake and Mouton favored the collaboration strategy in conflict situations. It requires that a person believe that the concerns of the other person are as important as one's own and adopt the goal of finding mutually satisfying solutions to problems and resolutions of issues, which takes time and effort. Gross and colleagues demonstrated that people in temporary task-oriented dyads preferred a problem-solving approach and were critical of a controlling approach to the problem.[23] Research by Manning and Robertson suggests that "skilled negotiators tend to use low avoidance and high collaboration modes of conflict handling. . . [they] also show a preparedness to use accommodation and compromise, whilst avoiding competition."[24]

When you don't have the time or effort or find collaboration to be a problem, you can consider using an alternative strategy. However, as a general rule, we would like to see you adopt the collaboration strategy more often because it contributes less toward long-term personal and relationship stress and most toward personal and relationship growth and satisfaction. Therefore, we would like to spend the rest of this chapter on a more detailed description of collaboration and its related tactics, in addition to providing some good reasons for using collaboration.

Low Personal and Relationship Stress

In general, stress "comes from demands and pressures of the recent past and anticipated demands and pressures of the near future."[25] Stress can be personal or relational in nature, or a combination of both. The five behavioral orientations result in differing levels of personal and relational stress, as reported in Table 5.3.

Personal stress occurs within a person and refers to wear and tear on one emotionally and physically. While a little stress is positive and pleasurable as when one experiences an up-lift associated with falling in love, seeing a great performance, or watching an exciting athletic event, other stressors such as strong feelings of anxiety, frustration, and anger that are associated with life crises such as a death of a family member, a divorce, a marriage, a new job, or a change in one's location may contribute to ulcers, heart disease, hypertension, migraines, and even suicide. Loneliness is also stress producing. Psychologists have long argued that stress improves performance, but only up to a point, at which efficiency drops off sharply.

Relationship stress occurs outside the individual and refers to wear and tear on a relationship. Whereas personal stress goes on within the individual, relationship stress goes on between two or more persons. In long-term relationships, "new social roles of the sexes" is frequently mentioned as a relationship stress producer. Because of the omnipresence of interpersonal conflict, a little relationship stress is normal and unavoidable, but in the extreme, relationship stress results in relationship dissatisfaction and deterioration, which eventually may result in social disengagement such as breaking up, divorcing, or losing a job.

TABLE 5.3   Degrees of Stress Underlying Five Conflict Strategies

Conflict Strategy	Degrees of Stress
Avoidance	High personal stress/high relationship stress
Accommodation	High personal stress/low relationship stress
Competition	Low personal stress/high relationship stress
Compromise	Moderate levels of both types of stress
Collaboration	Low personal stress/low relationship stress

TABLE 5.4   **Conflict Strategies and Effect on Relationship and Personal Growth**

Conflict Strategy	Personal/Relationship Growth
Avoidance	Low feelings of self-worth and relationship satisfaction; no personal/relationship growth
Accommodation	Low feelings of self-worth and relationship satisfaction; no personal growth; partners grow apart (high growth only for partner)
Competition	High feelings of self-worth and relationship satisfaction; high personal growth for self; partners grow apart (no growth for partner)
Compromise	Moderate feelings of self-worth and relationship satisfaction; moderate personal/relationship growth
Collaboration	High feelings of self-worth and relationship satisfaction; maximum personal/relationship growth

Source: Reprinted from *Letting Go,* by Dudley D. Cahn, by permission of the State University of New York Press. © 1987, State University of New York. All rights reserved.

As displayed in Table 5.4, the five alternative communication or conflict strategies vary in the degree and type of stress underlying them. Again, frequent reliance on collaboration to manage conflicts is the most advantageous alternative because it alone reduces one's emotional and physical stress as well as the stress on the relationship.

Another way of understanding how people respond to the relational stress caused by conflict is through the long-term strategies people may adopt. Unlike conflict strategies used at a particular time and place, these **relationship strategies** are general approaches to dealing with the conflicts that exist in a relationship. A comprehensive research program on strategies in conflict situations undertaken by Rusbult and her colleagues has identified four options that vary in their destructiveness.[26]

Exit strategy (leaving the relationship) and **neglect strategy** (ignoring the problem and its effect on the relationship) are destructive, whereas **voice strategy** (saying something about the problem) and **loyalty strategy** (diminishing the problem's importance in light of the good in the relationship) are considered more constructive. In comparison with men, Rusbult and her colleagues found that women were more likely than men to choose strategies of voice and loyalty and less likely than men to choose neglect as a strategy. Where partners are committed to their relationship (i.e., the rewards outweigh the costs), partners prefer loyalty or voice as alternative cognitive strategies in conflict situations. The greater the commitment to a relationship, the more likely they are to choose voice rather than loyalty as a strategy. However, where partners are not committed to remain in the relationship, partners prefer neglect or exit from the relationship as alternative cognitive strategies in conflict situations. The less the commitment, the more likely they are to choose exit rather than neglect as a strategy. This narrative shows a progression from neglect to voice to exit.

I finally confronted my former best friend about trying to steal my boyfriend from me. Because it took me four months to confront this conflict, I was hoping for a resolution, but not expecting one. Pam and I started growing apart a year ago as we became different people with different views. At first I wanted to blame Pam for the conflict, but I realized that I was to blame because I waited to confront her, I ignored her when she confronted me, and because I purposely distanced myself from her. In a letter, I told her that I forgave her and realized most of what happened was my fault. Pam wrote back and basically attacked me for everything I have done wrong since I met her. She also critiqued my letter! I am so frustrated because I tried to be the good person by carefully handling the conflict and forgiving Pam, and all I got in return was bitterness. We just can't be friends any longer.

Building on Rusbult's typology of conflict strategies in conflict situations, Healey and Bell argue that partners may cognitively progress through different strategies as dissatisfaction in a relationship grows.[27] At first, they might prefer loyalty as a strategy, hoping that the situation improves soon. They may turn to the strategy of voice when the situation does not improve, then decide on neglect, and eventually choose exit as the preferred strategy. Perhaps newly formed romantic couples prefer loyalty because they fear losing their partner who is not yet fully committed to the relationship. However, after commitment takes place such as engagement or marriage, they prefer the strategy of voice, but if conditions worsen, then they change mentally to neglect. Finally, when superior alternatives appear, they prefer exit as a strategy.

More recently, Fritz has examined which of the four strategies people are likely to use when faced with unpleasant work relationships.[28] Her results indicated that the choice of strategy depended upon one's position in the organization as well as perceptions of the problem. People tended to use exit when the problem was with superiors or peers; voice and loyalty were more likely responses with subordinates. People were more likely to choose neglect when they did not believe they could solve the problem and had little desire to try. Loyalty was associated with a desire to solve the problem, but the strategy of voice required that a person had a desire to solve the problem, a belief that he or she could solve it, a belief that the other wanted to solve the problem, and a belief that the problem inconvenienced the other person involved. It would seem that, at least in organizations, people do not want to engage in conflict without a reasonable chance of solving some problem.

5.2   Apply It

Write out a description of a conflict you recently experienced or observed. How would you have handled it using each of the four relational strategies (voice, loyalty, neglect, and exit)?

High Personal and Relationship Growth and Satisfaction

As depicted in Table 5.4, a comparison of the five strategies reveals that, if enacted and repeated often enough, they differ in their contributions to personal and relationship growth and satisfaction. By failing to include one's self interests, both avoidance and accommodation create conditions characterized by low feelings of self-worth and relationship satisfaction, and no opportunities for personal or relationship growth. By considering one's self-interests (but at the expense of others), competition creates conditions one may describe as high in personal growth, feelings of self-worth, and relationship satisfaction for the dominant party but low in personal and relationship growth for the other party to the conflict. Thus, it may happen that people who frequently use accommodation and those who tend to choose to compete are attracted to each other initially, but find that the stress and strain on the relationship as they grow apart often leads to relationship dissatisfaction for the one who gives in and eventual disengagement. By gaining some and losing some of one's interests, needs, and goals, compromise as a strategy contributes to moderate feelings of self-worth and relationship satisfaction, and moderate personal and relationship growth. Finally, by allowing for self-interests, encouraging effective listening, and promoting an integrative approach to problem solving, collaboration, if enacted often enough, is the only strategy that contributes to high feelings of self-worth and relationship satisfaction for both partners and maximum personal and relationship growth.

Derr offers support for the collaborative strategy when he argues that it promotes authentic interpersonal relations, is used as a creative force for innovation and improvement, enhances feedback and information flow, and increases feelings of integrity and trust.[29] When successfully utilized as a mode for resolving interpersonal conflict aimed at developing an integrated consensus through argumentation and perspective-taking, collaboration not only ends conflict but modifies the perspective of the individuals involved to a consensus framework that respects individual differences.

Meanwhile, Blake and Mouton argue that an improved quality of life and more efficient interpersonal relations result when the collaboration strategy of communication is frequently used in conflict situations. Evidence exists that their judgment is shared. One study found that across types of relationships and issues of conflict, respondents approve of collaboration strategies for conflict over the other orientations.[30] Without training in conflict resolution, many people see the concern for the other and concern for one's own goals as competing and believe that being self-oriented and task-oriented while at the same time demonstrating concern for others is difficult to do if not impossible.

Collaboration is necessary for genuine and mutual understanding. With training people can adopt a strategy of collaboration and find ways to develop mutually satisfying solutions to conflicts.

Phases of Collaboration

Given our emphasis on the desirability of collaboration, this section demonstrates how one might accomplish a collaborative process. Later, we use an extended example to illustrate it.

Clarification of Perspectives. When conflicting parties decide to confront one another in an effort to solve a problem, they need to clarify their points of view to one another. Suggested tactics for enacting a strategy of collaboration are presented in Table 5.5. Collaboration calls for understanding the other as well as one's own position and respecting one another. To do this, we need to understand that good, well-intentioned people may hold opposing views, which do not diminish their humanity in any way. This narrative reports one person's frustration with a friend who cannot accept other points of view.

> I don't know why, but often my friend and I get into huge arguments when we're driving somewhere. The other day he was talking about how repressed the U.S. is compared to Europe, and how we shouldn't have so many laws restricting our "natural inclinations." I

TABLE 5.5   Tactics Used to Enact a Strategy of Collaboration

Description	Nonevaluative statements about observable events related to conflict
Qualification	Statements that explicitly qualify the nature and extent of conflict
Disclosure	Nonevaluative statements about events related to conflict that the partner cannot observe, such as thoughts, feelings, intentions, motivations, and past history
Soliciting disclosure	Soliciting information from the partner about events related to the conflict that one cannot observe
Negative inquiry	Soliciting complaints about oneself
Empathy or support	Statements that express understanding, acceptance, or positive regard for the partner (despite acknowledgment of a conflict)
Emphasizing commonalities	Statements that comment on shared interests, goals, or compatibilities with the partner (despite acknowledgment of a conflict)
Accepting responsibility	Statements that attribute responsibility for conflicts to self or to both parties
Initiating problem solving	Statements that initiate mutual consideration of solutions to conflict

Source: Alan L. Sillars, Stephen F. Colletti, Doug Parry, and Mark A. Rogers, "Coding Verbal Tactics: Nonverbal and Perceptual Correlates of the 'Avoidance-Distributive-Integrative' Distinction," *Human Communication Research* 9 (1982) 83–85, copyright © 1982 by Sage Publications, Inc. Reprinted by permission of Sage Publications, Inc.

replied that laws are often there to protect others from what we'd like to do, and he got really loud and said no reasonable person could see it any other way than his. This is what he usually says when he's tired of trying to make his point and doesn't want to listen to what I have to say, so I dropped it.

Rigid Goal but Flexible Means.   When people collaborate, they are rigid in terms of the goal of developing mutually satisfying solutions, but they are flexible with respect to the means for achieving them. They are committed to a win–win outcome but are able to devise alternative ways to achieve it. Thus, they accept only high personal gains for themselves and their partners and tend to pursue many alternative paths in an effort to achieve a mutually satisfying outcome.

Developing Mutual Understanding.   Resolving differences in opinion or points of view, in a manner that is mutually advantageous to everyone involved, usually requires first that partners increase their range of perspectives, solutions, or alternatives. Understanding the perspective of another person does not necessarily mean agreeing. It means only that you make an effort to see the problem as the other defines it, without deciding on the validity of the other person's perspective.

It also helps for you to try to see the difference between what you want for yourself and what might benefit both of you. One way of doing so is to think about what you want as end points on a continuum with many intermediate views. For example, if you and I argue over a dollar we both see on the sidewalk, we could change it into 100 cents and then see that one might settle for 90, 65, or 50 cents. A continuum often opens the door to many alternatives not previously seen.

Another technique for generating mutual understanding involves reordering the partners' views on the matter at hand, or helping the other person to see that the problem can be defined differently than his or her first impression of it. Such a shift can create an entirely new perspective. For example, when two sales representatives are arguing over who first contacted a client, one might say that the other could spend the sales commission on dinner for the both of them. That might make the other see the situation in a whole new light. Realizing that there are other possible solutions to the problem, each person must take a new look at the matter.

Implementation of a Mutual Understanding.   While the discovery of a mutual understanding is often a challenging task, all the time and effort spent on its pursuit is wasted if appropriate measures are not taken to put the solution into effect. To implement means to undertake the solution as agreed on. Quite often, this requires a trial period. Sometimes minor adjustments are needed to make matters work out as intended.

In sum, Daniels and Walker describe the key aspects of collaboration as follows:[31]

1. It is less competitive.
2. It features mutual learning and fact finding.
3. It allows for exploration of differences in underlying values.
4. It resembles principled negotiation, focusing on interests rather than positions.
5. It allocates the responsibility for implementation across many parties.
6. Its conclusions are generated by participants through an interactive, iterative, and reflexive process.
7. It is often an ongoing process.
8. It has the potential to build individual and community capacity in such arenas as conflict management, leadership, decision making, and communication.

To illustrate the collaborative strategy in a real conflict situation, the following extended example is offered.

Case Study

Oganna and Adrian were married soon after graduation four years ago and each has worked ever since. This year they receive a $20,000 inheritance (left to both of them). Now Oganna wants to take a year off from work and use the inheritance to pay for a year of her schooling. However, Adrian is against her taking a year off from work and favors banking the inheritance instead.

After giving the matter considerable thought and preparing for a possible conflict situation, Oganna decides to discuss her idea with Adrian, so she suggests that they talk about it after supper. She begins the confrontation by telling Adrian that she is unhappy with her present job and realizes that he would like her to continue working, but she would like to quit her job. She then listens to Adrian, who says that he realizes that she doesn't like her job, he is concerned about their future finances, and would prefer they both continue to work while they invest the inheritance, so that it would grow into a sizable nest egg.

Oganna states that she wants to take a year off from work to attend a local university to acquire a master's degree in Business Administration, which she says may advance her career in the long run. Adrian, who likes his job, is adamantly opposed to her taking a leave of absence because after four years of their paying off debts for an automobile and furniture for their apartment, he says that he would like to put the money in a bank to earn interest.

Both Oganna and Adrian indicate that they must resolve these differences of opinion because the issues are creating a strain on their marriage. They also say that a completely satisfactory understanding must not break up their marriage, but at the same time, must not result in either one having to give up ambitions, needs, and goals. In other words, they are rigid in their goals of achieving a mutually satisfying solution but flexible in how they might go about achieving it. At this point in the confrontation, they also shift from sticking to their positions or wants (I want to quit and go to school; I want you to make money) to a discussion of their interests or needs. While Oganna says she wants to have a job that is more satisfying, Adrian points out his need for future financial security. So, they agree that a solution must enable Oganna to advance in her career; and yet it must provide greater financial security for Adrian.

While Adrian and Oganna appear rigid with respect to goals, they report that they are willing to entertain a wide variety of means for attaining them. Here they begin to brainstorm a variety of options. Oganna could earn her degree on a full-time basis, on a part-time status, or not return to college at all and do something else instead. Adrian, meanwhile, could bank all $20,000 or $10,000 or $5,000 or none at all. At this point, however, a premature understanding that consisted solely of Oganna agreeing to return to school on a part-time basis and Adrian banking $10,000 would result in a compromise with both persons receiving less than they desire. They agreed that they would rather find a solution that is more satisfying to them both.

In addition to increasing the range of perspectives, the partners would benefit by trying to discover new perspectives, solutions, or alternatives that are related to the matter at hand, such as time, money, interests, security, and status or other factors that were not considered at first. Perhaps, in the case of Oganna and Adrian, they may introduce a time dimension in at least two ways. Oganna could attempt to complete the degree in one year or spread it out over two years or more. Adrian could invest the entire inheritance for an indefinite period or invest all of it now and some of it later. Moreover, because Oganna expressed a desire to do something different, she could consider not doing some aspect of her work that is especially bothersome to her. Perhaps a vacation or a change in her job situation such as a different task, new co-workers, or a different department (or even a new job) would satisfy her need for a change.

An idea occurs to Oganna that might help Adrian view the situation in a different light. She decides to go so far as to suggest that she could not remain in a marriage where a husband was not more interested in her happiness, needs, and interests. In fact, she states that obtaining a master's degree may make her more valuable to her employer and better guarantee her tenure and advancement in the long run. However, she adds that Adrian needs to realize that neither Oganna's desire for time off nor Adrian's desire for financial security is achieved in the event of a marital breakdown, especially if it means divorce. The threat of severe financial loss at this time which neither party wants may motivate the couple to see the value of the newly discovered alternatives to the problem, to realize that there may be a way to reach mutual understanding, and to make an even greater effort to achieve it.

Hopefully, Oganna and Adrian use interpersonal communication skills that we identify as collaborative or integrative strategies (see Table 5.3). Both are analytic, conciliatory, and problem solving in focus, attempt to clarify the issues and facilitate mutual resolution of the problem, describe behavior, disclose feelings, ask for disclosure from the other person, ask for criticism from the other person, qualify the nature of the problem, support the disclosures or observations the other person has made, and accept responsibility for each one's part in the conflict.

Using the acceptable elements of the possible alternative opinions, points of view, and solutions, the partners work together to find a choice that meets the needs of everyone involved. In the case of Oganna and Adrian, an example of an understanding that is mutually advantageous is as follows. As soon as possible, they could take a three-week camping trip that they both want. Oganna could return to her job after the vacation and enroll part-time at the university for one year at which time she could request a leave of absence to attend to her studies full time, and then she could earn any remaining credits on a part-time basis. In the meantime, Adrian could bank most of the inheritance to draw interest for one year at which time Oganna could spend half of the inheritance on her education and the remainder could stay in the bank indefinitely. This solution has the potential of completely satisfying both Oganna and Adrian because while on a vacation with Adrian, Oganna is "getting away for a while" and on return she commences work on her degree and looks forward to a semester of full-time graduate student status next year, while Adrian banks most of the money for one year and half after that.

Although other agreements are possible, this is an example of how the collaborative strategy may actually enhance a relationship. During the confrontation and development of a mutually satisfying outcome, Oganna and Adrian have a greater understanding of each other's needs, desires, and beliefs. Each may believe that his or her position has a valuable contribution to make in the long run to their relationship, and that each needs to take the other's ideas into account in any decision the couple reaches. They may take pride in the fact that they asserted themselves and employed the collaboration strategy. As a follow-up, the partners need to reinforce these attitudes during the next few months to guarantee the successful implementation of the mutual understanding.

5.3 Apply It

Write out a description of a conflict you recently experienced or observed. If you had attempted the collaborative style, what actions would you have taken at each step of the conflict?

Manage It

When studying conflict management, we often come across the word *collaboration.* Authors frequently describe effective conflict resolution as collaborative. We are told that it is important to collaborate with others. What does this mean? How do we do it?

Collaboration is a style or strategy that effective conflict managers use. When we think of style, we think of fads or fashions. However, when the term is applied to conflicts, style is more like a personality or way of acting. People respond in a characteristic manner that reflects their preferred way of dealing with conflicts.

When enacting a conflict style, people also employ both strategies and tactics. While both styles and strategies refer to overall plans for dealing with conflict, styles differ from strategies in their scope. One selects a strategy as an overall plan for one situation only, but if a person has a tendency to select the same strategy again and again, we call it a conflict style.

A style or strategy is made up of specific behaviors or tactics. The collaboration strategy is applied to a conflict through the use of tactics such as paraphrasing, asking the other for more information, and so on. Tactics move a conflict in a particular direction in line with the overall plan. Thus, collaboration is a style when one collaborates across all situations whereas it is a strategy when one intends to collaborate in a particular conflict situation. The specific behaviors that a person manifests are the collaborative tactics.

We prefer to view overall plans for dealing with conflict situations as styles rather than strategies because the idea of conflict styles suggests that people are predictable, inflexible, and often unable to adapt to different situations or changing circumstances. If we say a person has a conflict style, we imply that their behavior is inevitable and they can't change. This view is problematic in the face of reality. Actual research shows that individuals switch from one strategy to another as a conflict progresses, suggesting that not everyone has a single preferred style. Moreover, little association was found between stated preference for particular styles and actual observed conflict behavior.

Several interpersonal communication skills or tactics are associated with the collaborative style or strategy. These include being analytic, conciliatory, and problem solving in focus; attempting to clarify issues and facilitate mutual resolution of the problem; describing behavior, disclosing feelings, asking for disclosure from the other person, asking for criticism from the other person, and qualifying the nature of the problem; supporting the disclosures or observations the other person has made; and accepting responsibility for everyone's part in the conflict.

Note that one of the above tactics or communication skills involves asserting one's own feelings. Although we may have been led in the past to think that assertiveness is not "nice," it plays a role in collaboration. Because assertiveness is so important in conflict situations and so difficult to learn, we devote the entire next chapter to explaining how to create effective assertive messages.

Although all five conflict strategies serve a purpose, there are advantages to employing a collaborative strategy. If both parties are willing, collaboration is the best way to resolve interpersonal conflicts because it produces less personal and relationship stress and the most personal and relationship growth.

5.1 Work with It

Answer the questions following the description of the conflict.

A and B married this past year, and A wants to spend the holidays with his/her side of the family. B wants them to go to his/her parents for the holidays. Neither wants to visit his/her relatives alone.

1. What effective confrontation steps could A and B take before, during, and after discussing the issue? How could they clarify their perspectives using I-statements?
2. What are their initial positions and what interests or needs lie behind them?
3. What phases of collaboration should they employ?
4. What additional techniques could they use?
5. What might their final agreement look like if it attempts to satisfy both of their needs or interests?

5.2 Work with It

Attempt to role play the conflict situation below in which you and another student in class employ the collaborative strategy as described in this chapter. Develop a list of the principles and techniques taught in this chapter and try to employ as many of them as you can. Then write out your answers to the questions provided below.

A and B were friends since high school, picked the same college to attend, and agreed to room together. After two years, A decides that he or she would like to see what it is like living with someone else for a change. B is against changing roommates because the two of them share each other's clothing, pooled money to buy their TV and microwave, and find each other highly compatible.

1. What effective confrontation steps did you take before, during, and after discussing the issue? How did you clarify your perspectives using I-statements?
2. What were both your initial positions and what interests or needs lie behind them?
3. What phases of collaboration did you employ?
4. What additional techniques did you use?
5. To what extent does your final agreement, if reached, satisfy both of your needs or interests?

5.1 Remember It

Write an essay in which you apply the ideas presented in Chapter 5 to your life situation. Make sure to address the following topics.

1. Describe real or imagined interpersonal conflict situations in which all five conflict strategies are illustrated and their two underlying factors.
2. Explain how you can apply each step of collaboration to analyze a successfully managed conflict.
3. What advantages or outcomes might you expect by collaborating in this conflict?

NOTES

1. Robert R. Blake and Jane Srygley Mouton, *The Managerial Grid* (Houston: Gulf, 1964); Robert H. Kilmann and Kenneth W. Thomas, "Developing a Forced-Choice Measure of Conflict-Handling Behavior: The Mode Instrument," *Educational and Psychological Measurement* 37 (1977), 309–325; M. Afzalur Rahim, "A Measure of Styles of Handling Interpersonal Conflict," *Academy of Management Journal* 26 (1983), 368–376.

2. Joseph P. Folger, Marshall Scott Poole, and Randall K. Stutman, *Working through Conflict,* 4th Ed. (Boston: Allyn & Bacon, 2001), p. 219.

3. Alan L. Sillars, Stephen F. Coletti, D. Parry, and Mark A. Rogers, "Coding Verbal Conflict Tactics:

Nonverbal and Perceptual Correlates of the 'Avoidance-Distributive-Integrative' Distinction," *Human Communication Research* 9 (1982), 83–95.

4. Robert J. Sternberg and Lawrence J. Soriano, "Styles of Conflict Resolution," *Journal of Personal and Social Psychology* 47 (1984), 115–126.

5. Rebecca Dumlao and Renee A. Botta, "Family Communication Patterns and the Conflict Styles Young Adults Use with Their Fathers," *Communication Quarterly* 48 (2000), 174–189.

6. Stella Ting-Toomey, John G. Oetzel, and Kimberlie Yee-Jung, "Self-Construal Types and Conflict Management Styles," *Communication Reports* 14 (2001), 87–104.

7. William W. Wilmot and Joyce L. Hocker, *Interpersonal Conflict,* 6th Ed. (New York: McGraw Hill, 2001), p. 130.

8. Suzanne McCorkle and Melanie Reese, *Mediation Theory and Practice* (Boston: Allyn & Bacon, 2005), p. 84

9. Wilmot and Hocker, 2001, p. 222

10. Ibid.

11. Anne Nicotera (Ed.), *Conflict and Organizations: Communicative Processes* (Albany: State University of New York Press, 1995), p. 26.

12. Boris Kabanoff, "Predictive Validity of the MODE Conflict Instrument," *Journal of Applied Psychology* 72 (1987), 160–163.

13. Barbara Mae Gayle, "Sex Equity in Workplace Conflict Management," *Journal of Applied Communication Research* 19 (1991), 152–169.

14. Charles Conrad, "Communication in Conflict: Style-Strategy Relationships," *Communication Monographs* 58 (1991), 135–155.

15. Wilmot and Hocker, 2001, p. 130.

16. Folger et al., 2001, p. 223.

17. Deborah A. Cai and Edward L. Fink, "Conflict Style Differences between Individualists and Collectivists," *Communication Monographs* 1 (2002), 67–87.

18. Blake and Mouton; Kilmann and Thomas; and Rahim, op. cit.

19. M. Afzalur Rahim, "A Measure of Styles of Handling Interpersonal Conflict, *Academy of Management Journal* 26 (1983), 368–376.

20. An interesting counterpoint to this idea is found in Julia Richardson, "Avoidance as an Active Mode of Conflict Resolution," *Team Performance Management* 1 (1995), 19–23, which argues that the lack of confrontation between management and teams can actually be an active strategy on the part of a less powerful team to accomplish their goals more covertly.

21. Folger et al., 2001, pp. 228–229.

22. Donna R. Pawlowcott, A. Meyers, and Kelly A. Rocca, "Relational Messages in Conflict Situations among Siblings," *Communication Research Reports,* 3 (2000), 271–277.

23. Michael A. Gross, Laura Guerrero, and Jess K. Alberts, "Perceptions of Conflict Strategies and Communication Competence in Task-Oriented Dyads," *Journal of Applied Communication Research* 32 (2004), 249–270.

24. Tony Manning and Bob Robertson, "Influencing, Negotiating Skills and Conflict Handling: Some Additional Research and Reflections," *Industrial and Commercial Training* 36 (2004), p. 108.

25. American Psychological Association, "The Different Kinds of Stress," retrieved October 26, 2005, from http://apahelpcenter.org/articles/article.php?id=21.

26. Caryl E. Rusbult and Isabella M. Zembrodt, "Responses to Dissatisfaction in Romantic Involvements: A Multidimensional Scaling Analysis," *Journal of Experimental Social Psychology* 19 (1983), 274–293; Caryl E. Rusbult, Dennis J. Johnson, and Gregory D. Morrow, "Determinants and Consequences of Exit, Voice, Loyalty, and Neglect: Responses to Dissatisfaction in Adult Romantic Involvements," *Human Relations* 39 (1986), 45–63.

27. Jonathan G. Healey and Robert A. Bell, "Assessing Alternate Responses to Conflicts in Friendship," in Dudley D. Cahn (Ed.), *Intimates in Conflict: A Communication Perspective* (Hillsdale, NJ: Erlbaum, 1990), 25–48.

28. Janie M. Harden Fritz, "Responses to Unpleasant Work Relationships," *Communication Research Reports* 14 (1997), 302–311.

29. C. Brooklyn Derr, "Managing Organizational Conflict: Collaboration, Bargaining, and Power Approaches," *California Management Review* 21 (1978), 76–83.

30. Tara L. Shepherd, "Content and Relationship Dimensions of a Conflict Encounter: An Investigation of Their Impact on Perceived Rules," paper presented to the Speech Communication Association Convention, Anaheim, CA, November 1982.

31. Steven E. Daniels and Greg B. Walker, *Working through Environmental Conflict: The Collaborative Learning Approach* (Westport, CT: Praeger, 2001), p. 124.

6 Effectively Confronting Others

OBJECTIVES

At the end of this chapter, you should be able to:

- Explain what it means to say that communication is a skill.
- List the six steps to confronting interpersonal problems.
- Explain how to prepare for a confrontation and to make a "date" to sit down and talk.

- List the four parts of an effective I-statement.
- Explain how you might consider your partner's point of view during a conflict.
- Explain how to make a mutually satisfying agreement and what it means to follow up on it.

KEY TERMS

communication skill
confrontation
confrontation steps
consequences statement
feelings statement

goal statement
imagined interaction
information reception
   apprehension
I-statements

personalized communication
problematic behavior statement
self-talk

Ideally, we would spontaneously assert ourselves in our everyday conversations when appropriate and let people know right away when there is a problem or when we have a feeling to express. If that were the case, there would be little need for a textbook such as this, and people would probably not use negative metaphors to describe conflict. In Chapter 2 we discussed misplaced and displaced conflicts and games, which occur because previously unresolved conflict and face issues cloud the current conflict issue. Other behaviors that can fuel destructive escalation are the "don'ts" in conflict: don't complain, don't be glib or intolerant, don't assume you know what the other is thinking, don't tell the other person how to feel, don't label the other person (as childish, neurotic, incompetent, and so on), don't be sarcastic, and don't talk about the past—stick with the here and now. This last "don't" is particularly important. When conflicts accumulate over a long period of time, a big bag of grievances results. Eight months ago, you lost the Acme account; last week, you offended another client; and so on. What matters most of all is right here, right now. One of the most threatening actions a person can do to another is hit the person with a bagful of complaints saved over a period of time.

Often assuming that they know what others are thinking, people can work through a conflict, arrive at the resolution stage, and then degrade the experience by saying something like, "Well, you won't like my solution anyway" or "You're just doing this because you have to." We all know that it is frustrating to have another person tell us what we think or what we plan to do, particularly if we have not decided yet.

The fact is that we just do not handle all of our conflicts as they arise. Because of this, there are times when we have to make a special effort to confront others, creating a unique situation that requires careful handling. This chapter describes a six-step process for confronting others when an issue or problem could threaten your relationship.

Confrontation as a Conflict Communication Skill

According to Remer and de Mesquita, "confrontation is viewed as an interpersonal invitation to identify self-defeating and harmful defenses… (interpersonal discrepancies, distortions, games, and smoke screens) and to achieve a sense of self-understanding resulting in a functional change in behavior."[1] Or, more simply, we define **confrontation** as a conflict process in which the parties call attention to problems or issues and express their feelings, beliefs, and wants to one another. So, if a neighbor's barking dog upsets you and could lead to significant deterioration in your relationship, then you are engaging in interpersonal confrontation when you consider the problem or issue, arrange to meet with the neighbor, tell him or her about the problem, observe the other's feedback, come to some sort of understanding, and reevaluate the outcome at some future date. Obviously, assertiveness plays a role in interpersonal confrontation. Whereas assertiveness was defined in the previous chapter as the ability to speak up for one's interests, concerns, or rights but in a way that does not violate or interfere with those of others, confrontation is viewed in this chapter as a conflict process event that involves dynamic interaction between the parties involved. Thus, confrontation involves a series of steps of which assertiveness is only one.

Because of the potential benefits, we need to know how to effectively confront others about conflicts that eat away at our relationship. We handle many of our everyday conflicts with little pomp and circumstance. If you are able to address a problem as it happens, a simple, "You know, it bothers me when you do that" may draw the other person's attention to the behavior and result in an agreement to stop or modify it.

However, we don't always confront problems as they arise, and often they become bigger because we have not dealt with them in a timely way. When problems are large, people often ask us: "How do you actually go about confronting someone when there is a big problem? My boyfriend is often late, my girlfriend wears a perfume that bothers me, my parents won't let me drive their car, my roommate leaves her clothes all over the place, my neighbor plays the stereo too loud late at night, so what do I need to say to them?" In this chapter we help you answer this important question.

In recent years, communication scholars have focused on the idea of "communication competence," which is knowledge that relates theories about conflict into thinking about conflict, allowing people to communicate well in conflict situations.[2] In this chapter, we apply this idea to conflict situations by describing communication skills that are useful in conflict situations. A **communication skill** is "the successful performance of a communicative behavior . . . [and] the ability to repeat such a behavior."[3] Because some communication skills are useful in conflict situations, we can also call them conflict communication skills.

Conflict communication skills are not innate; they are learned. We develop them through experience. The only way you learn how to handle conflict situations more competently is to work through the conflicts you encounter, trying to practice your new skills. Due to the complexity of the task, few successfully ride a bicycle the first time. Most fall off. Sometimes they are lucky and stop before hurting themselves. Soon, with a great deal of concentration, riding a bike is manageable, and then it becomes something that is almost second nature. The problem is that most of us are more willing to learn how to ride bicycles than we are to learn conflict communication skills. Communication competence takes knowledge about the way conflict works, knowledge of the skills that are used in conflict situations, and practice. This chapter discusses the skills associated with framing messages in conflict situations—specific message behaviors that have proven effective in various kinds of conflicts. The goal is to connect thinking about conflicts with acting in conflicts so as to choose the most effective behaviors possible. One way to do this is to use a six-step confrontation ritual.

6.1 Think about It

Think of a time when you felt that you handled a conflict well. What did you do that seemed competent to you? How do those behaviors contrast with a time when you felt you handled a conflict poorly?

The Confrontation Ritual: Six Steps to Successful Interpersonal Conflict Resolution

Rituals consist of a series of steps with a beginning and an end. There are six **confrontation steps** to move through as you confront another person. They are:

1. Preparation: Identify your problem/needs/issues.
2. Tell the person "We need to talk."
3. Interpersonal confrontation: Talk to the other person about your problem.
4. Consider your partner's point of view: Listen, empathize, and respond with understanding.
5. Resolve the problem: Make a mutually satisfying agreement.
6. Follow up on the solution: Set a time limit for reevaluation.

Although we would like to avoid giving the impression that all conflicts, large and small, are resolved by following six easy steps, it helps to know what to do and what not to do when confronting someone with whom you disagree. Also, keep in mind that when stopped at one step, we advise backtracking one or more steps to allow for a more thorough discussion before attempting to move forward. That being said, let's begin with the first step, preparation for confrontation.

Preparation: Identify Your Problem/Needs/Issues

"Preparation is the most extensive and, in many ways, the most important stage of the confrontation process."[4] This process is the stop and think portion of the S-TLC model. At this stage, self-talk is important. **Self-talk,** as you can guess, is verbalizing, either out loud or to ourselves, inner messages. People can talk themselves out of confronting others, they can talk themselves into it, or they can talk themselves into handling confrontation in negative, destructive ways. In Chapter 1, we noted that many people prefer to avoid conflicts, but this is not a good idea when a continuation of problems and unmet needs may do damage to a relationship, assuming that the other does not turn abusive if confronted. Asking yourself, "who, what, where, when, how," enables you to examine many more aspects of a situation to determine what the problem is, how it affects you and the relationship, and how you feel about it. You need to determine what you want (your goal). Ask yourself what is likely to happen if you don't receive what you want or what could happen to the relationship if you do. Once you have determined that you need to confront the other person, you need to try to think positively and encourage yourself to go through with it.

A way to prepare is through what is termed an **imagined interaction,** which is a form of intrapersonal communication in which you think about what you might say and another might say in response to you in a particular conversation.[5] Imagined interactions serve as a planning function. People who imagine interactions with others do not actually think about the interaction as they expect it to occur. Rather, they think about the interaction in an "if–then" kind of way: If he says "x," I will tell him "y"; if she says "a," I will say "b." In this sense, imagined interactions are much like cartoon strips. They are both visual and verbal, they happen sequentially, and the imaginer can rewrite the script if desired. Imaginers also have powers similar to comic strip creatures: They can control a conversation to their satisfaction, they can read the minds of characters, and they can travel through time or back up action if they want to replay it.[6]

There is a downside to imagined interactions. When people are asked about thoughts they have concerning conflict situations, only 1 percent report thinking about the other person's view in the conflict situation.[7] People do try to make sense of conflict situations, however, by answering two questions: Who or what is responsible for the conflict? and How serious is the conflict? Unfortunately, thinking about a conflict often makes it worse. People who think a great deal about a particular conflict tend to place the blame on the other person involved and overestimate the seriousness of it.[8] We find it useful to not simply think about the conflict, but to think about what the other person might say about it, what you would like to say, and to do so in a "competent way." That is, you don't want to practice negative or aggressive messages as you are imagining the conflict. Imagining yourself acting competently in the conflict situation is most likely to result in competent behavior. After preparing for the confrontation, now is the time to arrange for it.

Tell the Person "We Need to Talk"

Telling the person "We need to talk" may sound strange to you. To us, this step is like making an appointment or a reservation. We are simply saying that you need to arrange to sit down and talk with the other person.

You do this by asking the other person if you can meet and talk about something. Personally, we think you need to provide a little bit about the subject so that the other person has some idea about the topic of discussion, otherwise she or he may worry about something that has nothing to do with the meeting. You need to pick a time and place that is appropriate, but usually not over twenty-four hours from the time when you ask the other person to meet and talk. Working spouses, for example, usually don't want to engage in a serious discussion when they first arrive home from a hard day's work. Supervisors generally like to have some warning that a problem is afoot, and usually have less busy times when they can meet with employees about problem areas. The point is this: Try to anticipate the other person's schedule so that the time to talk doesn't become one more crisis in a day full of them.

Pick a place that is relatively private and free of distractions. It's usually not a good idea to try to talk with children, roommates, or others around or with the television set on. They are potentially distracting. An example of a way to ask for a meeting is: "I want us to talk about what happened last night. I know that now is not a good time, so can we discuss it tomorrow after your Modern World class? We could go for a ride and talk." Once you have made the arrangement to meet, consider the next stage, the actual confrontation itself.

Interpersonal Confrontation: Talk to the Other about Your Problem

This is the stage where assertiveness plays an important role because you call attention to a problem or issue and give voice to your wants, interests, or needs. We need to observe that we may appear to favor assertiveness in all conflict situations, so we need to point out that confronting others is not always advisable. You need to choose to assert yourself when the situation calls for it, however. Sometimes others cannot handle your assertiveness, and they may be someone who has a lot of influence over you or your future, such as your boss, teacher, parent, or romantic partner. Insecure people may become aggressive or passive-aggressive. One of the authors, Lee, likes to tell his students that the romantic, dating period is a good time to determine whether a future mate can handle one's assertiveness. When a problem occurs in your relationship, you can test your partner's ability to deal with conflict situations by confronting him or her. If that person turns abusive, walks out on you, becomes rigid and uncooperative, and you find yourself having to avoid or accommodate on all important concerns, you need to realize that such a person is likely to continue to mismanage conflict situations. On the other hand, if the person is not turned off by your assertiveness, takes you into consideration, and cooperates with you, then you may have discovered someone who is an effective conflict manager. The moral to the story is to try to surround yourself with people who are open with you and who can handle your assertiveness.

To illustrate an interpersonal confrontation, we use an extended example. The two characters in the conflict are romantically involved: George and Laura. George tends to avoid or accommodate in a conflict situation. He likes to smooth everything over. Laura, on the other hand, is more of a confronter, although she tends to want to please others. They have been dating for over a year and share many activities together. Their roles are fairly well defined. Lately, they have been spending more evenings at Laura's house, where she cooks dinner and they watch a movie on the VCR. Laura wants George to realize that she is not satisfied with the way they are spending time together. On this particular evening, after dinner, she asks him to talk instead of watching TV.

> **LAURA BEGINS BY SAYING:**   You know, we spend a lot of time at my place lately.
>
> **GEORGE:**   Oh?
>
> **LAURA:**   This is the third time this week you've come over for dinner and a movie.
>
> **GEORGE:**   Well, I really like being with you.

From the exchange, Laura has also learned that George dislikes change. Both parties need to not use sarcasm or threats. If they use the right words but speak in a sarcastic tone, their nonverbal expression can change the meaning completely.

> **LAURA:**   I really enjoy our time together, but I think that I am putting more effort into our getting together than you are. I buy the groceries, cook the dinner, and rent the movie.
>
> **GEORGE:**   You're right. I haven't brought anything the last few times I was over here.

Expressions of feelings go beyond what is observed. If Laura had simply started with "I think I am putting more effort into this relationship than you are," George might have been confused about the issue of the conflict.

> **LAURA:**   I guess I believe you're taking advantage of me.
>
> **GEORGE:**   I really don't want to take advantage of you. What do you want to do?
>
> **LAURA:**   I need to believe that I am special to you. I feel special when you take me out now and then.
>
> **GEORGE:**   But you know that I don't have a lot of money after school takes its cut. What are you talking about?

Despite a false start with a vague need, Laura is getting around to something specific. She probably does not mind fixing dinner as long as that is not all that she and George do together. If they pursue the issue, they might find some low-cost entertainment that they can enjoy. They must make their needs as specific as possible. Laura could state her needs as follows.

> **LAURA:**   But that's the point. We're both in school and on limited budgets. To be honest, I think you're taking advantage of me when you don't contribute anything to the evening. I don't think it's fair for me to buy everything.
>
> **GEORGE:**   I don't expect you to buy everything. I haven't this week, and I'm sorry. I really didn't think about it.

To express feelings constructively, we need to make our disclosures relationship-directed and proportional to the importance of the relationship. They need to reflect caring for the other. Like observations, they need to be personalized, well timed, and as specific as possible—"I'm upset" is not as helpful a message as "I'm upset because I am being taken advantage of."

We also need to express our wants in a conflict situation. Wants are specific actions requested of the other person to resolve the conflict. Telling the other person that you are dissatisfied with a situation is not enough. You must specify what you would like as a solution. Sometimes, one person in the conflict has a hard time framing wants so that the conflict can come to some sort of resolution. Frequently, people are better able to say what they don't want rather than what they do want. Moreover, when a person has difficulty framing her or his desires in a conflict, the tendency is for the listener to start suggesting solutions. If what the listener suggests is unacceptable to the speaker, the exchange can quickly degenerate into a "yes, but" scenario, with one person suggesting solutions and the other person vetoing each one as unacceptable.

To express wants constructively, we must focus on desired actions rather than our feelings, state the desired behavior explicitly, tell the other person what behavior we expect, and choose a want that the other person is capable of delivering. We need to also speak of wants instead of "not wants," stating our desires in positive rather than negative terms.

At this point, Laura needs to express some specific wants to see if George is willing to resolve the conflict in a way that might benefit them both.

> **LAURA:** I had an idea for next week. Tuesday is dollar night at the movies, and we could go for ice cream afterwards. Or you could surprise me—I really like it when you plan something. You don't have to do something big—you could make dinner. We could go miniature golfing, or bowling, or take a walk. I want to be with you, but I guess I don't want to have to do the planning and all the work.
>
> **GEORGE:** That seems fair. But does this mean no more dinners?
>
> **LAURA:** No, it just means that I want something besides our dinners. Okay?

A great deal was not addressed by this exchange. If Laura felt ambivalent about her relationship with George, she probably received little that would clarify it, except that he did seem willing to take more responsibility for their dating activities and did not seem to realize that his actions were viewed as taking advantage of her.

However, conflicts are best dealt with in small pieces. If the dating activities issue gets clarified, then Laura is better off waiting until later to deal with the issue of where the relationship is headed.

Laura also has to realize how important her part is in changing George's behavior. If she simply states her problem, and George agrees that it is a problem but then she goes back to the same pattern of fixing dinner for him, nothing has changed.

There are three principles demonstrated in the preceding conflicts. First, we need to request specific changes, both in the action requested and in the amount of change desired. One cannot just say, "I want you to change your attitude." What is an attitude? What does it look like? How much change is involved in producing a better attitude? Second, we need to want something that the other person is capable of doing. We need to ask whether we have correctly assessed the other person's ability to do whatever we ask. And third, we need to make reasonable requests. If Laura had wanted George to take her out to dinner twice a week, the request may be unreasonable considering his student status. Wants need to sound reasonable from the other person's point of view. Test your recognition of legitimate and effectively stated "want statements" in Apply It 6.1. Then move on to the next step, where you don your "effective listening cap" and turn your attention to the other person.

6.1 Apply It

Look at the following statements. Which statements clearly express specific wants? Circle the ones that do.

1. Let's get together for lunch.
2. I want us to spend more time together with the kids.
3. I want you to attend this class with me.
4. I wish we could play different kinds of music around here instead of yours all the time.
5. I want to stop feeling overwhelmed.
6. I don't want your pity!
7. I wish you'd get off my case!
8. I would like us to have one night a week just for ourselves.
9. I want you to exercise more.
10. I want you to put your dirty clothes in the laundry instead of on the floor.

Statements 3, 8, and 10 describe specific wants. Statement 1 is too vague—when should we get together? Statements 2 and 9 suffer from the same problem—how much is "more"? The want is not quantified. Statement 4 can create defensiveness by implying that the other "always" gets his or her way. Statement 5 does not suggest a solution. Statements 6 and 7 are statements we often say, but they do not really communicate. In the heat of a conflict, we can construe almost anything sympathetic as pity, and we can interpret almost any constructive criticism as overly demanding.

Consider Your Partner's Point of View

Researchers claim that empathy is an essential aspect of communication competence. "Empathic processes, or the tendency to consider another's beliefs and feelings, allow people to better judge appropriateness . . ."[9] Put yourself in the other's position and ask yourself how you would feel if requested to make the same change. Would you resent it? Would you think that such a request is reasonable? If you do not think it is, chances are the other doesn't either.

Assertiveness sounds self-oriented, but according to our view it is both self- and other-oriented. Self-orientation is standing up for your rights, interests, and concerns as discussed in the previous chapter. Other-orientation means that you are attentive to, adaptive toward, and interested in others participating in a conversation. We shift to an other orientation when we start asking questions like "What do you think? What do you want? How do you feel?" Other orientation is also seen in expressions of empathy and concern about the other's thoughts, wants, and feelings. It is manifested when listening well, providing relevant feedback to the other, and supporting and accepting what the other is saying as a true representation of who the other person is. Lane argued that both empathy and assertiveness are part of communication competence. She believes that we can assert ourselves empathetically, that is, maintain an orientation toward the other while pursuing one's own goals.[10] As discussed previously, this orientation is associated with collaborating, or exhibiting a high regard for both the relationship and for the issue at hand. Empathy is an orientation toward the other and is associated with the ability to take the other's perspective and assess the other's definition of the situation, for example, by being attentive and sensitive to cues in the situation.[11]

According to researchers, some individuals suffer from **informational reception apprehension,** which "triggers deficiencies in an individual's ability to receive, process and interpret, and/or adjust to information."[12] This concept is particularly relevant because one often fears what others may say in a conflict situation. They may blame us, bring up undesirable information, or remind us of past incidents. However, it is important that you open yourself to the other's point of view. Hopefully, you can see that the need to "hear the person out" outweighs the unpleasantness of what the other may say.

There are four skills for responding. You can rephrase. Another way of responding is simply to ask the other person what he or she means. Or you can provide a possible reason for the statement and see if it is correct. Finally, you can use an unfinished question and let the other person fill in the rest. In responding, you need to try to keep your temper under control. Act; don't react. You do not have to accept what the other person says if it is incorrect.

When we listen to another's feelings, sensitivity is important. Perhaps one of the most disconfirming actions we can take is to tell others that they have no right to feel the way they do. Focus on why others feel the way they do and what role those feelings play in the conflict rather than arguing about the legitimacy of the feeling. If George had challenged Laura, for example, when she said, "I get angry when you take advantage of me," by disparaging the feeling ("You can't really be angry over this"), she would have been less likely to continue the conflict episode to a mutually satisfactory ending. She more likely would have shut down and said, "Never mind. It doesn't matter," leaving both people feeling that the issue is unresolved.

Another disconfirming action is the response many people make when listening to others: "I know exactly how you feel." This is one "I" message that does not belong in conflict language. You make such a statement to someone close to you when you're sharing an excited exchange or discovering mutual interests. But in conflict, such a statement belittles others because it negates the uniqueness of the listener's experience, and, in essence, represents a play for power. The emphasis is on "I" (my wants, needs, desires, importance), not on "you" (your wants, needs, desires, importance). If you tell me how angry you are with me because I was on the phone when you expected an important call and I say, "I know just how you feel. Last week I didn't get an important call, either," whose feelings become the focus of attention? Mine do. How is it different if I respond, "I didn't realize that you were expecting a call" or "You're really angry, aren't you"? This response makes your feelings the focus of my attention and, in doing so, acknowledges my responsibility in the conflict and my willingness to make amends. After determining how the other feels about the issue or problem, you can do the next step, resolve it.

Resolve the Problem: Come to a Mutual Understanding and Reach an Agreement

An important step in resolving or managing conflict is coming to a mutual understanding and reaching an agreement. We sometimes find it helpful to put the agreement in writing for future reference ("You say I agreed to what?"). We need to request specific actions. The reason we request the action is shown in the expression of needs. Through the expression of specific wants, Laura and George may bring their conflict to resolution. Having reached an agreement, conflicting parties can give the outcome a try, and attempt the last step, review and reevaluation. Many interpersonal conflicts are resolved with rather simple agreements ("OK, I agree to do the dishes on days you work"). For more complicated ones, we make a number of suggestions for written agreements in Chapter 14, when we look at formal agreements that result from mediation.

Follow Up on the Solution: Set a Time Limit for Reevaluation

The entire confrontation process does not stop with an understanding, agreement, or resolution; it ends only after successful performance over time, which is determined (and more likely guaranteed) by a review at a later date, because a true resolution or agreement is one that works or is actually carried out. We suggest that you set a date with the other to return to the issue at hand to evaluate the progress made, reward yourself if successful, or to revise your agreement if not. After a few weeks, discuss to what extent the necessary changes have actually occurred.

Doing Conflict Messages

In our discussion of the above six steps to confrontation, we purposely strove for brevity to give you more of an overview of the confrontation process. We could say a lot more about each step. Because our students often want more help on specifically carrying out some of the steps, we are providing more details on exactly how to confront others. We hope these suggestions enable you to effectively resolve more interpersonal conflicts.

General Tips on Being Assertive

When you want to assert yourself, follow these suggestions.

- Stand tall, or if sitting, lean slightly forward, but don't crowd the other person—keep at least a couple of feet between you both.
- Look at the person, but don't stare (suggestion: focus on her or his forehead).
- Look serious, but don't frown, glare, or appear menacing.
- Speak firmly, calmly, slowly, and don't allow yourself to become verbally aggressive.
- Use open gestures, and avoid any threatening gestures such as arm waving, pointing, standing up, or making a fist.
- State your own point of view in terms of your needs, wants, interests, and concerns, but find something on which you both agree.

A confrontation ritual is most productive when those involved make an effort to be nonverbally engaged with each other as well as verbally engaged.

■ Use techniques for communicating emotion and active listening. Don't expect that effective communication always resolves a conflict; however, when an interpersonal relationship is at stake, we hope you try it.

Using I-Statements

Key to the whole confrontation is the ability for the grieving individual to use effectively worded **I-statements.** An interesting research finding indicates that as a conflict progresses, people tend to repeat what they have said previously or use a more restricted vocabulary in describing their problems. In addition, they use fewer words that overtly connect sentence parts with each other, making their communication more abbreviated and harder for the other to understand. The researcher concluded that

> As participants move from simple disagreement to conflict, their levels of anxiety increase and apparently their perspective-taking skills decrease.... [T]he speaker begins to use talk that is habitual and comfortable to the speaker, with less thought to the impact the words have on the other(s). Instead of "How can I say this so s/he understands (How can I persuade him/her)?" the response is to repeat what was just said with even less elaboration.[13]

Clearly the way we state problems in a conflict situation affects the other person's response. If we respond in kind with accusations or retaliation, we contribute to the competitive conflict escalation cycle described in Chapter 9. On the other hand, if we respond assertively with well-worded statements, we interrupt the cycle and switch to a more constructive one.

Assertive behavior reflects both our rights as a communicator (to express our feelings) as well as our responsibilities (to communicate those feelings in a way that reflects ownership of them). Probably the most important skill in conflict is the ability to use I-statements that personalize the conflict by owing up to our feelings rather than to make them the responsibility of the other person. Saying "I feel" and "I think" is far less threatening to the other person than saying "you make me feel" and "most people think." Unfortunately, we sometimes want to put the blame on the other person ("you make me") or to have the weight of a group's opinion ("most people think") rather than simply to express our feelings as our own. The ability to personalize communication comes from a basic assumption:

> If I experience myself as free, I am more likely to personalize my messages. If I am not free, I do not own my feelings. The two skills involved are (a) explicitly signifying that I am the one possessing the feelings, wants, and beliefs when that is what I mean and (b) refraining from holding others responsible for what is going on. Depersonalized communication is characterized by words like "they," "one," "it," and "people"; such words duck responsibility for what is going on and assign it to someone else.[14]

Central to the notion of assertiveness is responsibility—for your actions, for your feelings, for your words, and for the consequences of all of them. We must take responsibility for what we say in a conflict: We must own our feelings and try to state them as clearly as possible. In the previous chapter where we made the point that you have options and can choose assertiveness as appropriate, we explained how people are responsible for what they do and how they feel in conflict situations. This suggests that when we take responsibility for how we feel and act, we start to realize that in every conflict situation we have contributed to it in some way.[15] Interpersonal conflicts occur because we are interdependent (involved). As Folger and Poole say, "the key to resolving almost any conflict lies in gaining a perspective on how we ourselves contributed to it."[16] However, instead of owning what they say and how they feel, people often tend to express themselves in impersonal or generalized language or blame someone else for their feelings and behaviors. As the examples in Table 6.1 show, when you own up to your statements and feelings, you take responsibility for them.

A common type of responsibility avoidance is the use of "you-language." We often resort to blaming the other person for our behavior and feelings, but again we need to strive for the truth, accuracy, and take responsibility. You can see the difference between the statements in Table 6.2.

Assertive behavior is characterized by **personalized communication**—language using "I" statements (i.e., I think, I feel) versus "you" or depersonalized statements (i.e., you always, most people think). You may find that learning assertive behavior and I-statements challenges you. Two "misassumptions" about others lead us to prefer depersonalized communication over communication that owns our feelings. We tend to confuse our perceptions of the other person with their qualities. Suppose, for example, your roommate frequently leaves a wet towel on the bathroom floor and hair in the sink after bathing, which are you more likely to say to the other person (be honest!): "You're such a slob," or "It bothers me when you leave your towel on the floor and hair in the sink." The first statement puts all the

TABLE 6.1 Statements Demonstrating Responsibility

Escaping Responsibility	Taking Responsibility
He made me do it.	I did it.
She upset me . . . she made me angry . . . She riled me up.	I was angry.
The professor is too hard and insensitive.	I think that the professor is . . .
That was a great movie!	I liked the movie a lot.
Everyone knows that isn't true.	I don't believe it.
Adults don't behave like that.	I don't approve of your behavior.
Nobody likes her.	I don't like her.
Anyone with any sense at all would not . . .	I don't understand why you would not . . .
This is the way it has always been.	I don't want to change it.

blame on your roommate. With the second statement, you run the risk that your roommate may not care if it bothers you. And so the first statement seems less risky, but that is an illusion. Say to your roommate, "You're such a slob," and you create defensiveness. Even when joking, negative language creates an unsafe feeling for the other, resulting in defensiveness. Defensiveness, in turn, causes people to tune out your ideas.

Another misassumption that seduces us into depersonalized communication is thinking that others do not change much, and so we can predict their behavior. We can make some educated guesses about the way others react, and the better we know them, the better those guesses become. But making sweeping statements about the other person's behavior to make him or her "pay attention" belittles the other and indicates a lack of trust. We can say only that people respond to situational demands; we can estimate how they might perceive those demands and respond to them.

We need to overcome these misassumptions. Accepting responsibility linguistically is less likely to result in defensiveness from the other person. We need to express inferences

TABLE 6.2 Statements Demonstrating Responsibility

Escaping Responsibility	Taking Responsibility
You are too hard and insensitive.	I think that you are . . .
Your hair, hat, shoes is (are) terrible.	I don't like your hair, hat, etc.
You have a warped sense of humor.	I don't think you're being funny.
You're too sarcastic.	I don't like sarcasm.

or feelings about the situation as specifically as possible and link them to behavior in some way. Only then is the other person likely to understand what is meant. Even if you first state the observation that your roommate left towels on the bathroom floor before declaring, "You're a slob," the statement is not owned by the speaker. Poorly stated inferences often project judgments on the other without being personalized (e.g., "we think you're acting like a child"); are phrased in absolute, certain, or dogmatic language; or lack a context for the description (e.g., "she's so defensive").

Components of I-Statements

To make effective I-statements, we have devised the following form to guide you:

I feel . . . when I . . . because I (think, believe) . . . I'd like (want, wish) . . .

Table 6.3 contains four types of descriptive statements:

1. **Feelings statement:** a description of your feelings (e.g., feeling angry, neglected, offended, surprised, depressed, or unhappy).
2. **Problematic behavior statement:** a description of the offensive, upsetting, incorrect, selfish, problem-producing behavior (e.g., the other saying something insulting, nasty, or sarcastic, leaving clothes all over the room, or forgetting an important date).
3. **Consequences statement:** a description of the consequences the problematic behavior has for you or others (e.g., wastes your time, you have to expend the effort, you could lose friends, or your parents may get angry). The statement contains the word "because."
4. **Goal statement:** a description of what you want specifically (e.g., one may want the other to appear on time in the future or call if delayed). It states what you want, would like, prefer, hope for, expect, or ask (avoid using words like "demand," "require," and

TABLE 6.3   Examples of I-Statements

Feelings Statement	Problem Behaviors	Consequences	Goals
I feel annoyed	when I have to put gas in my car after you use it	because I end up having to take the time to get gas.	I'd like you to get gas after you use my car.
I feel depressed	when I hear about all the fun others are having	because the doctor says I have to remain inactive.	I'd prefer to talk about other topics.
I feel frustrated	when I study but still get a poor grade on a test	because this could hurt my grade in this course.	I would like to go over the chapters with you.

"or else"). A major challenge is identifying what you really want and stating your position in a clear way that specifically describes what it takes to satisfy you.

Notice that every part includes "I," and ideally, none contains "you." While in theory, the best I-statements do not contain "you," you may find it difficult to avoid saying "you" when describing the problem. Test your recognition of specific need/feeling statements in the following application.

6.2 Apply It

Look at the following statements. Which are correctly stated needs or feeling statements? Circle the correct statements.

1. I feel disappointed that you are backing out of this show after you agreed to help me with it.
2. You really irritate me when you don't show up for a date with me.
3. I need assurance I am loved in a language I understand.
4. I need for you to tell me where a class is going so that I can get excited about it.
5. I feel like a single parent around here.
6. You don't seem to contribute anything to our group project.
7. I feel frustrated when it seems that I have sole responsibility for planning our dates.
8. I feel like I am going crazy.
9. I feel insecure when we don't have at least the equivalent of a month's salary in the bank.
10. I am not the only person who's having trouble in your class.

Statements 1, 3, 4, 7, and 9 are correctly stated because they link the feeling to a current or desired behavior. Statement 2 is incorrect because the focus is on the other person creating the feeling rather than on the speaker owning the feeling. Statement 5 states something vague—what is the actual feeling and what would eliminate the feeling? Statement 6 denies responsibility for the feeling—blaming the other. Statement 8 is probably a legitimate feeling but does not tell the other why the feeling is there. Statement 10 uses "mob appeal" (a type of logical fallacy) to validate the feeling rather than personally owning it.

We need to point out that you can make longer I-statements than the above examples. You may choose to talk for a while about how you feel. Then discuss what it was that made you feel this way and why. Because confrontation is a challenge for many, it may take a while before you eventually say what you want. This form is presented only to ensure that you address all four components when presenting your side of the conflict.

Finally, I-statements won't work unless they are accompanied by a calm, nonthreatening tone of voice and facial expression. If one is to avoid being perceived as judgmental, one must sound nonjudgmental in both what is said and how one says it. Otherwise, even the best worded I-statements won't work because they are accompanied by upset and anger, which contradict the words.

6.3   Apply It

Fill in the blanks with words that complete the sentence using the formula:

I feel . . . when . . . because . . . I want . . .

- I feel _____ when I have to wait and wait because I hate waiting around and wasting time. I want to leave at the time we agreed on.
- I feel frustrated when _____ because I don't know what is expected of me. I would like some help on how to improve my grades.
- I feel angry at myself when we stay out too late and drink too much because _____. I want to get more sleep and cut down on my drinking.
- I feel frustrated when I am the only one who cleans up this place because it's not fair to me. I want _____.

Create your own I-statements:

- I feel afraid when _____ because _____. I want _____.
- I feel _____ when _____ because _____. I want _____.

Advantages of Using I-Statements

By asserting yourself in this way, you provide much needed information, demonstrate honesty, and reduce defensiveness in others.

- You provide necessary information because the other person doesn't need to "read your mind" to determine what you are thinking, feeling, and wanting.
- You reveal your honesty by telling others what is on your mind, what you prefer, or what is upsetting you.
- You reduce defensiveness in others because you are not assigning blame or blurting out accusations.

6.2   Think about It

When does assertiveness become aggressiveness? What guidelines do you need to develop for yourself in order to create assertive rather than aggressive statements?

Challenges Associated with I-Statements

"I get too mad to become nice."   Instead of using I-language, it is tempting to hit the other person where it hurts. This option seems particularly tempting when the other person has already hurt us. The nature of relationships, regardless of their setting, provides information that can embarrass or hurt the other person. When we are hurt, we are tempted to pull out this "albatross" and drape it around the other's neck. Aggressive communication laden with blame, anger, and accusations may seem warranted in a particular conflict situation, but such communication behavior only makes matters worse because the communication process has an immutable dimension to it: You cannot take back what you said. If you value your interpersonal relationship, you owe it to yourself and the other person to resolve the problem in a constructive and positive way. Owning your feelings, using the words "I think," "I feel," and "I want," minimizes the possibility of regret over what is said. I-statements make one more assertive without producing ill feelings and provoking retaliatory behavior.

Moreover, recall the S-TLC system presented in Chapter 3. You may need to stop and wait a few minutes, hours, or days until after you have "cooled down." Then, you may find it possible to express yourself using I-statements rather than abusive language.

"It doesn't sound right or normal for me to talk that way."   Many people have bad habits; they avoid, simply give in, or respond to conflict in aggressive ways. Meanwhile, what one learns, one can unlearn. The problem is that over time, one's habits feel "normal," and any new behaviors seem "artificial" at first and require effort to learn as new habits. As you see the effect of using I-statements on others, you may prefer to use them more often. You need to give them a try and see how they improve your interpersonal relationships.

Remember that as a last resort, you can walk away from a conflict. If you find yourself overwhelmed by the situation, unable to remain in control of your emotions, and unwilling to listen to the other, tell the other person you need to leave and talk later about the situation. Walking away is not wrong if the alternative is losing control of yourself and ruining any chance to bring the conflict to resolution. Also, consider the possibility of bringing in a third party to help.

Manage It

Teachers of conflict management are often asked by their students, What should I say? What should I do? They want specific suggestions as to how best express themselves in a conflict situation. To meet this need we have devised the following six confrontation steps to effectively manage interpersonal conflicts.

1. Preparation: Identify your problem/needs/issues.
2. Tell the person "We need to talk."
3. Interpersonal confrontation: Talk to the other person about your problem.
4. Consider your partner's point of view: Listen, empathize, and respond with understanding.
5. Resolve the problem: Make a mutually satisfying agreement.
6. Follow up on the solution: Set a time limit for reevaluation.

Although six confrontation steps may seem like a long list to remember, each and every step is an essential phase of the confrontation process. People often forget the last one, but we need to ensure that the process is complete and working as we intended.

People are responsible for what they do and how they feel in conflict situations; we should take responsibility for how we feel and act during a conflict. However, instead of owning what they say and how they feel, people often tend to express themselves in impersonal or generalized language. Or they often avoid responsibility for their feelings or their contribution to the conflict by using "you-language."

To help students create assertive messages for expressing their feelings, wants, and needs during the third step of the confrontation process, we encourage them to use personalized communication—language using I-statements (i.e., I think, I feel) versus "you" or depersonalized statements (i.e., "you always," "most people think"). These I-statements consist of four parts: "I feel (feeling statement) when I (problematic behavior statement) because I (consequences statement). I'd like (goals statement)."

In cases in which we value our interpersonal relationships, we owe it to ourselves and others to resolve the problem in a constructive and positive way. I-statements allow a person to assert him- or herself without producing ill feelings in others or encouraging retaliatory behavior. Any new behavior seems artificial at first and requires effort to learn and develop as a habit. While learning to speak assertively is important, we must not forget to consider our partner's point of view during a conflict. In step four, we should not forget the role of active listening, other-orientation, rephrasing, and sensitivity.

Just as in the last chapter on styles and strategies, collaboration is key. Only by working together can we develop a mutually satisfying solution. To ensure that an agreement is mutually agreeable, we need to follow up and re-examine the effectiveness of the agreement at a later date. Sometimes people think they are in agreement only to find out some weeks later that the understanding is not mutual.

We would like to say that confrontation always produces mutually satisfying results, but this is not true. Although confrontation works more often than not and sometimes with surprising results, there are times when the other person is uncooperative, the issue is too complex, and we don't have enough time or energy to do it right. As teachers, we authors encounter many pessimistic students who are reluctant to try the six steps; however, many report excellent results and a change of heart after applying them while confronting someone about a significant issue.

6.1 Work with It

Read the following case study and answer the questions that follow it.

There is a lot of uncertainty in my relationship with Ashley. First of all, we live in different states and the majority of our interaction is online or on the telephone. Because I am not there, I don't know what she is doing or who with. We also do not share many fun events or memorable moments together. I really miss her but I don't know how much she misses me. I find it difficult not getting interested in other people when I see her so seldom. We only get together on holidays when she comes home to visit her parents and see me or if I can scrape enough money together for a trip to see her. I don't know how to improve our situation.

1. How might the narrator prepare for a confrontation with Ashley?
2. How might he make a "date" to sit down and talk with her?
3. How might he word a four-part I-statement to tell her?
4. How might he consider her view of the situation?
5. How might the two resolve the problem?
6. How might they follow up on it?

6.2 Work with It

This exercise asks you to write about your experience after confronting someone in a conflict situation. Follow these steps.

First, Prepare and Plan for the Interpersonal Confrontation

- Read and understand the six steps to successful confrontation.
- Identify someone who is close to you and willing and able to work on this assignment with you as your confrontation partner. Choose someone who is a good friend, roommate, romantic partner, or relative of the same or opposite sex.
- Think about a problem you are having with this person. There is something bothering all of us at any given point in time. At this point we encourage you to choose a problem or conflict that does not involve scarce resources. It does not matter whether it occurred recently (something she or he said this morning) or happened some time ago, but you never forgot it. It does not matter whether the incident is a minor or a major problem, but you may have to decide whether you need to discuss this particular problem with this person. The other person does not have to know that you are doing this for an assignment unless you want to tell her or him.
- Go through the appropriate procedures to arrange to "sit down and discuss the problem" with this person. Plan ahead and follow the six steps presented in the chapter.
- Note that you are the one (not the partner) who is expected to use the constructive confrontation skills. The other person needs to reciprocate, but one never knows for sure. You can still do this assignment regardless of how cooperative the other person turns out to be.

Second, Discuss the Problem with the Person

- Incorporate the S-TLC system (Chapter 3).
- Be self-assertive (Chapters 3 and 4). State your thoughts and feelings openly, directly, and honestly; express positive feelings for the other person and for your relationship even during the conflict.
- Sit down and talk (Chapter 6). Engage in conflict collaboratively, remain calm, and lower your voice. Use I-statements (rather than "you-statements"), use the confrontation formula using I-language (When I . . . I feel, etc.), and use friendly questions.
- Paying attention to your conflict communication behavior, attempt to resolve the problem as best you can, but do not think that you have to resolve it in this one discussion. You can still write about the confrontation even if it is unsuccessful.
- Use active listening techniques; try to understand the other's point of view; try to feel what the other person is feeling; try to see the situation as the other does; accept, confirm, and validate the other person's feelings as legitimate and appropriate for her or him (confirmation); listen to what the other person is trying to say; mirror the other's expressed feelings; and respond with understanding.
- Describe problematic behaviors to the other person rather than evaluating or judging the other person; state your position tentatively, rather than "as the final word"; indicate a willingness to change your position if appropriate; use de-escalators to avoid escalating the discussion; try not to blame yourself or the other for the conflict; and treat the other as an equal.

(continued)

6.2   Continued

- Try to reach a collaborative solution using the steps to create one.
- Find out what you agree and disagree on to narrow down the conflict, emphasize areas of agreement before approaching topics where there is disagreement, and try to reach a compromise or, better still, a solution you are both satisfied with.
- Afterwards, discuss with the person the value of "sitting down to discuss the problem" in this manner. You may find that the other person is pleased by the way you dealt with this conflict.

Third, Write an Essay Summarizing Your Experience

- You do not need to supply much information about the problem itself. Do remember to define "confrontation." Use just a couple of sentences or at most a paragraph describing the background, history, problem, and so on.
- Write mostly on the following: Describe the confrontation from beginning to end, subdividing into six sections corresponding to the six steps (label each section with the name of the step), including your making arrangements, planning, and actual wording as you attempted to communicate in a way that avoided arousing defensiveness. (Yes, we really want you to describe in your own words what you actually said to the other.)
- We ask you to recall and write the actual wording used in steps two and three of the six-step process and any friendly questions you asked. Specify in detail the agreement and give details on how you two intend to follow up on the agreement.

6.1   Remember It

Write an essay as though you were writing a letter to a friend. Explain the six steps in the confrontation process, describe the components of an I-statement, and discuss why you believe these steps and statements are important in managing your conflicts.

NOTES

1. Rory Remer and Paul de Mesquita, "Teaching and Learning the Skills of Interpersonal Confrontation," in Dudley D. Cahn (Ed.), *Intimates in Conflict: A Communication Perspective* (Hillsdale, NJ: Lawrence Erlbaum Associates, 1990), p. 225.
2. Daniel J. Canary, William R. Cupach, and Richard T. Serpe, "A Competence-Based Approach to Examining Interpersonal Conflict: Test of a Longitudinal Model," *Communication Research* 28 (2001), 79–104.
3. Brian H. Spitzberg and Michael L. Hecht, "A Component Model of Relational Competence," *Human Communication Research* 10 (1984), 577.
4. Remer and de Mesquita, p. 229.
5. James M. Honeycutt, Kenneth S. Zagacki, and Renee Edwards, "Imagined Interaction and Interpersonal Communication," *Communication Reports* 3 (1990), 1–8.
6. Renee Edwards, James M. Honeycutt, and Kenneth S. Zagacki, "Imagined Interaction as an Element

of Social Cognition," *Western Journal of Speech Communication* 52 (1988), 23–45.

7. Denise H. Cloven, "Relational Effects of Interpersonal Conflict: The Role of Cognition, Satisfaction, and Anticipated Communication," Master's thesis, Northwestern University, Evanston, IL, 1990.

8. Denise H. Cloven and Michael E. Roloff, "Sense-Making Activities and Interpersonal Conflict: Communication Cures for the Mulling Blues," *Western Journal of Speech Communication* 55 (1991), 134–158.

9. Amy S. Ebesu Hubbard, "Conflict between Relationally Uncertain Romantic Partners: The Influence of Relational Responsiveness and Empathy," *Communication Monographs* 68 (2001), p. 402.

10. Shelley D. Lane, "Empathy and Assertive Communication," paper presented at the Western Speech Communication Association Convention, San Jose, CA, February 1981, p. 11.

11. Eugene A. Weinstein, "The Development of Interpersonal Competence," in D. A. Goslin (Ed.), *Handbook of Socialization and Theory and Research* (Chicago: Rand McNally, 1969), pp. 753–775; see also James B. Stiff, James Price Dillard, Lilnabeth Somera, Hyun Kim, and Carra Sleight, "Empathy, Communication, and Prosocial Behavior," *Communication Monographs* 55 (1988), 199–213.

12. Paul Schrodt and Lawrence R. Wheeless, "Aggressive Communication and Informational Reception Apprehension: The Influence of Listening Anxiety and Intellectual Inflexibility on Trait Argumentativeness and Verbal Aggressiveness," *Communication Quarterly* 49 (2001), p. 57.

13. Mae Arnold Bell, "A Research Note: The Relationship of Conflict and Linguistic Diversity in Small Groups," *Central States Speech Journal* 34 (1983), 128–133.

14. Herbert J. Hess and Charles O. Tucker, *Talking about Relationships,* 2nd Ed. (Prospect Heights, IL: Waveland Press, 1980), pp. 13–14.

15. Walter Isard and Christine Smith, *Conflict Analysis and Practical Conflict Management* (Cambridge, MA: Ballinger Publishing, 1982).

16. Joseph P. Folger and Marshall Scott Poole, *Working through Conflict,* 2nd Ed. (Glenview, IL: Scott Foresman, 1993), p. 56.

7 Cooperative Negotiation in Win–Lose Conflicts

OBJECTIVES

At the end of this chapter, you should be able to:

- Explain the difference between a tangible and an intangible conflict issue.

- Explain the assumption behind negotiation in which people try to minimize their losses and maximize their gains.

- Distinguish between competitive and cooperative negotiation and explain when each approach is most appropriate.

- Describe four ways to generate more options.

- Explain how one converts a potentially competitive negotiation into a cooperative one.

- Explain the negotiation tools of BATNA and fractionation.

KEY TERMS

aspiration point
bargaining range
BATNA
brainstorming
bridging
compensation
competitive negotiation
concession

control the process
cooperative negotiation
cost cutting
fractionation
interests
language of cooperation
logrolling
minimax principle

negotiation
objective criteria
positions
principled negotiation
resistance point
scarce resources
threats
thromise

In Chapter 2, we distinguished between two types of conflicts based on intangible and tangible resources. We said that intangible resources are emotional, mental, and psychological assets. Sometimes one doesn't know that the other would like more attention, cooperation, or a change in a relationship, so the other has to make his or her wants, needs, or interests known. In other cases, one may misunderstand what another wants or needs, so the other again must straighten matters out by explaining and clarifying her or his wants, needs, or interests. Conflicts involving resources that are not scarce are often resolved through interpersonal communication (as discussed in Chapters 3–6).

We also introduced you to conflicts based on tangible resources, which are hard, physical, or observable. We pointed out that, when tangible resources appear initially as scarce or in fact are scarce, conflicts involving them take more than basic interpersonal communication skills to resolve; they require more advanced problem-solving techniques for generating more mutually satisfying outcomes. In this chapter, you learn how to resolve conflicts even when they are over scarce tangible resources or at least those that initially appear as scarce. One way to do so is through negotiation and bargaining.

Negotiation is defined as "a particular type of conflict management—one characterized by an exchange of proposals and counter proposals as a means of reaching a satisfactory settlement."[1] By agreeing to negotiate, people are agreeing (1) to engage in a conflict by confronting others rather than avoiding it and (2) to try to find an outcome that is mutually acceptable to all those involved in the conflict by exploring various options in the conflict.[2] There are elements of negotiation that cut across cultural differences.[3] This chapter is not intended as a full-blown discussion of all aspects of negotiation, but rather focuses on tools used by negotiators for generating possible solutions.

The terms "bargaining" and "negotiation" are often used in place of each other. Unions might bargain for their new contract; two people contemplating marriage might negotiate a prenuptial agreement. Authors in this area of research claim that bargaining and negotiation are essentially interchangeable.[4] Both terms describe people in a conflict situation agreeing to common rules to manage their conflicts.[5]

In this chapter, we focus more on resolving tangible conflict issues involving **scarce resources,** in which there are not enough resources to go around. The resolution of these issues requires both interpersonal communication and negotiation techniques.[6] We also distinguish between competitive and cooperative negotiation in the hope that you use them when most appropriate. We conclude with specific suggestions on how to engage in cooperative bargaining, where we combine interpersonal communication skills with negotiation techniques. After reading this chapter you can engage in effective negotiation for resolving conflicts over tangible issues.

Negotiation Basics

One assumption behind negotiation is that people try to minimize their losses and maximize their gains—the **minimax principle.** This strategy is applied when both parties start bargaining with an **aspiration point** (their preferred option, which would maximize their gains) in mind. Both parties also have a **resistance point** (an identifiable amount that they are willing to concede to the other person with minimum loss). Between both parties exists a **bargaining range** of resistance points and aspiration levels. One implication of this idea is that one should expect to make some concessions. This is not the same idea as a compromise, where you settle for less than what you truly want to achieve an agreement. Rather, you may need to set a higher goal than you think possible, knowing that you may need to settle for less in order to obtain what you truly want. You must understand this basic principle if you are to engage in successful negotiation.

7.1 Apply It

Read the following statements. Circle the number of those statements that reflect situations involving scarce resources. Check your answers on page 283.

1. There is not enough time to divide between friends, partner, and children.
2. Your roommate didn't return a book or rental video as promised or returned the item late, incurring a fine.
3. Both sets of parents want their married children to spend the holidays with them.
4. Borrowed items weren't returned to you as promised.
5. One partner is private and closed and won't open up to the other partner.
6. Your parent received a job transfer, which necessitates moving, leaving friends, changing schools, and so on.
7. Two people are interested in the same person as a romantic partner.
8. One roommate shows disrespect and is inconsiderate to the other and her or his possessions, borrows without asking, and returns the items in an unsatisfactory condition.
9. Two domestic partners have conflict over failing to share domestic tasks and taking turns with chores.
10. One partner always blames the other for all problems experienced. One always criticizes the other for personal inadequacies.
11. One person needs assistance, help, or cooperation but isn't getting it where it could be provided.
12. Partners share only one television set, but they want to watch different channels at the same time.
13. Two roommates share one shower, kitchen, study room, or living room, but both want to use one or the other at the same time.
14. Partner does not appreciate other's efforts and time spent on both their behalf.
15. Two siblings share one car, and they both want to use it at the same time.

Competitive Negotiation

The two different approaches to negotiation are competitive versus cooperative. While in all negotiation, concessions made by one side benefit the other, the **competitive negotiation** pattern is an exchange in which one must start high, concede slowly, exaggerate the value of one's concessions, conceal information, argue forcefully, and outwait the other.[7] The competitive negotiator learns as much as possible about the other person's position without giving away her or his own position. Such negotiators believe that they must not show weakness in their positions or offer concessions too soon.[8]

If you decide to adopt this style of bargaining, you should base your decision on the demands of the situation. It is an appropriate style of bargaining when the parties have earned your distrust. The disadvantages of competitive bargaining are found in the climate it fosters between those in the bargaining situation. Competitive bargaining tends to foster (more) distrust, dissatisfaction, and resentment—it is "me versus you" rather than "both of us." Competitive bargaining can lead to an impasse and prevent agreement. The emphasis on secrecy makes it difficult to predict the responses of the other person. Still, because we sometimes are in situations that necessitate competitive bargaining, we should not simply reject it as a possibility, but choose it purposefully and sparingly as needed.

Cooperative Negotiation

In the fields of interpersonal and organizational communication, interest has shifted from competitive bargaining situations to integrative ones that encompass both formal and informal negotiation. **Cooperative negotiation** is an integrative form that combines formal bargaining techniques with many skills taught in basic interpersonal communication courses such as effective listening, assertiveness, supportive communication, and collaboration. Cooperative negotiation works best when the parties trust each other and the situation is one where mutually satisfactory outcomes are possible, even though the parties may not know that at the outset. One implication is that negotiators should assume that win–win solutions are always possible and work to achieve them because they often do in fact discover mutually satisfying outcomes eventually.

Given the various ways in which bargaining is studied, what findings can help us understand how bargainers reach mutual agreement through integrative behaviors in negotiation situations? Pruitt argues that integrative solutions occur when people are rigid in the goals they are pursuing but flexible in means they adopt for those goals. In cooperative negotiation, the parties' goals are mutual gain, but they are open to a number of ways to achieve a win–win solution. In addition, Pruitt claims that information exchange leads to integrative agreements only when bargainers believe that the other is truly concerned with both their own needs and the other person's needs.[9] Research supports Pruitt's claims.[10]

7.1 Think about It

In which common situations would you most likely resort to competitive negotiation? In which for cooperative negotiation?

Some Research on Tactics and Strategies in Negotiation

Concessions

Findings generated through game theory and study of simulated interactions by researchers in social psychology support collaboration over competition in negotiation. First, they suggest that, in general, bargainers who make concessions are more likely to elicit cooperative behavior from the other than are those who make demands or who make no concessions at all.[11] A person makes a **concession** when he or she grants something highly valued to the other person without asking anything in return, or when he or she drops a demand on the other. However, the person making concessions runs a risk of exploitation, which can occur when we trust people we shouldn't. For example, as Bostrum points out, "A bargainer who makes frequent concessions will probably be viewed as willing to settle for less than one who makes concessions only occasionally."[12] According to one study, people who made concessions quickly were exploited by other players who retaliated with a competitive strategy.[13] Because the greatest cooperation was found when a bargainer was slow to compete and slow to cooperate in reciprocating the other's behavior, we could say that trust takes time to build.

Second, other research has confirmed the utility of starting tough and becoming more cooperative later. However, recent research in the field of communication conducted by Tutzauer and Roloff indicates that one should use toughness in moderation: If combined with pressure tactics, it can create a perception of competition between bargainers and reduce the likelihood of mutually satisfying agreements.[14]

An implication of these findings is that bargainers should resist the temptation to make their final offer too soon. Neither person in the bargaining situation is likely to have full information on what the other's most desired position is. It takes some time to figure out the bargaining range involved.

Third, according to Pruitt and Kimmel, when people think in terms of long-term rather than short-term results, they are likely to cooperate more. This is especially true if those involved understand that they depend on one another, that exploiting one another is not likely to achieve a good outcome, and that cooperating with the other probably generates more cooperation.[15]

Threats

A competent negotiator is aware of his or her behavior and reputation as a negotiator. How people behave in a bargaining situation affects the way they are viewed by the others. Who the people are and what roles they play also affect outcomes. Throughout all the research on bargaining is the assumption that bargaining is a communicative behavior, and, as such, the actual messages exchanged by people in a bargaining situation are of interest. Perhaps researchers have paid the greatest attention to the role of threats and promises in the bargaining situation.

A person who consistently carries through on **threats,** or statements that link the other person's noncompliance with negative outcomes, gains greater cooperation than a person who does not follow through, and consistency in the fulfillment of promises lends greater credibility to both threats and promises. The consistency with which a person acts in regard to threats or promises made has a great effect on outcomes of the bargaining situation. If a person makes threats but fails to carry them out when compliance is not obtained, or makes promises that remain unfulfilled, then the person is unlikely to affect the outcome of the bargaining situation through the use of them.[16] However, consistency in carrying out one's threats does not create greater believability for one's promises. Obviously, one must also have the credibility to carry out a threat or fulfill a promise; that is, the fulfillment of the threat or the promise must not exceed one's power. In addition, the bargainer may use a **thromise**—a message that sounds like a promise (i.e., if you do x you will receive y) but operates like a threat because it is the noncompliance that may hurt the recipient, not simply failing to receive a benefit.[17] An example of a thromise is to say that you offer to continue providing something to the other if she or he does something in return. On the one hand, you are making a promise or commitment to some action, but on the other hand, you are threatening to stop something of use or interest to the other. Can you list a number of thromises you have made to others over the past several weeks or months?

Another aspect of the bargaining process concerns the explicitness with which promises, threats, and commitments are made—in other words, do not make early, firm commitments from which you cannot retreat without losing face.[18] This is challenging when constituents are involved. Research has demonstrated that bargainers who are representing others besides themselves, and are thus accountable to those others, are less likely to engage in compromise, concession, or other commitments than bargainers who are not accountable to their constituency.[19] If one makes a commitment and then finds it unsupported by his or her constituents, one can lose face in negotiating. Thus, tentativeness, such as the use of qualifiers (e.g., "that could work"), allows for more give and take in the situation until a final solution is reached. When one party firmly commits to a position, the other party has no choice but to concede or escalate the conflict. So, bargainers should make implicit, rather than explicit, commitments until the final details of the negotiation are settled. You should merely imply your promises and threats whenever possible to allow yourself to back away from the promise or threat should it become untenable.

Whether explicit or implicit, threats are a last-resort measure. A threat clearly defines one's resistance point, which you recall is the point at which you concede no further. Use a threat only when you are amply prepared to carry it through and have clearly thought out the consequences. In particular, if you are negotiating with your employer, threatening to quit is one of the worst bargaining options because it gives the employer an impression of having no choice in dealing with you.

Principled Negotiation

Fisher and Ury, who headed the Harvard Negotiation Project, developed a method they called **principled negotiation,** which consists of separating the people from the problem, focusing on interests rather than positions, generating a variety of possibilities before deciding what to do, and insisting on the use of an objective standard upon which to base the results.[20]

Separate People from the Problem

One of the most important actions we can take in a conflict is to keep our perceptions of the other person separated from our perceptions of the problem or issue. It is easy in a conflict to confuse how we feel about the issue with how we feel about the person involved with it. Because this can work in both positive or negative ways, our like or dislike of a person can cloud our decision-making processes.

An example of focusing on the problem rather than those involved is found in this narrative.

> As a driver of a school bus, I occasionally have conflicts with students, and sometimes these spill over to conflicts with their parents. That is usually when the principal, Bob, gets involved. Recently, parents complained that they felt I had falsely accused their son, Rick, of misbehaving on the bus. They saw the "referral for misbehaving" as an attack on their child by me. When the meeting occurred in the principal's office, they immediately began by attacking me and questioning my judgment as though I had something personal against their son. Bob really did a good job of separating their son and me (as people) from the problem, which was really Rick's behavior.

7.2 Think about It

Can you think of examples where people either focused on the other person or tried to deal with the problem or issue instead? Discuss the outcomes.

Focus on Interests Rather Than Positions

What is the difference between interests and positions? Think of **positions** as the final part of an I-statement (the goal part of the statement—what you want). Think of **interests** as needs that are satisfied by different positions. When a conflict is first identified and people begin to make their opinions about the matter known, it is easier to identify the various positions people have taken than it is to identify the interests each party has in resolving the conflict. For example, Jamie and Ray are shopping for a new car. Ray wants a particular car for $10,000. If Jamie wants the same car that Ray wants, both have the same position: They both want that car. Interests are needs such as transportation, housing, food, and so on, that are satisfied by both positions. For example, Ray really wants sharp transportation, but he can only pay $10,000 for it. If the car sales representative can show him such a car for $10,000, and he decides to buy it, then they can choose to satisfy the interests of both. Ray can have what he wants, and Jamie gets a car that satisfies her interest or need. People may change their positions, if you show them how to meet their interests or needs. Thus, a good way to resolve conflict (when over scarce resources) is to shift from positions (where we really want the same object) to interests (where different positions/wants may satisfy our needs).

Generate More Options

You need to identify both positions and interests in conflicts over scarce resources. Moving from positions (wants) to interests (needs) automatically expands your options for resolving a conflict in a more mutually satisfying manner.

7.2 # Apply It

For each of the following situations, identify and write out each person's position and interest that caused them to take that position.

1. Jennifer wants to use the computer so that she can research her paper. Cheryl wants to surf the Internet.
   - Jennifer's position: She wants to use the computer.
   - Cheryl's position:
   - Jennifer's interest: She needs to do research for a paper.
   - Cheryl's interest:

2. Dan wants the car to buy groceries. Scott wants it to "go somewhere."
   - Dan's position:
   - Scott's position:
   - Dan's interest:
   - Scott's interest:

3. Maria wants to cook dinner to try out a new recipe. Larry wants to go out to eat because he is hungry.
   - Maria's position:
   - Larry's position:
   - Maria's interest:
   - Larry's interest:

4. Rob wants to have his friends visit homecoming weekend (and stay in their small apartment). Diane, his roommate, wants to have her friends the same weekend.
   - Rob's position:
   - Diane's position:
   - Rob's interest:
   - Diane's interest:

Brainstorming.   You are probably aware that the first solution that occurs to you is not necessarily the best one. But how do you move beyond your first solution? **Brainstorming** is a process that requires you to list all possible solutions, irrespective of their initial feasibility. Not all the options are workable, but when you have examined all the possible solutions you can think of, it is easier to focus on one. An account of the results of successful brainstorming is related by this person.

At the car dealership I work for, the service manager knows many of his customers well, having served them for many years, but he still finds himself in conflict with occasional unhappy customers. He normally comes up with several remedies and presents them for the customer to decide what would make them the happiest or the most satisfied with the situation. The customers generally believe that he is concerned about them and about

Brainstorming is a way of generating more options in negotiation situations.

solving the problem. I've seldom witnessed times when he was unable to solve the conflict in a positive way.

There are other ways to generate more solutions in a situation involving conflict over scarce resources. Pruitt offers four techniques for increasing such options.

Cost cutting.   In **cost cutting,** one person reduces the price of an item so that the other is more easily able to accept and live with the solution. In the following negotiation examples you can see how one person reduces the price or cost to the other.

One of my co-workers Maria is planning a vacation with her husband and children, but the price of airline tickets is too much for all four of them to go right away (her kids are 17 and 18). Maria and her husband decided to leave on Friday night and have her kids fly out on Sunday morning. How this works I do not know—but I do know that they are saving money in the long run. It also works out for Maria and her husband because it gives them some alone time together. They still get a family vacation, but at a cheaper cost!

When a man came to buy a camper from my dad, he knocked off quite a bit more money, but not too much. That did the trick and the man bought it.

For Christmas one year, I received a few rings. Since my fingers are so small, I could tell right away that they were in need of sizing. When I went to the jeweler, I asked how much it was going to cost to have all five sized. He gave me an astronomical price. I mean they keep the excess gold anyway. But besides that, I asked if we could work out a deal. I mean I had quite a few rings, so he cut the price down about $20.00 or so. If he hadn't, I would have gone someplace else. I really didn't have time to argue. It's either you want my business or you don't. So in the end it worked out for both of us. I got my rings done, and he made his money. Plus, when I got home, I realized that one of the rings wasn't sized right, so when I brought it back, he fixed it for nothing.

My boyfriend is Scott. His family was planning a two-week vacation to St. Martin and wanted us both to go with them. I was busy with school and he was overloaded with work. We both really needed to take a vacation, but for financial reasons, Scott couldn't afford to take two weeks' vacation from work. After some discussion, we came up with the idea that I would leave a week early with his family and he would join us the second week. This worked great because I not only got the time to get away, which I really needed, but we also had a wonderful time together the second week. He really enjoyed the much-needed vacation, and he didn't have to take the full two weeks from work.

Compensation. **Compensation** occurs when Party A provides something of value (often monetary) to Party B to make up for losses caused by A's behavior or that result from A's demands. In the following negotiation example, one person argues for compensation—damages and harm occurred.

My conflict was with Fed Ex. I sent out four packages of breakable items for a client. We were under an extreme deadline. I packed the boxes carefully and marked, "GLASS!! HANDLE WITH CARE!!" all over them. The person filling out the air bill forgot to declare a value for the packages. Needless to say, they arrived broken. I was "compensated" for the damages. They offered me $100 per damaged box. Three boxes were damaged, so in turn, I received $300 to replace the damaged items and free shipping to resend the items. It took a lot of paperwork and fighting to get them to pay. Because no value was declared, they did not want to pay, but luckily it worked out. Considering the lack of options we had, it worked out for the better.

Logrolling. **Logrolling** is a process in which each side grants to the other those issues that the other gives top priority. Both parties make concessions, but not on those issues to which they give top priority. Conflicting parties have to want several items (not just one), but only insist on the top priority because of its importance and not the others because they are less important. In the following negotiation examples, both of the parties use logrolling.

I took a negotiation class, where we negotiated a labor contract with the management. (I was on the side of the union.) During our simulation, we discussed four different grievances: wages, sick leave, vacation, and holidays. Our side had more priority put forth for wages, while the management had a good argument for limiting vacations. What the two sides decided to do, was to allow our side to have our wage increase, while we took a cut back in vacation. So, wages (our top priority) was given to us, while we were okay with us taking shorter vacations.

I just wanted to watch a movie (top priority) while crocheting the other day and my housemate really wanted to play cards (top priority) and also liked to listen to music. You cannot listen to music (not his top priority) and watch a movie at the same time. Also, you cannot crochet (not my top priority) and play cards at the same time. Of course we argued about it first with neither of us giving in. We finally realized we were wasting time and getting nowhere so I agreed to play cards with him if we first watched the movie.

I wanted to help with finishing an installation job on a van, but my fellow worker Trish wanted to go to lunch before I did that same day. We discussed the matter and decided that Trish could help me first with the van and then she could go to lunch early while I would cover for her. Each of us had our main concern dealt with. We gave into the other on something that was low priority for ourselves but high for the other.

Recently, I visited a stereo store to buy a new FM tuner. I also needed a pair of surround speakers to make the whole system work like it should. During the discussion over FM turners and prices, it became clear that the sales rep did not want to reduce the price of the stereo receiver, but he discovered that I needed speakers. At that point, he threw in a pair of new surround sound speakers, which resolved the negotiation over price. I got what I wanted—the receiver and speakers. The seller got what he wanted—the regular price.

Bridging.   **Bridging** occurs when a new option is developed that satisfies both parties' most significant needs. Unlike the above examples, in the following three negotiation situations, no cost cutting, no compensation, and no more than one item for each side is involved.

My boyfriend and I are always trying to help each other out. Sometimes, when I need to use his car, he carpools with his friends on the way to work so that I can use his car. I also drop him off at his friend's house so that I can accomplish some tasks instead of the car sitting in a driveway. If I know that he is really busy with something, but still needs to get other tasks done, I take time out from my day to assist him. I do this also because I know he is not the best at multi-tasking.

When one of my high school friends was planning to visit a mutual friend and me, we looked around for an empty bed he could sleep in, but it seemed as though everyone was staying in town for the weekend. We were about to schedule his visit for another weekend, but it turned out to be OK for him to stay with his cousin's friend. They talked to each other on the phone, the arrangements were made, and a weekend was not wasted.

Yesterday my friend Kerry wanted to go to town and she needed someone to go with her, but I had to do laundry at my apartment complex. We decided that first I would go with her to town and then she would drop by my apartment so I could get my laundry, and I would do it in her dorm. We both got to do what we wanted to do; we just figured out a different option.

Minor or major new options may involve bridging. A renter may hesitate about renting a particular apartment because she wants to have a home office but no telephone jack exists in the second bedroom. The landlord may "bridge" the deal by installing a more convenient telephone jack. While that is a simple bridge, a more complicated one could occur.

7.3 Apply It

Write out examples of times you have used cost cutting, compensation, logrolling, and bridging in scarce resource conflicts. What clearly distinguishes each example as one type or the other?

Base Decisions on Objective Criteria

How do you know when the solution you have decided on is the best one for all concerned? One way is to try to base the decision on **objective criteria,** or guidelines we apply across a variety of situations to ensure fairness. Actually, we do this often in everyday situations when decisions are made on the basis of trade-offs, sharing, and turn-taking. For example:

- It's my turn this time to go first, and you can go first next time.
- Majority rules.
- Let's toss a coin or draw straws to see who gets it.
- He needs it more than she does.

These are common objective criteria we all use on occasion to settle everyday conflicts over scarce resources.

7.3 Think about It

Can you list some situations in which a different objective criterion is applicable? For example, list one that involves "majority rules" and others that involve other generally accepted standards.

Converting Competitive Negotiation into Cooperation

The principles of creating win–win outcomes are found in separating people from the problem, focusing on interests, brainstorming options, and finding objective criteria on which to base decisions. We next translate these principles into the following actions.

Seeking Commonalities

When you look at a half glass of water, do you see the glass as half full or half empty? A half full glass may make you feel happy, while a half empty glass may depress you. Your point of view makes a difference. We know, for example, that it is difficult to cooperate and collaborate with others if you start out focusing on what you disagree on with them. That disagreement may produce distrust and competition. If instead you focus on areas of agreement, you are more likely to trust and cooperate, as this narrative demonstrates.

> I once had a professor who divided his discussion class into two groups, which he assigned to different classrooms. He then gave each group different instructions, initially. He told one group that they would receive a group grade and to cooperate and work together to solve a problem. That group did end up working together and quickly solved the problem. While he gave the same problem to the other group, he told the group members that they were in competition with each other. He said he would give each student a separate grade based on

his or her individual contributions to the group. As expected, that group had a tough time working together and found it difficult to come to a consensus.

Talking Cooperation

Unlike some of the conflict messages we wrote of earlier that take responsibility for feelings and wants, the **language of cooperation** is "we-based." "We both want this." "We both think this." This is important to everyone concerned. Cooperative language is also tentative: "What would you say if. . . ." or "Do you think that's a good idea?" Cooperative language leaves space for people so that they aren't backed into corners.

Consulting before Acting

This skill is of paramount importance. Don't assume that you know what the other wants. Don't assume that you know what is best for the other person. Instead, check your statements to make sure they are right, or even more conservatively, ask what the other person wants before tendering an offer.

Communicating Frequently

As conflicts escalate, people have a tendency to shut down communication. They become entrenched in their positions, and conclude that since they are at an impasse, they should say nothing more. Although communication is not a magic cure-all for conflict, frequent and nonhostile communication keeps those in the conflict from making too many unchallenged assumptions about the other.

Controlling the Process, Not the Outcome

If an election is fair and honest, everyone has a good chance of getting elected. Controlling the election process can guarantee a fair outcome, but we still don't know who is going to be elected. We can have a similar approach to negotiating. By following the suggestions in this chapter for constructive ways to **control the process,** the parties can create the conditions for a fair and honest problem-solving discussion, but we can't predict the outcome with certainty. One has to have faith that creating a cooperative negotiation process should produce a mutually satisfying outcome.

Thinking Positively

People often resemble the characters in the children's book *Winnie the Pooh.* Some people are Rabbits, compulsive about everything, wanting to control all events. Others are like Piglet, worried that the sky might fall in. Some are happy-go-lucky Poohs, content to take life as it comes. And then there are the Eeyores. They're pretty easy to recognize. They make comments like, "I wasn't invited to the party, but I wouldn't have had fun anyway." Eeyores are not positive people, and their pessimism can really make it difficult for others to believe that they are making progress. Eeyores are the ones who shoot down all the solutions during a brainstorming session, who don't believe the parties can create any objective criteria to judge solutions to a problem, and who don't think any mutual interests exist when people are in conflict. Don't become an Eeyore!

Considering Your BATNA

When conflicts seem intractable, you could consider your **BATNA,** the acronym Fisher and Ury have given to the idea of one's "Best Alternative to a Negotiated Agreement." If you cannot come to some understanding with the other person, what is the next best alternative? Your BATNA is determined on a number of levels. For example, if you can't come to agreement today with the other person, what's next best? If you can't come to an agreement with this person in the foreseeable future, what are your other alternatives?

Engaging in Fractionation

In addition to calculating a BATNA, people in the conflict may also engage in fractionation in order to work through the problem.[21] **Fractionation** is a matter of breaking the problem down into its smallest pieces, and then dealing with each piece one at a time. This account shows how fractionation helped solve the problem of repairing a house.

> We bought a lovely little house in a great location. Unfortunately, despite its great layout and look, it needed a lot of work. I would have rather done all the remodeling at once—preferably before we moved in! That simply wasn't possible. So, we finished out the garage so my son could use it as a bedroom and we fixed the fence to keep the dogs in. We repaired the roof before winter rains came, and painted the house because it made sense to do it at the same time. Inside issues have taken much longer. Inside we made replacing the windows the first priority. After that we moved to refinishing the wood floors and replacing the old linoleum with tile. It will take about five years to get it all done, but it's a lot easier to handle one task at a time.

In this chapter, we have looked at ways of addressing conflicts over tangible resources (imagined or real) that appear to be win–lose. Successful resolution of these conflicts depends on our ability to assess the situation and decide how important it is to achieve our initial goal in the situation. Situations occur when we decide to back off the conflict, giving more importance to the relationship. At other times, we need to argue more forcefully. In most cases, though, finding a solution is a matter of learning how to "color outside the lines."

Manage It

In the preceding chapters we discuss how conflict managers can often clear up a misunderstanding by communicating their wants and listening to the other party. When confronted, the other often says, "Oh, I didn't realize you felt that way. Why didn't you say something sooner? Now that I know what you want, okay." While this often happens, there are other situations that are not as easily resolved. The problem lies in the inherent difference between tangible and intangible issues.

What is the difference between a tangible and an intangible conflict issue? Because intangible resources are emotional, mental, and psychological assets, they are not limited by nature. Consequently, such issues are often resolved through interpersonal communication. In contrast, tangible resources are physical and observable. Because tangible resources are often scarce, conflicts involving such issues take more than basic interpersonal communication skills to resolve; they require more advanced problem solving skills, in particular, negotiation techniques.

When confronted with a conflict over an intangible resource, skilled conflict managers follow the minimax principle to minimize their losses and maximize their gains. They start bargaining with an aspiration level but also have a resistance point in mind. One implication of this idea is that one should expect to make some concessions, so it pays to set a goal higher than one thinks possible to attain. Negotiators who make concessions are more likely to elicit cooperative behavior from the other party than are those who make no concessions at all.

Skilled conflict managers also strive for a win–win outcome. Such outcomes are more likely to occur when the parties trust each other and the situation is one in which mutually satisfactory outcomes are possible, even though the parties may not know that at the outset.

Whether we approach a conflict from a minimax principle or a win–win orientation, there are four principles of negotiation that govern the effective conflict management of tangible issues:

1. Do not confuse the problem at hand with the people involved.
2. Focus on the interests of the people involved rather than on their articulated positions.
3. Try to agree ahead of time on objective criteria.
4. Generate more options by cost cutting, compensation, logrolling, and bridging.

How do effective conflict managers convert a potentially competitive conflict into a cooperative one? They do this by seeking commonalities, talking cooperation, consulting before acting, communicating frequently, controlling the process, thinking positively, considering their BATNA, and engaging in fractionation

We have completed Part I. The preceding chapters explain exactly how to confront someone and how to better handle conflicts. This highly practical part of the text gives specific suggestions as to what one can say and exactly how to say it. It is our hope, as the authors, that students apply these basic conflict management principles in conflicts while in college and continue to use these ideas and techniques after graduation in future partnerships, family, work, and other important interpersonal relationships. Part II expands our skills in conflict management by examining theories of conflict behavior and factors that often lead to escalation in conflicts.

7.1 Work with It

Read the following case study and answer the questions that follow it.

> Last week I met with a colleague, the Division Chief for Right of Way (I am Division Chief of Planning), to discuss our mutual need to staff a receptionist position on the eighth floor of a new office building we will occupy beginning next month. She will have about eighty employees working on this floor, while my staff will total around forty.
>
> For security and customer service reasons we need to place a receptionist at a cubicle opposite the elevator where visitors can be greeted, screened, and directed as they enter the floor. We do not currently have this problem in our existing building as the organization has a guard hired to check visitors in and out of the only public entrance to the building.
>
> Since the Right of Way Division has twice the number of employees and many more visitors than we do in Planning, I attempted to convince her to agree to staff the position out of her budget. I have had some previous history negotiating with this Division Chief and have found her difficult to work with. This meeting was no exception. I tried to convince her that equity demanded she pay for the position or at least two-thirds of the costs. She refused, arguing that I should bear the entire cost because her budget had been reduced this fiscal year.
>
> After posturing for some time, it was clear that she was not going to budge in her negotiating position. I had more important issues on my plate that day and also I did not want to take this issue to our mutual boss, the District Director, to resolve. In light of this, I proposed that we split the costs 50–50, which she agreed to almost immediately. The problem I have is that this really is not a fair decision for my division and is another example of where I should have been more aggressive in sticking to my position, instead of looking for resolution through a compromise.

1. To what extent did the parties apply the four principles of negotiation (people, interests, etc.)? If not, how could they?
2. Did the parties use any of the four ways to generate more options (logrolling, bridging, etc.)? If not, how could they?
3. Did the parties incorporate any of the recommendations for converting competitive negotiation to cooperation (talking cooperation, fractionation, etc.)? If not, how could they?

7.2 Work with It

Recall a recent conflict you observed or experienced that concerned a tangible issue or problem that is a scarce resource (not enough time together or money, a single object or place you can't share, etc.). The conflict should be one that you resolved or have managed for the time being. Write a short description of the conflict, and then analyze it by answering the following questions.

1. How did you apply the four principles of negotiation (people, interests, etc.)?
2. How did you use one or more of the four ways to generate more options (logrolling, bridging, etc.)?
3. How did you incorporate the recommendations for converting competitive negotiation to cooperation (talking cooperation, fractionation, etc.)?

> ### 7.1 Remember It
>
> Write an essay as though you were writing a letter to a friend. Explain the four methods of generating more options (cost-cutting, logrolling, compensation, and bridging), and discuss how your friend might use them in an upcoming negotiation.

NOTES

1. Linda L. Putnam, "Bargaining as Organizational Communication," in Robert D. McPhee and Phillip K. Tompkins (Eds.), *Organizational Communication: Traditional Themes and New Directions* (Newbury Park: Sage, 1985), p. 129.
2. Joyce L. Hocker and William L. Wilmot, *Interpersonal Conflict,* 3rd Ed. (Dubuque, IA: Wm. C. Brown Publishers, Inc., 1991).
3. Laura E. Drake, "The Culture-Negotiation Link: Integrative and Distributive Bargaining through an Intercultural Communication Lens," *Human Communication Research* 27 (2001), 317–349.
4. Linda L. Putnam and Trisha S. Jones, "The Role of Communication in Bargaining," *Human Communication Research* 8 (1992), 262–280.
5. Linda L. Putnam and M. Scott Poole, "Conflict and Negotiation," in Fred M. Jablin, Linda L. Putnam, Karlene H. Roberts, and Lyman W. Porter, *Handbook of Organizational Communication: An Interdisciplinary Approach* (Newbury Park, CA: Sage, 1987), pp. 549–599.
6. Chapter 2 discusses the idea of scarce resources as a conflict issue in more detail.
7. David A. Lax and James K. Sebenius, *The Manager as Negotiator* (New York: Free Press, 1986), p. 32.
8. James A. Wall, *Negotiation: Theory and Practice* (Glenview, IL: Scott Foresman, 1985).
9. Dean G. Pruitt, *Negotiation Behavior* (New York: Academic Press, 1981).
10. See, for example, Melvin J. Kimmel, Dean G. Pruitt, John M. Magenau, E. Konar Goldband, and P. J. D. Carnevale, "Effects of Trust, Aspiration and Gender on Negotiation Tactics," *Journal of Personality and Social Psychology* 38 (1980), 9–22; Dean G. Pruitt and Steven A. Lewis, "Development of Integrative Solutions in Bilateral Negotiation," *Journal of Personality and Social Psychology* 31 (1975), 621–633; P. J. D. Carnevale, Dean G. Pruitt, and Steven D. Seilheimer, "Looking and Competing: Accountability and Visual Access in Integrative Bargaining," *Journal of Personality and Social Psychology* 28 (1973), 12–20.
11. V. Edwin Bixenstine and Kellogg V. Wilson, "Effects of Level of Cooperative Choice by the Other Player in a Prisoner's Dilemma Game," *Journal of Abnormal and Social Psychology* 67 (1963), 139–147; see also Marc Pilisuk and Paul Skolnick, "Inducing Trust: A Test of the Osgood Proposal," *Journal of Experimental Social Psychology* 11 (1968), 53–63; Gerald Marwell, David Schmitt, and Bjorn Boyesen, "Pacifist Strategy and Cooperation under Interpersonal Risk," *Journal of Personality and Social Psychology* 28 (1973), 12–20.
12. Robert N. Bostrom, *Persuasion* (Englewood Cliffs, NJ: Prentice Hall, 1983), p. 223.
13. Vertus E. Bixenstine and Jacquelyn W. Gaebelein, "Strategies of 'Real' Opponents in Eliciting Cooperative Choice in a Prisoner's Dilemma Game," *Journal of Communication Research* 15 (1971), 157–166; see also Samuel S. Komorita and Arline R. Brenner, "Bargaining and Concession Making under Bilateral Monopoly," *Journal of Personality and Social Psychology* 9 (1968), 15–20.
14. Frank Tutzauer and Michael Roloff, "Communication Processes Leading to Integrative Agreements: Three Paths to Joint Benefits," *Communication Research* 15 (1988), 360–380.
15. Dean G. Pruitt and Melvin J. Kimmel, "Twenty Years of Experimental Gaming: Critique, Synthesis and Suggestions for the Future," *Annual Review of Psychology* 28 (1977), 363–392.
16. Barry R. Schlenker, B. Helm, and James T. Tedeschi, "The Effects of Personality and Situational Variables on Behavioral Trust," *Journal of Personality and Social Psychology* 32 (1973), 664–670.

17. John Waite Bowers, "Guest Editor's Introduction: Beyond Threats and Promises," *Speech Monographs* 41 (1974), ix–xi.

18. Max Bazerman, "Why Negotiations Go Wrong," *Psychology Today* 6 (June, 1986), 54–58.

19. Richard J. Klimoski, "The Effects of Intragroup Forces on Intergroup Conflict Resolution," *Organizational Behavior and Human Performance* 8 (1972), 363–383; see also Michael E. Roloff and Douglas E. Campion, "On Alleviating the Debili-tating Effects of Accountability on Bargaining: Authority and Self-Monitoring," *Communication Monographs* 54 (1987), 145–164.

20. Roger Fisher and William Ury, *Getting to Yes: Negotiating Agreement without Giving In* (Boston: Houghton Mifflin, 1981), p. 11.

21. Ibid.

8 Social-Psychological Perspectives of Conflict

OBJECTIVES

At the end of this chapter, you should be able to:

- Explain the key concepts and assumptions that identify factors that play an important role in interpersonal conflict according to each theory.

- Explain key principles that describe how conflicts develop according to each theory.

- Show how one should manage or resolve interpersonal conflicts according to each theory.

KEY TERMS

anxiety
attribution theory
comparison level (CL)
comparison level for alternatives
    (CL_{alt})

psychodynamic theory
skill
social exchange theory
system
systems theory

theory
uncertainty

In the first part of this textbook, our purpose was to provide you with skills you could start using immediately to manage the conflicts that you experience. But skills alone, without an understanding of their origin in theory, are sometimes underused or applied improperly. In this portion of the text, we apply to conflict situations various theories that social psychologists created to explain why people behave the way they do. A **theory** is a means of explaining how something works. The way we explain conflict determines how we interpret it and choose our responses. The focus of a theory's explanation directs attention to that part of the conflict and assigns causes at the point of its focus.

Theories allow us to carry skills from one situation to another and to apply them appropriately within situations; a **skill** is a behavior that one can repeat at the appropriate time.[1] Theories allow us to understand what the appropriate time is.

There are several metaphors that can help explain the relationship between skills and theories. For example, having a toolbox does you no good unless you know what each tool is used for. Or, if you only know how to format a single page document in Word, having many other programs available to you doesn't do you much good. Further, not everything can fit into the format you understand. Understanding a program (a single skill) is not as helpful as understanding an operating system (a theory).

Another analogy concerning the relationship of skills to theory has to do with color. Why do some colors work together and some don't? We have color theory, which says that complementary colors (across the color wheel) create excitement, analogous colors (alongside each other on the color wheel) create a restful feeling, and so on. How do you know what color to use when?

The point about theories is this: If we don't understand theories, it is hard for us to repeat a successful conflict performance, because we don't know what we did right. Conversely, it is hard for us to avoid repeating a poor performance, because we don't necessarily know what we did wrong.

The key social psychological theories described in this chapter are psychodynamic, attribution, uncertainty, social exchange, and systems theories. Each emphasizes the role of the individual and her or his perceptual processes, the nature of the relationship that binds the conflicting parties, and the structures that shape conflict behavior in a relationship. They are about relationships in which there is interdependence and where a problem has occurred creating some dissatisfaction. Each theory adds an additional set of factors to determine more precisely the cause of the conflict. We study these theories because they call our attention to the key concepts, assumptions, and principles that lay the groundwork for developing techniques for the management of conflict. You are expected to apply these theories to conflicts in your life, to identify the key principle that explains the conflicts, and to suggest how best to manage them.

Intrapersonal Theories of Conflict

Psychodynamic, attribution, and uncertainty conflict theories, generated by researchers in psychology and social psychology, have focused on what individuals bring to the conflict situation and how that impacts the conflict process. The key concept that unifies these theories is their assumption that the way people act in conflict situations is due, in large part, to their individual dispositions and ways of thinking. The theories remind us that the individuals in the conflict play no small part in determining the direction that the conflict takes.

Psychodynamic Theory

Stemming from one of the most historically significant psychological theories, based on the work of Sigmund Freud and his followers, **psychodynamic theory** says that people experience conflict because of their intrapersonal states. Misplaced and displaced conflict (where the conflict is acted out with the wrong person or over the wrong issue), overblown conflicts (where the conflict receives more attention than it really deserves), and bickering (where the primary purpose is to hurt the other) are conflicts that are best explained by this theory. The following narrative illustrates a displaced conflict driven by psychodynamic tension.

When I'm going to leave for an extended trip, I often wind up fighting with my husband before I go over some insignificant but overblown issue. This time, I was really aware of the tendency, and we had avoided any major blowups. It took a toll, though, in my response to a neighbor's irritating comments at the shared swimming pool. Normally I simply would have left the situation, but I wound up telling him off in no uncertain terms. I was really embarrassed that I blew up—not only was the issue simply not worth the anger I felt, but I didn't even know this person before and now I feel like I have to avoid him.

Freud's theory explains how conflict occurs for the individual.[2] Freud conceived of the mind as a body of psychic energy that is channeled into various activities. Not only is the psychic energy channeled, but it is channeled into appropriate or inappropriate places. For the person in the narrative above, the tension created by trying not to fight before leaving on a trip gets channeled onto a "safe person," a stranger. People often displace or misplace conflict when they think that dealing with the other person directly is not possible or that it may make matters worse.

Three aspects of the human mind affect the way in which frustration, or more generally, psychic energy, is released. The principal component of the mind is the id, the unconscious aspect that "contains everything that is inherited, present at birth, or fixed in the constitution."[3] The id contains the libido, the source of instinctual energy, which demands discharge though various channels. The id operates on the "pleasure principle," a tension-reduction process in which tension from a bodily need is translated into a psychological wish in order to reduce the tension. The id seeks pleasure and avoids pain; it seeks only to satisfy its needs without regard for the cost of doing so.

Opposing the id is what Freud called the superego, containing both the ego ideal and the conscience. The ego ideal is an internalized idea of what a person would like to be. The conscience contains morals and other judgments concerning correct and incorrect behavior. As a parent does, it tries to punish a person for "immoral" behavior and reward a person for "moral" behavior through feelings like guilt or pride.

Mediating between the id and the superego is the ego, governed by the "reality principle," which attempts to "postpone the discharge of energy until the actual object that will satisfy the need has been discovered or produced."[4] The ego, in mediating between the id and the superego, plays a significant role in conflict situations—it tries to reconcile the desires of the id ("I want it all, and I want it right now") with the constraints of the superego ("Nice people don't throw temper tantrums"). The ego must constrain aggressive impulses and control the level of anxiety conflict creates.

The ego deals with aggressive impulses by suppressing them or redirecting them through a process of displacement. In displacement, the aggressive impulse is often redirected "toward a more vulnerable or socially acceptable target than the actual source of frustration. . . . Displacement is more likely when the true source of frustration is powerful or particularly valuable to the individual."[5] Coser argued that the process of scapegoating in groups results from displaced aggression, because members are afraid to blame the entire group for a situation.[6]

Anxiety is an additional product of frustration and tension, occurring when people perceive danger in a situation. People can become anxious when they think that someone may interfere with their goals, when they fear their own impulses in a situation, or when they disapprove of their own actions. The major impact of anxiety on a conflict situation is the rigidity and inflexibility it causes in people's responses to the situation.[7]

Psychodynamic theory explains how individuals respond to conflict situations, particularly in light of their aggressive impulses and their anxieties. The theory points out that people are not always aware of the motivations that drive their behaviors. When diagnosing conflict situations, an understanding of the foundations of psychodynamic theory reminds you that the first task is to determine who is involved in the conflict.

A key point to remember about psychodynamic theory is that it explains those conflicts that often arise out of nowhere. A common defense mechanism that occurs in conflict is displacement—taking out our frustrations on those perceived as less dangerous to us rather than confronting those persons who caused the original feelings in us. Frustration resulting from the internal battle between the id and superego often erupts into conflict with others. That frustration can originate from many sources, for example, tension, stress, insecurity, anxiety, hostility, sexual urges, or depression. The following narrative is an example of a displaced conflict due to internal frustration.

> I work in a retail store and I am often in charge of ringing people up at the register. I always make sure that when I ask for the next person in line that in fact the truly next person in line comes over or at least has a chance to. But when I asked for the *next* person in line, another lady who was not the next person in line came over. When I tried to get the proper person to come over, the woman that had come over started yelling at me. I calmly explained to her that it was part of my job to make sure that the next person in line had a fair chance to come over. She did not like this and went so far as to throw her credit card at me when paying. This made me absolutely furious and the worst part about it was there was nothing that I could say.
>
> So after I got off work I met my boyfriend at my house. Everything was going along smoothly until suddenly we got into a disagreement about whether we would go out that night or stay in. I was tired from working all day but he wanted to go out. Well I ended up blowing the whole situation out of proportion and I know that it was due to the tension I had held on to all day from the irate customer that I had dealt with earlier in the day.

This retail salesperson needs to learn how to deal more effectively with offensive customers so that she doesn't have so much pent up frustration. She may even need to take up a different line of work, one that is more supportive and doesn't create a lot of tension. Unfortunately, too many people do not do anything until after they have ruined one or more relationships with those who were the safe targets of their frustrations.

8.1 Think about It

Are there situations in your life where you are more likely to displace your anger or conflict with the other person than to deal with it directly? What characterizes those situations?

Apply It

This exercise is something you can start now and add to throughout the chapter. Take a piece of paper and draw two columns on it. In the left column, list your theoretical tools, starting with psychodynamic theory. In the right column, describe what your tool does in analyzing conflicts.

Attribution Theory

An attribution is an inference made about the causes of another's behavior. If I infer from your behavior that you are internally motivated and I don't approve of what you did or said, I could say that you acted that way because you are evil, angry at me, anxious, unmotivated, depressed, or unintelligent. For example, I don't like the fact that you beat me at cards, so I call you a cheat (as though you are a bad person who intended to cheat me—all internal attributions).

If I approve of what you did or said, I might attribute the behavior to an external source such as a run of luck, God, your parents, and so on. For example, I might credit your spouse for your success at your job.

Sillars argued that in a conflict situation, one makes conclusions about the other person's behavior and that those conclusions lead to theories to explain the conflict.[8] **Attribution theory** states that people act as they do in conflict situations because of the conclusions they draw about the other. Conclusions about the other are based on attributions about that person or on inferences about the meanings, causes, or outcomes of conflict events. Attributions are internal, related to the person's general personality, or external, related to the other person's circumstances. As you might suspect, attribution theory accounts for false conflicts—when we are assuming we are in conflict due to insufficient information or because of faulty conclusions we have drawn about the other person's behavior.

Sillars claimed attributions affect the way people define conflicts, interpret the other's behavior, and choose strategies to achieve their goals effectively within conflict situations. Furthermore, the process of making attributions about the other may discourage the selection of collaborative conflict strategies, because the process of attribution may shift the blame from oneself to the other. This reciprocal relationship between making attributions and the escalation of a conflict also can affect international conflict: The tendency to maintain attributional consistency (i.e., to generate an explanation of the other's behavior and stick to it) and consequent misinterpretation of information increases the likelihood of escalating conflict and prolonged hostilities in international conflict.[9]

People are most likely to perceive the other as aggressive and respond with anger and retribution when three conditions are met. First, the action the other person has taken is seen as a constraint to one's own alternatives or outcomes. Gabriel cannot act in the way he wishes because of Javier's actions. Second, the action taken by the other appears to have been done intentionally to do harm. Not only has Javier taken action that constrains Gabriel, but Javier appears to have done so in order to intentionally harm Gabriel. Third, the action taken by Javier is seen as abnormal or illegitimate. Gabriel sees no action on his

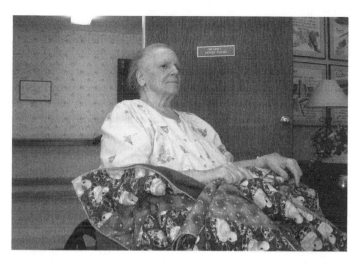

What kinds of attributions would you make about this woman, based on the setting in which you see her?

part that might have provoked Javier into acting as he did. Anger or retribution is less likely on Gabriel's part if Javier is seen as having acted without choice and because forces moved him in the direction taken. Anger and retribution are more likely if Gabriel sees Javier's action as arbitrary or whimsical.[10]

In a slightly different approach, Louis explained conflict by examining how people conceptualize it and attribute it to various causes.[11] According to her approach, conflict is a series of affective, cognitive, and behavioral phases. The perception of conflict arises when a person feels some frustration, thinks about the source of the frustration, and then acts in response to it. Frustration is thus the stimulus initiating a conflict episode. The person in this narrative allowed her frustration to build three years before saying anything about the conflict.

Before I was hired at my parish church, there had been no young women working in the office for over thirty years. I could tell that Monsignor was hesitant about hiring us three girls but he seemed to get more enthusiastic about it after we started working there. He gave us pet names and always had something nice to say. Then three weeks into the new schedule, he called a meeting. He told us that one of the parishioners had said we wore our skirts too short. Monsignor had defended us though, and everything seemed fine. Then six months into the job, I was working alone when a man came in and asked to speak to a priest. He needed money. While we were waiting for the priest to come, he began to make sexually suggestive remarks about me. I asked him to leave, and he did before the priest could arrive. I reported this the next day, and they added some security measures like a button to call the police directly. But when I came back to work, Monsignor was cold and professional toward me. This lasted three years, until I finally decided to write him a note and tell him that I was hurt about the way he was treating me. He wrote back and said he had felt bad that he wasn't there to protect me. So we had a conflict for three years because both of us thought we knew what the other one was thinking.

The context surrounding the frustration can reduce or enhance the interpretation of a stimulus as frustrating, depending on the importance of the context characteristic. If you are trying to study, for example, and your neighbor is making a great deal of noise, you probably feel frustrated. However, if it is Saturday night, and people generally socialize and make a great deal of noise on Saturday nights, you may not feel as frustrated as you would in the middle of finals week. Once you analyze the other person's behavior and make attributions about it, you decide on the choices that are available to you to reduce the source of the frustration.

One shortcoming in Louis' model is the assumption of rationality on the part of the individual. The explanation of the process of analyzing the source of a conflict and choosing responses is insightful, but it is unlikely that people always choose to act in such a rational manner when responding to conflicts. Some conflicts occur rapidly, with no time for thought or reflection. For conflicts that occur over a period of time, this model may illustrate how people decide they are experiencing a conflict; at the least, it is a reminder that the way that people judge the conflict situation and the other person's behavior affects the way that they choose their own behavior.

As you consider attribution theory, an important aspect to remember is that it explains retaliatory behavior. When we make internal attributions about another person (she wanted, he hates, she's stupid, he's evil, she's angry, etc.), it often results in name calling (you cheat, idiot, lazy good for nothing, etc.) and assigning blame (it's all your fault). Making external attributions for oneself is a way to avoid blame (it's my parents' fault that I am this way, I can't help that I didn't go to the right school) and to avoid giving credit to others where it is due (your spouse must have done it for you, you got the job because you graduated from the right school, you must have had connections, etc.).

Interestingly, we tend to make internal attributions to explain others' behavior when we don't like it, and external attributions when we are impressed. Meanwhile, we do the opposite for our own behavior. If I do something impressive, I like to take the credit for it (aren't I great!), but when it is nasty, I try to blame it on someone else (she made me do it). This is called the "attribution error."

> The other night my three friends and I played a card game called spades. My partner and I were not doing as well as the other team. I figured that somehow they were giving each other some kind of signals; so I finally stopped the game and accused them of cheating us. One of them responded by saying, "We are winning simply because of the luck of the draw." But the conflict escalated into a yelling match. Luckily, someone suggested that we change partners, which solved the problem. We went back to playing cards, but I still ended up on the losing side.

One interesting study looked at the way attributions were made about the use of humor by participants in a conflict episode. When humor was attributed to internal motives (e.g., "that person just enjoys jokes"), it had a negative outcome on the conflict resolution, but when humor was attributed to an external motive (e.g., laughing at the situation), it had a more positive effect on conflict resolution.[12] In another study, Sillars and colleagues found that conflicting spouses saw their own messages in more favorable terms than their partner's.[13]

8.2 ## Think about It

When have false attributions you have made about another exacerbated a conflict situation? Have there been times when making accurate attributions about the other has helped you?

8.2 ## Apply It

Add to the paper you started with Apply It 8.1. Write attribution theory in the left column, and explain how it helps you to analyze conflicts in the right column.

Uncertainty Theory

Uncertainty occurs at two levels. Conflict creates uncertainty within the relationship in which it occurs, and uncertainty also exists to different degrees within the particular conflict episode. **Uncertainty** in the conflict situation occurs when we have insufficient information to understand another's motives, goals, or behaviors or when we do not understand how another is responding to us.

Many events are capable of creating uncertainty in relationships: changes in the other person's behavior, the breaking of a confidence, a friend breaking off contact, a dating partner going out with someone else. Interestingly, nearly all the events recalled by people as those causing uncertainty are classified as conflict episodes.[14] Most people cannot recall anything that might have been a clue to events causing uncertainty, or they can recognize clues only in retrospect. Uncertainty in relationship does lead to increased communication with the other person, and when people communicate about events causing uncertainty, they are more satisfied. Those who do not talk about uncertainty-causing events generally express regret about avoiding the issue. As time passes, feelings about uncertainty-causing events become less negative.[15] Communication with the other, "doing" the conflict, is generally the best way to reduce uncertainty within a relationship. But there is a deeper level of uncertainty—that within the conflict itself.

Conflicts are inherently messy and filled with ambiguity. "The characteristic of conflict that is most difficult to capture in research is the chaos that pervades a heated argument or a long-simmering conflict."[16] There are three sources of ambiguity and disorder in conflict: the source of the conflict, the organizational complexity of conflict patterns, and the embeddedness of conflict in daily activities.

Issues in conflict are rarely singular or straightforward. Rational views of conflict assume that both people are able to identify the issue, develop straightforward goals about it, and move toward resolution through compromise or collaboration. However, the real case is that people may not share the same perception about the issue or may not agree on the conflict issue at all. They may think the conflict has arisen due to different causes; they may interpret the other's behavior differently than the other intends; and so on. Further, conflicts may exist simultaneously at different levels—superficial issues may also involve deeper relational implications. Mild conflicts generally reflect agreement concerning the deeper relational issues involved; in bitter and destructive conflicts, relational issues are entangled and difficult to resolve.

The complexity of conflict may also affect the level of ambiguity present. Whereas casual conversation is characterized by adherence to a set of cooperative principles, these principles are often violated in conflict when it is not in one's best interest to converse in a succinct, relevant, and orderly manner. In addition, patterns in conflict (beyond the broad stages of prelude, initiation, differentiation, and resolution) are difficult to identify. Most conversation shows a reciprocal pattern, in which message types are generally followed by similar types, but "conflicts often have a dynamic quality characterized by oscillation between aggression and withdrawal."[17] Further, participants in conflicts often introduce, drop, reintroduce, and expand topics in an unpredictable pattern, making it difficult for the other person to know where the conversation might lead.

A final source for the situations of uncertainty created by conflicts is the embedded-ness of conflict in our everyday lives. They can occur anywhere, at any time. Often we may feel surprised by them. It's rare that we can make an appointment for a conflict!

When a person is in an uncertain relationship, they tend to "test the waters," so to speak, in order to reduce the uncertainty they feel. They are alert and observe the other person's behavior. They'll look for positive behaviors, but may overestimate the meaning of a negative behavior (e.g., she looks upset—she's probably thinking about breaking up with me). Indeed, in a situation of uncertainty, this overemphasis on the meaning of the behaviors the uncertain person observes makes it harder to reduce the uncertainty. This conflict narrative demonstrates how uncertainty makes interaction between both people difficult.

> After a terrible conflict in which I felt physically endangered, I asked my partner to move out. She promised to reform, but the difficulty is that she doesn't really think she did any-thing wrong. So she'll say things that indicate she doesn't trust me. In the meantime, I'm worried about her losing her temper again, and I'm watching all the time to see what's going to happen. It's pretty hard for both of us to simply relax and be around each other.

People reduce uncertainty in conflict situations in one of three ways. First, they may choose to trust the other, although the ability to trust depends on past behaviors. Second, they may reduce uncertainty by taking the perspective of the other person. And third, they may reduce uncertainty by engaging in "imagined interactions," or thoughts about what they might say and what the other might do in a conflict situation.[18]

> Usually my boyfriend calls me on a regular basis about three times a week. The conflict I had with him arose when he didn't call me for an entire week. I had no idea why and really wondered what was going on. I automatically jumped to the conclusion that something was wrong, that he no longer wanted to be with me, and that he probably was seeing someone else. My confidence in him was shaken. When the weekend came, I decided to drive to his college and pay him a visit. I wanted to jump all over him, discourage the competition, and demand that he shape up. When I found him he was surprised to see me, and he acted like nothing was the matter. Come to find out, he was pledging a fraternity and was unable to

call me. I was so worried about my exams that I had forgotten about his pledge week. When I heard his excuse, I quickly dropped my demands, told him I was sorry that I forgot, and cooked him his favorite dinner. My confidence in him was immediately restored.

8.3 Think about It

What conflicts can you identify that were motivated by uncertainty? How could you have obtained more information before engaging in the conflict?

8.3 Apply It

Add to the paper you started with Apply It 8.1. Write uncertainty theory in the left column, and explain how it helps you to analyze conflicts in the right column.

Relationship Theories of Conflict

While the theories in the first section focused on the individual as a key element in conflict, this section considers theories of how the relationship between the people involved in a conflict affects the way the conflict is enacted and resolved. The two dominant theories of this type are social exchange theory and systems theory.

Social Exchange Theory

Developed by Kelley and Thibault, **social exchange theory** states that people evaluate their interpersonal relationships in terms of their value, which is created by the costs and rewards associated with the relationship.[19] A person's feelings about a relationship, according to this theory, depend on assessments of the amount of effort put into the relationship (costs) compared to what is received as a result of the relationship (rewards). People assess the costs and rewards associated with their relationships through what is termed the comparison level (CL) and the comparison level of alternatives (CL_{alt}). People enter into conflict when they believe that the rewards they are receiving are too little in comparison with the costs they must pay in the relationship.

According to social exchange theory, partners ask "What does a relationship have to offer? How valuable is it? Am I better off with or without the other?" Social exchange theory explains how people rate their relationships in terms of what they are giving and getting out of them.

Rewards are resources of exchange (money, goods/property, love, sex, affection, companionship or shared time, status, services, information), while costs detract (pain/suffering, loneliness, abuse, loss of self-esteem, lost of resources of exchange, loss of investments). Partners make two comparisons (CL and CL_{alt}) to determine their level of relationship satisfaction and relationship commitment.

CL and CL_{alt} emphasize the role of relationship satisfaction and commitment in interpersonal conflict. The **comparison level (CL)** is a standard with which people determine how satisfactory or attractive a relationship is. This standard reflects what people think they deserve. If the rewards of a relationship compared to its cost fall above the CL, then a person considers the relationship satisfying; if the outcome falls below the CL, the person is probably dissatisfied with the relationship. A person's CL is created by considering all the possible outcomes a relationship might have, either from direct experience in the relationship or by observation of other relationships.

The **comparison level for alternatives (CL_{alt})** tends to be applied when a third party enters the picture. The addition of a third party may lead a person to examine the current relationship and perceive inequity in it, in turn creating conflict. A person compares the rewards and costs of the present relationship with those of the alternative relationship, and if the current relationship's rewards exceed the alternative, they remain committed to it.

This narrative illustrates how a person begins to make changes in a relationship through a consideration of the rewards and costs.

> My mother graduated from high school early in order to marry my biological father and move with him to Germany, where he was stationed in the service. I was born a year later, and they divorced a few months after I was born. My mom then married Harry when I was about two. For the next fourteen years, I lived with my mom and Harry, seeing my dad on the weekends. I felt like I lived two separate lives. Home was where Mom and Harry were—in fact, I didn't call him my stepfather, I called him "Dad." My biological father didn't like that.
>
> My relationship with my biological father got worse over the years. I never enjoyed spending time with him and I even dreaded seeing him because he bad-mouthed my mom and Harry. My biological father resented the relationship I had with Harry and he kept trying to make me think Harry was a bad guy. He would use gifts as a way of making me visit him. He bought me lots of toys, took me fun places, and as I got older the gifts got more expensive—a television, a stereo, the promise of a car. I accepted these gifts with a clear conscience because I figured he "owed" me for the miserable weekends I spent with him.
>
> When I was sixteen, my biological father and I had a major confrontation over this pattern we had developed. I basically stood up to him and told him how I hated the way he bad-mouthed my mom and how I didn't want to spend any more time with him if he was going to be like that. My father comes from a culture where you don't argue with your parents, so when I stood up to him, he got upset and told me never to come back to his house. That was five years ago, and I have never spoken to him since that time.

The narrator in this conflict has a clear comparison level when she evaluates the relationship she has with her biological father. She has a good relationship with her stepfather, and wants only one family, not two. Her father appears satisfied with the relationship they had, but her dissatisfaction grows as the expensive gifts no longer are enough to make up for the unpleasantness of each weekend visit.

This conflict also illustrates the idea of CL_{alt}, which is the lowest level of outcomes a person may accept in a current relationship in light of available opportunities in other relationships. The more the outcomes in a relationship exceed the CL_{alt}, the more a person is committed to the current relationship, and the more dependent that person is on the relationship for psychological rewards. As time wears on, the rewards of the narrator's relationship with her father are too low for her to accept. The emotional cost of staying in the relationship is higher than the value of any gift her father can give her.[20]

Social exchange theory assumes that people choose their behaviors due to self-interest and a desire to maximize rewards while minimizing costs. However, choices are made with respect to rules of fairness: People generally expect rewards proportionate to contributions they make to the relationship, based on their perceptions of the rewards and costs involved.[21] So, even if a relationship is unsatisfactory at a particular point in time, if people think that it was a good relationship in the past and believe it might satisfy them in the future, they do not immediately abandon the relationship when problems arise.

From a social exchange point of view, conflict arises when one person in the relationship thinks that the outcomes are too low and perceives that the other may resist any attempt to raise the outcomes.[22] This is precisely what happened in the narrative. It is possible that the narrator could have convinced her father that continuing to bad-mouth her mother (particularly sixteen years after the divorce) was not appropriate. Such an outcome would have been the result of what social exchange theory terms cooperative joint action, where both people agree together to make changes in the relationship. Through independent action, the narrator could simply have continued her relationship with her biological father without expecting him to change, although this was unlikely as his behavior really bothered her. The actual outcome of the conflict was imposed joint action, where the narrator's father discontinued their relationship.

How people choose to alter their outcomes depends on the power held by each person in the relationship. Kelly and Thibault argued that the dependence of person A on person B constitutes person B's power, and vice versa. A person may have "fate control" over the other, the ability to affect the other's behavior regardless of what the other does, or may have "mutual fate control" over the other, the ability to make it desirable for the other to behave as the person wants.

Overall, social exchange theory leads to four insights about conflict behavior. First, the theory recognizes that people are often quite purposeful about the way they "do" conflict, calculating the costs of various options and weighing those costs against the potential rewards the options might bring. This strategic calculation is illustrated by the following conflict account.

> The other night my mom called me to ask me what I was doing for the weekend. I told her I was going to come home because I had some plans with friends. She wondered if I could do something around the house so that I could spend some time with my brother. I was upset because she knew I had already made plans, and she was going out also. I felt like I was being pushed to cancel my plans because my brother wasn't doing anything. I was very hurt and angry because she was not even thinking about canceling her plans with her new boyfriend. I thought the request was very unfair. Because my mom had started dating again, I was feeling pressure in our relationship because I felt like it was changing. Most of her free

time was spent in this new relationship, and I felt like she was only thinking of herself and failing to see how hard it would be for me to adjust to the change. As a result of the negative feelings, we didn't hang up the phone on a very positive note. I feel very upset when there are negative feelings between my mom and me, but I felt the situation was not approached fairly. However, I must communicate my feelings to my mom in order to understand her motives and actions.

The preceding account also illustrates a second concept emphasized by social exchange theory: the interdependence of those in the conflict. It is not possible, according to social exchange theory, to take steps to resolve a conflict without reactions from the other person involved.

The third social exchange theory concept is that conflict is a situation in which moves and countermoves take place. It helps us understand how people explain conflicts—when narrating a conflict episode most people use a move–countermove format: He did this, so I did that, and so on.

The fourth concept of social exchange theory is that people in conflicts choose actions based not only on their particular outcomes but also on their cost for the relationship.[23] People may deliberately avoid a conflict because the current costs of initiating one are too high. Conversely, they may engage in a conflict because the costs of not doing so are too high.

Although some people initially react to social exchange theory negatively, thinking it is wrong to use an economic model to explain relationships, social exchange theory does make sense. We don't like believing that we put more into a relationship than we receive. If we have hope of staying in the relationship, we work to increase our rewards relative to our costs. On the other hand, if the costs continue to rise without some increase in rewards, people tend to cycle out of the relationship—as they see conflict as creating too high a "cost" with respect to the "reward" they might receive, they do not communicate their concerns and eventually do not communicate at all.

Here is another example of a conflict that illustrates social exchange theory.

Before college began, a high school friend and I had a great relationship. We would hang out all of the time together and knew all of each other's secrets. We promised that even though we'd be going away to different colleges, we'd always stay in touch and be the best of friends. After graduation, we both got absorbed in our own college life and lost our close ties. She eventually got bored with college and decided to take some "time off," while I remained in school where I am extremely busy with work, family issues, and my boyfriend.

Over the past three months she has been trying to get me to come back home for a weekend and go out partying at the local bars with her. She won't give up and is very persistent that I spend more time with her, and she says that, after all of this time, I'm not living up to my promise. Recently we lost touch again when I was too involved with my local obligations to call her back or spend a weekend partying. When I finally did call her, she never returned my phone calls and I haven't heard from her since. I feel that she must have compared the lack of satisfaction of our present relationship to all the dissatisfaction she must be feeling and it is less satisfying than she expected. She had put a lot of time and effort into maintaining our present relationship, while I did not. She was clearly putting more into the relationship then she was receiving, and so she must have decided to end our relationship.

8.4 Think about It

What conflicts can you identify that were motivated by a desire to increase your rewards or to decrease your costs in a relationship? Were you successful? Why or why not?

8.4 Apply It

Add to the paper you started with Apply It 8.1. Write social exchange theory in the left column, and explain how it helps you to analyze conflicts in the right column.

Systems Theory

Systems theory is best summarized by Ruben, who took issue with the idea of equating conflict with breakdowns. Rather, he argued, if human relationships are thought of as systems, communication, and therefore conflict, is not only inevitable but also continual.[24] Ruben's view of conflict within a system turns to an entirely different assumption from previous theories: Rather than being a disruption in the normal state of affairs, conflict is the normal state of affairs within any system. Conflict is necessary for the growth and adaptation of a system. Without conflict, a system faces the possibility of stagnation and decay. Conflict is the primary way in which a system adapts to the demands of its environment. According to this view, then, the major defining condition of conflict is the process of reducing alternatives as the system adapts to changes and demands in the environment.[25]

Let's expand the idea of system. A **system** is a set of interrelated components acting together as a unit. A holistic perspective suggests that the unit (couple, family, team, organization, society, etc.) is key, not the individual. That is, while it helps to know what elements (people) are in a system (relationship), it is the system itself that is most important in helping us understand the behavior and conflicts within it. We know that people behave a certain way because they are married (marital system), or because they are friends (another system), or members of a group (yet another system). Because they are part of the system, they act accordingly. Thus, the interdependent relationship among the components (individuals) of the system is considered more important than the components themselves. As they say about systems, the "whole is greater than the sum of its parts."

A system also has some purpose—it is goal-directed and adapts to its environment through self-maintenance and regulation. Thus the system maintains itself in pursuit of a goal. The goal in a marriage is to stay married—and it is much harder than it sounds! There are financial strains, in-law strains, job strains, and more. Conflict arises as these external factors make keeping the relationship problematic.

From a practical point of view, conflict occurs within a relationship because a person in that relationship needs to adapt to demands of the other person or to demands in the environment surrounding the relationship. Here is an example of a conflict explained by systems theory, where the relationship (system) is in turmoil because of the inability of those in it to adapt to each other's demands and to the demands of the environment.

> Mike and Lori fight constantly. They dropped out of high school to get married very young and have a baby. Lori's parents were so much against the marriage that they cut off contact and support to the young couple. Mike has only one parent, his mother, who is living on welfare, is an alcoholic, and depends on Mike for some support. She wants to live with them, but Lori is against the idea. Mike lacks both an education and employment skills and continues to have trouble holding a job.
>
> Meanwhile, Lori claims that she is unemployable and wants to stay home to raise their daughter. Mike wants her to go back to school and get a job, while his mother could move in and take care of their daughter. During the first year, Mike felt that he had to locate and tear up all the credit cards in their home, because Lori was buying things for him, herself, and the baby, which he felt they couldn't afford. This is difficult because she keeps receiving new credit cards in the mail and tries to secretly use them. So, now they argue constantly over lack of money, his mother, her not working, credit cards, and his working off and on.

Perhaps the most important contribution of systems theory to theories of conflict and its management has been the idea that conflict is a normal part of interaction. Rather than seeing conflict as a disruption that occurs within an otherwise healthy and normally functioning relationship, systems theorists see conflict as an important part of a system that allows change and adaptation to various demands.

8.5 Think about It

What conflicts can you identify that were motivated by systems theory principles? How best might you deal with such conflicts?

8.5 Apply It

Add to the paper you started with Apply It 8.1. Write systems theory in the left column, and explain how it helps you to analyze conflicts in the right column.

Manage It

As we state at the beginning of this chapter, understanding theories can help us understand our conflicts better so that we can adapt to them more easily. Psychodynamic theory, for example, helps us understand that aggressive impulses result from internal conflict between the id and the superego, which produces frustration and tension. The internal conflict can arise from various places: tension, stress, insecurity, anxiety, hostility, sexual urges, depression, and so on. Psychodynamic theory explains displacement—taking out our frustrations on those perceived as less dangerous to us rather than confronting those persons who caused the original feelings. As we come to understand the theory better, we realize that we need to learn how to cope in positive ways so that we don't resort to displacing conflict and aggression when the internal conflict becomes too great.

Attribution theory helps explain retaliatory behavior—we respond the way we do because we assume we understand why other people behave as they do. Making internal attributions for others often results in name calling and assigning blame. We make external attributions for ourselves to avoid blame or to avoid giving credit to others. We tend to make internal attributions to explain other's behavior when we don't like it, and external attributions when others impress us. Meanwhile, we do the opposite for our own behavior.

We can discuss uncertainty theory at two levels. Conflict creates uncertainty within the relationship in which it occurs, and uncertainty also exists to different degrees within the particular conflict episode. Uncertainty in the conflict situation occurs when we have insufficient information to understand another's motives, goals, or behaviors or when we do not understand another's behavior.

According to social exchange theory, partners determine the value of their relationships. Social exchange theory explains how people rate their relationships in terms of what they are giving and getting out of them. Partners make two comparisons to determine their level of (1) relationship satisfaction (based on previous experiences) and (2) relationship commitment (based on rewards/costs of alternatives).

Systems theory also deals with relationships. A system has some purpose—it is goal directed and adapts to its environment—a type of self-maintenance or self-regulation. Thus the system maintains itself in pursuit of a goal. Conflicts happen as people adjust to the demands of other people in the system or to the demands of the environment on the system itself.

Sometimes people will say that a theory sounds reasonable but doesn't work in practice. Good theories are those we can put to use. The theories presented in this chapter are part of a conflict manager's toolbox—they help to make sense of conflict behavior and guide us in the competent choice of conflict management strategies.

NOTES

1. Brian H. Spitzberg and Michael L. Hecht, "A Component Model of Relational Competence," *Human Communication Research* 10 (1984), 575–599.
2. Calvin S. Hall, *A Primer of Freudian Psychology,* 2nd Ed. (New York: World, 1979), p. 28.
3. Ibid.
4. Ibid.
5. Ibid., p. 14.
6. Lewis Coser, *The Functions of Social Conflict* (New York: Free Press, 1956).

8.1 Work with It

Label the following statements by selecting either internal attributions (a) or external attributions (b). Check your answers on page 283.

1. "He did this to me because he wants to get even."
2. "She did this to me because she hates my guts."
3. "He did poorly because his parents expect the worst from him, so he delivers accordingly."
4. "He didn't show for the test because he is probably afraid he will fail."
5. "He made the test too hard, so I flunked it."
6. "Of course she didn't return the laptop. She is an idiot. What do you expect from an imbecile?"
7. "They keep tearing up the parking lots and that is why I was late to class."
8. "I've been in a slump, which is why I am not doing well these days."
9. "She's immoral and only wants you for your money."
10. "He treats you badly because you are so tall. He has a rotten attitude toward others taller than he is."
11. "Luck is against me. Maybe next time I will get lucky."

8.2 Work with It

Identify the theories that best explain the following conflicts. Check your answers on page 283.

1. Conflict situation: I blame my roommate for our current feud. All I can think about is getting even. Yesterday he took my car and returned it on empty. I thought I had plenty of gas so when I took off today I was shocked when I ran out on the way to classes. I had to walk into town and carry a can of gas back to the car three miles each way. I also missed my test. You want to know what makes me mad? I know that he had the money to buy gas, and he must have driven by at least three stations when going through town. He just wanted to get me into trouble with my professor and mess up my grades. He must hate my guts. I am going to retaliate. He has to meet an important study group tonight, and I am going to wait till he is ready to go to tell him he can't use my car. Let's see how he feels about flunking a test.
   a. Which conflict theory discussed in this chapter best explains this conflict?
   b. What is really the cause of the conflict?
   c. How could or should one resolve this conflict?
2. Conflict situation: I am anxious before flying on a trip; so I become irritable and wind up fighting with my partner before I go over insignificant but overblown issues.
   a. Which conflict theory discussed in this chapter best explains this conflict?
   b. What is really the cause of the conflict?
   c. How could or should one resolve this conflict?
3. Conflict situation: I am unhappy in my relationship because I have to do all the housework and my partner won't agree to do more. It seems unfair that I have to do more than my share. Why won't she help out?
   a. Which conflict theory discussed in this chapter best explains this conflict?
   b. What is really the cause of the conflict?
   c. How could or should one resolve this conflict?

8.1 Remember It

Write an essay as though you were writing to a friend. Tell your friend why he or she should understand the different conflict theories. Explain each theory and given an example of a conflict that is best explained by the theory.

7. Joseph Folger and Marshal Scott Poole, *Working through Conflict* (Glenview, IL: Scott Foresman, 1984), p. 15.

8. Alan L. Sillars, "Attributions and Communication in Roommate Conflicts," *Communication Monographs* 47 (1980), 180–200; Alan L. Sillars, "The Sequential and Distributional Structure of Conflict Interactions as a Function of Attributions Concerning the Locus of Responsibility and Stability of Conflicts," in Dan Nimmo (Ed.), *Communication Yearbook 4* (New Brunswick, NJ: Transaction Books, 1980), pp. 217–235.

9. Shawn W. Rosenberg and Gary Wolsfeld, "International Conflict and the Problem of Attribution," *Journal of Conflict Resolution* 21 (1977), 75–103.

10. Ibid., p. 103.

11. Meryl Reis Louis, "How Individuals Conceptualize Conflict: Identification of Steps in the Process and the Role of Personal/Development Factors," *Human Relations* 30 (1977), 451–467.

12. Amy M. Bippus, "Humor Motives, Qualities, and Reactions in Recalled Conflict Episodes," *Western Journal of Communication* 67 (2003), 413–426.

13. Alan Sillars, Linda J. Roberts, and Kenneth E. Leonard, "Cognition during Marital Conflict: The Relationship of Thought and Talk," *Journal of Social and Personal Relationships* 17 (2000) 479–502.

14. Sally Planalp and James M. Honeycutt, "Events that Increase Uncertainty in Personal Relationships," *Human Communication Research* 11 (1985), 593–604.

15. Sally Planalp, Diane K. Rutherford, and James M. Honeycutt, "Events that Increase Uncertainty in Personal Relationships II," *Human Communication Research* 14 (1988), 516–547.

16. Allan L. Sillars and Judith Weisberg, "Conflict as a Social Skill," in Michael E. Roloff and Gerald R. Miller (Eds.), *Interpersonal Processes: New Directions in Theory and Research* (Newbury Park, CA: Sage, 1987), p. 148.

17. Ibid., p. 153.

18. James M. Honeycutt, Kenneth S. Zagacki, and Renee Edwards, "Imagined Interaction and Interpersonal Communication," *Communication Reports* 3 (1990), 1–8.

19. John W. Thibault and Harold H. Kelley, *The Social Psychology of Groups* (New York: John Wiley, 1959); Harold H. Kelley and John W. Thibault, *Interpersonal Relations. A Theory of Interdependence* (New York: John Wiley & Sons, 1978).

20. Kelley and Thibault, pp. 8–9.

21. This concept of fairness is called "distributive justice" in George C. Homans, *Social Behavior: Its Elementary Forms* (New York: Harcourt Brace Jovanovich, 1961); it is called "equity" in Elaine H. Walster, G. William Walster, and Ellen Berscheid, *Equity Theory and Research* (Boston: Allyn & Bacon, 1978).

22. Folger and Poole, p. 24.

23. Folger and Poole, pp. 36–37.

24. Brent D. Ruben, "Communication and Conflict: A System-Theoretic Perspective," *Quarterly Journal of Speech* 64 (1978), 205–206.

25. Delmar M. Hilyard, "Research Models and Designs for the Study of Conflict," in Fred E. Jandt (Ed.), *Conflict Resolution through Communication* (New York: Harper & Row, 1972), pp. 439–451.

9

A Process View of Conflict

Phases, Stages, and Cycles

OBJECTIVES

At the end of this chapter, you should be able to:

- Name and explain the five stages or phases of constructive, successful conflict.

- Identify the five stages in a specific conflict that you experienced.

- Explain the steps in avoidance, chilling effect, and competition conflict cycles.

KEY TERMS

chilling effect
competitive conflict escalation
   cycle
conflict phase
confrontation avoidance cycle
cycle of behavior

differentiation phase
initiation phase
phase theory
prelude to conflict
process
resolution phase

schismogenesis
scripts
triggering event
undesired repetitive pattern (URP)

Whereas Part I explained specifically how to confront someone you know personally and collaborate with that person to create a mutually acceptable agreement, Part II delves deeper into the subject of conflict management by examining factors that escalate or de-escalate conflict. Recall that in Part I we recommended that you take a process view of conflict because processes are what people manage in social situations. While some conflicts may escalate and get out of hand, other conflicts may de-escalate and leave partners feeling better about their relationship. You need to learn about these process factors to better manage interpersonal conflicts. To meet this need, Part II examines the role played by anger, stress, saving face, forgiveness and reconciliation, and mediation in escalating or de-escalating conflict.

Communication scholars often look for patterns of interaction. In Chapter 1, we defined conflict as a problematic situation with certain characteristics. We defined conflict management as the behavior a person employs based on his or her analysis of a conflict situation. Two key terms for our consideration now are "situation" and "behavior." Both are embedded in a series of instances that follow one another (as in a video of people meeting, talking, and departing). Such a view of reality is, as Thomas argued, "concerned with the influence of each event upon the following events."[1] When we learn to take this view, we begin to see situations as phases or stages, reflecting a switch to a process orientation. If the series continues to repeat itself (like a perpetual motion machine), it becomes a cycle. A process view of conflict sees conflicts as a series of stages. In some cases, conflicts become cycles because they get bogged down in particular stages and repeat themselves. We are especially interested in cycles, where we can learn from the past and, it is hoped, intervene to prevent, stop, or change unwanted cycles.

Many writers argue that conflicts proceed through stages. In this chapter, we explore phase theory and the process model of conflict, and demonstrate how choices made in different stages of the conflict may contribute to productive or destructive outcomes. A **conflict phase** is a stage in the interaction that is similar across many conflicts. For example, as we mentioned in Chapter 1, most people understand that the statement "we need to talk" is an invitation to conflict, creating the first stage of interaction, called the initiation phase. Our purpose here is not only to identify the stages through which many conflicts progress, but also to suggest some of the behaviors that contribute to successful resolution of conflict and other behaviors that either go nowhere or cause the conflict to turn violent.

Phase Theories of Conflict

You may have noticed that your conflicts are often alike in the way they are played out: You have a complaint about another person, you point it out to that person, the other responds, the two of you go back and forth for a while, and then find a way to work matters out. **Phase theory** starts with the assumption that conflict unfolds in fairly predictable ways over a period of time and progresses through recognizable stages of interaction. When behaviors are fairly predictable, moving through various stages and creating the possibility of new movement through similar stages, we say that they are cyclic. A **cycle of behavior** exists when people sense repetitiveness in the way something happens. The academic school year is a cycle—you begin in August or September, work through the fall semester or quarter, take exams in late December, take a few days or weeks off, begin classes again, and end in May or June for the summer. It starts all over again the next year until you leave the cycle by graduating or by leaving school. Conflict cycles typically make people feel stuck because there is no apparent end to them.

In Part I, you learned specific behaviors that help resolve or manage a conflict. But managing conflict effectively also requires that we pay attention to the process of the conflict itself. While some conflicts may escalate and get out of hand, other conflicts may de-escalate and leave partners feeling better about their relationship. Our ability to contain conflict escalation depends not only on our knowledge of particular communication behaviors, but also on our understanding of the various processes involved in the way a conflict unfolds.

What does it mean to take a process view of something? A **process** is dynamic, on-going, and continuous (not static, at rest, or fixed). It is evolutionary in nature. Viewing objects, people, events, and social situations as processes means that we understand:

1. Processes have stages or phases of development through growth or deterioration.
2. They have a history in which a distinctive pattern emerges.
3. They consist of continual change over time.
4. They have ingredients that interact (affect one another).
5. At any given point in time and space, they represent some outcome, stage, or state of being (like a picture or a single frame in a film).

The way we talk about something often fails to reflect a process view—such as "the happy couple," "a divorced person," or "an ex-convict"—which suggests that people do not change, are not at one stage of a developing life cycle or relationship, or do not learn from their experiences and grow. Failing to see a conflict as a process explains why some people are not interested in learning how to manage it. So, we don't take a process view:

- when we see something as unchanging (e.g., he was a naughty child, so he is probably a problem adult),
- when we see something as having no history (e.g., nothing in your past is important or affects you today),
- when we see something at its present age only and not as a stage in development (e.g., you will always be this way and never grow old), or
- when we do not consider the ingredients that make up something (e.g., you do not consider how your goals, fears, and abilities, others' expectations for you, and your deadlines or time limits interact to create how you view yourself).

9.1 Think about It

In what ways do you take a non–process view of communication, relationships, or conflict? How can you change your thinking?

A process view of conflict, on the other hand, sees the conflict situation as dynamic, changeable, and moving towards some end. We usually know when conflict begins (we hear the words, "We need to talk"), and we usually know when a conflict ends (e.g., people reach an agreement and maybe shake hands or "kiss and make up"). We know that resolving conflict, however much we might want it, does not end conflict for us forever. We will engage in conflict again and again, and we have a pretty good idea how these conflicts will unfold.

Think about It

How have your conflicts typically played themselves out? Do you sense that there are patterns in your conflicts?

Patterns and Cycles in Constructive Conflict Processes

As depicted in Figure 9.1, a process view suggests that a successfully resolved conflict moves through a series of five recognizable stages, steps, or phases, with each stage affecting the next: the prelude to conflict (known as the frustration or latent stage in some theories), the triggering event (a behavior that at least one person in the conflict points to as the "beginning" of the problem), the initiation phase (where at least one person makes known to the other the presence of a felt conflict), the differentiation phase (where the participants work out the problem using various strategies and tactics), and the resolution phase (where those involved agree to some outcome to the conflict).

Prelude to Conflict

The **prelude to conflict** consists of the variables that make conflict possible between those involved. The prelude comprises four variables:

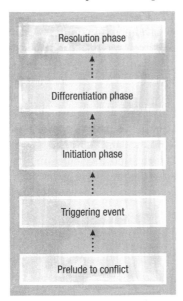

- the participants in the conflict situation (number, age, sex, etc.),
- the relationship between them (which may vary in closeness and distribution of power) and their conflict history,
- other interested parties to the conflict (including bystanders), and
- the physical and social environment of the conflict situation.

In the prelude to conflict, the potential for manifest conflict exists because of the people involved and the other social and physical factors that define the situation. Like the first block in a line of dominoes, these variables affect the course of conflict.

The Participants.   There is no doubt that the people involved in the conflict influence whether a conflict arises and on how it plays out. Participants vary in their temperament, attitudes, and outlook; they also

FIGURE 9.1   The Five Successful Stages of Conflict

vary in the amount of anticipation they experience concerning a conflict.[2] Nye pointed out that both individual characteristics such as defensiveness and frustration as well as interaction patterns such as competition create a potential for conflicts,[3] and Hample and Dallinger argue that those who take conflict personally often propel others into the same behavior.[4] When others are cooperative, we tend to reciprocate. When they are hostile or suspicious, it is difficult to cooperate with them.

Age of the conflicting parties is also a contributing factor. Among married couples, younger parties in conflict seem to react differently to one another than do their older counterparts. In comparison to retired and middle-aged couples, younger couples had a comparatively intense engagement style of interaction, characterized by alternation between analytic confrontation and humorous remarks.[5] Of course factors other than age may also contribute to differences in conflict behavior between younger and older married couples.

In addition to the ages of the people involved in the conflict, the number of people involved may also affect the way the conflict unfolds. Mack and Snyder suggest that the larger the number of people involved in a conflict, the more difficult it is to find a common solution, and the more likely it is coalitions will form.[6]

The Relationship.   The relationship between the conflict participants affects the way they perceive and react to a conflict. Are the participants in a hierarchical or equal relationship? How well do they know each other, both in breadth and depth of knowledge? Does one tend to dominate the other? How have they handled conflict in the past?

Research on serious conflict between dating partners who were considering breaking up suggests that when important issues are addressed it is better to express more affiliation and less forcefulness on one's own point of view. Additionally, dating partners expect emotional support from one another.[7]

The variable with the greatest effect on the enactment of conflict in a situation is the conflict history of the participants—how have they resolved the conflicts in the past? Because of high levels of uncertainty in a new relationship, conflicts may appear threatening. The relationship may not withstand scrutiny under the microscope of conflict analysis. If the participants have engaged in unsatisfactory conflict before, they may fear future conflicts or pollute the new conflict situation with unresolved issues from the past. Research suggests that negotiating pairs who were unsuccessful in a first round of negotiations were not successful in a second round of bargaining with the same partner, and even those who were successful after an unsuccessful first round had less positive outcomes than those who reached agreement the first time.[8] To the extent that conflict participants can approach the conflict in the "here and now," rather than dwell on what happened in the past, conflict history does not realize its negative potential.

Interested Third Parties.   Sometimes outsiders are present when conflicts occur. Often, this has a calming effect on the situation. Mack and Snyder claim, "The pressure for liquidation or control of social conflict from disinterested but affected bystanders is one of the primary limits on its duration, extension, and intensity."[9] At other times, bystanders may egg people on, hoping that the conflict escalates and turns into a brawl. "You tell him, Nick." "Don't let her say that to you, Joy Ann." "You go, girl." And at other times, the conflicting parties may ask the bystanders to participate. Whatever their role, people who have some stake in the conflict—either through participation or from its outcomes—play an important role in the escalation and containment of the conflict.

Morrill and Thomas found, for example, that conflicting parties were more likely to seek outside assistance in resolving the conflict if they had a less involved relationship.[10] Dating couples most often see same-sex friends as their primary supporters, rather than joint friends of the couple. In addition, women felt their position in the conflict was more legitimate when they had support from friends; for men, it was the absence of criticism that indicated legitimacy.[11]

Research examining how spouses confide about conflicts to their friends has resulted in some interesting findings as well. Where wives who experience overall satisfaction with their marriage confide about a conflict to a friend who also is satisfied with her marriage, the conversation is more problem–solution oriented in nature. But when unhappy wives complain to equally unhappy friends, the talk reinforces the conflict and creates a more negative perception of the situation.[12]

Third parties who are not physically present may still affect the outcomes of a conflict situation. In most decision-making situations, there are people who have an interest in the decision made. For example, if parents are deliberating over when an older child may have some privilege, the younger child has an interest in the decision, because it affects when he or she is allowed the same privilege. A teacher making a decision to change a grade for one student has as interested parties the rest of the students in the class. If flexible time is awarded to one employee, other employees have an interest in the decision. So, often when people are working out a conflict, they are doing so with respect to what they think others may think of the decision they make, irrespective of whether those third parties are physically present.

Some evidence suggests that, at least at the interpersonal level, how third parties perceive the behavior of those in conflict depends on their own aggressive tendencies. Results of one study indicated that generally, aggressive people interpret other's behavior as aggressive. However, knowing why a person is acting aggressively reduces impressions of aggressiveness. The research also indicated that people who shun communication see verbally aggressive persons as powerful.[13] Thus, the personality of the third party may influence how she or he views an interpersonal conflict and determine the constructive or destructive role that person plays.

The Physical and Social Environment.　Surprisingly little has been written about the effects of the physical environment on how a conflict is played out. Where a conflict is initiated, whether public or private, owned or shared, comfortable or uncomfortable, and so on, can certainly affect the way it is enacted. This narrative reports an observed conflict.

> I couldn't help but eavesdrop on the couple in the booth next to us in the coffee shop. They were trying to negotiate the details of their divorce. It seemed like they had chosen a public spot to try to control themselves, but as the hour went on they got more and more heated. Now and then one would say, "Okay, let's not shout at each other here." I really felt sorry for them.

The social environment, which is often tied directly to the physical setting, can also affect how people enact conflict episodes. Deutsch noted that any group of people tends to develop techniques, values, symbols, and rules for interacting with one another.[14] A social system has a purpose, determines the nature of membership in the system, and prescribes what behaviors are appropriate and inappropriate within the system. For example, a couple that thinks of conflict as normal probably engages in conflict in a fairly open manner where their children can observe the conflict and see how Mom and Dad work their way to an agreement, whereas a couple who thinks of it as abnormal may do their conflict in hushed tones behind closed doors because they are afraid to let the children see them fight. People develop a sense of where and when it is appropriate or inappropriate to engage in conflict. Thus, whether or not a conflict occurs and how it may occur is determined to some extent by the nature of the social system itself. To understand how conflict is played out, then, we need to have some understanding of the rules and procedures the people involved have created for dealing with conflicts.

9.1 Apply It

Write out a description of a recent conflict that you experienced or observed. What would have happened if there were more or less individuals involved as parties to the conflict? How would the addition or subtraction of interested third parties or bystanders affect the conflict outcome? What effect would changing the time or place have had on the conflict?

The Triggering Event

The **triggering event** or stimulus is a behavior that at least one person in the conflict points to as the "beginning" of the problem. Examples include saying something upsetting, doing something offensive, breaking a relationship rule, or not doing something one is expected to do by others. The triggering event is perceived when the person experiencing the conflict, Person A, observes one of the following behaviors in Person B.

- *Rebuff.* Person A asks Person B for a desired behavior and Person B fails to respond as hoped. For example, you ask your roommate to take a message for you while you are out and your roommate says no.
- *Illegitimate demand.* Person B places or imposes his or her wants, needs, desires, or demands on Person A. For example, you find that your roommate has borrowed your new leather jacket without permission.
- *Criticism.* Person B criticizes or finds fault with what Person A is doing, saying, or feeling without demanding or asking that Person A do something different. For example, your roommate tells you that the paper you are about to turn in is not even close to what the professor wants.
- *Noncumulative annoyance.* Person A realizes a difference in attitude, lifestyle, or opinion between him or her and Person B. For example, you are disturbed by a new political attitude expressed by your roommate and your roommate's efforts to change your thinking about the issue.

- *Cumulative annoyance.* Person A realizes a difference in attitude, lifestyle, or opinion between him or her and Person B and also realizes that it occurred more than once. For example, you realize that it really bothers you when your roommate gets drunk every Friday night and passes out on the couch in the living room.
- *Mutual cumulative annoyance.* Person A and Person B are mutually or interactively involved in the creation of a cumulative annoyance. For example, you and your roommate are purposely bothering each other—not taking each other's messages, bad-mouthing each other to friends, and so on.[15]

The Initiation Phase

The **initiation phase** or response occurs when at least one person makes known to the other that a conflict exists, such as reacting to another's upsetting comment, pointing out the offensive nature of the other's behavior, calling attention to the breaking of a relationship rule, or reminding the other that she or he is expected to do something the person is not doing.

The participants' issue assessment depends on their definition of the issue, and how they define the issue may depend on whether they define it solely in terms of their own concerns or mutual concerns, whether they see how the issue is tied to others, and how large they perceive the issue to be.[16] Given their assessment of the issue and the time and opportunity necessary to reflect, the persons observing the triggering event then choose to confront or avoid the conflict. The choice is the fulcrum of a dilemma: Conflict is necessary to clarify issues, but conflict is feared because of the feelings of vulnerability and frustration it can arouse.[17]

The Differentiation Phase

The **differentiation phase** or ongoing interaction pattern occurs when the participants use constructive or destructive strategies and tactics, presenting both sides of the story, moving back and forth, and escalating and de-escalating. Lasting anywhere from a few minutes to days or even weeks, this is the stage where the conflict becomes quite obvious. Although parties may view the open disagreement as "the conflict," from a communication point of view, the revelation of differences is the fourth phase in the interpersonal conflict process.

This phase serves a useful purpose by allowing both parties to explain how they see the situation giving rise to conflict and what they want to happen as a result of the conflict. Sometimes, only one participant wants to address the conflict; the other person avoids confronting the issues. The relationship, the conflict history of the participants, and their preferred styles in doing conflict all affect how the conflict escalates and how the other person views the escalation behavior.

Differentiation is so stressful that sometimes people cling to rigid behaviors that may have served them in the past but do not serve them well in the present.[18] There are several sources of rigidity in a conflict: personalization of the conflict, in which the conflict is seen as the result of who is involved instead of what is involved; stress of acknowledging opposing stands or hostile or emotional statements; uncertainty about the outcomes of conflict; or the heightened awareness of the consequences of not reaching a conclusion. In established relationships, the decision-making history and established ways of resolving conflict may heighten the problem of escalation, particularly when a conflict is resolved by forced compromise, resulting in clearly identified winners and losers. Early public commitment to inflexible positions may also create destructive differentiation as the middle ground between conflicting parties disappears. All these sources of rigidity may serve to create a competitive escalation cycle, when participants enter the conflict with a win–lose orientation, create threats to the other person's face, and suppress issues rather than resolving them.

When conflicts involve more than two people, the formation of coalitions may add a destructive element in the differentiation phase. Gamson argued that a full-fledged coalition situation is one in which the following conditions are present: There are more than two social units in the conflict, no single solution maximizes the payoff to everyone involved, no single party has sufficient resources to control the decision, and no singular party has the power to veto solutions. Predicting the composition of coalitions requires knowledge of how resources are initially distributed, what the payoff is for each coalition, and how inclined parties are to join with each other regardless of their resources. People joining in a coalition may demand from it a share of the payoff proportional to the amount of resources they contribute.[19]

As conflict progresses, Thomas argued, a number of different dynamics may occur. The participants may reevaluate their positions in the conflict; rather than giving in, they change their minds about the issue. Self-fulfilling prophecies may guide the conflict as participants react to what they think the other is doing. That is, if one person distrusts the other and expects the other to act in ways that are not mutually beneficial, the first person may interpret behaviors in light of that suspicion and react in accordance to them, thus confirming what the person suspected in the beginning. In addition, biases in perception occur, causing people to see their own behaviors as reasonable while viewing the other's as arbitrary. This can result in both participants underestimating their commonalities and missing the other's cooperative overtures or other signs of goodwill in the conflict. Cognitive simplification can also lead to black and white, win or lose thinking and away from the search for mutually satisfactory outcomes.

Research by Alberts and Driscoll focused on the pattern of interaction in conflict episodes that leads to escalation of the conflict or to containment.[20] The authors studied forty married couples, whose responses to a marital satisfaction scale were used to classify them as satisfied, dissatisfied, or mixed (one satisfied partner, one unsatisfied partner). The couples were videotaped as they discussed issues identified on their questionnaire as points of difference between them. Alberts and Driscoll found six patterns couples used to make complaints to the other person. Two in particular were found to escalate the conflict and make an agreement difficult to reach.

In the unresponsiveness pattern, one person makes a complaint, the other person tries to justify the behavior, the justification is denied, and then the discussion is abruptly terminated. This might happen, for example, if Maria tells her husband Raul that she thinks he could have put more effort into painting a door, and he responds that he did the best he could. Maria might say, "Well, it wasn't good enough," and walk away. The conflict never really escalates, but the issue is not resolved either. When partners in conflict are underresponsive to one another, it may lead to a point where one or both of those involved begin to think that conflict is simply not worth the effort required to engage in it.[21]

The escalation pattern is similar to unresponsiveness, except that a counter-complaint is made after denying the accusation. Escalation is a series of charges and counter-charges, a "well, you . . ." pattern, with no real engagement of issues but only a series of complaints.[22] Patterns that lead to conflict containment and agreement were labeled:

1. *Passed* (the complaint is ignored and then dropped). For example, a wife ignores her husband's mutterings about something that displeases him, even though she can hear them. She refuses to allow the conflict to emerge.
2. *Refocused* (the complaint is made but then is put onto a third party or an object outside of the relationship). For example, a husband tells his wife that he is really unhappy about her coming home late from work again, and she tells him that she was unable to leave a meeting even though she really wanted to do so.
3. *Mitigated* (the complaint is made but steadily watered down as the couple talks about the issue). For example, a spouse who believes in having dinner together every day might settle for three to four times a week because of the work schedules each spouse must fulfill.
4. *Responsive* (the participants listen to and validate each other during the interactions and respond to the complaint as a legitimate concern). Interestingly, satisfied married couples reflect each others' positive nonverbal behaviors while engaging in conflict, while dissatisfied couples tend to reflect negative behaviors even if the other person has switched to positive behaviors. Conflict managers should show responsiveness in nonverbal as well as verbal messages.[23]

Throughout the differentiation phase, participants may undergo goal revision as they examine whatever goals they came into the conflict with in light of the other person's response and decide whether it is still fruitful to pursue those goals. The number of issues being dealt with in the conflict may expand or, it is hoped, become more focused. Those in the conflict start to search for solutions, and once solutions are the focus of discussion, the conflict moves into the resolution stage.

The Resolution Phase

The **resolution phase** or outcome occurs when those involved agree to some outcome to the conflict. At this point, we are looking at a constructive conflict situation in which an incident progresses through stages until successfully resolved.

A successful conflict results in a win–win outcome, but at any point along the way, it can turn into a lose–lose or win–lose outcome. It can also end in one of two orientations: resolution (the participants never have to deal with the issue again) or management (the parties have dealt with the issue for now, but not to the satisfaction of all the parties involved, so the issue may come up again in the future). Resolution is a probable outcome when the agreement satisfies all concerned; management is more likely when one party is left dissatisfied.[24]

If the conflict is resolved, then a decision has been made by the parties to end the disagreement, and they are both satisfied with the outcome. When people are able to bring their conflicts to successful resolution, it reinforces positive thinking about conflict. Each successful conflict we engage in increases the chances that future conflicts are productive, because we learn that conflict isn't dreadful and something we must avoid.

9.2 Apply It

Take a sheet of paper and draw three columns on it. Describe three recent conflict-triggering events that happened to you that involved people you know well. For example, a person at work is always borrowing your materials without permission. Compare the way you responded to each of these triggers. Did you respond the same way in each case? If so, why? If not, why?

In examining the process model of conflict, you should realize that we have recast the event we call "conflict" as a process in order to examine in more detail the series of steps or stages from beginning to end. However, like fingerprints, not all conflicts are exactly alike. Some may follow the five-step sequence of events faster or slower, and there is often an uneven distribution of time within the model. For example, the prelude to conflict may occur over several months and the actual overt manifestations of conflict happen in a matter of minutes, or the opposite may occur.

Moreover, as we show in the next section, from this perspective, an unsuccessful conflict is one that becomes diverted at one of the stages. A conflict may begin to cycle through the phases and stop, or it may return to a previous stage when new issues are introduced and added to the conflict. As in examining any communication event, the model may illuminate, but may also distort our expectations. The model is used for explanation and analysis, not as a Procrustean bed into which all conflicts must fit exactly.[25]

The following are a few examples of how successfully managed conflicts proceed through the five stages.

Prelude.   For the first time in about two weeks, my dad, brother, and I were all in the same place at the same time. We went to dinner together, giving us our first chance in weeks to talk together. We had just ordered dinner when the inevitable question came up. What am I going to do after I graduate? I'm not used to sharing details about my life with him because he was never around when I was growing up to take part in my life. When the question came up this time, I had an answer. I told him about the progress I had made in job contacts and other possibilities I was considering. I especially want to travel during the summer with a sports team as a sports information director, but I had made no specific plans. Pop asked if I had sent in my application yet. I said that I hadn't.

Trigger.   My older brother, Stuart, chimed in that I'd better do it soon. This is when the conflict started. The tone in Stuart's voice was what set me off. He was using a condescending attitude toward me, which I hate.

Initiation.   I told him that it was none of his business; that he didn't need to tell me what to do.

Differentiation.   Stuart got mad, as usual, and told me that I was interpreting the situation wrong. He basically told me that I shouldn't feel the way I was because they were only showing that they care. This rubbed me the wrong way because I've had enough of people telling me how I should feel. I tried to explain how I felt but was interrupted several times with the response that I was wrong. I told him that I thought I was being more than fair in telling my family my plans and feelings.

Resolution.   At this point, my father intervened and made us both apologize to each other for making such a scene. We did and moved on to other topics that were safer to discuss.

Prelude.   Our daughter is not a morning person. My husband is one, but I am usually the one who drags her out of bed for school. The other morning I was having a hard time waking up, and I didn't worry too much about it because my husband was up and I didn't have to get up early. I finally got up just before my daughter had to leave.

Trigger.   My husband remarked "I got Jenny up for you." That really irritated me—when he says that it sounds like taking care of our daughter is a favor he does me instead of an obligation we both have.

Initiation.   I remarked that it really bothered me when he said that.

Differentiation.   He said that he realized that it would be easier for all concerned if he got her up this morning. I said I didn't like the way he said it.

Resolution.   He apologized and said he didn't mean it the way it sounded. He appreciated that I always got her up. He was just trying to reassure me that I didn't have to worry about getting Jenny to school. I told him I appreciated being reassured, but really needed to believe we were in this together. He agreed, and we dropped it.

Patterns and Cycles in Destructive Conflict Processes

A process view suggests that unsuccessfully resolved conflicts fail to move through the same five recognizable stages, steps, or phases characteristic of successfully resolved conflicts, and they enter destructive cycles of their own. After starting with the prelude phase, they are diverted at one of the subsequent stages: the triggering event or stimulus, the initiation phase or response, the differentiation phase or ongoing interaction pattern, or the resolution phase or a constructive outcome.

Many activities are repetitive. You probably arise about the same time each day, have a breakfast similar to the one from the day before, put on your clothes in the same order, and walk or drive to classes using the same route as always. Sometimes routines are nearly unconscious behaviors. Routinized events are **scripts** that we perform with little deviation each time we do them. People repeat similar behaviors each time they encounter the event. Without scripted events, it is more difficult getting through the day. Imagine having to make a new decision for each choice that confronts you!

9.3   Think about It

Think about several scripts that you perform regularly. What are the advantages and disadvantages of doing so?

A major disadvantage of scripted behavior is what Cronen and colleagues called an **undesired repetitive pattern (URP),**[26] or the feeling of being trapped in a set of circumstances beyond one's control. Those involved in URPs can have automatic, "knee-jerk" responses to one another: Something one of them says triggers an automatic response in the other, and the episode quickly escalates out of control. It happens when those involved have a pretty good idea of what the other is going to say next, or at least they think they do. URPs recur, are unwanted, and generally occur regardless of the topic or situation. Those in the URP have a feeling that the pattern is hard, if not impossible, to avoid.

URPs sometime have an escalation effect, in which each exchange between those involved gets increasingly intense. **Schismogenesis** (the escalation of the cycle) occurs when the behaviors of one person intensify the behaviors of another person.[27] Schismogenesis is complementary in nature when the exchanges balance each other (e.g., as one person becomes more dominant, the other becomes more submissive; as one person shows off, the other becomes more admiring, which leads to more exhibitionism). Schismogenesis is symmetrical when each person tries to outdo the other's behavior. Seeking revenge often leads to symmetrical schismogenesis, as blood feuds escalate through retaliation after retaliation.

The belief that conflicts are cyclical is widespread in the conflict literature. It is not the conflict occurring frequently within a relationship that makes it dysfunctional; it is rather the repetitive, unchanging, and negative way in which it recurs that creates dysfunctional conflict. When people are locked in a set of behaviors and seem unable or unwilling to change those behaviors, and when issues are not resolved in some way, conflict can become a destructive element in the relationship. Productive conflict behavior is flexible and varied; these destructive cycles are inflexible and unchanging.

Three dysfunctional conflict cycles are common:

- the confrontation avoidance cycle
- the chilling effect
- the competitive conflict escalation cycle

A key point is that issues are not resolved in any of the cycles, which stem, in large part, from the attitudes people have about conflict and from the way those attitudes are validated by their conflict behavior.

The Confrontation Avoidance Cycle

The first of the three dysfunctional conflict cycles is confrontation avoidance, which is depicted in Figure 9.2. Chapter 1 noted that the bulk of conflict resolution advice is slanted toward open conflict or confrontation, but we now know that not every conflict requires engagement. Some issues are better left alone. Either they are unimportant or they may take too much time and energy to deal with constructively.

The **confrontation avoidance cycle** is characteristic of those people whose first impulse is to avoid initiating conflict or to quickly withdraw when conflicts arise. In this case, we are saying that some people tend to avoid confrontation with most everyone and with most issues. We are not talking about a single instance of parties avoiding a conflict, but rather a

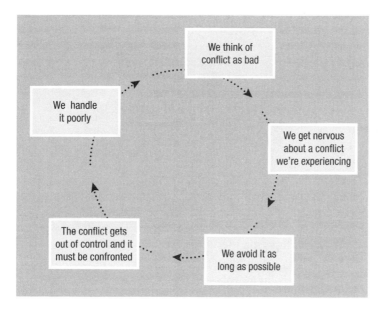

FIGURE 9.2   The Conflict Avoidance Cycle. The cycle begins
with the belief that conflict is something that we should avoid if at
all possible. Because we would like to avoid conflict, experiencing
one makes us nervous. Generally, something that makes us nervous is
something we put off. Unfortunately, many issues worsen when left
alone, so eventually we have to confront them. Our anxiety causes
us to handle the conflict badly. Our negative perception of conflict is
confirmed, and the cycle starts again.

pattern that an individual displays in responding to conflict. This type of conflict management
style is similar to the communication styles of shyness or reticence because it occurs across
situations and people. Typically, unsuccessful conflict management becomes mired down in
one of the first four stages, namely at stage two. It is at the choice-making portion of the initiation stage that people often get stuck in an avoidance cycle. When one sees confrontation in
general as something to avoid, she or he can easily decide to avoid the current confrontation.
If one cannot avoid this particular confrontation, the person who generally avoids confrontation has his or her negative perceptions reinforced when conflict is finally addressed after it
has gotten beyond the stage where productive resolution is possible.

In a conflict avoidance cycle, a conflict has a prelude stage (e.g., one or more of
the participants has a past history of poorly managing conflicts), followed by a stage two
triggering event (e.g., one partner forgets an important date), but instead of progressing to
stage three, initiation, the offended individual does not initiate the conflict because she or
he prefers to avoid most confrontations. Either the conflict isn't resolved, which hurts the
relationship, or issues build up until one eventually erupts, resulting in a mismanaged conflict. This is reinforcing because the pain associated with the previous conflict discourages
one or both partners from wanting to address future issues.

Bobbi Foote's conflict artwork depicts her desire to pretend conflict doesn't exist by keeping her head in the sand. Nevertheless, she does keep an eye out for problems coming her way.

For example, some spouses have learned in their marriages that they are better off avoiding some conflicts, as in Bill's case.

> **Prelude.**   This is a second marriage for both of us, and my wife brought three kids with her. Her oldest daughter seems really wacky to me.
>
> **Trigger.**   Her daughter's nutty behavior is a problem. Last week, she telephoned her boyfriend who is in Europe and ran up a $300 telephone bill. However, I don't comment on it, even though it is getting worse. I feel that it is not worth creating a scene.

There was no initiation stage (or differentiation or resolution), because Bill chose to avoid confronting his wife or her daughter. Thus, the issue is unresolved and may continue for years to come. Interestingly, this avoidance behavior is more typical of husbands than of wives in marital relationships.[28]

Roloff and Ifert claim that confrontation avoidance can serve useful purposes, as long as it eliminates arguing and does no damage to the relationship.[29] Sometimes, avoidance in the present allows for the reintroduction of a difficult topic at a later time.[30] However, if any participant in the conflict feels that leaving the issue unresolved is more costly than confrontation, avoidance is potentially destructive.[31]

This is not the same as avoiding particular topics within a relationship;[32] conflict avoidance involves delaying an important issue until it is too late, hoping it just goes away. In Bill's case above, the daughter is creating some problems that need attention, but Bill is avoiding the issues.

Hocker and Wilmot identified misassumptions about conflict.[33] Taken together, we can identify these behaviors as a confrontation avoidance cycle. Probably the most widespread misassumption about conflict, and the one that has the greatest chance of creating a confrontation avoidance cycle, is the notion that conflict is abnormal. People who experience conflict want to end it as soon as possible so that their lives can "return to normal"—harmony being the norm. The truth is that both excessive conflict and excessive harmony are abnormal. Harmony and conflict are processes in life; people move back and forth between them. Harmony in a relationship is desirable, but it does not allow growth because it does not allow change. Rummel noted that "the desire to eradicate conflict, the hope for harmony and universal cooperation, is the wish for a frozen, unchanging world with all relationships fixed in their patterns—with all in balance."[34] This misassumption affects the way people approach the study of conflict management. They are motivated to learn about conflict so they can do it better, and faster; their motivation is not to gain a true understanding of the process while they are in it.

Related to the notion that conflicts are abnormal is the idea that conflicts are pathological: They are symptoms of a system that is functioning incorrectly. Some conflicts are indeed pathological. We have all had the experience of observing people who continued a conflict long after it made any sense to do so. For the most part though, conflict is a sign that a system (an interpersonal relationship, a task group, or an organization) is functioning well and testing itself to make sure the boundaries are clear and understandable to those involved.

Another misassumption, perpetuated by numerous popular writings on conflict management, focuses on reducing or avoiding confrontation. Some people avoid conflict as long as they can, and therefore the problem continues.

At the risk of oversimplification, one could identify two basic approaches to conflict interaction—confronting and avoiding—although people may do both in different relationships. When dealing with an avoider, one may have to heighten the avoider's awareness of the conflict so that it is impossible to ignore. For example, a newly married couple may have different expectations about how to account for their whereabouts to the other. The wife may frequently leave the house without indicating a destination or return time. The more conscientious husband indicates that such behavior is worrisome but gets little response from his wife. Were he to copy his wife's behavior for a few days, she might realize how inconsiderate her behavior is. Communicating one's needs to the other is not necessarily the most effective way to resolve a conflict if the other does not understand the negative aspects of the behavior involved.

9.3 Apply It

Compare two conflicts in which avoiding worked in different ways—one conflict you avoided eventually resolved itself, and another you avoided that ended up getting worse because you put off confronting it.

The "Chilling Effect": A Diminished Communication Cycle

A special case of avoidance is called the **chilling effect,** in which one person in a relationship withholds grievances from the other, usually due to fear of the other person's reaction.[35] This cycle is presented visually in Figure 9.3. People are likely to avoid conflict in low-commitment

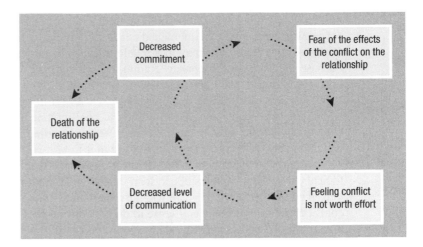

FIGURE 9.3   The Chilling Effect in Conflict. The chilling effect begins with the perception that conflict has negative effects. This fear leads us to believe that conflict is not worth the effort it would take to enact. When conflicts are avoided, however, other types of communication in the relationship decrease. A decrease in communication often leads to a decrease in a commitment to the relationship. After several cycles of decreased communication and decreased commitment, we may simply cycle out of the relationship altogether.

relationships, whereas in strong, committed relationships, conflict is more spontaneous and emotional.[36] Research indicates that a chilling effect is likely to occur when the other person appears to have attractive alternatives to the relationship with the withholder and when the other's commitment to the withholder seems weak. If you are worried that your friend does not care much about you and that your friend could easily leave the relationship, you are not likely to tell your friend when you have a grievance. Conversely, if you are not worried about my leaving because I have no alternatives and care about you, you are more likely to express your dislikes and desires. You have nothing to fear from conflict.[37]

A milder version of the chilling effect occurs when one avoids confronting another because she or he feels powerless to do so.[38] In stronger cases, even committed partners, who are sometimes trapped in abusive relationships, fear confrontation with their partners. The chilling effect is different from the avoidance cycle in that it exists only between two people rather than with everyone in general and includes an element of fear (afraid of the other or afraid of losing the other).

Here is another case of how unsuccessful conflict becomes mired down in one of the first four stages. In this example, the conflict has a prelude stage (e.g., one or more of the participants has reason to fear the reaction of the other person based on a past history of abuse during conflict), followed by a stage two triggering event (e.g., one partner does something that upsets the other), but instead of progressing to the stage three initiation (or later stages), the offended individual does not initiate the conflict because he or she again fears the outcome.

The chilling effect focuses on the negative aspects of the other person that irritate or anger the withholder. These negative aspects become areas of perceived incompatibility and evolve into ongoing conflicts. Sometimes the withholder describes the conflict to friends or other third parties but does not confront the irritating person; therefore the conflicts remain unexpressed. Generally, the withholder does not confront the other because of fear of damaging the relationship. However, a chilling effect is negative in desirable, ongoing relationships because it puts communication barriers between those involved, which undermines the relationship and mutual happiness for the partners.

There are two ways to respond to a threatening partner. First, in cases where one merely lacks the habit of asserting oneself, one may overcome this fear and learn to stand up to the other person, but this is not possible in cases where the partner is stronger, meaner, and better equipped to abuse. Second, people caught in controlling, abusive relationships have to seek outside help (usually the police, courts, or other authorities). The best time to counter abuse is the first time it happens, because after that it becomes more difficult to take action against it.

The Competitive Conflict Escalation Cycle

The third of the three dysfunctional conflict cycles is the **competitive conflict escalation cycle,** in which the conflict bogs down in the differentiation stage when competitive interests lead to divergence rather than integration. Figure 9.4 illustrates this cycle.[39] In this cycle, the participants are so concerned with winning that they are unable to respond to integrative messages, if indeed those messages even make it into the conflict interaction.

Prelude. I already knew where my favorite blouse was—it was in my sister's room. She seems to have this habit of borrowing whatever she wants without my permission. I went into her room and . . .

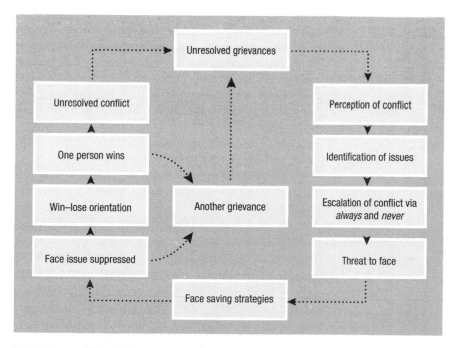

FIGURE 9.4 The Competitive Conflict Escalation Cycle

Trigger.   under her bed was where I found my blouse. I was so angry that I had KILL written on my forehead. I went searching for my sister throughout the house, like a lion searches for its prey. When I found her . . .

Initiation.   I brought up all the past times that she had taken something from me without permission, and then I accused her of "stealing" my blouse.

Differentiation.   She started screaming at me, and I called her a kleptomaniac. Neither of us was trying to de-escalate the conflict.

Resolution.   She stormed off to her bedroom and I went to mine. We haven't spoken for two days. But like past occurrences, we will eventually get over it. At least until something like this happens again!

A common occurrence, the competitive conflict escalation cycle is the third example of how an unsuccessful conflict becomes mired down in one of the first four stages, namely at stage four—differentiation. Here, the conflict has a prelude stage (e.g., one or more of the participants has a past history of poorly managing conflicts), followed by a stage two triggering event (e.g., one person takes something she shouldn't or a partner forgets an important date). The conflict moves through stage three, initiation, but gets mired down in stage four, differentiation, instead of progressing to the final stage, resolution. Like the preceding two destructive cycles, the resulting process takes on quite a different form from that of a successfully resolved conflict.

Pruitt and Rubin argue that competition in a conflict creates a pattern of interaction that intensifies the competition and the desire to outdo the other. Whereas the competition may start with more friendly competition, later moves become more unfriendly, increasing the number of issues in the conflict. As issues are introduced, the conflict is less likely to focus on a particular issue and is more likely to result in an irritating universal level such as "You're always bugging me." Moreover, although the conflict may have started with one person's desire to simply win, the desire to win is distorted into a desire to win coupled with a desire to hurt the other with the loss. More parties may become involved as the conflict escalates. The most difficult part about this process, though, is the fact that each competitive move creates a difficult to reverse transformation in the conflict situation, making it more and more difficult for those in the conflict to de-escalate because they see it as "backing down."[40]

There are a number of behaviors that contribute to escalation that we should avoid, such as the following.

- *Face threats:* The individual does not feel accepted by the other.
- *Blaming tendency:* Rather than focusing on the problem, people focus on one another. Blaming the other and holding oneself blameless is an almost guaranteed way to turn a conflict into an escalation cycle.
- *Counterattack:* One person brings up an issue, relatively focused, and the other person ignores it, issuing a counterattack.
- *Hostile verbal and nonverbal displays:* These are not the messages themselves, but the way in which messages are framed. Interruptions, talkovers, and expressions of disgust have been demonstrated to escalate conflict, particularly in parent–adolescent dyads.[41]
- *Distrust:* Certainly, some people do not appear to deserve trust, but in ongoing relationships one needs to give the other person a chance. Mistrust creates escalation cycles, and too much trust makes one too vulnerable, but somewhere in the middle is an attitude that allows two people to work toward an outcome that benefits both of them.

- *Rigidity:* There are several sources of rigidity in a conflict: personalization of the conflict, in which the conflict is seen as the result of who is involved instead of what is involved; stress of acknowledging opposing stands or hostile or emotional statements; uncertainty about the outcomes of conflict; or the heightened awareness of the consequences of not reaching a conclusion.
- *Coalitions:* Coalitions are frequent when three or more roommates live together, in class projects where the same grade is assigned to all the participants, in organizations where people depend on one another to do their jobs, and so on. Whenever possible, the parties should avoid coalition formation because it tends to lead to a win–lose or us versus them mentality that makes resolution of the conflict difficult.
- *Communication distortion:* This enables both participants to develop and maintain their distorted views of each other and feed their mutual hostility. As hostility and distrust increase, tactics tend to become more coercive.

Figure 9.5 illustrates how the negative conflict cycles spin off from the successful five stage model and subvert its productive nature. Thus, we may view the five-stage successfully managed conflict and its destructive spin off cycles as processes.

9.4 Apply It

Compare two conflicts, one that escalated and another that did not. What was the difference between the two? What were the outcomes?

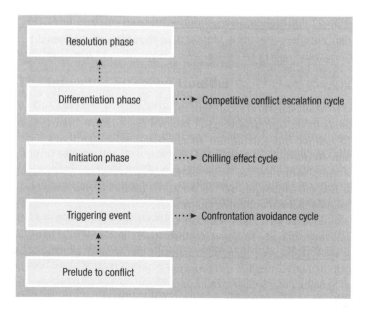

FIGURE 9.5 Destructive Conflict Spin Off Cycles

Manage It

In this chapter, we describe the process of conflict and different ways conflict unfolds as people begin to experience issues with someone close to them. The key to effective conflict management is an understanding of both what gives rise to conflict (what we have termed the prelude to conflict) and what occurs at the different stages in the process of conflict—the triggering event, initiation phase, differentiation phase, and the resolution phase.

The prelude to conflict sets the stage by identifying the people, place, and time of the conflict. At the next stage, a triggering event functions as a stimulus, often leading to the initiation of conflict, followed by the initiation phase, which is the response to a triggering event. The subsequent differentiation phase is the ongoing interaction pattern in which most of the conflict communication occurs. Finally, in the resolution phase conflict participants come to a mutually satisfactory agreement or outcome.

Often people will get caught up in destructive cycles that do not allow their conflict to progress to some satisfactory outcome. The conflict avoidance cycle is characteristic of a relationship between people whose first impulse is to avoid initiating conflict or to quickly withdraw when conflicts arise. Here is an example of how unsuccessful conflict becomes mired down in one of the first four stages, namely at stage two. In this case, the conflict has a prelude stage (e.g., one or more of the participants has a past history of poorly managing conflicts), followed by a stage two triggering event (e.g., one partner forgets an important date), but instead of progressing to stage three initiation, the offended individual does not initiate the conflict because she or he prefers not to engage in conflict.

The chilling effect conflict cycle has a prelude stage (e.g., one or more participants has reason to fear the other person's reaction based on a past history of abuse during conflict), followed by a stage two triggering event (e.g., one partner does something that upsets the other). Like the conflict avoidance cycle, instead of progressing to stage three initiation, the offended individual does not initiate the conflict because he or she fears the outcome.

The competitive conflict escalation cycle has a prelude stage (e.g., one or more of the participants has a past history of poorly managing conflicts) followed by a stage two triggering event (e.g., one partner forgets an important date) and moves through stage three initiation, but gets locked into stage four differentiation, instead of progressing to the final stage five resolution.

The way we view our relationship with the other person, our past successes and failures in enacting conflict with the other, how we identify an issue, how we assign blame, and how we voice our complaint all affect our pattern of interaction in conflict situations. Potentially productive conflict behavior exists somewhere in the maze of options. In each stage of productive conflict we can choose to spin off into the avoidance, chilling effect, and competitive cycles. As with the destructive cycles, productive conflict behavior stems from attitudes and beliefs about conflict.

When we see conflict as a normal part of relationships and when we listen to others and assert ourselves, we are less likely to become mired down in destructive conflict cycles. Becoming aware of behavior and ways of thinking about conflict can help us; the more we examine our behaviors at each stage of a conflict, the more successful we become in dealing with the conflicts in our lives.

9.1 Work with It

Using the process approach, read the following case study and determine what stages are illustrated. What type of nonproductive conflict cycle is illustrated by this case study? What do you think happens later in this situation? By applying the ideas learned in this chapter, analyze the conflict to see what has gone wrong and what other choices could have led to better outcomes.

> I was having dinner with my parents. When the topic of politics arose, I made a negative comment about the current U.S. president, in response to which my father called me an idiot. I felt my dad wasn't even listening to my point of view but rather looking for ways to criticize me. I told him that he wasn't listening. This in turn angered him and he told me that I'm someone impossible to carry on a conversation with. I told him that he was regressing to the way he treated me when I was a child. He then said, "When is your attitude going to change? Are you going to ever grow up?" I told him I was trying but felt that he was too demanding in his expectations of my maturity. As usual, my mother was eating without saying anything.

9.2 Work with It

Identify each of the stages (prelude, triggering, initiation, differentiation, and resolution) the following argument is going through. After doing this exercise, check your answers on page 283–284.

1. I work in a clothing store and since it is back to school time I have seen a lot of parent–child conflicts. I know that parents and their children are from two different time periods. I also realize that usually the parents are paying for the clothing, so they feel that they should have a lot to say about buying it. They have different ideas over what is cool, and what isn't. Just today I saw a boy having a disagreement over what to try on. The boy wanted to wear the big baggy pants, but his mother refused to let him get them. This disagreement went on for about five minutes. The whole time the boy constantly argued that this was the way everyone else wears them. Then the mother went into why they were so horrible. She complained mostly about how having the jeans dragging on the floor would bring in all the germs that he walked through. No matter what the boy said his mother would find something to disagree about. Finally the boy gave in and the mother got him to buy a pair of jeans that were much shorter.

2. A few weeks ago, my dad and I went to Subway to eat lunch. My dad planned on buying one sub and then getting the next free for me. Subway has this sticker accumulation deal where you get one sticker for every sub you buy. When you fill up the card you get a free sub, but they clearly state on the card that you can't redeem the full card for a free sub on the same day you filled it up. Meanwhile, my dad asked me to take a seat and wait while he got a sub. Of course he got a sticker for buying his sub and put it on his card, which filled his card up. He came over to me and left his order and then went back to order another sub. I guess he thought he could get away with something. When it came time to pay for the second sub, darned if he didn't turn in his card filled with stickers. When he did this, the owner responded with "you couldn't get the free sub the same day you fill up the card." My dad got angry and said that he was not willing to come back the next day to get his free sub. The owner proceeded to ring up my sub on the cash register, and my dad started yelling and cursing. The owner yelled back, and told my dad to leave the store. I tried to get my dad to calm down and just leave but he wouldn't. They both engaged in a shouting match for another minute before my dad stormed out of the store cursing, when the owner started to telephone the police.

9.1 **Remember It**

Write an essay in which you apply the ideas presented in Chapter 9 to your life situation. Make sure to address the following topics.

1. Define *process* and pick a successfully resolved conflict and describe it in terms of the five stages or phases of constructive, successful conflict.
2. Describe the steps of a real or imagined conflict in which the parties avoided confrontation. What is the outcome? (Save an example of a chilling effect for the next topic.)
3. Describe the steps of a real or imagined conflict in which one of the parties experienced a chilling effect. What is the outcome?
4. Describe the steps of a real or imagined conflict in which the parties engaged in a competition conflict cycle. What is the outcome?

NOTES

1. Kenneth W. Thomas, "Conflict and Conflict Management," in M. D. Dunnett (Ed.), *The Handbook of Industrial and Organizational Psychology* (Chicago: Rand McNally, 1976), p. 893.
2. Denise Haunani Cloven and Michael E. Roloff, "Cognitive Turning Effects of Anticipating Communication on Thought about an Interpersonal Conflict," *Communication Reports* 8 (1995), 1–9.
3. R. D. Nye, *Conflict among Humans* (New York: Spring Publishing, 1973), p. 94.
4. Dale Hample and Judith M. Dallinger, "A Lewinian Perspective on Taking Conflict Personally: Revision, Refinement, and Validation of the Instrument," *Communication Quarterly* 43 (1995), 297–319.
5. P. Zietlow and A. Sillars, "Life-Stage Differences in Communication during Marital Conflicts," *Journal of Social and Personal Relationships* 5 (1988), 223–245
6. Raymond W. Mack and Richard C. Snyder, "Cooperators and Competitors in Conflict: A Test of the 'Triangle' Model," *Journal of Conflict Resolution* 22 (1978), 393–410.
7. Amy S. Ebesu Hubbard, "Conflict between Relationally Uncertain Romantic Partners: The Influence of Relational Responsiveness and Empathy," *Communication Monographs* 68 (2001), 400–414.
8. See, for example, Kathleen M. O'Connor, Josh A. Arnold, and Ethan R. Burris, "Negotiators' Bargaining Histories and Their Effects on Future

Negotiation Performance," *Journal of Applied Psychology* 90 (2005), 350–362.
9. Raymond W. Mack and Richard C. Snyder, "The Analysis of Social Conflict: Toward an Overview and Synthesis," in Fred E. Jandt (Ed.), *Conflict Resolution through Communication* (New York: Harper and Row, 1973), p. 49.
10. Calvin Morrill and Cheryl King Thomas, "Organizational Conflict Management as a Disputing Process: The Problem of Social Escalation," *Human Communication Research* 18 (1992), 400–429.
11. Renate C. A. Klein and Robert M. Milardo, "The Social Context of Couple Conflict: Support and Criticism from Informal Third Parties," *Journal of Social and Personal Relationships* 17 (2000), 618–637.
12. Danielle Julien, Howard J. Markman, Sophie Léveillé, Elise Chartrand, and Jean Bégin, "Networks' Support and Interference with Regard to Marriage: Disclosures of Marital Problems to Confidants," *Journal of Family Psychology,* 8 (1994), 16–31; see also Danielle Julien, Nicole Tremblay, Isabelle Béllanger, Monique Dubé, Jean Bégin, and Donald Bouthillier, "Interaction Structure of Husbands' and Wives' Disclosure of Marital Conflict to their Respective Best Friend," *Journal of Family Psychology* 14 (2000), 286–303.
13. David L. Alloway and Janis F. Andersen, "Individual Differences of the Perceptions of Verbal Aggression," paper presented at the Western Speech

Communication Association Convention, San Diego, February 1988.

14. Morton Deutsch, "Conflicts: Productive or Destructive," *Journal of Social Issues* 25 (1969), p. 8.

15. Hal Witteman, "Analyzing Interpersonal Conflict: Nature of Awareness, Type of Initiating Event, Situational Perceptions, and Management Styles," *Western Journal of Communication* 56 (1992), p. 264.

16. Ibid.

17. Joseph Folger and Marshall Scott Poole, *Working through Conflict* (Glenview, IL: Scott Foresman, 1984), p. 60.

18. Ibid., p. 63.

19. William A. Gamson, "A Theory of Coalition Formation," in Claggett C. Smith (Ed.), *Conflict Resolution: Contributions of the Behavioral Sciences* (Notre Dame, IN: University of Notre Dame Press, 1971), pp. 146–156.

20. Jess K. Alberts and Gillian Driscoll, "Containment vs. Escalation: The Trajectory of Couples' Conversational Complaints," *Western Journal of Communication* 56 (1992), 394–412.

21. Also known as the demand/withdraw pattern of conflict, this has been tentatively linked to individual personality attributes by John P. Caughlin and Anita L. Vangelisti, "An Individual Difference Explanation of Why Married Couples Engage in the Demand/Withdraw Pattern of Conflict," *Journal of Social and Personal Relationships* 17 (2000), 523–551. Demand/withdraw patterns of conflict are also associated with low self-esteem and high alcohol and drug use in adolescents and parents; see John P. Caughlin and Rachel S. Malis, "Demand/Withdraw Communication between Parents and Adolescents: Connections with Self-Esteem and Substance Abuse," *Journal of Social and Personal Relationships* 21 (2004), 125–148.

22. Other research has shown that cross-complaining leads to escalation. See, for example, Ian Dersley and Anthony Wootton, "Complaint Sequences within Antagonist Argument," *Research on Language and Social Interaction* 33 (2000), 375–406. Additionally, cross-complaining is characteristic of distressed parent–child dyads. See Paul J. Lattimore, Hugh L. Wagner, and Simon Gowers, "Conflict Avoidance in Anorexia Nervosa: An Observational Study of Mothers and Daughters," *European Eating Disorders Review* 8 (2000), 355–368.

23. Danielle Julien, Mathide Brault, Élise Chartrand, and Jean Bégin, "Immediacy Behaviours and Synchrony in Satisfied and Dissatisfied Couples," *Canadian Journal of Behavioural Science* 32 (2000), 84–90.

24. Thomas, p. 895.

25. In Greek mythology, Procrustes was an innkeeper with only one bed. If his guest was too short for the bed, he stretched the guest to fit; if the guest was too long, he cut off the guest's legs to fit.

26. Vernon E. Cronen, W. Barnett Pearce, and Lonna M. Snavely, "A Theory of Rule-Structure and Types of Episodes and a Study of Perceived Enmeshment in Undesired Repetitive Pattern ('URPs')," in Dan Nimmo (Ed.), *Communication Yearbook 3* (New Brunswick, NJ: Transaction Books, 1979), pp. 225–240.

27. Gregory Bateson, *Naven,* 2nd Ed. (Stanford, CA: Stanford University Press, 1958).

28. Ann Buysse, Armand DeClercq, Lesley Verhhofstadt, Else Heene, Herbert Roeyers, and Paulette Van Oost, "Dealing with Relational Conflict: A Picture in Milliseconds," *Journal of Social and Personal Relationships* 17 (2000), 574–597.

29. Michael E. Roloff and Danette E. Ifert, "Conflict Management through Avoidance: Withholding Complaints, Suppressing Arguments, and Declaring Topics Taboo," in Sandra Petronio, *Balancing the Secrets of Private Disclosures* (Mahwah, NJ: Lawrence Erlbaum Associates, Publishers, 2000), pp. 151–163; Denise Haunani Solomon, Leanne K. Knobloch, and Mary Anne Fitzpatrick, "Relational Power, Marital Schema, and Decisions to Withhold Complaints: An Investigation of the Chilling Effect on Confrontation in Marriage," *Communication Studies* 55 (2004), 146–171.

30. Michael E. Roloff and Danette Ifert Johnson, "Reintroducing Taboo Topics: Antecedents and Consequences of Putting Topics Back on the Table," *Communication Studies* 52 (2001), 37–50.

31. Ibid., pp. 57–58.

32. See, for example, Laura K. Guerrero and Walid A. Afifi, "Some Things Are Better Left Unsaid: Topic Avoidance in Family Relationships," *Communication Quarterly* 43 (1995), 276–296.

33. William W. Wilmot and Joyce L. Hocker, *Interpersonal Conflict* 5th Ed. (Dubuque: Wm. C. Brown, 1998), pp. 9–11.

34. R. J. Rummel, *Understanding Conflict and War: The Conflict Helix,* Vol. 2 (Beverly Hills, CA: Sage Publications, 1976); "A Catastrophe Theory Model of the Conflict Helix, with Tests," *Behavioral Science* 32 (1987), p. 238.

35. Michael E. Roloff and Denise H. Cloven, "The Chilling Effect in Interpersonal Relationships: The

Reluctance to Speak One's Mind," in Dudley D. Cahn (Ed.), *Inmates in Conflict: A Communication Perspective* (Hillside, NJ: Lawrence Erlbaum Associates, 1990), pp. 49–76.

36. Lorel Scott and Robert Martin, "Value Similarity, Relationship Length, and Conflict Interaction in Dating Relationships: An Initial Investigation," paper presented at the annual meeting of the Speech Communication Association, Chicago, November 1986.

37. Ibid.

38. Theodore A. Avtgis, "Adult-Child Control Expectancies: Effects on Taking Conflict Personally toward Parents," *Communication Research Reports* 19 (2002), 226–236.

39. Several authors have noted that once a conflict is initiated, the greatest pressures are toward escalation rather than toward containment and management. See, for example, Morton Deutsch, "Conflicts: Productive or Destructive?" *Journal of Social Issues* 25 (1969), 7–41; Louis Kriegsberg, *The Sociology of Social Conflicts* (Englewood Cliffs, NJ: Prentice Hall, 1973); Dean G. Pruitt and Jeffrey Z. Rubin, *Social Conflict: Escalation, Stalemate, and Settlement* (New York: Random House, 1986); R. D. Nye, *Conflict among Humans* (New York: Spring Publishing, 1973).

40. Pruitt and Rubin, pp. 7–8.

41. Sherry L. Beaumont and Shannon L. Wagner, "Adolescent-Parent Verbal Conflict: The Roles of Conversational Styles and Disgust Emotions," *Journal of Language and Social Psychology* 23 (2004), 338–368.

10 Conflict Climate

Power, Distrust, and Defensiveness

OBJECTIVES

At the end of this chapter, you should be able to:

- Describe the role that climate plays in general in conflict situations.

- Describe specifically the role played by an imbalance of power in a conflict situation and explain how to equalize power.

- Describe specifically the role played by distrust in a conflict situation and explain how to create trust.

- Describe specifically the role played by defensive behaviors in a conflict situation and explain how to engage and encourage supportive behaviors.

- Explain how the concept of defensive behavior differs from that of power imbalance.

KEY TERMS

conflict climate
defensive behaviors
harmful conflict climate
healthy trust
imbalance of power

mixed motive situation
neutral speech
nurturing conflict climate
power
powerful speech

powerless speech
Prisoner's Dilemma (PD)
supportive behaviors
trust
unhealthy trust

As you move from one location to another, you are aware of changes in the emotional tone of voices, the looks on people's faces, their body movements, dress code, and room décor. If you enter a location where a party is held, you are likely to encounter noise, a crowd of young people, loud music, a lot of social interaction, and a dress code that fits the occasion. You might smell cigarette smoke and alcohol. Many partygoers view a party as a positive experience and conducive to socializing or else they would leave. Conversely, at another location such as a hospital's patient ward, you probably encounter quiet, highly restricted interaction and access by the public, no drinking of alcohol, smoking, or use of cell phones, and many people in a variety of medical uniforms. Perhaps you smell a sterile environment that you associate with hospitals. If you were not visiting a close member of the family who is a patient, you would probably want to leave the hospital as soon as possible, probably immediately at the close of visiting hours. Depending on the event or place, there is a climate or an atmosphere that makes you feel comfortable or uncomfortable in a psychological as well as physical sense.

In the previous chapter, we described conflict from a process point of view. We know that physical processes, such as plant growth, depend on their physical environments to nurture them. Similarly, social processes like conflict management depend on a nurturing social climate. Although the concept of social climate is difficult to describe in concrete terms, we are still aware of it and its effects on our interactions. Of the many factors or properties that are part of the climate, we limit our scope of a **conflict climate,** or the psychological atmosphere impacting a conflict, to these opposing concepts: imbalance of power versus equity, distrust versus trust, and defensive versus supportive behavior.

Conflict management fails when it suffers from a **harmful conflict climate,** consisting of an imbalance of power, distrust, and defensiveness, which foster accommodation (chilling effect) or competition (meeting force with force). We learned in Chapter 9 that one cannot expect the parties to cooperate if they fear the other and simply give in (accommodation) to avoid the wrath of the other (chilling effect), which is unlikely to produce a mutually satisfying outcome. Moreover, some may use force to combat force if caught in a competition conflict cycle that escalates and gets out of hand. Conversely, conflict management is successful in other situations because it benefits from a **nurturing conflict climate,** which encourages openness, assertiveness, and cooperation. We can expect to collaborate in a nurturing conflict climate, which is far more likely to produce mutually satisfying outcomes.

The purpose of this chapter is to describe the role played by the climate in conflict situations and to explain how to engage in specific behaviors that contribute to a nurturing or harmful conflict climate. To help you learn how to produce a nurturing conflict climate to more successfully manage conflict, we explain how to increase equality, trust, and supportiveness and how to avoid their negative counterparts. We begin by explaining the role of power in conflict climates.

Power Imbalance versus Equality

Recently my parents and I argued about my job. My parents don't want me to work while in school because they think it could interfere with my studies. But in reality they don't give me enough money to do what I want to do. While talking to my parents they feel that only their opinions are legitimate. They do not even consider what I have to say and very rarely even give me a chance to speak.

In general, **power** is the ability to influence or control events.[1] People have power over us to the extent that we depend on them. In addition, people have power over us to the extent that they can affect our goal achievement, and to the extent that they have resources we need to accomplish our goals. In our daily routine, we encounter people who are more or less powerful than we are, and these are often cases of legitimate power differences. Legitimate power recognizes that a situation exists in which someone must take control of a situation or the welfare or interests of the group may suffer. In such cases, we should hold that person responsible for performing certain leadership tasks, and we should grant him or her authority over us to successfully accomplish the tasks. Because we all vary in our capabilities and resources, power often shifts from one situation to another, creating opportunities for different people to have power over others at different times.

Power sometimes becomes a conflict issue when there is an **imbalance of power,** which occurs when one person works to obtain and hold more power than others and is threatening to the less powerful. Power imbalances can create worry, anger, and resentment in those holding less power.[2] In situations of imbalance of power, we do not expect to resolve conflicts unless the powerful person initiates and employs solution oriented behavior rather than power perpetuating behavior.[3] We have all heard of the expression, "two heads are better than one." However, in conflict situations where one person outranks the other, there is a high likelihood that only "one head" prevails, and the powerful party fails to seek the input from others for better ideas. Why surround yourself with advisors who are simply "yes men" or "yes women"? You could just as easily disband the group and make the decisions by yourself. In addition to making the best decision because of input from others, people are more satisfied in situations where they have some say or influence. However, they are less likely to speak up if they fear the consequences or believe that the powerful person may not listen to their ideas.

10.1 Think about It

How does it feel when you are in an unbalanced power relationship? What is it like to have more power? Less power?

Change needs to come from the powerful people. They must value the input of others and seek to focus more on resolving problems and less on perpetuating their power over others. Moreover, less powerful persons must also realize that power is not a finite quantity but something produced by human transactions.[4] People do not have reward or punishment power over another unless the other person grants them this power. Thus, in keeping with the transactional view of communication, equalizing power in a conflict situation is the responsibility of both the powerful and the powerless.

Does this surprise you? The suggestion that you challenge someone you perceive as the authority may strike you as unnatural, disrespectful, or even mutinous. However, when the powerful offer to work with you in a more equitable manner, it is our position that you should take advantage of opportunity. All too often, subordinates fail to adequately step into a position of authority and do not exercise responsible leadership. For example, when a professor offers to share the classroom with the students, they sometimes fail to adequately prepare themselves for their oral reports or class discussions. The students who take on the responsibility are also using the opportunity to exercise some authority and control in the classroom. As children grow into adults, they have to help themselves make the transition.

Let us next determine how the powerful might relinquish power to facilitate a more even playing field in a conflict situation.

Communication researchers who study power have identified three ways conflicting parties can reduce the imbalance of power in a relationship by redistributing it.

- The more powerful person can transfer power to the less powerful person. One way to do this is to take turns as to who has the power. Another way to share power is to give up some of the more obvious power resources and symbols of authority.
- The parties in a conflict can join forces and combine their power to greatly increase their chances of a mutually satisfying outcome.
- The conflicting parties can give power to the relationship that exists between them by increasing their interest (or investment) in their relationship.

We intend to discuss each of these ideas in more detail. Hopefully you can use this knowledge to improve the climate the next time you are in a conflict situation.

Giving the Less Powerful More Power

As noted above, the more powerful person can transfer power to the less powerful person. One way to do this is to take turns as to who has the power. With regard to some responsibilities in a relationship, there are times when person A is the more powerful person, and other times person B is the more powerful person.

The idea of sharing power may seem radical or even shocking to some people. After years of graduate study and passing extremely demanding exams, they have attained a Ph.D., M.D., D.D.S., or law degree, so the last thought they may have in mind is to sacrifice the status and power that comes with such extraordinary achievement. The same goes for people who have worked their way up the ranks and now are in charge of a military unit, classroom, civilian department, or division of a company. These people believe that they have earned the rank and deserve privileges and special treatment. We could say the same for those who worked their way up from the lowest to the highest levels of any organization and worked hard to attain a position of influence. Because they made great sacrifices, overcame difficult barriers, and demonstrated high abilities, they believe that they have paid their dues. Now we come along and ask them to share their hard-earned respect, power, and status with others. We can hear their response: *Forget it!*

> As a Captain, I once taught counseling to a group of high-ranking Army officers. When I finished a list of dos and don'ts for officers counseling enlisted personnel who had personal problems that might affect the performance of their duties, which included hanging one's military jacket and hat (both covered with rank insignia) on a coat stand before meeting with the individual, Colonel Johnson suddenly stood up, turned to face the class, and said, "I am a Colonel in the United States Army and when someone comes into my office to see me, he or she is going to know I am a Colonel." There was a moment of silence. I then asked the class, "How many of you would go to Colonel Johnson, if you had a personal problem?" Everyone laughed, and someone even said "No way." Not receiving the support for his position that he expected, the Colonel suddenly grew embarrassed, said he realized now that he had missed

the point, and sat down. He told me later that he hadn't really thought about the problems he created by "pulling rank" on people.

Obviously we tread on hallowed ground here. We recognize that we are asking a lot for privileged people to set aside their perceptions of themselves as outranking the rest of us, to treat us with mutual respect, and to work with us as their equals. However, consider the idea that "we are all in this boat together," in that we share a sense of purpose and the primary goals of the college class, athletic team, military unit, or work organization. Because there is a job to do, a task to accomplish, we should focus on the task and not on the preservation of status or power. The leaders and followers all benefit by success of the class, team, unit, or organization, so stop worrying about sharing power and actively seek ways to share it.

Another way to share power is to give up some of the more obvious power resources and symbols of authority. By removing his hat and jacket, loaded with rank insignia, Colonel Johnson gives up power resources and status symbols that intimidate subordinates. By abandoning a podium or large desk to sit with the students, a teacher does the same. Bosses who leave the secure confines of their offices to walk among their employees to see firsthand how they are doing and what they need are also giving up power resources.

Another way to share power is to make power resources accessible to everyone in the group. When leaders or authorities turn over responsibility and control to subordinates, they raise the subordinates' status and equalize the playing field. The aforementioned Colonel may appoint a subordinate to take command in his absence. When people in authority delegate tasks to subordinates, they need to delegate some of their power for them to do the job. The teacher may let students give reports or conduct discussions in class rather than lecture, thus giving them more responsibility for the learning that takes place in the classroom. Examples of power sharing follow.

The boss decides everyone's part-time work schedule. However, he notices low morale, frequent arguments over working hours, minor theft, and employees calling in sick. So, he announces a flexible work schedule allowing employees to turn in a schedule of preferred work hours. He also holds a meeting to discuss the problem of working during exam weeks and holidays. The employees see the problem of work coverage and that the boss better understands their school and home pressures. New workers are then added to the schedule just to cover difficult periods. Moral greatly improves, there are no arguments over working hours, and workers seldom call in sick. Minor theft also stops.

The students in a marketing class were assigned to work in groups, with one person designated as a group leader. In Lynn's group, she made it known that she had worked in a marketing company over the summer and "knew more than the others did." She started ordering group members around and made all the decisions by herself. As members lost interest in the project and started not showing up to group meetings, she began to do all the work by herself. Finally, it became apparent that the project was taking too much time, and she could not do a good job without help. With some effort, she was able to get everyone together to explain the problem. For the first time she listened to everyone's complaints about her role as leader. Lynn agreed to let the group have more say and help define her role along with everyone else's. She pointed out that everyone's grade depended on the quality of the group project. Everyone's knowledge, ideas, and thoughts then made the group stronger as a whole. By combining the power in the group, no one person was overwhelmed by the project and the final result showed the efforts of everyone.

Yet another way to share power is for the one with the least interest in a relationship to increase his or her level of interest. Perhaps the other person has a terrific personality or brings certain advantages to the relationship. Better yet, the one with the least interest might better appreciate the commitment and attention received from the other, and he or she should see that as a fair exchange for his or her own assets. After all, teachers need students to teach, leaders need followers, and bosses or supervisors need workers to do their jobs. In any case, the more powerful person may change his or her perception of the other and increase her or his own level of interest or investment in the other person, which may distribute power more equally.

One more way to share power is to rely more on a neutral speech, which we define as neither powerful nor powerless speech. **Powerful speech** refers to verbal and nonverbal messages used to dominate and control others. Powerful speech can occur in different degrees. At one level it includes interrupting others, speaking loudly, controlling the topic of conversation, and sounding like one knows he or she is right (implying that the other is wrong). At another level it also includes talking down to people, put downs, efforts to belittle others, interrupting the other, talking through the other, and talking louder than the other. At the extreme it includes very aggressive behaviors.[5] These could include verbal threats, swearing, name calling while shouting, standing up to the other, or standing over that person accompanied with menacing facial expressions.

Erickson and his colleagues identified some differences between powerful and powerless speech. Powerful speakers used more intensifiers (e.g., very), fewer hedges (e.g., I guess), especially formal grammar, fewer hesitation forms (e.g., uh, you know), more controlled gestures, fewer questioning forms (e.g., rising in intonation at the end of a declarative sentence), and fewer polite forms when addressing others. Some examples of how people gain and maintain their power in interpersonal relationships are found in gender studies. Van Dijk summarized this area of research as follows: "Women generally do more work than men do in conversation, by giving more topical support, by showing more interest, or by withdrawing in situations of conflict . . . men tend to interrupt men more often."[6] We hasten to point out that men's tendency to control conversation is not necessarily a legitimate endeavor, but the example does draw attention to domination techniques.

Powerless speech is talking up to others, making requests or asking questions (showing that one is in need or is uninformed), speaking softly, and sounding tentative, uncertain, or unsure of oneself. When people are nonassertive, as we discussed in Chapter 4, they also engage in powerless speech.

When one employs **neutral speech,** she or he does not talk down or talk up to the others but talks to them as equals and relies on objective language. People in authority may go by their first names and ask others to treat them as a colleague or an equal rather than as a superior. We are reminded of instances when a coach or military officer plays a game of ball with the players or the enlisted troops where the rules are equal for all who play.

The idea of neutral speech that is neither powerful nor powerless is similar to the distinction we made in Chapter 4 between assertive behavior on the one hand and either aggressive or nonassertive behavior on the other. Like the nonassertive individuals, power-less people fail to effectively stand up for themselves, while aggressive people do it in a way that violates the rights of others. Only assertive people treat others as they want the others to treat them by striving for outcomes that benefit both of them and not just one of them at the other's expense. The assertive behavior serves as a goal for the powerful (who must now take the other into consideration) and for the powerless speakers (who must now stand up more for themselves).

While we have discussed many ways in which the powerful may, at least temporarily, set aside their power resources and symbols, enhance their interests in the relationship, and rely more on neutral speech, we now ask what the powerless can do to equalize the conflict situation. Power shapes the perceptions people have of their choices and their estimations of the other's behavior in conflict situations. Like all perceptions, we need to consider alternate views of situations. Maybe you have more power than you think, or the stronger person may relinquish more power to you if you ask for it, but you are choosing to remain powerless.

10.2 Think about It

Under what conditions are you likely to use powerful speech? Powerless speech? Neutral speech? Why?

10.1 Apply It

Think of a particular relationship where there is an imbalance of power. List the power resources and power symbols associated with that relationship and the powerful speech cues of the person in author-ity. Are there any power resources or power symbols that the stronger person has overlooked or not utilized? How might the person's use of power affect the situation if a conflict should arise?

Combining Forces to Manage the Conflict

The parties in a conflict can join forces and combine their power to greatly increase their chances of a mutually satisfying outcome. Using only one's own resources is limiting; instead, combine resources to accomplish the job. This approach differs from the above example, in that the parties focus together on managing a specific assignment, task, or problem. Rather than argue over which one of us should do the project, let's do it together. If we combine our resources, we can probably do it in half the time or at half the cost of tackling it by ourselves. Because it takes a lot of time and effort, achieving the difficult goal of finding a mutually satisfying outcome to a conflict is more easily managed if both conflicting partners work together for that purpose.

Giving Power to the Relationship Itself

The conflicting parties can give power to the relationship that exists between them by increasing their interest in the relationship. We do this by acknowledging our relationship, making commitments to it, and taking it into consideration as we behave. For example, when two people marry, they change their perspectives on themselves and each other, because they now have their marriage to consider. This also happens if romantic couples have children. They may change their perspectives on themselves because they have a family or children to take into consideration. Now they engage in actions because they are married or because they have a family. Whatever the relationship, it can become a third entity that can exercise power over the partners. As married persons, fraternity brothers or sorority sisters, roommates, friends, or romantic partners, we don't engage in some behaviors and do engage in others for the sake of the relationship. This change in perspective of who we are and of our relationship to one another results in our delegating some of our power to the relationship itself. As conflicting parties, we might decide to recognize the value of our friendship, roommate status, romantic relationship or marriage, family, or organization and engage in conflict in a way that allows the relationship to have power over us. When this occurs, friends, romantic partners, or organizational members do not threaten each other or expect to behave entirely independent of each other. They do take actions that contribute to the goals and needs of the social or work unit as well as their own individual goals and needs. While striving to satisfy their own wants or needs, they also ask themselves what is best for the relationship, group, or organization.

When we think of the power others have in our relationships, we are likely to think they have our best interests at heart and do not use power in ways that hurt us. This brings up the factor of interpersonal trust, which is another property of a conflict climate.

Distrust versus Trust

My best friend, Marilyn, and I knew each other for about a year. I was interested in another guy who also was friends with my best friend. Meanwhile, an ex-boyfriend was trying to come back into the picture. I didn't think Marilyn would tell my new love interest about my ex, but I was wrong because she did. You would think she would have had my best interests at heart, and she would have been concerned about how the situation would affect me, her friend, in the end. After that situation I felt plenty of distrust toward her.

Just as an imbalance of power produces a harmful conflict climate, so does the violation of trust. **Trust** is the belief that another is benevolent or honest toward the trusting individual, and that the other person's caring transcends any direct benefits the other receives as a result of caring.[7] In other words, we trust others when we think they have our best interests at heart and do not wish to hurt us. Trust reflects "people's abstract positive expectations that they can count on partners to care for them and be responsive to their needs, now and in the future."[8] As Jenn says,

A strong, healthy trust absolutely solidifies the status between my mother and me. I know that I can confide in my mother because, at the end of the day, she only wants the best for me.

Our trust of another person is generally reflected in the way we orient toward them nonverbally in conversation.

Although it doesn't always seem that she has my best interests in mind at the time, she has rarely led me in the wrong direction. As in any relationship, this trust is sometimes tested, but ultimately this trust endures.

To a great extent, trust is earned. If our actions warrant it, we gain the trust of others over time.

I was a counselor last summer at a "sleep-away summer camp," where kids don't see their parents for two weeks. One of the campers, who is named Neal, and I established trust for one another early on. He was the smallest camper for his age and, although he could defend himself when he got into fights with others, I often found myself protecting him from the bigger campers who would pick on him. This interaction created a mutual trust for one another. I began to trust that he would refrain from getting into fights with other campers, and he would trust that I would discipline other campers for picking on him.

Although trust depends on the previous actions of those involved, it still requires a leap of faith.[9] Most people go ahead and act as though a sense of security about the other is justified, because evidence for trustworthiness is seldom conclusive. The feeling that the other is benevolent toward oneself allows a person to move forward on the assumption that the other is trustworthy.[10] The tendency toward trust, according to Holmes and Rempel, is seen as a "contingency rule," a preferred way of acting within a relationship if the characteristics of the relationship warrant it:

If we think in terms of readiness to trust, we also avoid creating an unrealistic caricature of a trusting individual as a blind optimist. If anything, there is some evidence to suggest that distrusting individuals react less effectively to the features of particular relationships than do trusting individuals. People who distrust the motives of others tend to have more rigid and narrow expectations and to provoke the very reactions they fear.[11]

Healthy trust is distinguished from pathological trust or suspicion. Deutsch argued that what characterizes **healthy trust** (or healthy suspicion) is flexibility and responsiveness to changing situations. Conversely, **unhealthy trust** (or suspicion) is typically inflexible, rigid, and consistent in actions toward others, without regard for the situation.[12] Those who trust pathologically have a tendency to confuse risk-taking and trusting situations, overestimating the probability of getting what they want or underestimating the negative consequences of not getting what they want. Pathologically trusting persons may also overestimate the benevolence of the trusted person or overestimate their power to affect the trusted person's behavior. Pathologically suspicious persons make opposite assumptions. Either extreme makes it difficult to act effectively with respect to others. An example of pathological trust is illustrated by the following conflict between two roommates.

> I own a great deal of expensive photography equipment, which I keep at my apartment because I often do my studio work there. My roommate has this weird idea that the world is safe—he leaves doors and windows unlocked all the time. He comes from the Midwest, where "people are decent" and he never locked a door in his life.
> This conflict used to arise when I would come home in the afternoon and find the apartment wide open. Sometimes, if he went next door he would leave the door standing open, but most of the time he would go to work and leave everything unlocked and the windows wide open. If I confronted him, he would fall back on the fact that if God wanted us to have our material possessions then He would make sure that they were not stolen (since everything is God's and He lets us keep them or take them away).
> Then an incident happened. Without telling my roommate, I loaned my television to a friend. When my roommate came home early to an unlocked apartment, he found the set missing. Well, he panicked and called the police and had them looking our apartment over until I came home and straightened everything out. This taught him just how he would react in a real robbery situation and that he should exercise more caution in securing the apartment. After that incident, he did decide to lock the doors.

What direct effect does trust have on conflict situations? Research seems to indicate that, to begin with, trusting individuals are more likely to assume positive implications of behaviors than are distrusting individuals. Although they do not deny the negative elements in their relationships, they limit the implications negative events have for the relationship; distrusting individuals overemphasize the importance of negative events. Trusting individuals tend to see negative events in a larger time frame, stabilizing perceptions and making conflict less threatening.[13]

This tendency to see events in the larger time frame was tested with married couples. Prior to the videotaped discussion of a difficult issue in a couple's relationship, researchers measured the trust couples had toward one another by having the couples respond to semantic differential items concerning their expectations of each other's behaviors. Following the discussion, the researchers had the couples watch the videotaped discussion and had each partner independently rate any behaviors of the other that had positive or negative effects on them. After viewing the tape, the couples again completed semantic differential scales, which asked for perceptions of the partner's actual behavior during the interaction, then for their inferences for why their partner was acting that way.

The results were most interesting. Couples who trusted one another were more optimistic, and they tended to report that their partner's motives were positive, even to the extent of saying that the other person's motives were more positive than their own. People who had high trust for their partners usually did not change their opinions of the other person's behavior. The authors

> speculated that the confidence and clarity of the core attitudes held by trusting individuals lead them to react affectively to the partner's behavior in a relatively automatic, positive way and that little consideration of its meaning typically takes place. The potential cost of this process is that individuals may take acts of caring for granted if the implications of events are not elaborated.[14]

How does one engender trust? People gain the trust of others when they:

- perform cooperative actions,
- avoid suspicious activity, and
- reciprocate in trusting ways.

10.3 Think about It

When have you ever lost your trust in someone? How did you react to the loss of trust? How was the trust restored?

We can see how trust or distrust develops in an exercise called the **Prisoner's Dilemma (PD).** PD is a played like a game based on a familiar situation: Supposedly, two people are caught burglarizing a building and are brought separately to the police station. These are their options: If both of them remain silent, they both go free, but an incentive to speak the truth exists—if only one confesses, the one confessing receives a reward and goes free and the other goes to jail. If both confess, they both go to jail. In order to both benefit the most, then, they must trust each other to act in each other's best interest and not just one's own. However, to cooperate first (by remaining silent), if the other chooses not to cooperate, results in the worst outcome for the person acting first. This is called a **mixed motive situation,** because those involved have incentives to both cooperate and compete, but they can choose to stick with just one.

Whether or not one "wins" the game depends on the choice to openly cooperate or compete. The best outcomes occur when both people trust each other and choose to cooperate; the worst occurs if both people distrust each other and choose to compete. Both parties gain the most by choosing less for themselves but more for them both. To cooperate, we must think that you are not taking advantage of us. Then we trust you and choose to cooperate with you.

The notion that you can choose to maximize your gains and expect others to choose to lose is unrealistic and unsupported by research.[15] If we think that you are trying to maximize your gains at our expense, we distrust you and choose to compete. When played in class, some students become angry when they find that they can't trust the opposition and resort to competition. They often accuse the others of ruining the game. Emotionally intense and lively discussion usually follows the PD exercise.

One interesting issue connected with trust and cooperation is the illusion of self-interest. Often, if a person sacrifices his or her own goals for the group, the group gains but the person making the sacrifice loses. In some cases, though, the person making the sacrifice sees making a moral choice (i.e., sacrificing on behalf of the group) as serving their own interest. The altruistic choice is reframed as self-serving because it is in line with the person's moral outlook.[16]

Criticisms of the PD paradigm are widespread. Perhaps the most serious concerns the artificial and limited conditions under which communication can take place in PD simulations. However, the simulation has increased our understanding of trust and suspicion in conflict situations. In a similar game situation called "the sequential dictator," researchers found that participants usually reciprocated altruistic moves made by the other.[17]

10.2 Apply It

Arrange to play the Prisoner Dilemma game with other members of your class, some as individual contestants, others as pairs, and some with three members on each team. At the conclusion of the game, compare the competitive and cooperative styles of different teams and their outcomes. Discuss feelings about the opposition that chose one style over another.

A harmful climate includes distrust, whereas a nurturing climate manifests trust. We cannot say enough about the importance of trust in conflict situations. The next section examines the role of defensive and supportive behavior in the conflict climate.

Supportive Behavior versus Defensive Behavior

The other day, I told my husband that when I asked him to do any chores around the house he never completed them. Even tonight when I asked him to empty the dishwasher, he left two baking dishes on the counter. I said "You always leave dishes out when emptying the dishwasher." Well, having said all that, I have to admit that I was overstating things. He does complete many chores, and he hadn't left the dishes out in a long time. He apologized but

TABLE 10.1 Defensive versus Supportive Climates

Defensiveness Arises From		Supportiveness Arises From
Evaluation	versus	Description
Control	versus	Problem orientation
Strategy	versus	Spontaneity
Neutrality	versus	Empathy
Superiority	versus	Equality
Certainty	versus	Provisionalism

said he was upset that I accused him of not helping more. I don't know why I made such accusations. I guess I am afraid he would take me for granted.

It was time for the annual review where I work, and my supervisor strutted around looking like he was almighty high and powerful. He asked me to come into his office to administer my review. When I entered, to my surprise not only was my boss present but so was a friend of his who is a supervising manager from another department. My boss zipped through a lot of points very quickly. When he was finished, without asking for any input from me, he asked me to sign it. I told him that I did not have enough time to digest all that he said and I was not sure I agreed with some of it. I wanted to take time and go over it point by point and defend the inaccuracies. I was also uncomfortable discussing some of the points in front of the other supervisor. It was at that moment that he said, "I am your supervisor and this is your review." It was like he was ordering me to sign it.

To collaborate successfully, you and your partner must try to establish an atmosphere of support that encourages openness and cooperation and avoids creating a threatening, defensive conflict climate. In a seminal article, Gibb identified communication behaviors that are defensive or supportive (see Table 10.1).[18] These behaviors play a role in their respective conflict climates because they either encourage people to become closed and hostile toward one another or encourage them toward greater openness and cooperation.

According to Gibb, **defensive behaviors** consist of evaluation, control, strategy, neutrality, superiority, and certainty, while **supportive behaviors** involve nonjudgmental description, problem orientation, spontaneity, empathy, equality, and provisionalism.[19] It helps to consider these behaviors as opposites in pairs.

- An *evaluation* consists of praise and blame, while a *nonjudgmental description* is worded in a way that does not ask the other to change behaviors or attitudes.
- *Control* refers to attempts to dominate another's behavior, whereas a *problem orientation* is a focus on the issue rather than one's rank.
- While *strategy* suggests hidden motives and agendas, *spontaneity* is straightforward and free of deception.

- *Neutrality* refers to a lack of concern for the welfare of others (i.e., "that is not my problem"), while *empathy* involves taking an interest in others.
- *Superiority* means "pulling rank" on others, versus *equality,* which expresses a willingness to enter into participative planning.
- *Certainty* appears dogmatic because it refers to statements that consist of "all" or "every," such as "you always do that to me" or "everybody does it," while *provisionalism* suggests tentativeness, a desire to withhold one's judgment until all the facts are in.

What is the relationship of defensive behavior to the concept of power discussed earlier in this chapter? You may notice that a few of these behaviors are sometimes associated with people in positions of power, such as evaluation (critical), control (domination), neutrality (uninterested in subordinate's problems), and superiority ("pulling rank"). We do not want to confuse the subject of defensiveness by associating it with power. Defensive behaviors are associated with anyone, even those in subordinate positions, so these behaviors may appear irrespective of power. They are more consistently associated with the feelings of inadequacy, insecurity, fear, or uncertainty that make one turn defensive in a threatening situation. To the extent that powerful people manifest defensive behaviors, they probably also experience feelings of insecurity about their roles as supervisors, leaders, or parents.

In the following narrative, we added Gibb's key terms in parentheses to connect this example with his description of a defensive climate. How would you feel if you were the husband or wife in this marriage? What impact does this husband have on the management of conflicts between him and his wife?

> As a husband, I intentionally exercise a lot of influence over my wife (control). I do this by having only one car and keeping track of our household finances (strategy). I give my wife a certain amount of money for the week, and I tell her that after she has gone grocery shopping, she can have what is left over to spend on herself. That way she is rewarded for finding the best deals and getting the most for our money (evaluation). She complains to me that I am too tight, but I don't listen because managing the grocery money is not my problem (neutrality). I want her to think of me as the boss (superiority) and that I know what is best for us (certainty).

As you read this narrative, how do you think the husband and wife feel? As it turns out, he is insecure and is afraid of losing control of their marriage. Do you feel sympathy for the wife? One would not expect that his forceful hand would result in any mutually satisfying outcomes.

Now consider this next narrative. We again added Gibb's key terms in parentheses to connect this example with his description of a supportive climate. How would you feel if you were the husband or wife in this marriage? What impact does this husband have on the management of conflicts between him and his wife?

> I don't criticize my wife (nonjudgmental description). We tackle problems together regardless of what the problem is. I don't think that either of us is better at solving problems than

the other, but together we can come up with the best way to spend and save money (equality). I believe that what is important is that we come up with the best solution to a problem (problem orientation) rather than think I have to make all the decisions for us. I value her input. I don't first attempt to solve the problem and then try to convince her of the solution (provisionalism), but rather wait until we can discuss it together, because I value her input (spontaneity). I care about her feelings, wants, and needs, so I want to take her into account (empathy).

One would expect that by working together in a supportive rather than a defensive manner, the couple would develop more mutually satisfying outcomes when in conflicts.

Although the above listing of defensive and supportive behaviors that make up harmful and nurturing conflict climates may appear in an "either–or" format, typically climates exist somewhere in between such extremes. This means that every conflict climate has some degree of defensiveness and supportiveness. However, the nurturing conflict climate has more supportive than defensive behaviors, while the harmful conflict climate has vice versa.

Mutually satisfying outcomes are more likely to occur when communicators participate in the decisions, agreements, solutions to problems, and resolution of conflicts that affect them. When we confront another, we need to express our needs and feelings, which is sometimes difficult to do, because we may feel vulnerable. To the extent that we feel safe enough to assert our interests, needs, and goals, listen to the expression of others, and cooperate in the process of achieving an understanding, the more likely we feel free to cooperate and collaborate.

10.3 Apply It

Take a piece of paper and draw two columns on it. Compare two past or present conflict situations, one in which the other engaged in supportive behavior and another in which the other resorted to defensive behavior. What role does the supportive or defensive behavior play in each conflict situation? How do you feel about the other person in these relationships?

Manage It

Climate is something we usually associate with the weather. When weather reports announce hurricanes, typhoons, or tornadoes, we see these as hostile, dangerous, and harmful climatic conditions. In contrast, a warm sunny day in the summer means quite the opposite, as we pack our bathing gear and head for the beach. Similarly, we can classify communication climates as hostile and harmful or warm and friendly.

One purpose of this chapter is to describe the role played by climate in conflict situations. An imbalance of power, distrust, and defensive behavior create a hostile, dangerous, and harmful conflict environment, in which competition produces unsatisfactory outcomes for one or both parties. Equity, trust, and supportive behavior create a warm, friendly, and nurturing conflict environment that is more likely to produce mutually satisfactory outcomes.

Another purpose of this chapter is to explain how specific factors contribute to a nurturing or harmful conflict climate. Of the many factors or properties that are part of the climate, we limit our scope to these bi-polar concepts: imbalance of power versus equity, distrust versus trust, and defensive versus supportive behavior.

The more powerful person in the conflict situation has greater latitude in creating a balance of power. Although it is difficult to embrace the idea of giving up power, sometimes doing so is one's best option in resolving conflict. At the very least, de-emphasizing power differences will lead to a more cooperative conflict climate. Those with less power in the situation should also exercise choices that minimize the power difference by using power-neutral language and by refusing to act powerless in the situation.

The climate of a conflict situation is also affected by the level of trust we have for one another. Although people generally will trust others, conflict makes trust more difficult to maintain. People maintain the trust of others when they continue to act in cooperative ways, avoid suspicious activity, and reciprocate in trusting ways to the actions of the other.

Critical to our success in conflict situations is the use of communicative behavior that is supportive and non-threatening. The most significant steps toward creating a supportive climate are found in communication that describes behavior rather than judges it, and that is oriented toward solving problems rather than assigning blame. By focusing on description and problem-solution, one's communication creates a "we-orientation," unlike the "you-orientation" arising from defensive behaviors. The "we-orientation" of a supportive climate is also created through an attitude of empathy rather than an attitude that is neutral and unconcerned, and by a sense of equality with the other rather than a position of superiority. Finally, a supportive climate is created spontaneously rather than through behavior perceived as strategic, and through talk that suggests the conversation is still in process rather than certain and final.

The concept of defensive behavior differs from that of power imbalance. While a few defensive behaviors are sometimes associated with people in positions of power, such as evaluation (criticizing), control (being dominating), neutrality (lacking interest in subordinate's problems) and superiority ("pulling rank"), defensive behaviors may appear irrespective of power. They are more consistently associated with feelings of inadequacy, insecurity, fear, or uncertainty that make one turn defensive in a threatening situation. When powerful people manifest defensive behaviors, it is an indication of feelings of insecurity about their role as supervisor, leader, or parent.

Communicators who create nurturing climates are more likely to create mutually satisfying outcomes because they participate in the decisions, agreements, solutions, and resolution of conflicts that affect them. If we feel safe enough to assert our interests, needs, and goals, listen to others, and cooperate in the process of achieving an understanding, we are more likely to cooperate and collaborate.

10.1 Work with It

Read the case study and answer the questions that follow it.

My roommate has a habit of borrowing my things without always returning them. I had just bought a new computer, and was in the process of getting it all set up. Space is a precious commodity in university housing. My roommate has had a laptop computer for over a year that obviously requires less space to operate than does a full-sized computer like mine. He also has a printer that is about half the space of mine. Prior to my computer being shipped, we realized we would need another desk in the room. We were able to find one that barely fit in our room, and we moved it in. The new desk was half again as big as the one already in the room, and he started using it first.

Once I got my computer partially set up, I realized that it was going to be a tight fit to squeeze all the equipment into the available space, and I asked my roommate if we could switch desks. He quickly and firmly replied "No." I asked why not, since my computer took up so much more space, and it was already cramped in the corner where my desk is, without even having all the equipment set up. He replied that he simply liked the bigger desk so that he could spread out more. I half jokingly said I would pay him to switch, and he said, "This isn't a barter system, and you can't bid on this desk." I reminded him that he has used the smaller desk for a year and a half without any problems whatsoever.

My roommate then reminded me that he was in this room a year before I moved in. He also felt he was a better judge of arranging the place than I was. "You always have such stupid ideas," he said.

1. Define power and describe the role played by an imbalance of power in this situation. How might the parties equalize power?
2. Define trust and describe the role played by distrust in this situation. How might the parties regain one another's trust?
3. Define defensive behavior and describe the role played by defensive behaviors in this situation. How might the parties engage in more supportive behavior?

10.1 Remember It

Write an essay in which you apply the ideas presented in Chapter 10 to your life situation. Make sure to address the following topics.

1. Define climate, power imbalance, distrust, and defensive behavior and describe the role that climate plays generally in conflict situations.
2. Pick a conflict situation, real or imagined, describe the role played by an imbalance of power, and explain how to equalize power in that situation.
3. Continuing on with the conflict situation, describe the role played by distrust and explain how to create trust in that situation.
4. Describe the role played by defensive behavior and explain how to engage and encourage supportive behavior in that conflict situation.

10.2 # Work with It

Think of two different conflict situations with individuals you know well and see often.

■ In the first situation, the other person is subordinate to you (you have some authority over her or him at home, work, or school).

■ In the second situation, the other person is superordinate to you (has authority over you at home, work, or school)

Your purpose is to describe the communication and conflict patterns that exist in the two types of interpersonal relationships where you are superior or subordinate. Although you are to write about both relationships, divide each relationship into two parts. In the first part, describe how the powerful person (you in one case; the other in the next case) might try to retain all the power and use it against the other. Also, try to describe the likely outcome of the conflict as a result of holding most of the power. In the second part, describe how the parties might redistribute the power in a way that would benefit the relationship, group, or organization. Again, try to describe the likely outcome of the conflict as a result of trying to create a balance of power.

When you discuss your two relationships, describe the verbal and nonverbal communication patterns. Do you find that you use the same communication behaviors for both persons, or do you find that you tend to use some with one person but not the other? Also, thinking of each person one at a time, go through the list of examples of powerful, powerless, and neutral speech and determine which ones you tend to do with each person and which they use with you.

As you analyze the imbalance of power and its effects on your relationships, also consider the role of trust and defensiveness. Do you trust each person equally well? Do they trust you equally well? Are you more defensive or supportive with one another?

NOTES

1. Joseph Folger, Marshall Scott Poole, and Randall K. Stutman, *Working through Conflict,* 5th Ed. (Boston: Allyn & Bacon, 2005), p. 108.

2. Cathryn Johnson, Rebecca Ford, and Joanne Kaufman, "Emotional Reactions to Conflict: Do Dependency and Legitimacy Matter?" *Social Forces* 79 (2000), 107–137.

3. Larry Powell and Mark Hickson, III, "Power Imbalance and Anticipation of Conflict Resolution: Positive and Negative Attributes of Perceptual Recall," *Communication Research Reports* 17 (2000), 181–190.

4. Andrew King, *Power and Communication* (Prospect Heights, IL: Waveland Press, 1987), p. 138.

5. Loreen N. Olson, "Compliance Gaining Strategies of Individuals Experiencing 'Common Couple Violence,'" *Qualitative Research Reports in Communication* 3 (2002), 7–14.

6. Teun A. van Dijk, "Structures of Discourse and Structures of Power," in James A. Anderson (Ed.), *Communication Yearbook 12* (Newbury Park, CA: Sage, 1989), p. 33.

7. Robert E. Larzelere and Ted L. Huston, "The Dyadic Trust Scale: Toward Understanding Interpersonal Trust in Close Relationships," *Journal of Marriage and the Family* 42 (1980), 595–604; John G. Holmes and John K. Rempel, "Trust in Close Relationships," in Clyde Hendrick (Ed.), *Close Relationships* (Newbury Park, CA: Sage, 1989), pp. 187–220.

8. Holmes and Rempel, p. 18.

9. John K. Rempel, John G. Holmes, and Mark P. Zanna, "Trust in Close Relationships," *Journal of Personality and Social Psychology* 49 (1985), 95–112.

10. Larzelere and Huston, p. 596.

11. Holmes and Rempel, p. 190.

12. Morton Deutsch, *The Resolution of Conflict* (New Haven, CT: Yale University Press, 1973), pp. 170–175.

13. John Holmes, "The Exchange Process in Close Relationships: Microbehavior and Macromotives," in Melvin J. Lerner and Sally C. Lerner (Eds.), *The Justice Motive in Social Behavior* (New York: Plenum, 1981), pp. 261–284; John K. Rempel, "Trust and Attributions in Close Relationships," unpublished doctoral dissertation, University of Waterloo, Ontario, 1987.

14. Holmes and Rempel, p. 205.

15. Gary Bornstein and Zohar Gilula, "Between-Group Communication and Conflict Resolution in Assurance and Chicken Games," *Journal of Conflict Resolution* 47 (2003), 326–339.

16. Jonathan Baron, "Confusion of Group Interest and Self-Interest in Parochial Cooperation on Behalf of a Group," *Journal of Conflict Resolution* 45 (2001), 283–295.

17. Andreas Diekmann, "The Power of Reciprocity: Fairness, Reciprocity, and Stakes in Variants of the Dictator Game," *Journal of Conflict Resolution* 48 (2004), 487–505.

18. Jack Gibb, "Defensive Communication," *Journal of Communication* 11 (1961), 141–168.

19. Ibid.

11 The Escalation of Conflict

Stress and Anger

OBJECTIVES

At the end of this chapter, you should be able to:

- Explain how stress affects your communication behavior in a conflict situation.

- Identify sources of stress in your life.

- List ways to deal constructively with stress.

- Determine whether you are anger-in, anger-out, or anger-controlling.

- Explain how anger can negatively affect a conflict situation.

- List ways to effectively control your anger and express it in constructive ways.

KEY TERMS

ABC approach	distress	repression
anger	eustress	secondary emotion
anger controllers	hyperstress	stress
anger-ins	hypostress	stressors
anger-outs	projection	sublimation
defensive coping mechanisms	rationalization	ventilation approach
displaced conflict	reaction formation	

Why do some conflicts escalate? Why are there times when we feel out of control? Why is it that sometimes we can deal with an issue calmly and at another time the same issue sets off an emotional reaction in us? These are important questions if we want to understand how conflicts escalate and sometime turn violent.

While conflict, by our definition, does include the words, stress and anger, most of us associate them with interpersonal conflict. Do you or someone you know have trouble controlling their anger or dealing with life stresses? If so, you probably would welcome some suggestions that you could use or pass on to others who need help. Even if you do not have a problem at the moment or do not know anyone in need of help, you still may want to learn about anger and stress to prepare yourself for the future or to position yourself so that you can help others some day. As you read, you may see that what you have learned as basic interpersonal communication skills and conflict management skills are useful in dealing with stress and anger.

In this chapter we explain the factors that contribute greatly to the escalation of conflict, primarily stress and anger. We view these key factors behind escalation as "before" and "after." Before the conflict situation, stress may make it such that one cannot cope with one more frustration, an upsetting event, or a bad experience. Along comes a conflict, and the stressed out individual explodes. After the conflict situation, anger may "cause" one to lose control and turn verbally abusive or physically violent. You are expected to identify the sources of stress in your life and list ways to constructively deal with it. You are also expected to determine your way of handling your anger and explain alternative ways to deal with it.

Stress and the Escalation of Conflict

There's a bumper sticker that reads, "If you're not living on the edge, you're taking up too much space." There are people who like stress. They like to live fast, drive fast, and eat fast. They may even like conflicts! But these people are generally the exception.

Many people believe that conflicts cause stress in our lives. Usually, interpersonal conflict textbooks highlight the idea that conflict is stressful. Of course, when we are focused on an upsetting problem, dreading a confrontation with someone in authority, and looking at conflict negatively, we are likely to experience stress. However, we also believe the opposite: The stress we are feeling in our lives often erupts into conflict with others. To the extent that you accept our philosophy and welcome the techniques and skills offered in this book, you should find that conflict management and resolution will reduce your stress and make your life more enjoyable.

In this section, we take a unique view of stress based on the observation that when others explode, jump all over us, or overreact in a conflict situation, we usually find that they have other personal problems (or stresses) that make it difficult for them to behave more predictably. These past problems have produced stress and one more problem now is too much for them. So, here we consider the situation in which stress contributes to the escalation of conflict. We'll define stress, describe many common sources of stress, suggest ways to deal with stress, and explain stress's impact on conflicts you have with others.

Walker and Brokaw define **stress** as something that "arises when the perceived demands of a situation exceed the perceived capacities for meeting the demands"; we would add that stress also occurs when we fear that the demands on us might exceed our capacities, even when we have not been given a reason to fear.[1] Both negative and positive events are stressful. Few people would doubt that an IRS audit is stressful, and almost all people find enduring a root canal a high-stress situation. On the other hand, getting married, we presume, is a happy occasion, and yet it causes a great deal of stress as the bride and groom make arrangements, meet their new in-laws, and commit themselves to one another. Giving a dinner party is also pleasurable, but the demands of preparation may cause stress.

Selye has identified four kinds of stress.[2] A good kind of stress, **eustress** is a short-term stress that encourages us to take more seriously and expend more energy on important activities. For example, a hitter stepping up to the plate in a major league baseball game experiences eustress—he is psyched up to perform. A student getting ready to write a paper about a subject he or she has mastered also is experiencing eustress. We experience eustress when we have control over the situation. We know that we are able to make choices and have the necessary resources to meet the demand.

A second kind of stress is **distress.** This arises when we don't feel control over the situation, or when the source of stress is unclear. Generally, distress arises over a period of time. For example, if someone at work harasses you once, you may feel uncomfortable but probably feel little distress. However, if over a period of time you are unable to predict how this co-worker may respond to you, and you are harassed repeatedly despite requests to the co-worker to stop, you are likely to experience distress.

Hyperstress is a kind of stress frequently experienced by students. This happens when too many tasks and responsibilities pile up on us and we are unable to adapt to the changes or cope with all that is happening at once. If in the same week that you have three midterms, your parents call you to tell you they are divorcing, your car won't start, and you receive notice of several bounced checks, you are definitely a candidate for hyperstress.

Finally, people may experience **hypostress,** or underload. This happens when we're bored or unchallenged by our situations. If you are employed in a job that is repetitive and requires little adaptation on your part, you may experience hypostress and find yourself more and more unwilling to go to work.

11.1 Apply It

Take a piece of paper and draw three columns on it. In the first column, identify the various sources of stress you have in your life. In the second, indicate whether the stress factor is positive (leading to eustress) or negative (leading to distress, hyperstress, or hypostress). In the third column, list ways you can reduce the negative stress factors.

When stress occurs, our reaction to it unfolds in three stages.[3] First, we experience alarm, where our hearts beat faster, blood gets redirected to skeletal muscles, and so on. Essentially, your body is preparing to fight or run away. Second, we experience resistance. Our temperature, blood pressure, and breathing are still high, and our body releases hormones that affect us both physically and emotionally.[4] Finally, if stress is not relieved, we experience exhaustion. We become more susceptible to illness or even collapse because we have few physical and emotional reserves left.

One source of stress is competing demands on our lives, as NaniLii Paxton has depicted in her conflict art.

Sources of Stress

Stress can arise from a number of sources in our lives. Sometimes, we experience stress because there is a disparity between the kinds of activities we are engaged in and how we see ourselves (e.g., a moral person doing an immoral act). **Stressors,** or sources of stress, can include:

- anticipated life events (e.g., graduation)
- unexpected life events (e.g., the death of a loved one, the loss of a job, or too much happening at once)
- the need to make a decision (e.g., should I go to grad school or marry or . . . ?)
- struggle among the various roles we play and how much time and attention we should give to each one (e.g., you're all these roles: a student, a child, a friend, a part-time worker, and a romantic partner)

Responses to Stress

Some people respond to stress negatively through **defensive coping mechanisms,** or methods we have learned through experience that help us to feel less stress, at least in the short run. While some of these are external such as eating too much, drinking, using drugs, driving dangerously, and taking unnecessary risks, others are internal and consist of various messages we create for ourselves in order to make sense of a situation. We make sense of our engagement in these nonsubstantive conflicts by producing defense mechanisms such as rationalization, repression, projection, reaction formation, sublimation, and displacement.

Rationalization occurs when we defend questionable behavior or our reactions to stress with reasons that simply aren't connected to the behavior. "I blew up at you because I am having a really bad day," is a reason. Is it a good one? Many people accept it occasionally, but not as a regular reason for behavior. We expect others to contain their stress and not take it out on us. **Repression** occurs when we try not to think about our situation. Sometimes, we manage to hide the painful thought so well that we "forget" about an important (but stressful) event we were to attend. Scarlett O'Hara vocalized this process in *Gone With the Wind* when she would say, "I won't think about that today. I'll think about that tomorrow." Some people use **projection** when they are stressed. They attribute what they are feeling to others rather than owning the feeling themselves. If you really would rather not room with your roommate any longer, you may accuse him or her of wanting to move out rather than admitting it yourself. Another means of negative coping is **reaction formation,** when people do the opposite of their true feelings. Some homophobic persons engage in reaction formation. Those who are most afraid that they are homosexual, or who sometimes have homosexual urges, rage about how wrong homosexuality is.

When people negatively cope through **sublimation,** they put their efforts toward something socially desirable in order to deal with the stress of some event in their life. For example, sometimes people who believe that their parents don't approve of them cope by working hard and achieving a great deal in life. But the achievements aren't meaningful to them, because they haven't dealt with the source of the stress and substantive conflict issue, which is parental disapproval.

A final means of negative coping with stress is **displaced conflict,** which occurs when people engage in conflict with a "safe" person rather than the person who is actually involved in the conflict. This is the "kick the dog" syndrome, and certainly is negative for the dog!

11.1 Think about It

Which of the negative stress coping mechanisms do you tend to use? How can you reduce your reliance on these negative mechanisms?

You'll probably agree that these nonsubstantive conflicts are a negative coping strategy and you should avoid engaging in them. But how do you cope with stress in a positive way? Personal characteristics affect the way people respond to stress. Some people, for example, are simply "hardier" than others. They are involved in their jobs and families, they believe they can control their lives, and they see change as a challenge rather than as a threat. Can you become hardy? It is partly a matter of the way you think about stressors, and, as we show you below, you can change your way of thinking.

Probably the most important tool available for managing stressful events is our thought process. How we think about matters affects the way we perceive the events we experience. This in turn has a major impact on how we choose to respond to them, and whether we engage in conflicts with others. McKinnon and colleagues claim, "The way in which a stressor is interpreted, more than the stressor's properties, predicts the intensity, nature, and duration of physiological and psychological response."[5] We can't escape decisions. We nearly always experience the pressure of time and role demands.

We begin with the observation that the same event produces different reactions in people. Some interpret practically any event as good, others as indifferent, and still others as a disaster. We believe that the difference lies in our way of thinking about the event. Our approach to stress management is called the **ABC approach:**

A = the activating event or stressor
B = our relevant beliefs or thoughts
C = consequences or effects and reaction to the stressor

Of course, it is nice to change "A" and eliminate the stressor from our lives. There are two ways to do that: change the environment (turn off the computer if it is stressing you today) or change environments (pick up and leave; go somewhere else). Unfortunately, each life event we encounter (courtship, weddings, childbirth, taxes, death, applying for jobs, promotions, etc.) all produce some degree of stress. So, we don't always want to eliminate the stressor or can't even if we want to. In such cases, we can change B and interpret, perceive, or label the activating event in a more constructive or positive way. When you cannot easily change your circumstances, we are suggesting that you change yourself (or at least the way you think).

Let's begin with a common activating event (A)—someone rejects you. Maybe she or he doesn't ask you to go shopping, or vote for you, or call you when you want her or him to. It is at this point that we want to impress on you that you have a choice as to what to think (B). Here are two alternatives (perhaps more occur to you):

1. I am awful, no one accepts me, I am always rejected by others, I am a worthless person, I deserve this because I am unpopular, I wish someone could do some magic and change me into a better person.
2. I don't like this, I wish it hadn't happened, it was unfortunate, undesirable, we would have had a lot of fun together, I am good company, they don't know what they're missing, I'll go do something I know that I want to do.

If you choose to think option 1, the consequences (C) are likely that you become upset and disorganized, panic, suffer severe anxiety, and maybe even go into depression. The next person to say or do the wrong behavior may push you over the edge and you explode. If you choose to think option 2, the consequences (C) are likely that you feel sorrowful initially, and perhaps a bit regretful, irritated, or frustrated. However, there is no need for you to overreact and put yourself down. You can figure out a way to make the best of the situation. The next person to say or do the wrong action is not adding fuel to a raging fire, so you can respond in a constructive or positive way if you find yourself in a conflict situation.

The key point here is that if you choose option 1, you upset yourself. This is a self-fulfilling prophecy in that if you expect the worst, you are likely to receive it. Here is a list of thoughts that contribute to stress and the escalation of conflict: irrational thinking, ineffectual thinking, self-damaging thinking habits, self-damning, wishful thinking, intolerance, pessimism, expecting the worst, perfectionist thinking, expecting some magic, being superstitious, being dogmatic, blaming, or damning others for everything. In addition, being too other-directed (or accommodating) is a problem, as one thinks too much about what others think of her or him. If your self-acceptance depends on what others think, you lose control of who you are—which is a stressful event! On the other hand, being too self-directed (or competitive) is also a problem when people think they must win every argument, always come out on top, and have to show up the opposition. If your self-acceptance depends on being Number One, the fear of failure is a constant source of stress.

So, how can you control your thoughts so as to reduce your stress? The first step is to discover the ways in which your "self-talk" contributes to your stress. Consider how these different ways of thinking about the same event, shown in Table 11.1, can increase or reduce stress.

We're not suggesting that you ignore the reality of the situation when you engage in supportive self-talk. What we are suggesting, however, is that if you can avoid "doom and gloom" thinking about situations and focus on the power and choices you do have within them, you can reduce your stress level. Ellis claims that it is not the events themselves that cause stress but how we talk to ourselves about the events that causes our stress.[6] Consider how this person handled a stressful situation.

> There's a co-worker who is really unpredictable. I never know if he's going to snarl at me or say hello. It really depressed me, and I'd slink around the hallways hoping I wouldn't run into him. But whose life was being ruined? Mine. So, I decided I'd cheer up and greet him. To heck with him if he wants to be nasty. At least I'll know I acted like a nice person.

Helpful self-talk is rational. Three unhelpful kinds of statements are "shoulds," "awfuls," and "overgeneralizations." "Shoulds" have to do with the expectations we have for ourselves, for others close to us, and for the world in general. "Should" statements also contain words like "ought," "must," and "have to." Some of the shoulds are unreasonable, and create expectations that are impossible to meet. Consider how this person responds to "shoulds."

TABLE 11.1 The Effect of Self-Talk on Stress

Situation	Self-Talk Increasing Stress	Self-Talk Decreasing Stress
Romantic	I'll never find someone like him/her again.	I enjoyed my time with him/her and I know there's someone else out there.
Failing a test	I'm so stupid. I won't pass.	I can take other actions to bring up my class grade. I can study differently next time.
Getting a speeding ticket	Everyone was speeding. Why me?	I was going over the speed limit. I intend to concentrate more on my driving.

Three of us meet regularly to gripe and complain to each other as well as encourage each other. All three of us came from rotten families and we have committed to letting go of the negative messages of our childhood. All three of us have lots of "shoulds" in our lives—I should parent better, I should spend more time with my spouse, I should work harder, I should this, I should that. When one of us starts to talk this way, we tell that person to stop "shoulding" on him- or herself.

Recognizing when you are "shoulding on yourself" is one way to escape negative self-talk. Another kind of negative self-talk includes "awful" statements. When people talk about how horrible their circumstances are, or the fact that it is simply unbearable, it is pretty easy to start thinking that nothing can change. Continuing self-talk that makes change seem unlikely probably results in situations that do not change.

The final means of negative self-talk, "overgeneralizations," contains words like "always," "never," "everyone," and "no one." Overgeneralizations happen when people think one event is indicative of their entire life. You failed a test, so you're a complete failure. Someone didn't listen to you in this one instance, and that person never listens to you, and so on.

Negative self-talk is a poor means of controlling your thoughts in a situation. It leads to stress, and the need for more self-talk. When you are in a situation where you cannot control other people's responses, you still have control over your own. Recognizing that is a way of reducing the stress that you feel about the situation.

11.2 Apply It

Take a piece of paper and draw three columns on it. In the first, list two or three stressors you are facing right now. In the second, list the kind of negative self-talk you are engaging in about that stressor. In the third, write a different self-talk message that can help reduce your stress level.

The Impact of Stress on Conflict

We argued earlier in this chapter that stress is often a cause of conflict, rather than the other way around. Walker and Brokaw suggest several ways to avoid and alleviate stress.

First, we can avoid stress by minimizing the number of irrational thoughts we entertain. We can monitor our emotional reactions to problematic situations, and ask what feelings different events are arousing in us. We can attempt to find the trigger event and determine why it caused stress for us. We can record our self-talk and make sure it is positive rather than negative. When you write down what you are saying to yourself such as something like, "I am a failure because I received an F on this algebra test," it is easier to see that it is irrational. By writing down your self-talk, you can also dispute your irrational beliefs by writing down rational statements instead. If your negative self-talk includes a statement like, "I'll never understand this subject," you can dispute that by listing what you already do understand and listing places where you can seek help on this section.

Second, we can try to find the humor in the stressful situation. Some research suggests that the "tendency to tell jokes and stories . . . predicted perceiving events and situations in one's life as more predictable and controllable."[7] This is especially important when stress levels are excessive.

Managing stress once it occurs can also head off the escalation of conflicts that occur because of it. Walker and Brokaw suggest these steps:

- work off stress through physical exertion
- enjoy yourself by rewarding yourself with some pleasure
- talk it out with a trusted friend who may move you toward doing something about it (not the same as venting anger)[8]
- give in occasionally when in a quarrel
- do something for others
- have some close friends
- eat sensibly
- get organized
- rehearse stressful situations ahead of time
- do your most difficult task first (or as the saying goes, "Eat a frog first thing in the morning and it's the worst thing you'll have to do all day.")
- learn to say "no"
- learn to accept what you cannot change
- avoid self-medication (alcohol, drugs, etc.)
- live a balanced life
- get enough sleep and rest
- get involved with others
- don't act like a superhero
- exercise regularly
- take care of yourself
- learn to relax

If you are doing your best to alleviate stress as it occurs, and to avoid bad stress when you can, you are much less likely to engage in destructive conflicts. When we are stressed, it is more difficult to practice good communication skills. Empathy is a difficult skill to acquire. It is hard to hear another person out and want to respond to them. Keeping stress at an optimal level is a way of ensuring competence in communication situations.

11.3 Apply It

What makes you really angry? For one day, keep a journal of the way you are reacting to problems around you. You can do this by keeping track of your data in three columns. In the first, list the situation to which you reacted angrily. In the second column, rate how angry you were, with 1 = mildly irritated, 5 = extremely angry. In the third column, write down why you thought you were angry. How might you have reacted differently?

The Process of Anger

Anger is a strong feeling of displeasure, a synonym for antagonism and rage. It is often an emotional response to a conflict situation that disrupts a calm state. What does the feeling of anger do to you? Does it feel threatening? How do you respond physically to an interpersonal conflict situation? Perhaps your heart rate increases, you may perspire, your breathing rate may increase, and your muscles may tense. Sometimes, we are not even aware of these changes, as this narrative suggests.

> I had invited my work group over to my house, for a Christmas party. I guess I assumed that not everyone would show up, and I really had hoped a particular person would not. I like entertaining and normally don't find it upsetting, but within a half-hour of his arrival I had a headache that wouldn't stop. I realized that my neck was really tense and my leg muscles hurt. He came into my house and I was ready for a fight, even though he was polite and cheerful.

Do you think you may lose control of your anger? Or does it work as an impetus for change or make you more productive? Because we experience anger, it is important to understand what anger is and how to manage it. How we deal with our anger depends on our mental processes, our physical responses, and our verbal responses.

Dealing with Our Own Anger: Three Processes

People tend to fall into three different categories depending on how they deal with their own anger: anger-ins, anger-outs, or anger controllers. **Anger-ins** are people who have a hard time even admitting that they are angry. Their response to anger is generally avoidant and passive. They may sulk around, expect you to read their minds, and become even angrier. Eventually, they might become bitter or resentful toward the object of their anger and turn passive-aggressive, thereby burning dinner or forgetting to give you an important telephone message. Anger-ins generally aren't people who respond with overt hostility. They tend to:

1. engage in nonassertiveness, avoidance, accommodation
2. talk to someone else about how they feel rather than confront you
3. exhibit passive-aggressive behavior

Contrary to popular conceptions of the way men and women act, males score consistently as "anger-ins."[9] It is common knowledge that the suppression of anger can lead to stomach upset and ulcers, depression, and heart disease.

Perhaps you are tempted to talk out your anger with someone other than the offensive person, like a friend, parent, colleague, or bartender. This is called the **ventilation approach,** where we vent our anger but not to the person who we are blaming for it. However, it is not that we express our anger; it is the way in which we express it. When you talk about how angry you are to a sympathetic listener, they often reinforce your feelings. With reinforcement, you are likely to magnify the wrong done to you and minimize the part you may have played in the problem. The biggest problem with the ventilation approach is that simply expressing anger, without directing it toward the person responsible or toward problem solving, actually increases it, particularly when we rehearse repeatedly through different tellings. Ventilating through aggressive behavior is not an instinctive catharsis for anger. It lowers our inhibitions about acting aggressively and makes us more prone to aggressive behavior. Talking out anger does not rid us of it: Talking rehearses the anger and makes us feel it even more deeply. In addition, tantrums and rages do not forestall neurosis: They increase it.

We would suggest, then, that these anger-in behaviors are ways of how not to respond to conflict:

- Tell everyone but the person involved about the conflict.
- Don't let the other party know what you want, need, prefer.
- Don't tell the other person that she or he has offended you.

Anger-outs are the exact opposite of the anger-ins, because they are people who are quick to express their anger, vocally or physically. They express their energy outward rather than hold it in. These are the door slammers and screamers. If they continue in their anger, they may humiliate the object of their anger or slander or ostracize that person. Sometimes, they are moved to bully the other or damage that person's reputation. They tend to engage in:

1. automatic reactions, are quick to criticize, blame, and accuse
2. minor aggressive acts such as bickering
3. verbal aggression
4. physical aggression, force

Does one sex tend to have a greater number of "anger-outs?" Actually, "men and women are equally likely to keep quiet when they feel angry, or talk it out, or scream it out, or even get violent. . . . It does not depend on gender and it does not depend on personality."[10] One should not overlook the social context and the consequences of anger. You don't want your expressed rage to result in another person physically attacking you. Likewise, these anger-out behaviors are ways of how not to respond to conflict:

- When the other person says what is bothering him or her, come back with a "Well, you . . ." response and attack, accuse, or deny.
- Listen closely so that you can pick apart what the other person is saying.
- Argue over the way something is stated rather than what is being said.
- Call the other person names.
- Remind the other person of every stupid behavior he or she has ever done with respect to the issue at hand.
- Disregard the other person's feelings. Tell the person, "You shouldn't feel that way."
- Tell people that you know their situation better than they do (i.e., "I know exactly how you feel").
- Make threats.

- Fail to cooperate if it isn't your idea (i.e., "If I can't have my way, I won't do anything at all").
- Indicate that nothing can change and you're both doomed to failure anyway.
- Ask the impossible of the other person.

While many people are either anger-outs or anger-ins (that is why we have textbooks on conflict management), people can choose to become **anger controllers,** who are those who practice S-TLC. Anger controllers do not let their feelings control how they respond in conflict situations. They tend to:

1. collaborate and work together toward mutually satisfactory solutions (Chapter 5)
2. use assertive communication behavior; talk to the person about how they feel (Chapter 4)
3. employ the steps of the interpersonal confrontation ritual (Chapter 6)
4. negotiate (Chapter 7)

11.2 Think about It

Are you a person who tends to blow up, do you express your anger calmly, or do you simply not express it at all? What are the outcomes of expressing anger in this way?

However, before conflicting parties can collaborate, assert themselves, follow the interpersonal confrontation ritual steps, and negotiate in a cooperative manner, they need to gain control over their feelings. Controlling anger is a matter of (1) practicing new habits so that we don't lash out during our flight-or-fight anger episodes and (2) learning to express the underlying emotion when we experience the slow-building kind. How we learn to control anger depends on the more general habits we have about it.

Before Expressing Anger

The mental process of anger is a stage where we can best control the process. When someone is late, when someone has disappointed you, when someone has said something hurtful, how do you frame the event? Your interpretation of the event is probably the best indicator of how angry you feel and how you choose to express it. Do you assume that the other person has hurt you on purpose? Do you look beneath the person's behavior? Do you look for causes that are beyond the other person's control? We are not suggesting that you consistently make excuses for another person. But the kinds of inferences, assumptions, or conclusions you make about another in a conflict situation affects the way that you respond to the other. When you believe the other has acted in a way that constrains your behavior, that such action was intended to harm you, and that such action is uncalled for, you respond with anger. Further, we tend to draw different conclusions about others than we do about ourselves—we make excuses for our failures but attribute the failures of others to personal shortcomings. So, how are you making assumptions about the other? Is it possible that the other is innocent of intent to harm you, as this person suggests?

> It may make me sound like Pollyanna to say this, but I do find that if I say, "Thanks for missing me," rather than accusing another driver of "not having the brains God gave an amoeba," my blood pressure generally doesn't rise and my anger is momentary rather than lasting. In addition, if I try to assume that a person cutting me off simply didn't see me rather than assuming he or she is an idiot, I also contain the amount of anger I feel while driving. It takes practice, and quite honestly, it's harder on a day when I'm tired or upset about something.

In general, when you find yourself in a situation where you are becoming angry, there are three sets of specific techniques that have proven useful for many people: Take time out, relaxation exercises, and self-talk.

Take Time Out.   Exit temporarily if you can. Some people report that counting backward from twenty (or ten or fifty) helps them cool off.

> A student visited her teacher at his office to discuss her grade on the last test. She was unhappy about it and would not accept responsibility for her grade. The teacher tried to explain how the grade was derived and how we could improve in the future, but the student became angry. Suddenly she stood up and bolted out of the room. The teacher thought the situation unfortunate, especially for the student who probably would continue his anger with the teacher to her own detriment. But after twenty minutes, the student suddenly appeared at the teacher's office door and in a nice manner, said, "I shouldn't have acted like that. I was upset and started to lose it. I thought it best to leave and cool off. Now I want to find out what I have to do so that I can do better on the next test."

Relaxation Exercises.   Controlling your physical responses is also helpful. Shut your eyes, tighten muscles (clench your fist, tense your body), and fantasize your anger—imagine it, feel it all over your body, and then suddenly release the tension and picture something serene and relaxing. Monitor your body as you release the different muscles. Breathe slowly and regularly. Concentrate on relaxing your muscles—tense them up and then release them again. Being aware of how you are physically responding to the situation can help.

Self-Talk.   Engage in helpful self-talk before, during, and after a conflict. Before a potential conflict (if you expect it), tell yourself, "I'm not going to let so-and-so get to me." During the encounter, tell yourself that the other doesn't know what she or he is saying, is really upset at something, and doesn't mean to hurt you psychologically. After successfully surviving a potentially threatening situation, compliment yourself for getting through it. Tell yourself that you have really improved in the way you handle situations like that.

Expressing Anger Effectively

In addition to calming our emotional reaction in a conflict situation, we can choose how we respond to anger provocations. Anger is best expressed and most effective when several conditions are met.[11]

1. You must direct your anger at the target of the anger. Suppose, for example, you are really angry with your boss because your hours were changed without consulting you, and they now conflict with your classes. You probably do not believe that you can yell at your boss, so instead you go home and slam objects around the house and yell at your roommate (displaced conflict). The trouble is that such actions are unlikely to reduce your anger. Instead, you are probably angrier when you are done, because you find additional shortcomings with your boss as you remember all the other inequities you have experienced in your job.

2. Expressing anger has to restore a person's sense of justice and of control over the situation while not inflicting harm on the other person. Going into your boss's office and screaming might feel good, but he or she is unlikely to change your hours. And if your boss changed your hours simply because of forgetfulness rather than because of a malicious intent, screaming at the boss is too severe a reaction for the situation.

3. Expressing anger gives a person a sense of control over the situation if that expression changes the behavior of the other person (your boss says, "I'm sorry, I forgot that you had class on Monday and Wednesday afternoons") or if it provides new insights (you realize you cannot work for this person and must find a new place of employment).

4. It is best to express anger not when angry but after cooling down. Recall in Chapter 6, we recommend that when you realize that a conflict exists, begin by saying, Stop! Don't become so upset that you start to lose control of yourself. Instead, try to calm down and cool off. To gain greater control over your mental faculties, take a time out. We suggest that you exit temporarily to calm yourself, go for a glass of water, count down from 100, or stop discussing the problematic topic for a while to allow time for the air to clear.

5. For the effective expression of your anger, the target must not retaliate in anger. This last condition is unfortunately the hardest to create. We have yet to meet more than a handful of people who can let others express anger at them without responding in kind. To help meet this last condition, we must express anger responsibly and with tact. Tavris noted, "The result of the ability to control anger is that people feel less angry, not more."[12]

If one chooses to do so, how is it best to express one's anger to the offender? Of course, the best verbal response to anger is contained in the skills we discussed in Chapters 4 and 6. Express anger responsibly, and choose the assertive option for communication rather than the aggressive or passive-aggressive.

If we choose to avoid expressing our anger to the person, what other techniques can we employ? Anger-ins need to take time to think about why they are angry and what they would like to change in the situation. Rather than thinking about ways to get back at the other person, anger-ins must focus on problem solving.

Anger-outs, on the other hand, need to find some way to dissipate the energy that accompanies their anger. Physical exertion, like running or other exercise, helps to focus the anger-out. Would you believe that something like housework, particularly cleaning toilets, is helpful? (And quite symbolic!) Art and music are also ways anger-outs can learn to express anger in healthy ways. Once the energy of the anger has worn off, the anger-out needs to reflect on the situation and discover the source of the anger.

Overall, dealing with anger requires first that we build habits of positive rather than negative response to anger-provoking situations. It is also necessary that we determine the underlying source of the anger and that we decide what, if anything, we need to do to alleviate that source of anger. These specific actions help contain the escalation of conflict.

- Be aware of your behavior.
- Try to anticipate the effect that your words and actions have on others. It does minimize the amount of conflict you need to experience.
- Try to keep the other focused on the here and now. Past history should stay out of the conversation as much as possible.
- Be open to what others have to say. Let them say what they are feeling and accept it as a legitimate feeling, if not a legitimate criticism.
- Negotiate acceptable boundaries with others.
- Do not react to or act on everything a person says. Consider Aesop's fable of a man, his son, and the donkey. A man and his son are walking from the countryside into town alongside the donkey. In response to one person's criticism that they are not using the donkey efficiently, the man puts his son on the donkey. Another person criticizes, so he rides the donkey while the boy walks. Another person criticizes, so both ride the donkey. Another person criticizes, and they decide to carry the donkey, strung upside down on a stick over their shoulders. On the town bridge over a river, they accidentally drop the donkey into the river, and, being bound, the donkey drowns. *Don't drown the donkey!*

Anger as a Secondary Emotion

When we say that anger is a **secondary emotion,** we mean that its origin is in other emotions such as fear, disappointment, hurt, and frustration. According to Hocker and Wilmot, anger is a secondary emotion based on "frustration of unmet needs or thwarted desires."[13] Other communication scholars suggest that the primary emotion is the fear that occurs when our personal security is threatened or our self-esteem is attacked. Some psychologists claim that anger and hostility are cover-ups for insecurity, loss, and sadness.[14] If we are angry at or with someone, we feel more righteous about our emotions, and it is easier for us to lay the responsibility at the other person's feet, than if we say, "I fear . . ." or "I am disappointed." Anger protects us; admitting our fears or disappointments may make us feel vulnerable.

The realization that anger is a cover-up for other emotions we are reluctant to admit suggests that another trick to controlling emotion is to determine what unmet need or desire is being frustrated that creates the fear or hurt. For example, a teacher may feel frustrated because not all members of her class may pass an exam. Her fear is that she is not teaching as well as she could or should. So if she gets a lot of questions during a review session prior to the exam, the teacher may suddenly turn angry and accuse her students of not studying enough. Her apparent anger is really a response to her fear that the students may fail and make her look bad as a teacher. Once the teacher realizes that, she is much less likely to act angry toward her students.

11.3 Think about It

Under what conditions have you found yourself expressing your anger appropriately? How was the situation different from a time that you felt your anger was out of control? What do you think you could do to duplicate the situation under which you expressed your anger constructively?

Responding to Another's Anger

One of the more difficult challenges we must face in a conflict is the anger and possible rage an anger-out person is feeling. Often, our fear about the way another may react affects our ability to solve a problem, as this narrative suggests.

> Over the years, my husband has become calmer, but he still can lose his temper over unimportant issues pretty easily. When he loses his temper, he scares me. He's a big guy, and seeing all that muscle tense up makes me want to hide. I kept trying to hide a credit card bill from him, because I was afraid to tell him what a mess I had made. I was afraid he might even hit me when he found out. He finally picked up the mail before I did, and I prepared myself for the worst.

When you are dealing with someone who is extremely angry, it is important to do what you can to stay calm and not feed his or her anger. Often, people are loudly angry because they fear no one listens to them unless they yell and scream. Listening and reflecting are important skills in responding to another person's anger.

Equally important is acknowledging the importance of the source of anger. If you say something to the effect of "I can't believe you are reacting this way" or "I think you are being childish," you fuel that person's anger rather than subdue it. When a person is on the verge of rage, it is not the time to express your anger about the situation. You need to focus on calming that person down before raising any issue of your own. If your attempts to acknowledge the other person's source of anger and the legitimacy of her or his feelings fail, and the person continues to rage and fume, it is often a good idea to exit the situation. Saying something such as "I can see you're really angry, and I think I'd like to give you some time to cool off before we talk about it" acknowledges that you sympathize with the other and have a commitment to work out whatever problem is there, but postpones the conflict until both people are calm and ready to talk about it.

We not only need to know how to respond to anger-outs, but we also need to adapt to anger-ins. Anger-ins probably have the hardest time figuring out what the underlying issue is. Give anger-ins a safe space where they can express their thoughts. They need to figure out why they're really angry.

Manage It

Do stress and anger cause conflict or result from it? Clearly, we feel both when we experience a conflict. Almost as frequently, though, we experience a conflict because of the stress and anger we are experiencing in our lives.

Stress and anger share three features. First, they both arise from other events. We feel stress because of challenges outside our control and because of how we perceive our life events. We feel anger when hurt, or disappointed, or frustrated. Researchers classify both anger and stress as secondary kinds of emotions. We deal with them most effectively if we can change how we view the events that produce stress and anger.

Second, although anger and stress are causes of conflicts that often escalate and get out of hand, both result from poorly managed conflicts. A conflict in itself creates stress and motivates us to take some kind of action, either destructive or constructive. In addition, if we are dissatisfied with the outcome of a previous conflict, we may continue to resent others or want to seek revenge.

Third, when we are angry or stressed we find it difficult to communicate competently. We forget that assertive, not aggressive or avoiding, responses lead to productive outcomes.

Stress appears in many aspects of our daily lives: jobs, finances, romance, tests, papers, teachers, time pressures—the list goes on and on. Stress often leads to anger, sometimes inwardly directed. At other times, we direct our anger at our friends, romantic partners, family members, or colleagues. We can cope with stress most effectively by changing the way we feel about the sources of stress in our lives.

Just as the way we respond to stressors affects how we experience or avoid conflict, the way we express our anger plays a role in the resolution of conflict. Both anger-in and anger-out responses lead to unproductive outcomes. We need to learn to express our anger appropriately, at the right time to the right person over the right issue. In addition, we can take a "time out," engage in relaxation exercises, and engage in helpful self-talk. For both stress and anger, we must find the underlying emotion driving them. When we do so, we tend to respond effectively.

Most importantly, though, both stress and anger are unavoidable. However, we can control them. We can learn to rid ourselves of thoughts that contribute to stress and to manage other sources of stress as they arise. We can learn to express anger constructively. We can learn how to better manage our conflicts by first learning how to manage our stress and anger.

11.1 Work with It

Read the following case study and answer the questions that follow it.

> With my roommate Elena, there is a sense of uncertainty right now because I am not sure whether she is coming back next year to room with me. We have been the best of friends since our first days in elementary school, and I can't imagine anyone else as my roommate. I realize that this uncertainty is making me edgy and irritable. Everything she does right now is getting to me. I don't like it when she comes in late and wakes me, doesn't study when I do, and is too busy with her other friends to eat with me. We aren't seeing each other any more and here we are roommates!
>
> Anyway, yesterday she left the room and took my laptop computer with her without asking me. I really erupted. I went hunting for her and found her in the library lobby typing notes while discussing possible upcoming test questions with a couple of her classmates. I went right up to her and grabbed my laptop. I really told her off and left with it. She and her friends just stared at me.

1. How would you apply the principles of stress management to this case study?
2. How would you apply the principles of anger management to this case study?

11.2 Work with It

Apply the ABC model to the major stresses in your life by listing the following in a four-column table.

1. List activating events or stressors (triggering events, people, places, situations) in your life. Indicate which are temporary or short-lived stressors and which are longer term. Identify each as annoying or anger producing and disappointing or depression producing.
2. List consequences (physiological effects/body reactions, behavioral effects, psychological effects—negative coping and defense mechanisms).
3. List your internal pressures (irrational beliefs, self-damnations, thoughts, assumptions, wishful thoughts, intolerances). These are to include "should statements," "awfulizing statements," "overgeneralizations," and self-talk (or irrational beliefs).
4. List the positive coping mechanisms that you would like to use.

11.1 Remember It

Write an essay about the role of anger in recent conflicts in your life using the following as subtopics.

1. Describe conflicts in which you are one or more of the following: anger-in, anger-out, or controller.
2. What were the triggers that aroused your anger? What were the prevailing conditions or the time and place that affected how you handled your anger?
3. What actions by you or others contributed to the escalation or de-escalation of anger?
4. Positive techniques you used or would have liked to use for controlling your anger.

11.2 Remember It

Write an essay in which you apply the ideas presented in Chapter 11 to your life situation. Discuss the following topics.

Part A
1. Explain how stress affects your communication behavior in a conflict situation.
2. Identify sources of stress in your life.
3. List ways to deal constructively with these stresses.

Part B
1. Diagnose your own general anger level.
2. Explain how anger affects your communication behavior in a conflict situation.
3. List ways to effectively control or express your anger in that situation.

N O T E S

1. Velma Walker and Lynn Brokaw, *Becoming Aware,* 6th Ed. (Dubuque, IA: Kendall Hunt, 1995), p. 315.

2. Hans Selye, *Stress without Distress* (New York: J. B. Lippincott, 1974).

3. Thomas Berstene, "The Inexorable Link between Conflict and Change," *The Journal for Quality and Participation* 27 (2004), 4–9.

4. These hormones are often tied to the perceived power a person has in the relationship; see Timothy J. Loving, Kathi L. Hefner, Janice K. Kiecolt-Glaser, Ronald Glaser, and William B. Malarkey, "Stress Hormone Changes and Marital Conflict: Spouses' Relative Power Makes a Difference," *Journal of Marriage and the Family* 66 (2004), 595–612.

5. William McKinnon, Carol S. Wiesse, C. Patrick Reynolds, Charles A. Bowles, and Andrew Baum, "Chronic Stress, Leukocyte Subpopulations, and Humoral Response to Latent Viruses," *Health Psychology* 8 (1989), p. 391.

6. Albert Ellis, "Overview of the Clinical Theory of Rational-Emotive Therapy," in Russell Grieger and John Boyd (Eds.), *Rational-Emotive Therapy: A*

Skills-Based Approach (New York: Van Nostrand Reinhold, 1980), pp. 1–31.

7. Nathan Miczo, "Humor Ability, Unwillingness to Communicate, Loneliness, and Perceived Stress: Testing a Security Theory," *Communication Studies* 55 (2004), p. 222.

8. Barbara A. Winstead, Valerian J. Derlega, Robin J. Lewis, Janis Sanchez-Hucles, and Eva Clark, "Friendship, Social Interaction, and Coping with Stress," *Communication Research* 19 (1992), 193–211.

9. Carol Tavris, *Anger: The Misunderstood Emotion* (New York: Touchstone, through Simon and Schuster, 1989), p. 203.

10. Ibid.

11. Ibid., pp. 152–154.

12. Ibid., p. 189.

13. William Wilmot and Joyce Hocker, *Interpersonal Conflict,* 6th Ed. (New York: McGraw Hill, 2001), p. 250.

14. John Gottman, Robert Levenson, and Erica Woodin, "Facial Expressions during Marital Conflict," *Journal of Family Communication* 1 (2001), 37–57.

12 Impression Management in Conflict Situations

OBJECTIVES

At the end of this chapter, you should be able to:

- Explain the role of face and face saving in conflict.

- Explain the difference between positive face and autonomous face.

- Identify at least three preventative strategies you can use to avoid threatening the other person's face in a conflict situation.

- List three general ways and three specific techniques you can use to support another's face in a conflict situation.

- Compare and contrast three conflict situations using the repair sequence: one where you offer an account, one where you make a concession, and another where you offer an apology.

KEY TERMS

account	disclaimers	positive face
acknowledgment	excuses	preventive facework
apologies	face	remedy
autonomous face	impression management	repair sequence
concessions	justifications	reproach
corrective facework	offending situations	supportive facework

A fundamental assumption that underlies our approach to interpersonal conflict is this: People are motivated to create and maintain favorable impressions of themselves; that is, they engage in **impression management.** By *impression,* we mean what sociologist Goffman termed **face,** or people's image of themselves.[1] Not only are people striving to present and save face, this motivation may create a conflict situation. A person may not think she is smart, but if someone else accuses her of being stupid, the remark is likely to offend her. In fact, the remark may so anger her that she walks out of the room and has nothing more to do with the other person. Face is something that lurks behind the scene and may or may not make a difference in a conflict situation. However, when aroused, it may make all the difference in the world.

In addition to creating conflict situations, threats to face can also exacerbate conflict situations. According to Tracy, any interaction is potentially face-threatening;[2] but in conflicts, where people face incompatible goals or activities and share the feeling that the other is somehow interfering with their own pursuit of rewards and goals, face threats are present. As discussed in Chapter 9, one source of competitive conflict escalation cycles is the introduction of face issues, which add an extra issue to the initial conflict problems. Because face is so important to people, they try to repair their damaged image before the initial conflict issue is settled. Threatening the other person's face is a good way to guarantee that the conflict does not enter the resolution phase. Thus, the introduction of face issues into a conflict can escalate the severity of the conflict, making it difficult for people to resolve the original issue. "At its best, effective face support permits us to achieve (however fleeting) relationship nirvana. At its worst, persistent face loss can create bitter enmity and personal agony."[3]

When people lose face they may also seek retaliation, as demonstrated in recent studies. Aggressive responses to face-losing situations are more likely when people believe that the other person in the situation has caused it.[4] Such situations are as mild as someone criticizing you in public (e.g., a teacher criticizing a student in class) or teasing you. It is sometimes more serious, such as one friend picking a fight with another in public.

This chapter discusses the concept of face and impression management in more detail to show its importance in conflict situations. We want to address an important skill in developing competent conflict management behavior and that is the ability to maintain one's own impression and that of others to avoid escalating the conflict and to restore a relationship if face is lost. You are expected to identify people's face, and list techniques to prevent the loss of face, and list general and specific ways to support the other's face in conflict situations. To help you in this regard, we begin with an explanation of the role of face in conflict situations.

Understanding the Demands of Face

Defining Face

The concept of face is fundamental to who we think we are. According to Goffman, we all have images of ourselves, and we project that image (our face) in interactions with others.[5] As we interact, we also look for confirmation of the face we present. The projection of face is cooperative—as long as the image we project seems consistent and believable, others accept it and respond to it as presented. For example, we act like competent teachers and trust our students to support us in our roles. Similarly, they act like prepared and motivated students and expect us to respect their image of themselves. Of course, the situation is made more complicated by the many factors that affect our perceptions, understandings, and actions, but this example can give you an idea of how we use face in everyday interaction.

The mutual cooperation involved in projecting face is a principle of interaction that is taken for granted. Being able to create and sustain an identity for oneself, as well as helping the other person to create and maintain an identity for him or herself, is a fundamental component of communication competence, according to Cupach and Metts. In the past, intercultural communication researchers claimed that everyone has face concerns during conflict, but members of different cultures present, protect, lose, and save face in different

People try to create impressions in a variety of ways. What kind of impression do you think the owner of this Shar-pei puppy is trying to create?

ways because of different levels of face concerns. However, recent research suggests that these cultural differences are not as great as we think.[6]

Positive and Autonomous Face

In a seminal work, Brown and Levinson concluded that people experience two kinds of face needs.[7] **Positive face** means that people want others important to them to like and respect them. A person's positive face is supported when others appear to value what the person values, express admiration for the person, or show acceptance of the person as a competent individual. **Autonomous face** (often referred to in the literature as "negative face") occurs when people do not constrain or impose on others. When others respect a person's independence, the person's autonomous face is supported.

> Autonomous [or negative] face is the desire to maintain one's own autonomy. Individuals in any culture want to be shown proper deference and respect and not have their privacy and space invaded, their resources spent, and their actions restricted without just cause.[8]

The desires for positive and autonomous face, under the best of circumstances, can create a dilemma. One may communicate support of another's positive face by expressing admiration for that person, spending time with that person, and so on, but by doing so, one can encroach on the person's autonomy. Supporting a person's positive and autonomous face requires a balance under the best of circumstances. Consider how these competing needs are threatened in a conflict situation.

wow! →

I would say that the biggest conflict in my life arises when my girlfriend gets emotional. Of all the girlfriends I have had, I have never dated one as emotional as my current girlfriend. The conflict usually comes when I have had a hard day and still have work to do in the evening. My girlfriend will come over and yell at me for ignoring her and not really loving her, because I have been gone all day. When I try to tell her I have been busy and I still have much to do, the conflict becomes worse. She starts to cry and becomes crazy. At this point, I cannot deal with the situation and want to hide under a rock. The conflict usually has to defuse itself by me leaving and not speaking to her until later that evening or the next day. When she becomes calm, the situation is resolved, but sometimes it can last for a week or so.

While the man's positive face is supported by his partner's desire to spend time with him, his autonomous face is threatened by her need for too much of his limited time. According to O'Sullivan, it is unlikely that people would perceive a particular encounter as strictly positive or negative.[9] So, in the above example, the man's and his partner's conflicts would arise out of the need to support both positive and autonomous face.

Sometimes face threats occur unexpectedly. A study of 911 calls, for example, claims that the required questions for information asked by the operators "can threaten callers' desire to be treated as trustworthy, intelligent, and of good character, as well as threaten their need to feel unimpeded in their requests for timely police service."[10] And while most of us would agree that being told we are cared for is good, a directly affectionate message, while supporting our positive face, might threaten our autonomous face.[11]

12.1 Think about It

How have you seen issues of autonomous and positive face create conflicts in your experience? What have you done to resolve issues of autonomous and positive face? Are the strategies you use for each different?

To help solve the dilemma posed by competing desires for positive and autonomous face, we offer a before, during, and after set of recommendations. Before committing loss of face, people may take steps to prevent it. During interaction, they can go a step farther by supporting the other's face in general or specific ways. Finally, if a threat to face is made, they can use corrective facework: Using constructive responses to loss of face in a conflict situation.

Preventive Facework

Preventive facework forestalls becoming embroiled in face-saving issues during conflict situations by avoiding or minimizing threats to face. One way to use preventive facework is to try to see the situation from the other's perspective—how the issue affects the other and the other's self-image. Another way is to accept what the other person says at face value (no pun intended). Unless there is a good reason to the contrary, it is best to accept what the other person says as an accurate reflection of his or her feelings.

A third way to avoid face-saving issues is to accept the other person's right to change his or her mind. No one can predict the future with any degree of accuracy. The fact is that goals change, people change, and life changes. To treat a change in goals as a sign of the other person's insincerity or instability threatens the other person and sets up future conflicts concerning that very issue.

Fourth, people can also avoid threats to face by avoiding face-threatening topics (which is almost impossible in a conflict situation) or by employing communication practices that minimize threats to face. Research by Sereno and colleagues indicates that in intimate relationships, expressing conflict issues in a nonassertive manner rather than assertive was seen as more appropriate by those responding to the questionnaire. The authors suggested that this approach may allow the person hearing the complaint to maintain a "positive self-image, and to reaffirm that the actor still had a positive view of the receiver and of the relationship."[12]

The last approach of avoiding threats to face consists of communication practices such as politeness and **disclaimers** (additions to the message that soften the forcefulness of the message) that help to minimize threats to face before they happen.

> [As] a face-saving measure, individuals routinely adopt a politeness strategy that may involve sending less direct, more equivocal hedges. Building upon this notion others have catalogued the ways in which people use tactful messages, side stepping explicit disagreement in order to save face.[13]

This narrative illustrates how to maximize a face-threat.

> Just recently, my mother was expressing her dissatisfaction to me about the host in the dining room at the retirement home where she lives. She had come a little late to lunch and found that "her" table had dishes all over it. Instead of moving to a different table or asking someone to take away the dishes, she turned to the host and said, "When are you going to start doing your job?" As she told me the story, she was amazed that the host had subsequently been rude to her. I tried explaining conflict message skills to her, but someone with as much practice at engaging in nasty behavior as my mother is not likely to change.

In the above conflict situation, for example, the person making the complaint could have used either of the following disclaimers to soften the effect of the complaint:

- *Hedging:* indicating uncertainty and receptivity to suggestions. "Is this my table? It doesn't seem to have gotten cleared yet."
- *Cognitive disclaimer:* asserting that the behavior is reasonable and under control, despite appearances. "I don't want to sound demanding, but I'd really like to sit down now and the dirty table is bothering me."

Other disclaimers available in a conflict situation include:

- *Credentialing:* indicating you have good reasons and appropriate qualifications for the statement you intend to make. "I am your friend and I care about you, so I want to say . . ."

- *Sin license:* indicating that this is an appropriate occasion to violate the rule and one should not take the violation as a character defect. "Well, this is a special occasion and . . .")
- *Appeal for suspended judgment:* asking the other to withhold judgment for a possibly offensive action until it is explained. "Hear me out before you get upset . . ."[14]

12.1 Apply It

Imagine that you have to say something potentially face-threatening to a friend. Explain how you could use each of these disclaimers to soften the complaint:

- hedging
- cognitive disclaimer
- credentialing
- sin license
- appeal for suspended judgment

Supportive Facework

When in a conflict with someone, use **supportive facework** to help reinforce the way the other is presenting himself or herself. In a general way, people want others to like them, respect them, encourage them, consult them, include them, appreciate them, reward them, make references to them, ask them for their opinion or input, smile at them, greet them warmly, help when needed, and make them feel safe. Ask yourself if you do the following when in a conflict:

- Do I try to make the other feel important?
- Do I try to make the other look good to other people?
- Do I try to make the other think that they are winning?
- Do I try to make the other feel secure?
- Do I try to make the other believe that I am honest and trustworthy?

We can support others in a general way by what we do and what we say. If we don't include, consult, ask, reward, or help others, they may feel put down by our actions. It is also possible to put people down verbally by insulting them or showing disrespect.

We can also support others in a more specific way. To do this, you need to determine what traits or characteristics the other perceives in himself or herself and point out the ones you have in common or are capable of supporting.

- You like to fish? Well, so do I.
- I like people with red hair.

- You're a jogger, so let's jog together next time.
- You have taken three classes from Professor Hamad. I hope to take a class from her soon.
- We both want to lose weight.

When people say they don't like others with a particular color hair, and you have that hair color, they may put you down. Because they say they don't exercise regularly, you may see that as some kind of disapproval for your doing it. If their goal in a conflict is to inflict serious mental harm on you, they can resort to verbal abuse and put you down. If their goal is to solve a problem, then they want to avoid abuse in favor of face support.

12.2 Think about It

What are your general and specific face needs? In general, what actions could others take that would show support for your face needs? What specific actions could they take?

Corrective Facework

When a threat to face has been made, you should use **corrective facework,** or statements meant to ameliorate the effect of face-threatening messages. When you are the one whose face has been threatened, one means of corrective action is simply to act as though no threat to face has been made, ignoring the action that caused a face threat. This is a good strategy for minor issues, but ignoring a major face threat may result in a larger conflict later on.

Other forms of corrective action have been generated by Thomas and Pondy, who viewed impression management (ensuring that the image one projects is the one that others perceive) as critical in moving a conflict to its resolution phase.[15] People's beliefs about the other's intent affect the conflict strategies they choose and how they interpret the other's strategies. Thomas and Pondy found that when people were asked to recall what conflict resolution mode they had used, the majority (74%) were most likely to recall using "cooperative" modes: collaboration, compromise, and accommodation. However, the majority (73%) also recalled that the other person in the conflict had been competitive rather than cooperative. Thus, people are not being perceived as cooperative even when they think they are being cooperative.

The authors identified a number of ways in which people can work to manage the impression they make in a conflict to help ensure that the image they project is the one the other person perceives. Some of their suggestions are these:

- The first activity is scanning, or checking out the perceptions being created. We can question the other to confirm that we are "on the same page."
- A second activity is explaining, used when we perceive that the other has not taken our message in the way we meant it.

Repair Rituals

What should we do if we realize that we have offended the other person? We have available to us a ritual known as a repair sequence, which has these phases or steps:

- **Offending situation:** the other's behavior is seen as intentionally hurtful, whether or not that person did intend it
- **Reproach:** request for an explanation of an offense from the one offended
- **Remedy:** an account, concession, or apology supplied by an offender
- **Acknowledgment:** evaluation of the account supplied by the one offended

The **repair sequence** is a specialized version of the conflict process where a triggering event is followed by initiation, differentiation, and perhaps resolution. The difference is mainly in the relationship of the issue to the episode. Whereas in conflict both people perceive that the other is interfering with their goals or engaging in incompatible activities, in a repair sequence there is a clear distinction between the offender and the offended party. The offender has created a problem (that is, the offender has not acted in accordance with the face she or he has created for the other person) and must explain his or her actions. Let us consider each of the phases or steps in the repair sequence.

Offending Situation.   **Offending situations** are those in which a person believes that the other has acted in an intentionally hurtful way. Usually, the offense is face-threatening in nature. Nothing is more awkward that having to continue interacting with a person who has offended you and refuses to acknowledge it or appears unaware of it.

Reproach.   People are unlikely to walk away from an offense without saying anything at all, although that can happen on occasion, especially when the consequences are minimal. In more significant cases, one can call attention to an offense by simply commenting on it or confronting the offender and asking him or her for an explanation (e.g., "What do you have to say about the broken window?"). In some cases, one can make an offender aware of an offense even by remaining silent. The other may perceive this as "the silent treatment," realize what caused it, and come forward with an explanation. Finally, the offended party may also use nonverbal cues (e.g., slamming doors, dirty looks) to let the offender know an offense has occurred, which assumes that the offender knows what he or she did to upset the other.

Remedy.   Reproaches create a need for us to take an action that rectifies matters. However, it is possible that an offender may respond to a reproach by refusing to act, the most aggravating response. Refusals include denying that one was even involved in the offending event or that the event took place (which may mean lying). A person can also refuse to act by turning the reproach around and questioning the right of the offended person to make a reproach. In cases where one cannot deny the event or one's role in it, there are three types of actions an offender can take to restore a relationship: offer an account (through excuses or justifications), make a concession, or offer an apology; one can also act in a way that combines any of these.

An **account** is explanation for behavior when questioned. Accounts are also part of the conflict interaction (when a person is challenged on an issue and must respond) or its aftermath (when a person tries to explain what was done and said in a conflict situation). Accounts serve an important function in that they explain how people interpret the situation at hand. Through the process of requesting and providing accounts, people in offending situations come to establish, manage, and change the meanings of the situation.[16] Research on accounts has examined such diverse situations as managing instances of failure in organizations, reasons for the breakup of marital and romantic relationships, and distressed marriages locked into a blaming–accounting cycle.[17]

Accounts may take the form of excuses or justifications. **Excuses** admit that the offense occurred but deny responsibility for it. The offender can claim

- impairment (e.g., "I was drunk"),
- diminished responsibility (e.g., "I didn't know"),
- scapegoat status (e.g., "they made me do it"), or
- that she or he is a "victim of a sad tale," in which the offender recounts a series of misfortunes that have resulted in the way the offender is today. Sad tales are often the staple of courtroom drama, in which defense attorneys try to prove their client incapable of responsibility in a crime.

In contrast to offering an excuse, the offender may choose to offer a justification, which diminishes the meaning of the offense rather than diffusing responsibility for it. **Justifications** may acknowledge that an act was committed while claiming that

- it hurt no one (e.g., "it was just a practical joke"),
- the victim deserved it (e.g., "he hit me first"),
- other people who have committed similar offenses were not punished,
- he or she had good intentions when choosing to commit the offense, or
- the offense was needed because of loyalty to others (e.g., the reasons used by various political subordinates when explaining why they broke various laws).

Because not all excuses or justifications are acceptable, the offender may need to make some sort of concession. **Concessions** admit the offender's guilt and include apologies and offers of restitution. When an excuse or justification is not acceptable, the offender must make some concession or offer an apology.

Apologies are admissions of blameworthiness and regret on the part of the offender.[18] Apologies are a means of impression management used to restore or minimize damage done to one's identity and to stave off potential punishment from the person offended. Apologies allow a person to admit to blame for an action, but they also attempt to obtain a pardon for the action by convincing the offended person that the incident is not representative of what the offender is really like.[19] According to Schlenker and Darby,

> If the apology is viewed as sincere by the audience, the actor appears to have repented, appears not to require further rehabilitative punishment, and should be forgiven. The social interaction can then return to its normal course and the actor has minimized the negative repercussions.[20]

Schlenker and Darby have identified several levels of apology, which are used progressively by actors as the offense committed becomes more serious and as the actor's responsibility for the offense increases. An apology can include a simple "pardon me" or something more complicated, including statements of remorse (e.g., "I'm sorry"), offering to help the injured party, self-castigation, or direct attempts to obtain forgiveness. In one study, respondents were asked to imagine that they had bumped into another person in a public place, either in a crowded shopping mall or in a hallway at school between classes. The degree of felt responsibility was manipulated by explaining that the actor was either knocked from behind, thus bumping into the victim, or had not been paying attention and bumped into the victim without noticing. Offenses of varying degrees were that the victim had been bumped on the arm (low), knocked to the ground but was unhurt (medium), or knocked to the ground and was moaning in pain (high). Respondents were asked whether they would use one of the levels of apology, respond in nonapology (e.g., saying or doing nothing, or responding nonverbally), or respond in justification ("I'm glad to see you're not hurt") or excuses ("I didn't see you").

12.2 Apply It

Recall a time when someone required an account from you for your actions. Write out a description of the situation, and then provide a message that would fit each of these account categories: excuse, justification, and refusal to account.

Acknowledgement. After an account has been rendered, the offended party responds with an acknowledgement in one of several ways.

- The most mitigating way is to honor the account, accepting its content and signaling, verbally or nonverbally, that the "score is even."
- The offended party may retreat from the reproach, dropping his or her right to make it (e.g., "I didn't know that you were forced into action").
- The offended party may also simply drop or switch the topic, moving away from the reproach without resolving the issue.

More aggravating is rejection of the account, either by taking issue with it (e.g., "I can't believe you expect me to believe you") or by simply restating the reproach as though no account was given.

Responding to Others

In a recent study, Benoit and Drew examined the ways in which people respond to impression-management strategies. They had people rate how appropriate and effective various strategies are when someone has damaged one's impression. The scenario was one in which person A bumps into person B, spilling something on B's favorite coat. B accuses A of ruining B's clothes, and A replies with denial ("I didn't do it"), evasion of responsibility for the event ("it was an accident, it wasn't my fault"), reducing the offensiveness of the event ("it's not that bad"), corrective action ("I'll have the clothing cleaned"), or apology ("I'm so sorry"). The results indicated, not surprisingly, that apologies and offering some corrective action were seen as the most appropriate and effective ways to restore one's image in this kind of circumstance.[21]

12.3 **Think about It**

What kinds of apologies work on you? When someone has offended you, which are you most likely to accept? Least likely? Why?

A newly developing area of communication study is online conflict that occurs in real time chat rooms or asynchronous discussion such as Usenet newsgroups. In their study of online conflict, Smith, McLaughlin, and Osborne found that few people replied to reproaches in Usenet newsgroups and seldom completed the traditional repair sequence.[22]

How can you explain this difference between online and face-to-face encounters? We suggest that it is much easier to "walk away" from an offending situation online than it is face-to-face, especially where there is a relationship between the parties involved. In many of these online offending situations, there is no (previously established) relationship to repair. When face-to-face, if you call me on the carpet for something I said or did, I may feel obligated to respond and seek your acceptance of my excuse, apology, or concession, but in an online discussion group, I might find it easier and less awkward to simply exit the discussion.

Smith's research is corroborated by others examining the difference between face-to-face (FTF) conflict and conflict in computer mediated communication (CMC). Zornoza and colleagues, for example, found that negative conflict behaviors were more frequent in CMC than FTF, and the number of positive conflict management behaviors actually decreased over time.[23] In addition, Dorado and colleagues found that there were higher levels of avoidance and lower levels of forcing in computer mediated negotiation, while face-to-face negotiation displayed more forcing and compromise.[24] Finally, Hobman and colleagues' research indicated that CMC groups displayed more process and relationship conflict than FTF when first starting, but those differences disappeared after the first day.[25]

Manage It

Some other cultures more openly discuss face and face saving techniques than we do here in the United States. However, the concept is no less important for Americans. One of the primary reasons conflicts escalate or get out of hand is due to face-threats.

The truth is that people everywhere are motivated to create and maintain favorable impressions of themselves; this impression or image people have of themselves is called "face." There are two types of face that are important to every one of us, positive face and autonomous face. A person's positive face is supported when others value what the person values, express admiration for the person, or show acceptance of the person as a competent individual. Autonomous face is the desire people have for freedom from constraints and impositions. When others respect a person's independence, the person's autonomous face is supported.

The desires for positive and autonomous face, under the best of circumstances, can create a dilemma. Supporting a person's positive and autonomous face requires balance. This balancing act is referred to as impression management.

Impression management means ensuring that one's message is not mistakenly taken as face-threatening. To do this, an effective conflict manager adds to the message (before the other receives it) disclaimers such as hedging, cognitive disclaimer, credentialing, sin license, or appeal for suspended judgment.

Once engaged in conversation with another, an effective conflict manager can employ general ways and specific techniques to support another's face in conflict situations. In a general way, people want others to like, respect, encourage, consult, include, appreciate, and reward them. They want others to ask them questions, greet them warmly, help them when needed, and make them feel safe. We can also support others in a more specific way. To do this, we need to determine what traits or characteristics the other perceives in him- or herself and point out the ones we have in common or are capable of supporting.

In a conflict situation in which we lose face, we can employ a repair sequence to regain it. A repair sequence has these phases or steps: the offending situation, a reproach (request from the offended person for an explanation of the other's offense), a remedy (an account from the offender such as an excuse or justification, a concession, or an apology), and an acknowledgment (evaluation of the account).

When the violation creates more than an offending situation, a relational transgression occurs, which we examine in the next chapter. When relational transgressions occur, reconciliation is necessary to restore the relationship, or, if that is not possible, forgiveness is needed to help those involved make sense of the situation so that they do not carry the hurt into other relationships.

12.1 Work with It

Read the following case study and answer the questions that follow it.

A long-lasting conflict centered on the amount of time and affection Frank's wife, Judy, was spending on their cat, Lucky. This conflict took place a number of times, usually whenever Frank was feeling neglected. Whenever Judy entered the house, she lavished the cat with affection. In fact every time she passed the cat in the hallway, she would stop and caress her, talk to her, and go out of her way to make the cat feel loved. From his perspective, Frank felt that Judy always had time to give the cat the affection she needed (and more) while never having time to provide the affection he felt that he needed. It had become natural for her to seek out the cat and make over her while Frank had to ask or make an appointment. He inferred from her actions that she was never too busy for the cat but rarely had enough time for him. He was jealous of a cat.

From Judy's perspective, the cat was helpless and her lavishing attention was only because the cat was so "cute and defenseless." Judy didn't realize that Frank would really enjoy short, quick doses of affection throughout the day like she was giving the cat. Because of a few instances where Judy interrupted Frank while he was working intensely on something and he responded a bit negatively, she also felt that he might put a damper on her affectionate overtures toward him by not being responsive, or by failing to "purr."

1. What is the likely outcome of this conflict situation?
2. How could the characters have supported one another's face using general techniques?
3. How could the characters have supported one another's face using specific techniques, and what would then have been the likely outcome?
4. Describe the steps in the accounting sequence as they would apply to this conflict.
5. What role could accounts or concessions play in this case study?

12.2 Work with It

Read the following case study and answer the questions that follow it.

> A group of us live together in a sorority house. One of our sisters, Gina, is normally quiet and easygoing. However, one day she suddenly verbally attacked each one of us and accused us of plotting against her behind her back. I said to her, "What? Where is this coming from?" We were all shocked at her suddenly different behavior. She even threw a textbook at one of her sisters and stormed out of the room. That evening she rejoined the group but said nothing about the incident. At first, a couple of us raised the issue, but she just smiled and said, "I don't know what you are talking about."

1. Is this an offending situation?
2. Does a reproach occur?
3. Was a remedy offered? If not, what might it be? As for acknowledgment, what remedies would likely receive rejection from the narrator? What remedies might receive acceptance?

12.1 Remember It

Write an essay in which you apply the ideas presented in Chapter 12 by explaining the role of face and face saving in a recent conflict, real or imagined. Make sure to address the following topics.

1. Explain the difference between positive face and autonomous face in this conflict situation.
2. Identify at least three preventative strategies you could use to avoid threatening the other person's face in this conflict situation, including at least one specific disclaimer you could use or could have used.
3. List three general ways from the chapter and three specific techniques you can use to support another's face in this conflict situation.
4. Describe the accounting sequence and an apology that you could use for this conflict situation.

NOTES

1. Erving Goffman, *The Presentation of Self in Everyday Life* (New York: Overlook Press, 1959); *Interaction Ritual: Essays on Face-to-Face Behavior* (New York: Pantheon Books, 1967).
2. Karen Tracy, "The Many Faces of Facework," in Howard Giles and W. Peter Robinson (Eds.), *Handbook of Language and Social Psychology* (New York: John Wiley & Sons, 1990), pp. 209–226.
3. William R. Cupach and Sandra Metts, *Facework* (Thousand Oaks: Sage Publications, 1994), pp. 15–16.
4. Sandra Metts and William R. Cupach, "Situational Influence on the Use of Remedial Strategies in Embarrassing Predicaments," *Communication Monographs* 56 (1989), 151–162; William R. Cupach and Sandra Metts, "The Effects of Type of Predicament and Embarrassability on Remedial Responses to Embarrassing Situations," *Communication Quarterly* 40 (1992), 149–161.
5. Goffman, op. cit.
6. John Oetzel, Stella Ting-Toomey, Tomoko Masumoto, Yukiko Yokochi, Xiaohui Pan, Jiro Takai,

and Richard Wilcox, "Face and Facework in Conflict: A Cross-Cultural Comparison Of China, Germany, Japan, and the United States," *Communication Monographs* 68 (2001), 235–258; John Oetzel, Stella Ting-Toomey, Martha Idalia Chew-Sanchez, Richard Harris, Richard Wilcox, and Siegfried Stumpf, "Face and Facework in Conflicts with Parents and Siblings: A Cross-Cultural Comparison of Germans, Japanese, Mexicans, and U.S. Americans," *Journal of Family Communication* 3 (2003), 67–93.

7. Penelope Brown and Stephen Levinson, *Politeness: Some Universals in Language Usage* (Cambridge: Cambridge University Press, 1987).

8. Steven R. Wilson, Carlos G. Aleman, and Geoff B. Leatham, "Identity Implications of Influence Goals: A Revised Analysis of Face-Threatening Acts and Application to Seeking Compliance with Same-Sex Friends," *Human Communication Research* 25 (1998), p. 65.

9. Patrick B. O'Sullivan, "What You Don't Know Won't Hurt Me: Impression Management Functions of Communication Channels in Relationships," *Human Communication Research* 26 (2000), 403–431.

10. Sarah J. Tracy, "When Questioning Turns to Face Threat: An Interactional Sensitivity in 911 Call Taking," *Western Journal of Communication* 66 (2002), p. 152.

11. Larry A. Erbert and Kory Floyd, "Affectionate Expressions as Face-Threatening Acts: Receiver Assessments," *Communication Studies* 55 (2004), 254–270.

12. Kenneth K. Sereno, Melinda Welch, and David Braaten, "Interpersonal Conflict: Effects of Variation in Manner of Expressing Anger and Justification for Anger on Perceptions of Appropriateness, Competence, and Satisfaction," *Journal of Applied Communication Research* 15 (1987), p. 137.

13. Renee Edwards and Richard Bello, "Interpretations of Messages: The Influence of Equivocation, Face Concerns, and Ego-Involvement," *Human Communication Research* 27 (2001), p. 598.

14. J. Hewitt and R. Stokes, "Disclaimers," *American Sociological Review* 40 (1975), 1–12.

15. Kenneth W. Thomas and Louis R. Pondy, "Toward an 'Intent' Model of Conflict Management among Principle Parties," *Human Relations* 30 (1997), 1089–1102.

16. Richard Buttny, "Accounts as a Reconstruction of an Event's Context," *Communication Monographs* 52 (1985), 57–77.

17. Gail T. Fairhust, Stephen G. Green, and B. Kay Snavely, "Face Support in Controlling Poor Performance," *Human Communication Research* 11 (1984), 272–295; William R. Cupach and Sandra Metts, "Accounts of Relational Dissolution: A Comparison of Marital and Non-Marital Relationships," paper presented at the International Communication Association Convention, Honolulu, May 1985; Richard Buttny, "Blame-Account Sequences in Therapy: The Negotiation of Relational Meanings," *Semiotica* 78 (1990), 219–247.

18. Barry R. Schlenker and Bruce W. Darby, "The Use of Apologies in Social Predicaments," *Social Psychology Quarterly* 44 (1981), 271–278.

19. Barry R. Schlenker, *Impression Management* (Monterey, CA: Brooks/Cole, 1980).

20. Schlenker and Darby, p. 272.

21. William L. Benoit and Shirley Drew, "Appropriateness and Effectiveness of Image Repair Strategies," *Communication Reports* 10 (1997), 153–163.

22. Christine B. Smith, Margaret L. McLaughlin, and Kerry K. Osborne, "Conduct Control on Usenet," *Journal of Computer-Mediated Communication,* 2 (1997), retrieved on April 7, 2005 from http://jcmc.indiana.edu/vol2/issue4/smith.html).

23. Ana Zornoza, Pilar Ripoll, and Jose M. Peiro, "Conflict Management in Groups that Work in Two Different Communication Contexts: Face-to-Face and Computer-Mediated Communication," *Small Group Research* 33 (2002), 481–508.

24. Miguel A. Dorado, Francisco J. Medina, Lourdes Munduate, Immaculada F. J. Cisneros, and Martin Euwema, "Computer Mediated Negotiation of an Escalated Conflict," *Small Group Research* 33 (2002), 509–524.

25. Elizabeth V. Hobman, Prashant Bordia, Bernd Irmer, and Artemis Chang, "The Expression of Conflict in Computer-Mediated and Face-to-Face Groups," *Small Group Research* 33 (2002), 439–465.

13 After the Conflict

Forgiveness and Reconciliation

OBJECTIVES

At the end of this chapter, you should be able to:

- Distinguish relational transgressions from other types of problematic situations.
- Explain which relational transgressions are hardest to forgive.
- Distinguish forgiveness from forgetting and reconciliation.

- Explain the advantages of forgiveness and reconciliation following relational transgressions.
- Describe the steps one must take to forgive.
- List and explain the steps in the forgiveness/reconciliation loop.

KEY TERMS

core relational rules
deception
emotional residues
forgiveness
forgiveness/reconciliation loop

helping orientation
reconciliation
relational transgressions
revenge
self-fulfilling prophecy

transforming the meaning
truth bias
unforgiveness
victimization

In the previous chapter, we introduced the idea of an offending situation, which exists when people have acted in ways that threaten the face of another person or that seem intentionally hurtful. Accounts, concessions, and apologies are ways of rectifying problematic situations. But when "offending situations" take on crisis proportions and become more intense than a simple face management problem, we call them relational transgressions.

How do we handle a conflict situation involving a relational transgression? In this chapter, we discuss conflict situations that involve central relational issues, the nature of forgiveness, its effects, the means people use to forgive one another, and the ways in which we may reconcile our differences. You are expected to learn how to distinguish forgiveness from forgetting, distinguish reconciliation from continuing an existing relationship, explain the advantages of forgiveness and reconciliation following relational transgressions, and identify the means you should use to forgive others following conflict interaction.

Relational Transgressions

Relational transgressions are extremely problematic situations in which core rules of a relationship are violated, leaving high emotional residues. We'll explain each of these elements—rules and residues—in turn.

Core relational rules define our expectations about the way we should behave toward others as well as the way they should behave toward us. We treat strangers one way, friends another way, and our romantic partners still another. We relate to our parents differently from our more distant relatives. Part of the socialization process has taught us the rules that govern each type of social relationship such as romantic pairings, friendship, and being roommates. Relational transgressions occur when those rules we take for granted as "sacred" are broken by someone important to us.

In a committed romantic relationship, for example, a core relational rule is that you should not cheat on your partner. Metts asked respondents to rate relational transgressions in order of their difficulty in resolution and found that sexual infidelity was identified as the most difficult to deal with.[1] But sexual infidelity in romantic relationships is not the only relational transgression.

Another romantic relationship rule consists of intentional deception and lies. **Deception** is generally classified as "the conscious alteration of information a person believes to be true in order to significantly change another's perceptions from what the deceiver thought they would be without the alteration."[2] Certainly, "social lies" and lies used to avoid sticky situations (e.g., "I really can't go with you to the beach because I have to study") are part of our social fabric, whether or not we approve of them. They become a relational transgression, however, when the lie breaks core relational rules.

Another rule is that you should not physically abuse those you love. One expects his or her partner to love and protect, not hate and abuse the other. This occurs because as we develop romantic relationships with others, we tend to take a **helping orientation** toward them: We assume that they love us and desire to help rather than hurt us, as we do them. Clearly, violence in an interpersonal relationship constitutes a relational transgression, a violation of expected behavior. Violence, when it occurs, is an event progressing from an out-of-control conflict episode, and it creates an issue that the relational partners have to deal with if they are to continue their relationship.

Rules govern our friendships as well. One rule is that you should not lie to your best friends. Lying to an acquaintance about why you do not want to go to the beach is different from lying to your best friend, because best friends are supposed to trust each other. This is particularly true because as we develop friendships with others, we tend to develop a **truth bias** toward them: We assume that they tell us the truth.[3] This truth bias makes us more vulnerable and less accurate in detecting deception when it occurs. In addition to the cognitive effects, research indicates that the more involved people are with another person, the more intense their negative emotions when they discover that the person has lied to them. In addition, the more important the information lied about, the more intense negative emotions are on discovering the deception. The more important the issue that is lied about, the more likely it is that the future of the relationship is in jeopardy.[4] Lying to one's best friend is a relational transgression.

Another kind of relational transgression in friendships involves a violation of personal property, as in the following narrative told by Justin.

> When I arrived back at school after spring break, my roommate said that he needed to talk to me. From his nonverbal behavior I judged that this was something important. We sat down and began our talk; actually, I mostly listened. Scott proceeded to tell me that he had taken "a bold step of faith" and that he believed God had led him to destroy all of my records and compact discs. He said that they were hindering me from being all that God desired me to be. As I listened to him, I became quite confused because this action seemed irrational, unbalanced, and incorrect. Yet previously I had valued his judgment and wisdom. Also, we had a close relationship and this violation of trust damaged that respect and our friendship. When he finished talking, I didn't say a word. Scott left and I went to seek the advice of a wise friend. Later, I talked with Scott and told him that, while in principle he might be right, his actions were wrong. He agreed to repay me for all of my music, but it may take a long time to restore our friendship, particularly since I'm not sure he is really sorry for what he has done.

Justin experienced a large scale relational transgression—not only because Scott destroyed his music collection, but also because his roommate presumed to make a decision he believed would benefit the narrator without taking into account the narrator's point of view. In a friendship, one could expect that Scott would try to convince Justin to take such action himself rather than make a unilateral decision for him. While Scott admits breaking a relationship rule by destroying Justin's recorded music collection, a more convincing explanation was called for. The one offered fell short of rectifying the situation.

In addition to violating core relationship rules, relational transgressions produce highly **emotional residues** in a relationship; that is, people experience lingering emotional responses to the memory of the transgression. Transgressions result in negative emotional, cognitive, and behavioral responses. For the student losing his entire music collection, emotions of anger, disappointment, and disbelief replaced his originally positive feelings for his roommate. He had to think about the level of responsibility to which he would hold his roommate, and he had to decide what to do about the situation. After a relational transgression, people rarely reconcile instantly, but rather over a period of time.[5] Further, reconciling for a fear-based reason (e.g., I'm afraid of losing my partner) rather than a relationally-based reason (e.g., I care about this person), has negative implications for the relationship.[6]

13.1 Apply It

What constitutes a transgression in your relationships? Compare two relationships you are in, one with a close friend and one with an acquaintance, and list three transgressions in order of their importance to the relationship. How are the lists different?

The Role of Forgiveness and Reconciliation in Conflicts

The need to study forgiveness and reconciliation is based on the assumption that conflicts are cyclical and repetitive (see schismogenesis, URP, competitive escalation cycle, and chilling effect in Chapter 9), affected by what has come previously and affecting what comes after. Forgiveness and reconciliation are related but separate processes with the former preceding the latter. **Forgiveness** is a cognitive process that consists of letting go of feelings of revenge and desires to retaliate. **Reconciliation** is a behavioral process in which we take actions to restore a relationship or create a new one following forgiveness. The evidence indicates that forgiveness is an important mental process that should follow traumatic conflict. Reconciliation, on the other hand, involves a series of actions we may choose to avoid, particularly if the offender is likely to violate us again. (As the saying goes, "Fool me once, shame on you; fool me twice, shame on me.")

Research has begun to measure what forgiveness feels like to those who forgive and what it looks like to those observing it. One study examined forgiveness as described by people who had experienced instances of forgiveness or unforgiveness with an important person in their lives. The respondents wrote descriptions of their situations, and then the researcher analyzed them, looking for descriptions of communication and relational rules that were broken and how those situations were remedied. Confirming previous models of forgiveness, the researcher concluded that forgiveness is a process that starts with anger over a transgression and moves toward **transforming the meaning** of the event,[7] or changing the way we view the event in light of other events in our lives. Cognitively, forgiveness is characterized by a reduced focus on the other person and the transgression as a defining event in one's life (in unforgiveness, one might obsess over the source of hurt), affirmation of the other as an individual, lack of desire for revenge, and a rejection of the role of victim. The affective dimensions of forgiveness include the presence of positive feelings and absence of negative feelings toward the other.[8]

We can distinguish forgiveness from both unforgiveness and revenge. **Unforgiveness** "is a cold, emotional complex consisting of resentment, bitterness, hatred, hostility, residual anger, and fear . . . [it] occurs when people ruminate about the transgression, their reactions to it, the transgressor's motives, the consequences, and potential responses."[9] **Revenge** is based on the notion of "an eye for an eye." One wants to follow evil with more evil. Revenge characterizes the process of violence in which each aggressive act is followed by more aggressive behavior. The best way to stop the cycle is to switch to forgiveness and perhaps reconciliation. In Figure 13.1, we offer some suggestions that help one make this switch.

Dimensions of Forgiveness

Forgiveness does not obligate us to reconciliation or creating a new relationship. It is not simply forgetting that something happened. It does not release the other person from the consequences of his or her behavior. It does not deny anger. It does not put us in a position of superiority. It is not a declaration of the end of all conflict or of ever risking again with the other person (or anybody else). It is not one way.[10] When forgiveness takes any of these forms,

FIGURE 13.1   Forgiving Another Person

- Understand that forgiveness is a process.
- Start by acknowledging how the other hurt you.
- Allow yourself to experience anger.
- Don't adhere to the "victim" stage.
- Find people to support your forgiveness process.
- Recognize that the other person may not treat you any differently than in the past. Focus, then, on your responsibility in the situation and your responses to it.
- Try to see the other person as someone like yourself—human, having flaws, and making mistakes. This helps you escape from the villain/victim mentality.
- Try to see yourself as a person like the other—capable of hurting people, capable of doing something wrong (not necessarily that you are capable of the same offense). This helps you escape from a position of superiority with respect to the other.
- Think about what you have learned from the situation, and how you have grown as a result of it. Events usually have a positive and negative side to them, so you may often switch from a negative view to a positive view of the same event.

There is an obtrusive and onerous quality to the "forgiving" so that one feels the need for protection against such "righteousness." . . . [It] seems to nurture the memory of past injustice, to precipitate fresh "injustice," or to broodingly fantasize injustice yet to come.[11]

We do not forgive to become martyrs to the relationship. We forgive because it is better for us, and better for the other person. We forgive because we want to act freely again, not react out of past pain. Our difficulty in understanding forgiveness often stems from our need to see justice done where pain has been inflicted. But Volf takes issue with this: "If forgiveness were properly given only after strict justice had been established, then one would *not* be going beyond one's duty in offering forgiveness; one would indeed *wrong* the original wrongdoer if one did not offer forgiveness. . . . But that is not how we understand forgiveness. It is a *gift* that the wronged gives to the wrongdoer."[12]

Some actions, Smedes argued, are not worth forgiving, largely because they are not worth doing conflict over such as annoyances, slights, or disappointments. "It is wise not to turn all hurts into crises of forgiving. . . . We put everyone we love on guard when we turn personal misdemeanors into major felonies."[13] Smedes said that the best indicator that we have forgiven is when we can think of the person who has hurt us and wish that person well.

13.1 Think about It

Is there an event in your life that you find difficult to forgive? What is it? What makes it so difficult to forgive the other person? If you are not experiencing a difficult event now, describe a past event that you found difficult to forgive.

Forgiveness Is Not a New Concept

Teachings on the necessity of forgiveness and reconciliation between estranged individuals are at least as old as recorded civilization. Virtually every culture has a concept of transgression or sin against the gods, a particular god, or others, and most address the process by which sin is erased or forgiven.[14] Surviving excerpts of Babylonian wisdom literature, predating the biblical exodus out of Egypt and the giving of Jewish law, exhort,

> When confronted with a dispute, go your own way; pay no attention to it. Should it be a dispute of your own, extinguish the flame. . . . Do not return evil to the [person] who disputes with you; requite with kindness your evildoer, maintain justice to your enemy, smile on your adversary. . . . Do not let evil sleep affect your heart; banish misery and suffering from your side.[15]

The concept of forgiveness is a central concept in all major religions, as well as a core value of the Judeo-Christian culture.[16] Philosopher Hannah Arendt claimed that forgiveness is an essential characteristic of the human condition.

> The discoverer of the role of forgiveness in the realm of human affairs was Jesus of Nazareth. The fact that he made this discovery in a religious context and articulated it in religious language is no reason to take it any less seriously in a secular sense. . . . [A]spects of [his] teaching . . . are not primarily related to the Christian religious message but sprang from experiences in the small and closely knit community of his followers, bent on challenging the local authorities in Israel.[17]

Conflicts arise largely because we believe that someone has "transgressed" against us; we enact conflicts so as to correct the transgression. Forgiveness and reconciliation are processes that occur after people engage in conflict. Still, one author noted,

> Forgiveness has often been considered a problematic virtue because it can be difficult to justify in practice, particularly if it is not conditioned by repentance, judgment, or restitution. . . . Saints or saintly people, those at the point of death, and those at a great temporal or physical distance from an offense are more easily portrayed as forgiving or receiving forgiveness.[18]

1 3 . 2 Apply It

Do an Internet search using the terms forgiveness, reconciliation, and revenge. What kinds of sites do you find? Which term produces more sites? Why do you think that is?

Why Don't People Forgive?

"Don't get mad—get even" reads a popular bumper sticker. Why should we forgive? Do people not deserve punishment when they have hurt us? And why would we want to restore a relationship with a person who has hurt us? Several lines of research explain the need for forgiveness.

1. One study examined the way people describe transgressions, how they have come to forgive or not forgive the other person, and whether or not they attempted reconciliation. When people report that they have not forgiven the person who offended them, the primary reason for not forgiving is that they have not received an apology or an explanation from the other. Since the other has admitted no wrongdoing, they are not willing to forgive. In addition, people report refusal to forgive when the other continues in offensive behavior.[19]

2. They also might believe that by withholding forgiveness, they can prevent the transgressor from hurting them again.[20]

3. Sometimes people learn to forgive while in short-term therapeutic intervention, but revert back to a play of unforgiveness over time.[21]

4. People with higher levels of empathy find it easier to forgive others, although they may have difficulty forgiving themselves for offenses they have committed.[22]

5. Age is a factor. One study found that college-aged students, whose primary report of issues requiring forgiveness is hurts from dating relationships, believe it more difficult to forgive than any other age group.[23]

6. Sometimes, being hurt has created a loss of face for the person who was offended, and forgiving the transgressor would cause an even greater loss of face.

7. Others do not want to give up their right to hold a grudge; it gives them a sense of power to hold their hurt over the other's head.

8. Fear of vulnerability is a barrier to forgiveness.[24]

9. Some people don't forgive because they prefer the role of victim.

10. Some have argued that forgiving a wrongdoing too soon, particularly a criminal one, is a sign of insufficient self-respect.[25]

11. And, perhaps most importantly, some people don't forgive because no one offers support for doing so; in fact, people often think a forgiving person is stupid or naive.[26]

Advantages of Forgiveness

Where there is no forgiveness, there is discomfort, lack of communication and cooperativeness, and avoidance, which can create awkward situations at work or in one's family. Any interaction with the other is a matter of obligation rather than a matter of choice. However, it is important not to engage in what one writer calls *cheap forgiveness,* which is a "compulsive, unconditional, unilateral attempt at peacemaking for which you ask nothing in return . . . when you forgive cheaply, you seek to preserve the relationship at any cost, including your own integrity and safety."[27] Cheap forgiveness is often driven by fear of the offender's anger, fear of the offender leaving, or fear of harming the offender. It is based on an unhealthy need to preserve a relationship that may not survive the cost of avoiding the conflict.

Most writers in the area of forgiveness have argued that holding onto grief and hurt is psychologically unhealthy.[28] Holding grudges constitutes an egocentric position wherein we view those who have hurt us only in terms of what we need, what we wish, or what we long for.[29] It puts us in the position of judge, a position that few of us are qualified to hold.

> [Revenge] is based on the belief that . . . it is possible to measure the magnitude of an offense, to receive an equal amount of retribution somehow balances the account. An unforgiving attitude assumes that how one feels about past events is based on an economy similar to that of money and that a person thus feels poor and deprived if he or she has not sought an equal measure for all the wrongs committed against them. Revenge is a zero-sum game.[30]

By placing blame on other people, we relinquish our control over our emotions and give that control to another.[31] Research examining social adjustment and the ability to forgive found a high correlation between the two: As a person's social adjustment score went up, so did the person's ability to forgive.[32] More recent research on the role of forgiveness in counseling and mental health has demonstrated that teaching people about forgiveness and training them in "forgiveness strategies" helped increase recovery from divorce (restoring positive feelings about oneself, etc.), decreased feelings of guilt, and decreased feelings of depression and anxiety.[33] A lack of forgiveness accompanied by resentment and bitterness is a stress factor leading to burnout.[34] Linn and Linn argued that "forgiveness is at least as important a discovery for treating emotional illness as penicillin is for treating physical illness."[35]

1 3 . 2   Think about It

Seven years ago a thief broke into your home, went through your personal belongings, and stole many of your possessions. He was caught, much of your property was returned to you (but some was damaged), and he was sentenced to seven years in a state prison.

Are you now in a position to forgive him for what he did to you? Should we forgive all convicted felons after they serve their time in prison? Do you feel differently if the crime was committed against you? Would you feel differently if you were the one convicted?

Not only is forgiveness related to our psychological health,[36] it is related to our physical health as well.[37] Research on cancer patients has discovered four personality traits characteristic of people prone to cancer. The first trait is a tendency to hold resentments and an inability to forgive. The second trait is a tendency toward self-pity, and the third is a poor self-image (related to one's inability to forgive oneself). The fourth trait was a poor ability to develop and maintain a meaningful long-term relationship.[38] Senior citizens who manifested greater abilities to forgive others reported better physical health than those who reported less ability to forgive others.[39]

Harms resulting from the inability to forgive often involve anger and fear. Anger is part of the flight-or-fight response to stressors: Fear underlies how we respond to a situation, which turns to anger as our unmet needs are frustrated. We experience physical dam-

Working out forgiveness of our past hurts is often something we do on our own. Solitude, a quilt by Ruth Anna Abigail, depicts this sometimes lonely process.

age when this flight-or-fight mechanism, which was designed for short-term emergency responses to situations, becomes a long-term ongoing response.

> Except in the case of trauma (physical damage from a car accident, house falling, radiation, etc.), anger and guilt play a role in triggering most physical damage to our body. . . . Tensions and frustrations lower the immunization mechanism of the body, thus opening the door for bacteria and viruses to cause physical illness.[40]

Moving beyond Victimization

If reconciliation is not advisable, the offended person may forgive without engaging in communication with the transgressor. This is why we say that the reconciliation step is optional. One may chose to forgive without reconciling. In some cases, it is appropriate to forgive at a distance, so to speak, when the other person has not changed, has shown no willingness to change, continues to engage in offensive behavior, or poses harm to us mentally or physically. Under these conditions, contacting the other and becoming vulnerable again by expressing our anger and our hurt may cause more harm than good, so we forgive for our own sake—to let go of the offense, to move on with our lives, and to approach new relationships freely.

We tend to look for others outside of ourselves to blame. But it is the ability to move beyond **victimization** or the feeling of being a victim that leads to a state of forgiveness:[41]

> [W]hile the victim phase may be a useful part of recovery, it is not sufficient as a total approach to recovery. . . . [W]hat survivors have in common, among other things, is that they do not accept the label or identity of victim. . . . Forgiving has nothing to do with memory loss. There is no need to forget injustices and injuries, or pretend they never happened, and some events must never be forgotten. But that is quite different from letting them dominate one's present state of mind.[42]

> We had a family friend who lived with us throughout my childhood years. He molested me numerous times over the course of my childhood. I never told my parents until long after he had died. I thought I had worked through most of my forgiveness issues when I found out that my parents had let him live with us knowing that he had served time in jail for child molesting. What were they thinking? How could they let him spend time alone with me? How couldn't they know? I had forgiven my molester, and I had stopped thinking of myself as a child abuse victim, but in some ways it was harder to forgive my parents.

You may never experience a traumatic event like physical or sexual assault, or have someone lie to you about an important issue.[43] In the course of your everyday conflicts, however, you may at times think you are victimized (used, manipulated, or abused) by another. Perhaps the feeling results from having secrets you told to the other in trust used as weapons against you later in a conflict. It may arise from having your personal possessions taken or destroyed.

Forgiveness is a process. It may take days, weeks, or years. Forgiveness allows us to act freely again. Without it, we are held by the event that victimized us; with it, we move forward. It is "reframing of how one views the world. . . . [It is] in reality a case of acting in one's own enlightened self-interest."[44]

> I am unable to forget the time I took a trust and openness class in which the topic was "Someone in my life whom I want to forgive." As a group exercise, we discussed the steps to forgiveness and then we each had to contribute a personal experience of unresolved and unforgiving conflict with someone. You would not believe what happened. Adult men and women alike told shocking stories of wrongs done to them, and they talked about their anger and rage. The facilitator told us that we have suffered long enough. He asked us to picture our antagonists as children. Picture what was being done to us as being done to them as little children. He said we know that people do to others that which was done to them often as children. He asked us to free them from their wrongs and see them as the wronged, needy people they are. Instead of distancing us from those who had wronged us, he brought us together as mutual victims who are suffering together. I have difficulty believing what then happened. There were changes and healing like I have never seen before. We were all overwhelmed by what was happening. Some cried, some held hands, some hugged the facilitator and then one another. I couldn't help but wonder what would happen if everyone in the world went through a group experience like this.

If you cannot disengage people from their past, you enslave yourself to an ugly emotional affair. You may have unresolved conflicts with others, especially with family members. These unforgiving experiences are now serving as a barrier between you and that person, preventing you from having the positive relationship both of you need. Someday you may realize that these people are only doing the best they know how. They brought "past baggage" with them. Now you are in a good position to drop the baggage you are carrying in favor of new tools. You no longer have to act based on your past. As you move forward in your new ways, you can also let go of your feelings that "justified" your old ways. You can stop seeking revenge and choose to forgive. A new outlook, it is hoped, alters or re-establishes a much needed relationship. If the other doesn't respond, drop it. Forgiveness is your benefit alone to enjoy.

Past Forgiveness: Reconciliation

Recall that we differentiated reconciliation from forgiveness. Whereas forgiveness is a cognitive process that consists of letting go of feelings of revenge and desires to retaliate, reconciliation is a behavior process in which we take actions to restore a relationship or create a new one. Because they are different processes, forgiving the other cognitively does not necessarily lead to reconciliation behavior. Many people forgive, but at a distance. They let go of their need for revenge, but do not choose to put themselves in a position where the other can hurt them again.

However, for some people reconciliation has advantages. They may want to re-establish a prior relationship or convert it into a different one.

Steps to Reconciliation

How do we go about forgiving and opening ourselves to reconciliation? We believe that this process consists of the following six steps.

1. Sometimes, the transgressor explains her or his offensive behavior and offers an apology.
2. When this occurs, the offended person either accepts the account and apology or simply decides that it is no longer in her or his best interest to harbor feelings of anger, resentment, and revenge (even in the absence of an explanation and apology).
3. The offended person actually lets go of any feelings of anger, resentment, and revenge. Forgiveness is a process that starts with anger over a transgression and moves toward transforming the meaning of the event. To help you with this, see the list of suggestions in Figure 13.1.
4. If reconciliation is desired, the offended person may communicate her/his forgiveness to the transgressor. Sometimes, people do not state their forgiveness but simply behave in ways that communicate it.
5. A prior relationship is re-established or converted into a different one.
6. Actions confirm forgiveness/reconciliation; behavior constitutes the reality.

Let us consider each of these steps in turn and explain them more fully.

The Account and the Apology.   The transgressor may explain her or his offensive be-havior and offer an account and an apology. When people report to communication re-searchers that they have not forgiven the person who offended them, the primary reason for not forgiving is that they have not received an explanation and an apology from the other. Because the other has admitted no wrongdoing, they usually are not willing to forgive. In addition, people report refusal to forgive when the other continues the offensive behavior. Clearly, the process should begin with the transgressor understanding, recognizing, and admitting the offensive nature of his or her behavior, offer an account, follow the explana-tion with an apology, and ask for forgiveness. We say that this step is optional because not all offenders explain and apologize; where it is to one's advantage, the offended person may choose to forgive without the transgressor taking the first step.

As indicated above, except in cases of sexual infidelity and emotional attachment/intimacy (to someone else), research shows that people tend to let the transgressor off the hook by accepting accounts and apologies. In explaining behavior to the offended party, research indicates that the transgressors tend to rely most on justification or apology.

Acceptance of Account and Apology.   The offended person may chose to forgive the other if the transgressor has changed or is truly sorry for the transgression. The offended person makes a judgment call. Some people are willing to change, do in fact change, realize the errors of their ways, and are truly sorry for their transgressions, and others are clueless. The offended person needs to separate those who warrant forgiveness from those who do not. In deciding to forgive the other, the offended person must decide that it is a good idea to let go of any feelings of anger, resentment, and revenge.

Reconciliation without Talking about the Offense.   In the absence of an explanation and apology, the offended person may decide unilaterally that it is no longer in her or his best interests to continue feeling angry, resentful, and revengeful. Harboring such feelings is costly and drains one emotionally. Of course, when hurt by someone we trust and care for, it takes some time before we reach a point where we question the value of maintaining these feelings. If you are deciding to forgive without actually having discussed the trans-gression with the offender, it helps to keep these points in mind:

- With few exceptions, forgiveness is not equated with forgetting about the transgression.
- Forgiveness is generally conceived of as a process through which people move on with their lives after experiencing some hurt.
- Forgiveness involves reframing the event: One reframes the event so that it becomes less central in a person's life or in the life of a relationship.
- Forgiveness also includes reframing our perception of the other person: We see the person who hurt us in a different light. We may come to again value the other person—that is, we see that person as having worth regardless of the hurt he or she has caused us. We may see the other as equally precious. We may decide to trust again and take risks until it is seen by both people as authentic; however, forgiveness is not necessarily equated with the restoration of trust. We may love that person again.

■ When we forgive, we recognize that we cannot change the past; we know that we can influence future events; we accept the fact that the past is past.

Forgiveness Is Communicated.   The offended person decides whether or not to explicitly communicate his or her forgiveness to the offender. If it is not communicated explicitly, the offended person behaves in ways that imply forgiveness has taken place. In some cases, we may choose to restore or alter the relationship when the other person convinces us that he or she has truly changed or no longer poses a threat to us emotionally or physically. If we decide to restore the relationship eventually, then it is important to risk telling the other about our hurt. It is a risk because, as research shows, the other person may tell us that our feelings are not justified or that we have no right to feel hurt. Such an action makes it more difficult to forgive the other.

It is easier to forgive when the other person admits guilt or offers an account and an apology. Even so, depending on the offense, we may have a problem in trusting again. A frequent question asked is "Does this mean I have to trust the other person like I did before?" We think the answer is no—unless the person earns your trust over time.

We believe that forgiveness is more than the simple healing of wounds. Barbara Kingsolver writes in *The Poisonwood Bible* that

> If chained is where you have been, your arms will always bear marks of the shackles. What you have to lose is your story, your own slant. You'll look at the scars on your arms and see mere ugliness, or you'll take great care to look away from them and see nothing. Either way, you have no words for the story of where you came from.
>
>   Tall and straight I may appear, but I will always be Adah inside. A crooked little person trying to tell the truth. The power is in the balance: we are our injuries, as much as we are our successes.[45]

Injuries heal, and scars do remain. But the difference between forgiveness and simply moving on is that there are stories for where you have been. You neither ignore your scars nor focus on their ugliness. Injuries are not forgotten, but they do not always dictate the way you behave. We believe that forgiveness occurs when we no longer define our emotions, our desires, or our behaviors in terms of our injuries. Those scars become a part of us, not the whole of what we are.

Transforming the Relationship.   Reconciliation results in a transformed relationship between the parties in the transgression—we may feel less enthusiasm than before, we may feel better than before, or we may create an entirely different type of a relationship. For example, a relational transgression is often a reason for separation between spouses. Let us assume that two spouses are unable to forgive one another and seek revenge in the courts, where they spend most of their financial assets, expend considerable time, effort, and emotion seeking revenge against each other, and reaffirm their negative opinions of the other spouse. She blames him for his infidelity and he blames her for laziness and squandering. The courtroom is filled with anger and resentment. They may think they have no reason to communicate or relate to one another ever again, and they may not have to if the divorce occurs early in their marriage and they have no children. However, suppose they were married several years and do have children. Issues related to alimony and child support may make it unlikely that the spouses can avoid each other in the years to come.

Let us say that in another case, a couple with children suffer a relational transgression followed by a temporary separation, but then decide to "kiss and make up." In addition to forgiving each other, let us say that they also restore their relationship and continue as husband and wife. All assets remain in place, and the spouses continue as parents to their children. In this case forgiveness and reconciliation restored the relationship. Of course, the relationship may not be exactly the same, because the spouses may have agreed to some changes to the issues that led to the conflict in the first place, but we would say that in most respects life is continuing as before the blowup. If the couple is willing, though, the relationship can become stronger than it was before the transgression, but this takes considerable time and effort at reframing the transgression.

In still another case, let us consider a family where the spouses suffer a relational transgression and decide to forgive one another, but they want to convert their relationship (that is, they no longer want to remain husband and wife). However, due to the need to maintain alimony and child support, they want to continue to work together in the future. They end up divorced but maintain open lines of communication and consult each other from time to time. Perhaps the ex-husband continues to maintain the residence where his ex-wife and children live. Maybe the ex-wife visits her ex-husband when he is ill or in the hospital. Maybe they decide to share the same home (not together), with each living there for six months, so that the children can remain in one school. While the nature of this relationship may vary in its degree of warmth, former spouses may redefine their relationships as friends who help each other, especially in times of need and as parents as they continue to take care of their children while separated physically.

Actions Confirm Forgiveness and Reconciliation.   The role played by actions is found in research examining **self-fulfilling prophecies,** in which people act toward us in the way that we expect. If you act toward the other as though he or she is not trustworthy, the other may begin to act in untrustworthy ways. If you act toward the other as though the relationship is strained, he or she may come to believe it is strained and act in ways that reflect this belief.

13.3 Apply It

Write out a description of a conflict involving a relational transgression that moved through the reconciliation process. Describe what happened at each step of the process. How long did it take? Was it worth it to you? Why?

Normal life ceases [when we do not feel forgiven]. . . . [W]e feel forgiven when we get back to the familiar routine. . . . This return to normalcy may be an illusion. Logic tells us that life can never be quite the same after monumental hurt. Even if the wound has healed there

The descision to initiate reconciliation with another person is like walking through a door, as depicted in Possibilities, *a quilt by Ruth Anna Abigail.*

will still be scar tissue. But the more the present mirrors the past, the greater the assurance of pardon.

Although some heard the statement, "I forgive you," the words themselves had little impact. Offenders look for confirmation in deed. If the victim's response mirrored reconciliation, the assurance of pardon was unnecessary.[46]

As discussed in the previous section, reconciliation does not mean you simply forget what happened, but you do move forward in your relationship, rebuilding trust and re-establishing intimacy. Acting in ways that signal forgiveness creates expectations of a renewed relationship or a different relationship and the possibility of change. Reconciliation means acting in ways that do not lock the present situation into constant re-examination of the offense.

Social construction theory suggests that we make our social worlds by the way we talk about them, and we act within our social worlds based on the way we have made them through our talk. For example, a couple that is beginning to date might say, "We are just friends," and act accordingly. Later on, they may agree to move to a definition of "dating partners." This change in the definition of their relationship occurs with a change in their behavior toward one another. In a circular way, their affectionate behaviors increase because they change the definition of the relationship, and as the affectionate behaviors increase they give labels to their relationship that define it as more serious. Thus, in the communication/reality loop, the way we communicate about our behavior helps to constitute the reality of it. As we describe our behavior, we affect the way we behave; as we behave, we affect the way we describe our behavior.

The process of forgiveness and reconciliation works in the same way.

1. After forgiving one another, we tell each other that the act is forgiven, which allows us to act without reference to the offense.

2. In turn, we feel better about our relationship with one another and can talk about our relationship without reference to the offense.
3. In turn, our actions confirm what we said so that our behavior constitutes the reality of our forgiveness.

We call this a **forgiveness/reconciliation loop.**[47] Some evidence for this kind of reconciliation loop was found in a study of married couples who had enacted forgiveness; three of the means used to communicate that forgiveness had taken place were a return to mundane rituals (signaling that the relationship is "back to normal"), expressions of nonverbal affection, and the use of empathy to understand why the other had committed the offense.[48]

This model is a good example of a communication approach to conflict resolution. Within this forgiveness/reconciliation loop, reconciliation is a social construction: Those in a fractured or stressed relationship must create a meaning for the concept they term forgiveness and must create the actions necessary to make forgiveness seem real to them. Constructing reconciliation is the process of integrating what has become problematic into the realm of the unproblematic in relationships. Small conflicts may only cause people to temporarily pause and ask about the fit of the conflict into the total relationship. Transgressions interrupt their everyday reality, forcing them to reconcile vastly different pieces of the relationship. Accounts and apologies offer new definitions for the offense and its role within the relationship; reconciliation is the process of enacting that new definition so that it becomes permanent.

Thus, expressing forgiveness after conflict becomes a self-fulfilling prophecy when enacted correctly: We say forgiveness is possible; we act toward the other as though we have forgiven; the other, in turn, feels forgiven; and we are able to have a relationship that has moved beyond a relational transgression to where the transgression no longer defines the relationship. Here we have a communication process (involving verbal and nonverbal language, attributions, expectations, and confirmation) that is also a conflict resolution process. When any of these steps break down—if we say we forgive but do not act as though we have, or if we continue to refer to the offense as though it has not passed—forgiveness is almost impossible. Instead, we become victims of the relational transgression, and the transgression defines us and our relationship with the other. We can avoid the role of victim by forgiving and reconciling with the transgressor.

13.3 **Think about It**

Return to the incident you described in Think about It 13.2. What would it take for you to forgive the other person? What are the consequences of forgiving the other person? Of not forgiving the other person?

Although some therapists think that forgiveness is grasped quickly in some cases, most researchers in the field argue that the process of forgiveness takes time. The key in getting to the point of forgiveness is the ability to transform the meaning of the event that has occurred and to see it as an event among many in a relationship instead of the central event that defines the quality of the relationship. It is time-consuming and cannot occur if people are not willing to explore and reconcile the different feelings that arise as a result of transgressions.

13.4 Think about It

Anne Lamott wrote that "not forgiving is like drinking rat poison and waiting for the rat to die."[49] Are there times when we should not forgive? How does this affect us?

Manage It

It is not an overstatement to say that forgiveness is the most important part of conflict management. We can properly analyze a serious conflict involving relational transgressions, choose the right strategy, say all the right words, and come to an agreement without actually letting go of hurt associated with the conflict. If we cannot forgive the hurt and truly reconcile with the other person, if we cannot transform the meaning of the event we have experienced, we tend to repeat our mistakes in ways that often become increasingly more destructive.

Why do we re-engage in destructive conflict without forgiveness? The reason lies in the fact that relational transgressions involve core relational issues and leave emotional residues. Not every conflict necessitates our entry into forgiveness and reconciliation processes. But the conflicts that involve outcomes important to us in our intimate relationships almost certainly leave behind bad memories and bad feelings, including memories and feelings that we must come to terms with if we want to live differently in the future.

When we decide to forgive, we first give up our rights to revenge and retaliation. We give up our right to change the future based on the past. Forgiveness begins with a decision to reduce our focus on the transgression as a defining characteristic of our relationship with the other person, or indeed, our entire lives. The ability to move beyond victimization leads to a state of forgiveness.

Reconciliation is a behavior process in which we take actions to restore a relationship or create a new one. Once we forgive the other for the relational transgression, we do not have to reconcile unless we want to. We may wish to forgive at a distance and not communicate our forgiveness to the transgressor, or we may decide that we wish to re-establish a relationship or create a new one, so we choose to reconcile.

Critical to our understanding of both forgiveness and reconciliation is the understanding that they are not one-time events. Often, we return to an event cognitively and emotionally, but we deal with different parts of it. Wuellner notes that

> All [the] aspects of forgiveness are intertwined, one part nourished by another . . . We could think of our forgiveness as a great garden that we explore or a beautiful, complex house with winding passages and unexpected rooms.[50]

Like the ability to analyze conflicts and the ability to effectively communicate feelings and desires, the effective use of forgiveness and reconciliation strategies to cope with difficult conflicts characterizes the competent conflict manager. Through the processes of forgiveness and reconciliation, we can forge new relationships or repair former ones and move forward by letting go of the past. We must understand the kind of response necessitated by various transgressions and develop a repertoire of responses designed to remediate problematic situations. Of all the skills in conflict, we must learn how to put a conflict into perspective and move forward, otherwise our relationships become unstable; without forgiveness, our relationships eventually come to an end.

13.1 Work with It

Analyze the case study below in terms of the key ideas discussed in this chapter. You, personally, may not want to forgive anyone in this case study, but you are asked to take the necessary steps in forgiveness as an exercise to illustrate and apply the process. We selected a case study rather than have you describe an actual situation in your life so that you might analyze the conflict situation objectively and see ways to implement the suggestions in this chapter. Note that we are not suggesting that this couple continue their relationship, but rather we are recommending that forgiveness and reconciliation play a role.

Write an essay on the case study below in which you answer the following questions. What did David do that upset Maria? Does his behavior constitute a problematic situation or a relational transgression, and why? What probably makes it difficult for Maria to forgive David? What would he and she have to do for her to forgive him? Why would forgiveness and reconciliation help Maria? Apply the steps of forgiveness to this situation and describe what Maria must do at each step if she is to truly forgive him. Explain how she might forgive him but not forget the incident and not continue the romantic relationship.

Three months ago, David and I had tickets to see Harry Connick, Jr., in concert. We had just started seeing each other when we bought the tickets and planned to attend the concert. A few days before the concert, David came to my house late that night to tell me he had a ton of studying to do on the day of the concert, because he had a huge midterm on Thursday that he had to receive an "A" on. He made me understand, after hours of continuous explanation, how he really felt it was best to give the tickets to his cousin because he couldn't afford not to study the night before the exam. I understood, but I was really bummed out. I sort of wished David would give me the tickets so I could still go to the concert, but he felt it was unfair that I go to the concert while he stayed home and studied. He said that he would make it up to me with something better.

I went over to his house the next day so we could spend some time together and celebrate his doing well on the test. David said, "I lied, okay. I said it. I went to the concert. I didn't want to tell you. I didn't think I would feel this bad about it. I wasn't thinking, so I didn't tell you that I took Tina instead of you."

My face dropped to the ground and all I kept thinking was "Why? Why? *Why?* Tina? Why would you take your ex-girlfriend instead of me? You promised to take me. What about your test? Was that a lie too?" I didn't give him a chance to explain, I just told him I couldn't accept him lying to me, that it wasn't fair. Then I stormed out of his place. I wanted so badly for him to realize that the best person for him just walked out the door and wasn't ever coming back. I didn't want to listen to him. I was so angry that nothing could change the way I felt.

David finally called me and explained to me the real issue that he avoided telling me. He explained that before we started going out he and Tina had agreed to continue their relationship as friends. He said that he had originally bought the tickets for them to go to the concert together, but then we started dating, and he wasn't sure how I would feel about his friendship with Tina. David explained that he didn't know what to do. He avoided telling me, thinking I would never find out.

13.1 Remember It

Write an essay in which you apply the ideas presented in Chapter 13 to your life situation. You have the option here of describing a real or imagined situation in which someone has committed a difficult to forgive transgression against you. In other words, if a real transgression is too sensitive or something you are not ready to talk about, or you have none to share, then you can describe an unreal situation in which you imagine that someone has done something you would find hard to forgive. Make sure to address the following topics.

1. Define and distinguish relational transgressions from other types of problematic situations.
2. Describe a real or imagined relational transgression.
3. Explain the advantages of forgiveness and reconciliation following such a relational transgression.
4. Explain how you can forgive (i.e., how to transform the meaning) but not forget the transgression.
5. List the actual steps you should take (ritual) to forgive others following such a relational transgression.

NOTES

1. Sandra Metts, "Relational Transgressions," in William R. Cupach and Brian H. Spitzberg (Eds.), *The Dark Side of Interpersonal Communication* (Hillsdale, NJ: Lawrence Erlbaum, 1994), p. 4

2. Mark L. Knapp and Mark E. Comadena, "Telling It Like It Isn't: A Review of Theory and Research on Deceptive Communications," *Human Communication Research* 5 (1979), p. 271.

3. Steven A. McComack and Malcolm R. Parks, "Deception Detection and Relationship Development: The Other Side of Trust," in Margaret L. McLaughlin (Ed.), *Communication Yearbook 9* (Beverly Hills: Sage Publications, 1986), pp. 377–389; James B. Stiff, Hyun J. Kim, and C. N. Ramesh, "Truth-Biases and Aroused Suspicion in Relational Deception," paper presented at the International Communication Association Convention, San Francisco, May 1989.

4. Steven A. McComack and Timothy R. Levine, "When Lies Are Uncovered: Emotion and Relational Outcomes of Discovered Deception," *Communication Monographs* 5 (1990), p. 121.

5. David M. Droll, "Forgiveness: Theory and Research," Doctoral dissertation, University of Nevada, Reno, 1985.

6. Michael E. Roloff, Kari P. Soule, and Colleen M. Carey, "Reasons for Remaining in a Relationship and Responses to Relational Transgressions,"

Journal of Social and Personal Relationships 18 (2001), 362–385.

7. Neil Robert Fow, "An Empirical-Phenomenological Investigation of the Experience of Forgiving Another," Doctoral dissertation, University of Pittsburgh, 1988.

8. Susan Helen Wade, "The Development of a Scale to Measure Forgiveness," Doctoral dissertation, Fuller Theological Seminary, 1989.

9. Everett L. Worthington, "Unforgiveness, Forgiveness, and Reconciliation and Their Implications for Societal Interventions," in Raymond G. Helmick and Rodney L. Petersen (Eds.), *Forgiveness and Reconciliation* (Radnor, PA: Templeton Foundation Press, 2001), pp. 172–173.

10. Robert D. Enright and Robert L. Zell, "Problems Encountered When We Forgive One Another," *Journal of Psychology and Christianity* 8 (1989), 52–54; David Augsburger, *Caring Enough to Not Forgive* (Ventura, CA: Regal Books, 1981).

11. R. C. A. Hunter, "Forgiveness, Retaliation, and Paranoid Reactions," *Canadian Psychiatric Association Journal* 23 (1978), p. 171.

12. Miroslav Volf, "Forgiveness, Reconciliation, and Justice," in Raymond G. Helmick and Rodney L. Petersen (Eds.), *Forgiveness and Reconciliation* (Radnor, PA: Templeton Foundation Press, 2001), p. 41.

13. Louis Smedes, *Forgive and Forget: Healing the Hurt We Don't Deserve* (San Francisco: Harper & Row, 1984), p. 15.

14. James Hastings (Ed.), *Encyclopedia of Religion and Ethics* (Edinburgh: T. & T. Clark, 1974), pp. 528–571.

15. W. G. Lambert, *Babylonian Wisdom Literature* (London: Oxford University Press, 1960), pp. 101, 109.

16. Donald Hope, "The Healing Paradox of Forgiveness," *Psychotherapy* 24 (1987), 240–244.

17. Hannah Arendt, *The Human Condition* (Chicago: University of Chicago Press, 1956), pp. 238–239.

18. Thomas Trzyna, "Forgiveness and Time," *Christian Scholar's Review* 22 (1992), pp. 7, 8.

19. Roxane S. Lulofs, "Swimming Upstream: Creating Reasons for Unforgiveness in a Culture that Expects Otherwise," paper presented to the Speech Communication Association Convention, San Antonio, TX, November 1995.

20. Julie Juola Exline and Ray F. Baumeister, "Expressing Forgiveness and Repentance: Benefits and Barriers," in Michael E. McCullough, Kenneth L. Pargament, and Carl E. Thorsen, *Forgiveness: Theory, Research, and Practice* (New York: The Guilford Press, 2000), 133–155.

21. James N. Sells and Leslie King, "A Pilot Study in Marital Group Therapy: Process and Outcome," *Family Journal* 10 (2002), 156–166.

22. Ann Macaskill, John Maltby, and Liza Day, "Forgiveness of Self and Others and Emotional Empathy," *The Journal of Social Psychology* 142 (2002), 663–665; see also Varda Konstam, Miriam Chernoff, and Sara Deveney, "Toward Forgiveness: The Role of Shame, Guilt, Anger and Empathy," *Counseling and Values* 46 (2001), 26–39.

23. Michael J. Subkoviak, Robert D. Enright, Ching-Ru Wu, Elizabeth A. Gassin, Suzanne Freedman, Leanne M. Olson, and Issidoros Sarinopolous, "Measuring Interpersonal Forgiveness," paper presented at the American Educational Research Association Convention, San Francisco, April 1992.

24. Richard P. Fitzgibbons, "The Cognitive and Emotional Uses of Forgiveness in the Treatment of Anger," *Psychotherapy* 23 (1986), 629–633.

25. Joshua Dressler, "Hating Criminals: How Can Something that Feels So Good Be Wrong?" *Michigan Law Review* 88 (1990), p. 1454.

26. Doris Donnelly, *Learning to Forgive* (Nashville, TN: Abingdon Press, 1979).

27. Janis Abrahms Spring with Michael Spring, *How Can I Forgive You?* (New York: Harper Collins, 2004), p. 15

28. Michael E. McCullough, Steven J. Sandage, and Everett L. Worthington, Jr., *To Forgive is Human* (Downers Grove, IL: InterVarsity Press, 1997).

29. Heinz Kohut, "Narcissism and Narcissistic Rage," *The Psychoanalytic Study of the Child* 27 (1972), 379–392; Jared P. Pingleton, "The Role and Function of Forgiveness in the Psychotherapeutic Process," *Journal of Psychology and Theology* 17 (1989), 27–35.

30. Donald Hope, "The Healing Paradox of Forgiveness," *Psychotherapy* 24 (1987), p. 240.

31. Gershen Kauhnan, *Shame: The Power of Caring* (Cambridge, MA: Shenkinan Publishing, 1980), p. 95.

32. James G. Emerson, *The Dynamics of Forgiveness* (Philadelphia: The Westminster Press, 1964), used the Rogers and Dymond q-sort test of emotional adjustment, adding items concerning feelings about one's ability to forgive (Carl R. Rogers and Rosalind F. Dymond, *Psychotherapy and Personality Change* [University of Chicago Press, 1954]).

33. Mary F. Trainer, "Forgiveness: Intrinsic, Role-Expected, Expedient, in the Context of Divorce," Doctoral dissertation, Boston University, 1984; Mellis I. Schmidt, "Forgiveness as the Focus Theme in Group Counseling," Doctoral dissertation, North Texas State University, 1986; John H. Hebl, "Forgiveness as a Counseling Goal with Elderly Females," Doctoral dissertation, University of Wisconsin, 1990.

34. Frank Minirth, Dan Hawkins, Paul Meier, and Richard Flournoy, *How to Beat Burnout* (Chicago: Moody, 1986).

35. Matthew Linn and Dennis Linn, *Healing Life's Hurts: Healing Memories through Five Stages of Forgiveness* (New York: Paulist Press, 1978), p. 39.

36. Robert J. Murray, "Forgiveness as a Therapeutic Option," *Family Journal* 10 (2002), 315–331.

37. Unforgiveness is related to negative health outcomes, although forgiveness is not necessarily related to positive ones according to Carl E. Thorsen, Alex H. S. Harris, and Frederic Luskin, "Forgiveness and Health: An Unanswered Question," in Michael E. McCullough, Kenneth L. Pargament, and Carl E. Thorsen (Eds.), *Forgiveness: Theory, Research, and Practice* (New York: The Guilford Press, 2000), pp. 254–280.

38. Jeanne Achterberg, Stephanie Matthews, and O. Carl Simonton, "Psychology of the Exceptional Cancer Patient: A Description of Patients Who Outlived Predicted Expectancies," *Psychotherapy: Theory and Research and Practice* 6 (1976), 13–14.

39. Judith A. Strasser, "The Relation of General Forgiveness and Forgiveness Type to Reported Health in the Elderly," Doctoral dissertation, Catholic University of America, 1984.

40. Linn and Linn, pp. 36–37.

41. An interesting account of this movement is found in Debbie Morris with Gregg Lewis, *Forgiving the Dead Man Walking* (Grand Rapids, MI: Zondervan, 1998).

42. Carol Tavris, *Anger: The Misunderstood Emotion* (New York: Touchstone through Simon & Schuster, 1989), pp. 314–315.

43. For those who have experienced childhood trauma, two excellent resources are James E. Kepner, *Healing Tasks: Psychotherapy with Adult Survivors of Childhood Abuse* (San Francisco: Jossey-Bass, 1995); and Gina O'Connell Higgins, *Resilient Adults: Overcoming a Cruel Past* (San Francisco: Jossey-Bass, 1994).

44. Hope, p. 242; see also Albert Ellis and Robert A. Harper, *A New Guide to Rational Living* (North Hollywood, CA: Wilshire Book Co., 1975), who claim that forgiving leaves us sane and realistic.

45. Barbara Kingsolver, *The Poisonwood Bible* (New York: HarperTorch, 1998), pp. 594, 595.

46. Em Griffin, "Accountability and Forgiveness: Saying the Tough Words in Love," paper presented at the Speech Communication Association Convention, Denver, November 1985, pp. 18, 26.

47. Roxane Salyer Lulofs, "The Social Construction of Forgiveness," *Human Systems* 2 (1992), 183–198. The model is based on John Shotter's Communication/Reality Loop from *Social Accountability and Selfhood* (Oxford, England: Basil Blackwell, 1984).

48. David L. Palmer, "The Communication of Forgiveness," paper presented at the annual meeting of the Speech Communication Association, New Orleans, November 1994.

49. Anne Lamott, *Traveling Mercies* (New York: Anchor Books, 1999), p. 134.

50. Flora Slosson Wuellner, *Forgiveness, the Passionate Journey* (Nashville, TN: Upper Room Books, 2001), pp. 151–152.

14 Mediation as Third-Party Intervention

OBJECTIVES

At the end of this chapter, you should be able to:

- Describe the difference between formal and informal mediation.
- Define mediation and contrast it with the other ADRs.
- Explain when a third party should intervene as a mediator.
- Describe the role of the mediator.
- List and describe the steps of mediation.

KEY TERMS

adjudication
ADRs
arbitration
behavioral commitments
caucus
common ground

communication rules enforcers
conciliation
dispute
framing
intake
mediation

mediators
ombudsperson
reframing
rules

Up to now, we have concentrated on those concepts, principles, and skills that are most useful when you personally are involved in a conflict with someone you know. You can apply what you have learned so far to better manage or resolve the conflicts you yourself are having with others.

This chapter is different in that it focuses on what you need to know to help others who are having a conflict. Perhaps they invite you as a third party to intervene on their behalf. The nature of the conflict is different because it is one that the conflicting parties cannot handle by themselves. They need the help of a third party—a role you can perform after you study the subject of mediation.

In this chapter we apply the principles taught in formal mediation training to the management of conflicts in informal or everyday settings. Basic information is provided on mediation concepts, skills, steps, and techniques, so that you can help your friends, family, and co-workers resolve their interpersonal conflicts. However, if you want to practice mediation on a more formal basis, you need certification, which means mediation training by an approved university program or state agency. For our purposes, you need to learn how to explain the alternatives to dispute resolution, define mediation and dispute, describe the role of the mediators, explain when it is useful to include mediators in conflict situations, explain the advantages and limitations of mediation, and effectively perform the steps you would take to mediate an informal dispute. We begin first with an overview of the dispute resolution process in which mediation is one alternative.

Alternatives to Dispute Resolution

Mediation is one alternative to what is called dispute resolution. In fact, you cannot fully appreciate the idea of mediation without first understanding the concept of a dispute. A **dispute** is defined as "a conflict that has reached a point where the parties are unable to resolve the issue by themselves due to a breakdown in communication, and normal relations are unlikely until the dispute is resolved."[1] Not all conflicts are alike. Conflicts become disputes when participants realize that they confront a communication barrier, preventing normal relations. The parties seek help from a third party because they cannot resolve the issues by themselves.

When a dispute occurs, the conflicting parties sometimes resort to violent means. Our prisons are full of people who took "justice" into their own hands by taking violent action against someone with whom they disagreed. For those who use their heads instead of their fists and guns, the following alternatives to dispute resolution (**ADRs**) exist:

- **Conciliation:** a neutral third party practices "shuttle diplomacy" by traveling back and forth between conflicting parties who are unable to meet together for any one of a variety of reasons.
- **Ombudsperson:** one who cuts through the red tape on behalf of individuals who feel abused by the larger system (often governmental agencies) in which they work, study, or seek support.
- **Arbitration:** a neutral third party considers both sides of a dispute and makes a decision, which is more binding than that of a judge in the legal system if both parties have agreed in advance to abide by the decision (no appeal).
- **Adjudication:** a neutral judge and jury in the legal system hear attorneys who prosecute or defend people and decide a case, which either party may later appeal.
- **Mediation:** a neutral third party facilitates communication between the conflicting parties so that they may work out their own mutually acceptable agreement.

14.1 Think about It

Did you receive mediation training in elementary, middle, or high school? Did you find the training useful? What disputes did you mediate? If you did not receive such training, would you like to? Does your college or university offer mediation training?

We are focusing on mediation in this chapter because many studies have found that mediation produces superior results to adjudication.[2] Most importantly, it also has unique advantages that appeal to communication scholars:

1. Mediators help to restore communication and normalize relations.
2. Mediation allows for full participation by the conflicting parties.
3. Mediation has a high success rate. It is estimated that "once the disputants have agreed to mediate, at least 80 % of the time they are able to work out an agreement that is acceptable to both of them."[3]

Formal versus Informal Mediation

As it turns out there are several different approaches to mediation, each with its own set of techniques, but the approach advocated here does not require the mediators to take sides, engage in psychotherapy, or play the role of advocate. Rather, **mediators** are viewed here as unbiased facilitators of communication between the parties in a private setting. In many formal settings where it is normally more satisfying, cheaper, and faster than litigation, this form of mediation has become a popular alternative. In such formal settings, one party typically calls a local mediation center for a mediation, and a first meeting between the parties and mediators usually occurs within the next few days or weeks. In any case, community and school mediations are often free or offered on a sliding scale that is cheaper than lawyers' fees.

In formal mediations, satisfactory agreements are often worked out at a single mediation session lasting one to three hours, although complex cases such as divorce settlements involving child custody may require weekly sessions until all the details are worked out. Evidence indicates that parties are more satisfied with mediated agreements than they are with the courtroom decisions of judges and juries and are more likely to comply with mediated agreements than they are to court orders because they have more control in the resolution of their dispute.[4]

There are formal programs that train and certify mediators. Community and campus dispute resolution centers offer mediation for a wide range of conflicts including noisy neighbors, sexual and racial harassment, minor assault, breach of contract, landlord–tenant and buyer–seller disputes, small claims, bad checks, trespassing, and a variety of interpersonal issues such as gossip and rumors, misunderstandings, friendship issues, and post-breakup disputes.[5] Mediation is a method of parental intervention in children's disputes.[6] Rapidly becoming a popular alternative to the courts,[7] divorce mediation is a branch of family mediation that deals with issues associated with child custody, visitation, child financial support, and the redistribution of marital property. Today, divorce mediation training is offered to workers from a wide variety of occupations, including family law attorneys[8] and family counselors and therapists.[9] However, communication among the mediator and disputants lies at the basis of all these mediation training programs. Before one can deal with child custody, emotional issues associated with divorce, the children's interests, or dispose of marital property, the mediator must create a communication climate that is conductive to a mutually satisfactory settlement.

For those who have gone through formal training, it is clear that it offers a practical application of many skills taught in undergraduate interpersonal communication and conflict management courses. In the follow sections, we apply the formal mediation process to the management of everyday conflicts. First, we focus specifically on the role of the mediator.

The Role of the Mediator

The mediator is defined as "an impartial third party who has no authoritative decision-making power."[10] Although it may seem as though the mediator plays only a minor role, the mere introduction of a third person converts a private affair into a matter of social concern. Compared to private conflicts that tend to occur in the privacy of one's own home or involve only the partners themselves, mediation brings conflict to a social, public, and cultural level. The Chinese refer to this phenomenon as "the principle of three."[11] From the Chinese perspective, a culture of two is not a public affair and encourages a win–lose situation when two individuals engage in conflict. However, in a culture of three, the third party is there to remind the disputants that their behaviors are being viewed by others, thus bringing the behavior under social control and increasing the likelihood of social justice. The mere presence of mediators enables them to encourage cooperation rather than competition, strive for reasonable decisions that meet social concerns, and create and enforce rules to guide the interaction.

In informal situations, people can help others without their being formally trained and certified. Thus, everyone can benefit from receiving training that is available to the general public and is similar to that required for certification. The focus on mediators' attitudes, skills, and knowledge can form a basis for orienting third parties to their role as mediator. Basically, mediators attempt to create a safe and constructive environment to encourage the disputants to communicate, cooperate, and work out their own mutually satisfying solution.

Who should take the role of the "third person" and function as the mediator? First and foremost, mediators are neutral. This means that mediators are unbiased, and there is no reason for them to take one party's side against the other. In formal or informal cases, it is not a good idea to mediate if one knows one party better than the other. Mediators must also make every effort to demonstrate their neutrality by equalizing the speaking time, giving the same amount of time and attention to both parties, and not spending time alone with one of the parties without spending the same amount of time with the other during the mediation. Certainly, mediators are not to take sides in the dispute.

Second, because mediation offers the disputants an opportunity to openly talk to each other about their feelings, needs, goals, and reasons for behaving as they do, mediators must maintain confidentiality. They are not to make public the names of the conflicting parties, disclose the words spoken during the mediation, or retain notes after terminating mediation. In formal cases, trained mediators learn rules that cover a few legal exceptions, which they include in their opening remarks and make explicit on the mediation consent form, which is signed by both parties before mediation begins. In informal settings, mediators can simply state in their opening remarks that the mediation is considered confidential and ask the parties if they can agree to keep what is said "among us." It is this guarantee of confidentiality that makes self-disclosure possible in mediation.

Third, the mediators are competent in communication. In practice, you must manifest these effective communication behaviors:

- Be descriptive rather than judgmental.
- Be specific.
- Focus on behaviors that one can change.
- Give feedback when it is requested.
- Give timely feedback making it as close as possible to the behavior being discussed.
- Speak only for yourself. ("I understand you to say . . ." "I take it that you feel . . ." "I want you both to . . ." "I prefer to keep my opinions to myself.")
- Check what you see or hear with the other parties.[12]

Fourth, mediators are trained to facilitate communication by encouraging cooperation and discouraging competition between the parties.[13] Essentially, a mediator's objective is to create a safe and constructive environment for the parties to discuss emotional and substantive issues and reach agreement.[14] The process of mediation is successful to the extent that it moves from a competitive to a cooperative orientation because competition creates a defensive communication climate and cooperation creates a supportive atmosphere. Competitive communication is self-promoting because it serves as a vehicle through which individuals attempt to distort the other's perceptions of the situation in order to obtain an advantage. A cooperative orientation consists of behaviors characteristic of organized action (e.g., working together) and a thought process known as consensus (e.g., shared understanding, actual agreement). It also facilitates attempts to discover areas of common interest regarding issues.

Fifth, mediators have no decision-making power with respect to the outcome of the mediation. Initially, the parties often have expectations about the role of the mediators such as expecting them to solve their problems. Mediators must resist the temptation to solve the disputants' problem and need to inform the parties that they have no authoritative decision-making power.[15] However, because many disputants who enter mediation have found it difficult to communicate, relate, or work with each other in the past, mediators instruct the conflicting parties in constructive communication by announcing and enforcing communication rules. This topic is described in detail in the next section.

14.2 Think about It

What experience, training, and abilities do you possess that would make you a good mediator? Where are you weak? What could you do to become a better mediator?

We just described the role of the mediator. To understand how mediators gain control over the mediation process to produce mutually satisfying outcomes, we need to examine in detail a particular approach to mediation known as the rules or structural approach and the mediator's responsibility as a communication rules enforcer.

Mediators as Communication Rules Enforcers

To appreciate the idea that mediators primarily control the communication process to give them greater influence over the outcome of the interaction, one must understand how mediators create and enforce communication rules. According to Lulofs and Cahn (2000), mediators are trained to create and enforce rules to give the mediator greater control over the outcome of the interaction.[16] **Rules** are obligations (they tell us what we must say, what we should say) and prohibitions (they tell us what we had better not say in certain situations). We know that a rule exists largely when we have broken it and face some sort of sanction. For example, at a friend's wedding, it is customary to congratulate the groom and convey best wishes to the bride. Saying "congratulations" to the bride is considered in poor taste, and if you do so, others may give you a disapproving look. The rule is there, but it is not a strong one because so many people forget and get away with congratulating brides. On the other hand, laughing at a funeral is almost unheard of. It is prohibited, and anyone who breaks the rule gets escorted out of the room. This rule explains why there isn't more laughing at funerals.

Thus, a pattern of behavior is rule-governed when there exists mutual expectations or a consensus regarding what is appropriate behavior in a given situation. Although rules are social conventions, which are violated or changed by individuals or groups, it is argued that when people know the rules, they tend to conform to them. Mediation is viewed as a structured social activity guided and defined by rules designed to convert competitive orientations and actions into cooperative ones. According to Allen and Donohue,

> Successful mediators lay down rules at the beginning of the session. . . . The rules enforced by the mediator go beyond explaining the legal status of the mediator and mediation. The mediator also establishes rules for behavior during the session. The mediator limits the agenda for the session and the tone of the discussion. If disputants decide to call each other names and dwell on the issues . . . the mediator can and does exercise the option to ask the disputants to stop discussing those issues or change their use of language.[17]

It is no accident that even early practice in divorce mediation was based on a rules approach.[18] As **communication rules enforcers,** mediators establish and enforce the rules by which participants interact. Some common rules that are useful for directing the communication process toward positive outcomes are as follows:

- taking turns to talk without interruptions
- talking without expressing hostility to one another
- creating a positive climate with no put-downs
- focusing on the future (what the parties will do) rather than the past (what was done)
- striving for a win–win solution with no one feeling dissatisfied or agreeing to something unacceptable
- striving to solve the problem rather than attacking or blaming the other person
- being honest and sharing your thoughts and feelings without fear of criticism or publicity

- adhering to time constraints set by mediator
- agreeing to abide by additional rules as announced by the mediators during the session

Anxious to delve into an actual mediation? You need first to study the steps mediators take from the beginning to the end of the mediation.

14.3 Think about It

Have you studied rules in other communication courses? What are communication rules? How do mediators enforce communication rules?

The Mediation Process: Step by Step

In an effort to pull together much of the advice and principles of mediation, we have devised a list of steps that are common to mediating both (1) formal disputes conducted by certified mediators in divorce, community, or organizational settings and (2) informal disputes conducted by noncertified (but trained) third parties in family, friendship, or workplace settings. Once the conflicting parties realize that a dispute exists, the following steps are taken:

1. One or both disputants seek mediation, or mediators talk them into it (the intake process).
2. The mediators bring the disputants together and make an opening statement.
3. Following the mediators' opening statement, they ask each person to take a few minutes to describe the dispute from his or her point of view without interruption.
4. The mediators find common ground on which to build agreement.
5. The mediators write up the final agreement.
6. The mediators end the mediation.

In the rest of this chapter, we explain and illustrate these steps in detail. Let us begin with the fact that the conflicting parties realize that a dispute exists. This is to say that they are at a point where they realize that they cannot manage the conflict without help. They initiate the mediation process by taking the first step, which means requesting that someone take the role of third party and mediate their conflict.

The Intake Process

In formal mediation, the preliminary phase in which the parties seek help from a third person, who decides to intervene, is called **intake.** While informal mediations are often less methodical and sometimes seem quite chaotic initially, the parties eventually end up with someone who agrees to help them resolve the dispute. They may engage in "intake" without calling it that.

The decision to include a third party to mediate the conflict is an important one and involves the realization that such a person is necessary and that the parties must pick an appropriate person for the role. Both disputants may seek help from a third person, who becomes the mediator. If only one seeks help, the third person may contact the other disputant to see if she or he is agreeable to mediating the dispute. If neither disputant seeks help, a third person who is aware of the dispute may contact the disputants to see if they are agreeable to mediating the dispute.

Who should take the role of the "third person" and function as the mediator? As discussed above, mediators are neutral and unbiased, have no decision-making power with respect to the outcome of the mediation, must maintain confidentiality, communicate with competence, and encourage cooperation and discourage competition between the parties. This rules out people who are more involved with or familiar with only one of the conflicting parties, those who think they know what is best for the parties and dominate the mediation by talking most and advising them, people who can't keep secrets, who are not competent communicators, or those who encourage competition between the parties.

Opening Statement

Obviously, if mediation is to take place, mediators must arrange for a first meeting with the disputants where they make an opening statement. After all, mediators are responsible for initiating, managing, and terminating the mediation sessions. Mediators must select a location free of interruptions and distractions. The conflicting parties should sit and face one another with the mediators at the end of the table.

At the first meeting, mediators make an opening statement, where they explain the purpose and process of mediation, including their role as facilitators of communication and lay out the communication rules that structure the mediation. At this initial meeting, mediators make the following clear to the disputants:

- That their participation in mediation is voluntary and the mediator or conflicting parties may terminate it at any time.
- That the mediator is unbiased (impartial toward either disputant).
- That what is said in mediation is confidential.
- That the goal is a written agreement with which both parties are satisfied or at least comfortable.
- That the disputants are to try to work out a mutual agreement between them with the help of the mediator, who is an unbiased facilitator of discussion, and does not make decisions for the disputants (not a judge or jury).

The mediators also inform the participants that they are to adhere to a few communication ground rules to include the following:

1. The parties are encouraged to talk to and look at one another rather than at the mediator.
2. The parties are asked to take turns talking without interruptions.
3. The parties are required to adhere to time constraints set by the mediator.
4. The parties are asked to strive to solve the problem rather than attack or blame the other person. Mediators have to help the parties learn to talk without expressing hostility to one another and to create a positive climate with no put-downs (focus on the problem, not the other person).

5. The parties are encouraged to focus on the future (what they can do) rather than the past (what was done).
6. The parties are told that they can openly share thoughts and feelings without fear of criticism or publicity.
7. The parties are required to strive for a win–win solution with no one feeling dissatisfied or agreeing to something either party finds unacceptable.
8. The parties are asked to agree to abide by additional rules as announced by the mediator during the session.

Mediators also use the initial remarks as an opportunity to re-establish communication between the disputants and redirect it in a more positive direction. For example, mediators encourage the parties to look at each other rather than at them.

All of this sounds like a lot for an opening statement, and it is. Sometimes not everything is included in the opening statement, but the mediators add to it as the mediation continues. As you gain experience mediating, you can keep the opening statement to essentials and then add the other rules and suggestions later as the need arises.

14.1 Apply It

Now it is your turn. Imagine yourself as a mediator and write an opening statement for the following case.

> Two roommates, Mr. X and Mr. Y, have differences of opinion on what they like to listen to on the stereo, what they like to eat, when they have visitors, when they wake up or quiet down at night, and when they use the room for study.

Note the essential items that the mediator chose to include in the following opening statement. Do you agree with his or her choice?

> I am glad that you both decided to try mediation and am pleased that you have asked me to help out here by serving as mediator. Let me start off by saying that your participation is entirely voluntary. I don't see any reason to say anything to others, so if you want to keep what we say just among us, that is fine with me. Is that what you want to do? OK, my role here is to help you work out your own agreement, one that you both feel comfortable with. In addition to not making your decisions for you, I must avoid siding with either of you or showing any favoritism. I may stop you to ask you questions, and I may make some notes, so that I can keep track of the issues and help you write up a mutually acceptable agreement. During the session, I may have to establish some ground rules. For example, let's agree right off not to engage in any name calling, and if the conflict escalates, I'll have to stop the session.
>
> I am going to ask each of you to tell us your side of the story, while I try to write down the key points, so we can discuss them. When one of you is talking, the other is not to interrupt. Are there any questions? If not, let's begin with Marisa. After hearing your side of the story, then Georgia can tell us hers.

Describing the Dispute

Mediators usually begin with the person who initiated the complaint against the other. For example, a neighbor who is upset about the other neighbor playing basketball in the driveway early in the morning, which annoys him, is probably the person who initiates the complaint (against the noisy neighbor). This person describes the problem from his or her point of view, explaining what happened and how she or he feels about it. The other person listening must not interrupt the speaker, but must hear out the speaker in his or her entirety. As soon as the first party finishes the opening statement, mediators ask the other party to explain what happened from her or his point of view, again without interruption. After each opening statement, mediators summarize back to the disputant the issues raised and how the mediators believe that the disputant feels about them. Mediators ask for confirmation of their summary from that disputant, and sometimes ask disputants to summarize what they heard from the other party. From these opening remarks, mediators identify the issues that are to comprise the agenda for discussion. At this early stage of the mediation, mediators may tolerate some venting of feelings for a short period to help get them out of one's system, but later they discourage the strong expression of feelings, which can escalate the conflict.

Sometimes it is useful for mediators to **caucus,** in which the mediator steps aside with one disputant for a private discussion to request the disclosure of information that the disputant doesn't want to make in the presence of the other. This technique is especially useful when the parties are at an impasse. In the private meeting, the mediator may help one of the parties to better understand how to contribute more positively to the discussion. To maintain an unbiased position, it is important that the mediator meets with both parties, separately of course, for about the same amount of time. Mediators should ask permission from each party before introducing into the discussion something disclosed in the caucus.

14.2 Apply It

Read the following case study, which is based on the opening statements of the disputants, and identify the issues that the conflicting parties should discuss.

> These two disputants are romantic partners, living in the same house and relying on only one car to drive to campus and town. Robert decided that he needed a "break" from his involvement with Cherene, which she initially agreed to. He wanted to stay in the same house (and move to another bedroom) and share the car. They had shared a bank account, but he withdrew half of the money and opened a new account of his own. Cherene had originally signed for the apartment, so she felt obligated to pay the rent, but she didn't have enough money now in her account to pay the bills unless he would give her his share of the expenses, and lately he became reluctant to do so. As time went on, she continued to act as his primary romantic interest even though he was looking to distance himself from her. That is why she told everyone she knew that "everything was fine between them." Consequently, he became more and more aggravated with her actions and his reactions hurt her a great deal. When he said that he might bring home other female friends of his, she told him that he better not do that, or she would do some serious damage to the car (which was originally his). Robert had met her parents, and they were visiting this next weekend. Because they liked him, she didn't want to tell them about Robert's recent behavior. There is a lot of miscommunication between the two since and the situation is progressively getting worse with many quarrels and screaming matches.

Note that in the case study for Apply It 14.2, the mediator might want to caucus with each person and ask him or her how one truly feels about the other person and the relationship. Do they love each other? Do they want out of the relationship entirely but don't know how to do it? Each person may not want to talk about these feelings in the presence of the other but may open up to the mediator. The mediator might help convince the other person to strive for more openness and honesty later when they resume the mediation.

Common Ground

Mediation sessions usually begin with a broad and confused discussion of issues seen from competitive orientations, but when mediators are successful, the discussion proceeds to more detailed and specific statements out of which cooperation and consensus (shared meanings) emerge. The techniques mediators use are fractionation, framing, reframing, and common ground.

The mediators begin with the easiest issues to resolve, leaving the most difficult for last. While thinking about the issues and discussing them, the mediators may rely on a useful technique for resolving conflict over an issue called fractionation. This technique involves breaking down complex issues into smaller, more manageable ones. After separating issues into their smallest components, the mediators can ask the disputants to deal with each issue one at a time, which builds a feeling of success on small issues, until the larger issues are successfully resolved.

Another technique is known as **framing,** where mediators ask neutral or friendly questions that avoid blame or passing judgment and summarize issues. One more technique is **reframing,** where mediators restate negatively loaded, biased, or accusatory statements made by one of the parties in more neutral terminology or restate positions in a way that makes the disputants look at the issues differently. Finally, mediators highlight **common ground,** which consists of attitudes, values, behaviors, expectations, and goals the parties share and can serve as a basis for an agreement.

As soon as it seems appropriate, the mediators ask the parties what they want as an outcome of the dispute. Sometimes people do not know what they want and need time and encouragement to determine what they want. Once the wants are expressed, sometimes the opposing party discovers that the want is not what she or he expected to hear or as extreme as originally thought. This clarification of wants may lead to a quick settlement, but oftentimes it does not. In any case, the mediators succeed in getting the positions on the table as soon as possible.

Because the parties' interests and needs are broader than their specific positions or wants (see Chapter 7 for a discussion of interests versus positions), the mediators facilitate discussion of the interests that lie behind positions taken by the disputants. For example, the mediators discover that the complaining neighbor wants the other neighbor to stop playing basketball, but what he really needs is to sleep in mornings without noise and interruption. However, the opposing neighbor says he wants to play basketball in the morning, but what he really needs is practice at shooting baskets sometime most days. As it turns out, he doesn't really need to shoot baskets in the early morning.

In addition to discovering interests and needs, the mediators also reframe the disputants' statements and positions. The mediators do this by helping the parties restate their comments in less offensive language and reword their utterances as proposals. For example, the mediators might say, "You say that your neighbor's basketball is keeping you awake in the early morning, but are you asking that he play later in the day instead?"

As the discussion progresses, the mediators request proposals or solutions to the problem that would satisfy the interests and needs of both parties. The mediators also help the parties brainstorm alternative proposals. In many group communications, students of communication learned how to brainstorm solutions to problems. The idea is not to criticize or limit the proposals in any way, but simply to create as long a list as possible. Sometimes one suggestion, even if corny or ridiculous, triggers the parties to think of something better. Brainstorming plays an important role in expanding the range of options for reaching an agreement.

Throughout the discussion, mediators identify, highlight, and reinforce points of agreement, encourage positive contributions, and show attentiveness by responding verbally or nonverbally to comments by both parties. This positive feedback encourages the parties to continue the mediation and work toward agreement.

Try seeking common ground, perhaps as a member of a small group. Consider the list of issues you discovered from the above case study, involving a dispute between two romantic partners, Robert and Cherene. See if you can fractionate any of the issues into sub-issues. Then brainstorm solutions to the problem. Determine a list of points you think the two might agree on.

Final Agreement

Usually, the mediator keeps track of areas of agreement as the mediation progresses, so that eventually she or he has a rough draft of all points of consensus. Mediators learn early on in their training that wording of these commonalities is important. While it helps to list the different points of agreement, mediators need to employ the following format and say that "X agrees to this . . . Y agrees to that . . ." Mediators attempt to keep the agreement simple. They use clear, specific details (spelling out who, what, where, when, how). It helps to think of the agreement as a list of **behavioral commitments** because it enumerates the specific observable actions each party needs to take to fulfill the agreement. When there are comediators, one usually takes the responsibility of keeping track of this list of behaviors, while the other encourages the conflicting parties to communicate effectively. In developing the agreement, mediators should strive for balance or "something for everyone." The agreement also needs to address questions of feasibility and practicality because the parties should find the agreement workable. Finally, the culminating step occurs when the mediators ask both parties to sign the agreement.

Because it is important that mediators take a neutral role, they should not comment positively or negatively about areas of agreement. Mediators are not the ones agreeing to the behavioral commitments, so they should refrain from commenting one way or another. This is not a negotiation in which both are trying to win the most they can from one another. Sometimes, one party settles for less than expected in a mediation simply because he or she knows that the other is more likely to live up to the agreement. Of course, the mediators can raise questions of feasibility. Is this idea doable? Can each of you actually do this?

In the following scenario, we offer an initial draft of the behavioral commitments as an example.

> Daria, who is a communication major and college senior living at home, often finds herself in the middle when her mother and her teenage sister engage in conflict. Both have come to rely on her to help them resolve their conflicts (or play the role of mediator). In this case, the sister wants more freedom and responsibility, which her mother is against before the mediation.

After facilitating the mediation, in which both parties explain their views, Daria, who has kept track of areas of consensus during the mediation, drafts an agreement as follows:

Agreement between Mother and Sister dated _____.

Mother agrees to not wait up for the sister to return when out with friends or on a date on Friday and Saturday nights.

Sister agrees to tell her mother whom she is with, the places they plan to go, and return home by 1 A.M.

Mother agrees that sometimes plans change and sister may go places not originally intended.

Sister agrees to not go to places that her mother is concerned about (namely, Mr. G's in town, Mathew's home when his parents aren't there, Linsey's home when her parents aren't there).

Mother agrees to stop criticizing her boyfriend to his face.

Sister agrees to come home by 10 P.M. on school nights.

Mother agrees to let her use her car in cases where she has to meet her friends.

Sister agrees to not drive and drink alcohol.

Signed by _____ (Mother) and _____ (Sister)

Witnessed by _____ (Daria as mediator)

As you consider the above case, keep these points in mind. First, as mediator, Daria personally may not think this is a good agreement. She may think the mother is too strict or too lenient or the daughter too young or too old, but as mediator, she is not the one who is bound by this agreement. If this is what the mother and sister agree to, then Daria should keep her opinions to herself and encourage the two parties. Second, although the sister probably initiated the complaint, Daria tried to balance the agreement so that each party leaves the mediation with something she wants. Also, rather than say something vague or indefinite, such as "Mother doesn't want sister going out just any old time, staying out as late as she wants, or going to places that she doesn't approve of," Daria strove for specificity by clarifying the exact days, times, and places or people by name. Finally, Daria kept responsibilities clear by using the simple format, "X agrees to do . . . Y agrees to do . . ." Although mediators don't keep notes of the mediation after it is terminated, Daria may want to keep a copy of the agreement for future reference if the participants think that is a good idea or do not object.

14.3   Apply It

Read over the following scenario and draft an agreement using the format, "X agrees to this and Y agrees to that." Strive for balance as much as possible.

One roommate cares about the cleanliness of the apartment, but the other has shown no interest. However, in the course of mediation between roommates over their messy apartment, they agree to divvy up the household chores and times/days to do them.

Imagining the typical chores and considering a reasonable schedule for the two roommates, draft an agreement that you intend to ask both roommates to sign. Use the appropriate format recommended in this chapter

Children as well as adults can be trained to mediate in conflicts of their own making or of those around them.

Ending the Mediation

The mediators give each disputant a copy of the handwritten, signed agreement. Where appropriate, the mediators set up a date for reviewing and evaluating the agreement. They thank the parties for using mediation and wish them well. Unlike formal mediation, the mediators in an informal dispute usually do not need to file paperwork, have the agreement typewritten, or mail it to the disputants.

14.4   Think about It

Why should communication majors make good mediators? Why might lawyers and psychotherapists find it difficult to effectively play the role of mediator?

The agreement, whether written or not, culminates the process of mediation. The process as a whole works well in many everyday situations. Even young children can learn conflict mediation, making a difference in their lives and the lives of those around them.[19]

Following training in mediation in class, some students of one of the authors made comments such as these:

> I could relate to this subject because it reinforced my training as a Resident Assistant on campus. I have dealt with different issues in the building where I lived, where I have used mediation to solve conflicts among residents and staff members.

I did not realize that I act as a mediator almost daily at work. I work with children. Children often find themselves in some sort of dispute or conflict with one another, it is my job to act as a mediator for them so that they can work out their own mutually satisfying outcomes.

Teachers, day care providers, and others who work with kids are mediators all day long. Mediating conflicts between children may seem simple or small, but they are important to the children involved.

I think mediation happens almost every day on a more informal level. This can happen between roommates, families, coworkers, and so on. If there is a problem, a third party might intervene to help the resolution run more smoothly.

I thought this subject helped me to see different ways of handling conflict situations and how important it is to sometimes have a third party involved. Many times I find myself in conflict with someone and we cannot come to a resolution but with the help of someone else we come to a resolution that is fair to both of us. I see that having a neutral third party can be very helpful when trying to deal with certain issues.

Like these students, we hope you may find mediation useful in your everyday life.

Manage It

The study and practice of effective mediation is a natural fit for students of communication and conflict. Unlike other alternatives to dispute resolution (ADRs) such as conciliation, ombudsperson, arbitration, and adjudication/litigation, mediators are neutral third parties who facilitate communication between the conflicting parties so that the conflicting parties can work out their own agreement.

Many universities offer credit and some states provide training that leads to certification in mediation. While there is a need for fully trained, accredited mediators, there is an even greater need for us all to practice mediation skills to help those who are important to us when they have a dispute. For those who have gone through formal training, it is clear that it offers a practical application of many skills taught in undergraduate interpersonal communication and conflict management courses.

When should a person intervene in other people's conflict? Help is probably needed when the dispute has reached a point at which the two parties are no longer able to resolve it on their own. A typical mediation usually proceeds through the following steps:

1. One or both disputants seek mediation or a mediator may talk them into it.
2. The mediator brings the disputants together and makes an opening statement.
3. Following the mediator's opening statement, each person takes a few minutes to describe the dispute from his or her point of view without interruption.
4. The mediator finds common ground on which to build agreement.
5. The mediator writes up the final agreement.
6. The mediator ends the mediation.

When drafting the agreement, mediators need to employ the following format: X agrees to this, and Y agrees to that. The mediators should attempt to keep the agreement simple. They use clear, specific details (spelling out who, what, where, when, how). It helps to think of the agreement as a list of behavioral commitments because it enumerates the specific observable actions each party needs to take to fulfill the agreement. In developing the agreement, the mediators should strive for balance or "something for everyone." The agreement also needs to address questions of feasibility and practicality—both parties should find the agreement workable. Finally, the culminating step occurs when the mediators ask both parties to sign the agreement.

This chapter concludes our presentation of the core concepts involved in effective conflict management. The afterword presents an overall view of the effective conflict manager.

14.1 Work with It

Apply the chapter objectives to the following case study.

> My mother allows my 13 year old sister, Leanne, to publish a blog [online journal]. She did not know what Leanne was writing about online until she started receiving long distance telephone calls from older men asking for her by name. Both my mother and sister complain to me about the other. My mother tells me that she would like to start reading her blog daily and would like to delete any content that she finds inappropriate. Leanne tells me that her blog is like a diary, and she doesn't want her mother to read it. Both are really upset with each other.

1. Define mediation and explain whether you think a third party should intervene as a mediator, and why.
2. Describe the role of mediator for whomever intervenes as a third party.
3. List and briefly describe the steps the third party should go through for this hypothetical mediation.

14.1 Remember It

Write an essay in which you apply the ideas presented in Chapter 14 to your life situation. Make sure to address the following topics.

1. Define mediation and contrast it with the other ADRs.
2. Create a hypothetical mediation and explain when a third party should intervene as a mediator.
3. Describe your role in this mediaton.
4. What rules would you choose to enforce and why?
5. List and briefly describe the steps you would go through for this hypothetical mediation.

14.2 Work with It

Take turns playing the role of mediator or co-mediator and conflicting parties, so that everyone has an opportunity to role play a mediator. Then, discuss the mediation and ways to improve it.

You may wish to devise your own role play. If not, then select one of the following situations to mediate and assign roles of two conflicting parties and one or two mediators. If needed, others may serve as observers, but they cannot participate in the mediation. Mediators should start with their opening statements and follow the mediation steps.

1. Family members: Your father and his sister (your aunt) have asked you to mediate their dispute. Your father thinks that your aunt took an expensive piece of furniture from their father's house after he passed away without discussing it with him. Your aunt took care of their father in his final days and had a key to his house. Your aunt was also in control of their father's finances and your father thinks she took all his money during his final days. Now your father is angry at his sister.

2. Two romantic partners, Lacey and Henry, are living in a house with a third person, you. You treat them both equally. Recently Lacy decided that she wants to watch some TV programs, even though they were on the same time as sports. Meanwhile, Henry wants to watch the sports on the weekend and some weekday nights. The negative atmosphere is so bad in the house that you asked each of them to let you mediate the conflict, and they both agreed to let you do it.

3. Two romantic partners are having a conflict over time management. He wants to spend time with his buddies and even invites one or two to join them when they go out together. She doesn't approve of all of his friends and finds two to be offensive and a bad influence on him. She wants to go out more often as just the two of them. She also wants more time with him without his buddies hanging around.

4. Two roommates: Ms. X spends too much money. She likes to buy a lot of clothes. She never has enough for meals or gas, so she is always asking her roommate, Ms. Y, for food or gas money. She wants money to help pay for her books and sometimes doesn't have enough to help pay their room expenses. Ms. Y is fortunate to have enough money, but thinks it is unfair that her roommate isn't pulling her share and needs money from her so often. Ms. X often doesn't pay back the money she owes her roommate.

5. Two roommates: Bryon comes home late and rowdy from the local bars Thursday, Friday, and Saturday nights. Roommate Lee has Friday classes and needs to go to work early every weekend.

6. Two sisters: A borrows B's clothes without her permission. B occasionally snoops through A's room and tries to find her diary and other personal items.

7. Married seniors: Husband recently retired and now spends all his time in the house. He doesn't do any household chores and gets in his wife's way.

8. Two neighbors: Pearson's dog barks, and when loose makes messes in his neighbor's yard. Recently the dog ripped open the garbage container when the neighbor placed it at the end of the drive for pickup.

NOTES

1. Nancy A. Burrell and Dudley D. Cahn, "Mediating Peer Conflicts in Educational Contexts: The Maintenance of School Relationships," in Dudley D. Cahn (Ed.), *Conflict in Personal Relationships* (Hillsdale, NJ: Erlbaum, 1994), p. 79.

2. See, for example, Robert E. Emery, David Sbarra, and Tara Grover, "Divorce Mediation: Research and Reflections," *Family Court Review* 43 (2005), 22–37; Frank E. A. Sander and Robert C. Bordone, "Early Intervention: How to Minimize the Cost of Conflict," *Negotiation* 21 (2005), 1–4; Lisa B. Bingham, "Employment Dispute Resolution: The Case for Mediation," *Conflict Resolution Quarterly* 22 (2004), 145–174.

3. Bruce C. McKinney, William Kimsey, and Rex Fuller, *Mediation: Dispute Resolution through Communication,* 2nd Ed. (Dubuque, IA: Kendall Hunt, 1990), p. 146.

4. Dudley D. Cahn, *Conflict in Intimate Relationships* (New York: Guilford, 1992).

5. Claire Danielsson, "A Holistic Approach to Dispute Resolution at a Community Mediation Center," in Dudley D. Cahn (Ed.), *Conflict in Personal Relationships* (Hillsdale, NJ: Erlbaum, 1994).

6. Afshan Siddiqui and Hildy Ross, "Mediation as a Method of Parent Intervention in Children's Disputes," *Journal of Family Psychology* 18 (2004), 147–159.

7. James A. Wall, Jr., John B. Stark, and Rhetta L. Standifer, "Mediation: A Current Review and Theory Development," *Journal of Conflict Resolution* 45 (2001), 370–391.

8. Stephen K. Erickson and Marilyn S. McKnight, *The Practitioner's Guide to Mediation: A Client-Centered Approach* (New York: John Wiley, 2001).

9. Robert Coulson, *Family Mediation: Managing Conflict, Resolving Disputes* (San Francisco: Jossey-Bass, 1996); Stephen A. Giunta and Ellen S. Amatea, "Mediation or Litigation with Abusing or Neglectful Families: Emerging Roles for Mental Health Counselors," *Journal of Mental Health Counseling* 22 (2000), 240–252.

10. Nancy A. Burrell, William A. Donohue, and Mike Allen, "The Impact of Disputants' Expectations on Mediation: Testing an Interventionist Model," *Human Communication Research* 17 (1990), p. 106.

11. Wenshan Jia, "Chinese Mediation and Its Cultural Foundation," in Guo-ming Chen and Ringo Ma (Eds.), *Chinese Conflict Management and Resolution* (Stamford, CT: Ablex, 2001), p. 290.

12. Joyce L. Hocker and William W. Wilmot, *Interpersonal Conflict,* 4th Ed. (Dubuque, IA: Wm C. Brown, 1995), p. 238.

13. Jean Poitras, "A Study of the Emergence of Cooperation in Mediation," *Negotiation Journal* 21 (2005), 281–300.

14. Cahn, op. cit.

15. Jordi Agustí-Panareda, "Power Imbalances in Mediation: Questioning Some Common Assumptions," *Dispute Resolution Journal* 59 (2004), 24–31.

16. Roxane S. Lulofs and Dudley D. Cahn, *Conflict: From Theory to Action* (Boston: Allyn & Bacon, 2000).

17. Mike Allen and William A. Donohue, "The Mediator as an Arguer," in J. W. Wenzel (Ed.), *Argument and Critical Practices* (Annandale, VA: SCA, 1987), p. 280.

18. O. J. Coogler, *Structured Mediation in Divorce Settlement* (Lexington, MA: Lexington Books, 1978).

19. See, for example, Candice C. Carter, "Conflict Resolution at School: Building Compassionate Communities," *Social Alternatives* 21 (2002), 49–55; David W. Johnson and Roger T. Johnson, "Implementing the 'Teaching Students to Be Peacemakers Program,'" *Theory into Practice* 43 (2004), 68–79.

The Ideal Conflict Manager

A lot has happened since you encountered Chapter 1 and started to read about managing conflicts in your interpersonal relationships. By now you realize the common occurrence of such conflicts in our everyday life. You are more aware of the many alternatives that confront you, necessitating an analysis of the conflict situation, so that you may choose the best option.

In this afterword, we take a broader, more encompassing view of conflict management. First, we present a notion of conflict proneness, and suggest ways that we can head off conflict in our lives. Next, we summarize most of what you have learned as eighteen key conflict management principles or skills.

Conflict Proneness

Many of us suffer from conflict proneness because we take ourselves too seriously, don't enjoy what we are doing, or fail to see the humor in our everyday affairs. We may feel overworked, under pressure, or unable to meet the demands at home, at work, or at school. Fearing that we are falling behind or not succeeding in achieving our goals, we are conscious of the fact that we are not playing for fun. Instead, we are concentrating entirely on the end result. Athletes do this when they focus only on winning or outperforming others. These conflict prone people are not happy, having fun, or enjoying life. There are numerous reasons why modern living is stressful and depressing.

We all know people who say that they are too busy. They say, "You know how it is—work, work, work—too many problems, too much to do and not enough time. My life is overwhelming." Obviously, jobs are a major source of unhappiness in some cases. In his scholarly treatment of the subject, Brenner adds,

> [M]oney is important, but I believe that how we earn it is even more important . . . there is a great letdown in our sense of joy from life, and in our self-respect, as a result of things we do that we are unconsciously apologetic for, or feel guilty about, in the course of our daily work. And to a person who is unhappy, life cannot be fun.[1]

Why are people not happy? There are many reasons. Consider this person's account.

> I have a good friend who was, for a time, homeless. He moved to this state without having a job lined up and found he couldn't get one. He ran through his resources and wound up

living out of his car. It has really affected him. It's hard for him to spend money even on necessities, because he's terrified of being homeless again. The fact that he's making good money now and banking a good portion of it doesn't matter. As far as he's concerned, another rainy day is just around the corner.

People who take life too seriously often end up turning to alcohol, nicotine, or other drugs, become addicted to sex, gambling, or the Internet, or buy homes, cars, or vacations that they can ill afford.

We start our life as children with an obvious demand for joy. Even as adults, there is a child hidden in each of us, and this child would like to come out and play. However, later we learn to take everyday activities too seriously, such that they become obligations that usually rob us of fun, joy, and merriment. Our preoccupation with achievement, whether in winning or outperforming others, makes us feel insecure. According to Brenner, "Unfortunately, the traditional repression of play, humor, and wit deeply changed our ability to enjoy life and to be content. It has turned us into severe, aggressive, function-oriented rather than people-oriented creatures."[2]

It is not enough that we take matters too seriously. Sometimes we turn play and fun activities into work. Professional sports serve as an example in which some players no longer enjoy the game. The same is said of some entertainers and actors who have lost the joy of playing before others. Those situations show the negative elements that also are sometimes found in work and serious situations that are not viewed from a play or fun perspective.

Let's take something that should be fun like a vacation. Often people say they need a vacation to recover from their vacation! Why is that? Part of the reason is that they spend a great deal of time planning it, working overtime to pay for it, worrying that the experience might not live up to their expectations, and obsessing about how many tasks may pile up on their desk by the time they return to work.

We need to take ourselves less seriously, see the humor in our everyday activities, and enjoy life more. We need to adopt the attitude that "it is not whether we win or lose but how we play the game." Half the fun is getting somewhere, not just getting there. This means that we have to allow more time, plan some fun activities into our lives, learn to laugh more, and avoid making situations more complicated than they need to be.

Essentially, there are three different ways of lightening up. First, we can make a distinction between work and play. We can view work as what we do for the sake of something else, while play is what we do for its own sake. So, we can add to our week a few entertaining and fun activities in an effort to balance work. You certainly could give this solution a try; however, it may not work because a few fun events in the evenings or on weekends are not enough to balance forty, sixty, or eighty hours of a demanding job during the week. Moreover, these types of activities may lose impact if they are passive rather than active. Watching a movie is somewhat relaxing, but more benefit is gained from taking a walk or playing a game with someone.

The second way to lighten up is to take the view that "play is an attitude of mind that may pervade any human activity."[3] It isn't our actual experiences but what we make of them that gives meaning to our existence. It has been said that life is easier than we actually make it. It's as though we need to give ourselves permission to have fun. Mahan argues that

> [W]hat we'd most like to do is chuck the whole project of improving ourselves and with it our incessant and obsessive monitoring of our 'progress' toward whoever it is we think we ought to be . . . we long for a kind of self-forgetful yet fully engaged sense of immediacy, for a more graced and gracious way of being in this world, one that cuts deeper than the surface imagery sketched by our infernal preoccupation with some soon-to-be success or failure. . . .[4]

We can change the way we feel about our everyday activities at home, work, or school. We must find joy in the work we do. This is far more encompassing than the first solution. It is a matter of seeing our work as a game, as a type of play. Miller puts it another way: Not that we should start playing and stop working, but rather, we should work as if at play, because that is what we are doing anyway—playing at work.[5]

We need to take ourselves less seriously, treat matters more gamefully, and designate all our activities as games that we play. We need to make the decision that if we must do our everyday activities, we might as well enjoy doing them. We need to catch ourselves every time we take ourselves too seriously. When we do that, we become alive—we lighten up.

The third solution is termed *integration:* one understands that joy and pain are often found in the same place, and one can value both. Goldingay remarks:

> So many things we achieve are achieved only through struggle and conflict, not in easy ways. . . . I have so longed to find somewhere in life some corner where joy is unmingled with pain. But I have never found it. Wherever I find joy, my own or other people's, it always seems to be mingled with pain. . . . The bad news is that there may be no corner of reality where joy is not related to pain. The good news is that there is no corner of reality where pain cannot be transformed into overflowing joy.[6]

Developing a Playful Spirit

How does one adopt a playful spirit or attitude? Play theorists encourage us to lighten up and to develop a playful attitude toward life in a way that best suits our personality and psychological makeup. For example, while waiting at a red light, we could count the cars streaming through the intersection. We can play games like these to reduce the seriousness of situations. We use the following techniques:

- Don't blame yourself for everything that goes wrong or doesn't pan out. If you look for them, you can often find situational factors, which you could learn to accept rather than blame yourself.
- See irony in problematic situations.
- Visualize absurdities. Make a joke to yourself of something negative.
- Ask yourself: Am I happy right now? What can I do now to be happier?
- Learn to say "No," without feeling guilty.
- Take on a new role that is more enjoyable than the present one.

- Do something you can succeed at, especially after failing at something else.
- Take time off or time out; take a vacation; pay for a massage.
- Do something physical: Exercise or join a health club.
- Do something social: Throw a party for your friends.
- Hang a sign in your room or workplace: Success is happiness!

We can learn from those older people who grasp a playful attitude. The recent upsurge of "Red Hat Clubs," where women celebrate the fact that they're over 50 and deserve the label "Queen Mother," is an example of this playful attitude.

The use of humor in conflict situations is a double-edged sword. On one hand, used appropriately, it can alleviate some of the stress in the situation and help people express some of their negative emotions in a less harmful way. Appropriate humor may also help maintain social order, channel hostility, or assist people in saving face. If the humor is inappropriate, however, it can also make the conflict situation worse. The ability to use humor in a conflict situation, though, is an indicator of the level of trust in it—those who trust one another can laugh together.[7]

But what if other people think that everything is just a big joke to you? If your parents are paying for your college education, your boss is taking a chance in hiring you, or your teachers think that you only do superior work if you take their assignments very seriously, then you fear that they may misinterpret your behavior. We are not saying that you have to act silly in the presence of others. You may accomplish much of what we suggest covertly or mentally. We can change our views, talk to ourselves in a constructive manner, and make light of matters as a mental state. We can feel less guilt and less anxiety. Meanwhile, we can still work hard, and do what is possible or what it takes to keep a job or earn good grades. Neale claims that "Those who have observed children at play have no doubts about their seriousness."[8] Rahner adds:

> The same things that give human play its unique character—the light-hearted relaxing of the mind, the charm of a certain smiling contempt for mundane things, the wisdom of ease and detachment—also make it possible for a person to kick the world away from oneself with the airy grace of a dancer, and yet, at the same time, press it to one's heart.[9]

According to Sutton-Smith, a playful spirit contributes to well-being and is associated with being an emotionally, socially, physically, and mentally healthier person.[10] Approaching our environment as a game to be played as well as taken seriously can convert an unhappy life into a happy one—or at least reduce one's conflict proneness.

Conflict Management Principles

We believe the following principles describe an Ideal Conflict Manager (ICM).

1. *The effective conflict manager does not view conflict negatively, but rather sees opportunities for personal and relationship growth in conflict situations.* The most important step in managing conflict is to adopt a mindset that embraces conflict as an opportunity

This watercolor painting by Lynn Palmer titled Every Conflict Tells a Story *reflects a healthy view of conflict. There may be some painful spots involved, and there may even be places where the conflict is derailed or stalled, but overall, conflict yields positive results.*

while recognizing the risks involved in it. Your other skills in conflict depend on your ability to transform how you think about conflict in general. Cloke remarks:

> We can all recognize that in order to resolve our conflicts we have to move towards them, which is inherently dangerous because it can cause them to escalate. It is somewhat more difficult for us to grasp that our conflicts are laden with information that is essential for our growth, learning, intimacy, and change, that they present us with multiple openings for transformation and unique opportunities to let go of old patterns.[11]

This mindset recognizes the importance of personal responsibility for one's actions and encourages flexibility in oneself and in others within the conflict situation. The mindset also recognizes that communication works no miracles but that it usually helps when managing conflicts. Most importantly, this mindset rejects easy solutions and recognizes the complexity of conflict situations and their outcomes.

The accompanying conflict art illustrates the ICM mindset. It recognizes the inherent danger in conflict; at the same time, it demonstrates the positive outcomes that can arise from conflict handled well.

2. *The effective conflict manager understands the nature of interpersonal conflict.* Truly competent conflict managers view interpersonal conflict as a problematic situation with the following four unique characteristics: the conflicting parties are interdependent; perceive that they seek incompatible goals or outcomes or they favor incompatible means to the same ends; the perceived incompatibility has the potential to adversely affect the relationship if not addressed; and there is a sense of urgency about the need to resolve the difference.

> Sometimes I think conflict is like leftovers you forget about in your refrigerator. If you don't eat them or throw them away, they start growing things all on their own. And the longer you put off cleaning them out, the worse it is to take care of them. No matter how well I cook, there are always leftovers to contend with. No matter how well I am getting along with other people, there will always be tensions to resolve.

By viewing conflict this way, we quickly realize that conflict is inevitable because as relationships become closer, more personal, and more interdependent, we find that more conflicts occur, trivial (minor) complaints become more significant, and feelings become more intense.

3. *The effective conflict manager takes a transactional approach to communication and conflict.* A competent conflict manager sees communication as a transactional process by which people make or create meaning together. Such an approach recognizes that communication (and by extension, conflict) isn't something we do "to" one another, but something we do "with" one another (like teamwork or a dance). It takes two people to make the conflict, and it takes two people to manage or resolve it.

> One of the things I did following my husband's request for a divorce was to look over my prayer journals from the years preceding it. Over and over I prayed that God would make me a better wife, more understanding, and so on. But it didn't matter how good or understanding I was when my husband wasn't willing to change or meet me even part of the way. I tried and tried and tried, but it took two. I couldn't do it alone.

The advantage of the transactional model is that we recognize the importance of both people's behavior in the conflict situation. One person acting "competently" in a conflict situation, using good communication skills, usually cannot bring the conflict to a successful resolution.

4. *The effective conflict manager recognizes the role of choice in conflict situations.* Although we think conflict is inevitable, the competent conflict manager does not think that interpersonal violence or verbal aggression is a natural outcome of conflict. Violence is a choice we make or reject. By realizing that we have options in a conflict situation and by learning nonviolent solutions to problems, setting an example in our daily lives, and raising our children to resolve interpersonal conflicts peacefully, we are helping to reduce a serious social problem.

Effective conflict management can change potentially destructive conflict into productive conflict, containing expansion of the issues, number of people involved, costs to the participants, and intensity of negative feelings. Effective conflict management can attenuate the desire to hurt the other person and to get even for past wrongs and move us away from reliance on overt power and manipulative techniques. It features an awareness of options in conflict situations. Along with these characteristics, a productive view of conflict situations includes flexibility and a belief that all conflicting parties can achieve their important goals.

Probably the most important factor that affects your ability to put the advice in this book into effect is to remember that you always have choices in conflict situations. Even when you believe that everything is happening too fast or that you must deal with problems that arise suddenly, you still have choices as to how you act or react with respect to the other person.

5. *The effective conflict manager analyzes conflict by identifying its type to determine the appropriate response.* As researchers have explored the concept of conflict, they have identified different types of conflict situations that require different ways of dealing with them; as such you enhance your effectiveness as a conflict manager by learning these different types. Conflict managers choose among behavioral options based on their analysis of the conflict situation. Whether the conflict occurs in an interpersonal relationship or in a business, we might think that taking time to analyze the conflict is too costly. However,

> While the time to fully understand all the driving forces of a challenge is a luxury few can afford in a competitive business environment, acting precipitously with inadequate diagnosis and insight is an even more costly indulgence.[12]

Taking the time to analyze your conflicts helps you recognize when, for example, you are engaged in an unreal conflict: a situation in which you may have insufficient information (false conflict), you may blame the wrong person and issue (displaced conflict), or you may avoid the real issue by concentrating on an easier one (misplaced conflict). You may more easily recognize that you are engaged in a game with the other person, and that recognition, along with an understanding of the rules in operation, can help you bring some closure to it. Conflict management is essential for real conflicts, but we can often eliminate unreal ones by apologies or increased understanding of all the circumstances.

The effective conflict manager sees when he or she is faced with a real conflict and can tell the difference between conflicts requiring attention and those that are mere disagreements or overblown conflicts. The ICM also recognizes that conflicts over tangible issues may require different methods to resolve than conflicts over intangible issues.

6. *The effective conflict manager employs the S-TLC system.* As a competent conflict manager, you know that we need to stop, think, listen, and communicate (the S-TLC system) with the other person. By following these four steps, one can often resolve interpersonal conflicts through basic communication skills.

Stop means that we don't react blindly to the other person. Instead, try to calm down and cool off. Try to use the suggestions for taking a time out to gain control of your mental faculties. When we take time out, we can then consider our options in a conflict situation, and try to exercise them rationally.

Taking a time out gives you time to get your act together. *Think* means we analyze the situation to try to know what is really happening within it and the range of possibilities. At an elementary level, try not to take the conflict personally. At a more advanced level, think about changing the other, the situation, or yourself. Think about your goals, wants, and needs and those of your partner. Try to think optimistically, and tell yourself that you can handle the situation. When thinking about a conflict becomes difficult, a "right-brain" approach to analysis, called mind-mapping, might work. However, beware of interference from a trained incapacity, which occurs when a person's abilities and talents actually limit the person's thinking. Because the behavior has become generally beneficial (in nonconflict situations), the person expects it to work in conflict situations, where inappropriate.

Listening means that we consider the other person's opinion important, and that we try to hear and understand it before we make a point of saying what's on our mind.

You know that you have communication options when in a conflict situation. When communicating nonassertively, you can avoid a conflict altogether or accommodate (by simply giving in) to the desires of the other person. When choosing a competing conflict style, you may communicate aggressively or passive-aggressively. You communicate aggressively when you force your will on another person in a way that violates socially acceptable standards. You can also choose to communicate in a passive-aggressive manner by imposing your will on others through the use of verbal or nonverbal acts that appear to avoid an open conflict or accommodate to the desires of others, but in actuality are carried out with the intention of inflicting physical or psychological pain, injury, or suffering. Aggressive communication behavior is seldom if ever warranted except in situations of self-defense, and passive-aggressive behavior is not recommended except when confronting the other may result in physical harm to you. Finally, you can choose the compromising (where you only receive some of what you want) or collaborating conflict styles (where you and the other both obtain what you both want) and communicate assertively by speaking up for your interests, concerns, or rights in a way that does not interfere with the interests or infringes on the basic communication rights of others.

7. *The effective conflict manager knows when to use the appropriate communication option in a conflict situation.* Effective communicators are frequently assertive, sometimes nonassertive, or rarely aggressive depending on the occasion, time, location, the other person, and their own needs. If you understand the communication considerations described in this chapter, you are in a better position to decide when it is appropriate to use one type of conflict communication behavior or another.

In conflict situations competent communication behavior occurs when people have the knowledge to behave skillfully, are able to apply that knowledge in a particular situation, and are able to repeat their performance in similar situations. Competent conflict behavior is a matter of learning skills of analysis and skills of communication and then applying them in conflict situations. One success does not mean you have achieved competency any more than one failure means that you may not achieve it.

8. *The effective conflict manager knows how to collaborate.* Competent conflict managers know the advantages of employing a collaborative strategy: It produces less personal and relationship stress and the most personal and relationship growth.

When collaborating, you clarify perspectives and focus on a goal of mutual satisfaction, but remain flexible in the means to achieve that goal and work together to develop a mutually acceptable outcome. To collaborate effectively, you need to include your interests, feelings, and needs. Then you need to listen to her or his interests, feelings, and needs, to see if you can support them in future interaction. Finally, you need to see if the other is willing to collaborate and invest the time and effort to develop understandings that are mutually advantageous, or if the other prefers to avoid, accommodate, compromise, or compete.

Hopefully, you use interpersonal communication skills that are associated with collaborative or integrative strategies. You are analytic, conciliatory, and problem solving in focus, attempt to clarify the issues and facilitate mutual resolution of the problem, describe behavior, disclose feelings, ask for disclosure from the other person, ask for criticism from the other person, qualify the nature of the problem, support the disclosures or observations the other person has made, and accept responsibility for each one's part in the conflict.

9. *The effective conflict manager knows how to appropriately confront others.* Confrontation is a conflict process in which the parties call attention to problems or issues and express their feelings, beliefs, and wants to one another. There are six steps to confronting interpersonal problems. They are:

- Preparation: Identify your problem/needs/issues.
- Telling the person "We need to talk."
- Interpersonal confrontation: Talk to the other person about your problem.
- Consider your partner's point of view: Listen, empathize, and respond with understanding.
- Resolve the problem: Make a mutually satisfying agreement.
- Follow up on the solution: Set a time limit for reevaluation.

10. *The effective conflict manager knows how to effectively word an I-statement.* Competent conflict managers know that assertive behavior is characterized by personalized communication—language using "I" statements (i.e., I think, I feel) versus "you" or depersonalized statements (i.e., you always, most people think). They can list the four parts of an effective I-statement, which are an effective way to take responsibility for yourself and assert yourself if they take the following form: "I feel . . . (feeling statement) when I . . . (problematic behavior statement) because I . . . (consequences statement). I'd like . . . (goals statement)."

You need to consider your partner's point of view during a conflict. Don't forget the roles of active listening, other-orientation, rephrasing, and sensitivity.

Because people are responsible for what they do and how they feel in conflict situations, we are competent to the extent that we take responsibility for how we feel and act. However, instead of owning what they say and how they feel, people often tend to express themselves in impersonal or generalized language. Another common type of responsibility avoidance is the use of you-language. We often resort to blaming the other person for our behavior and feelings, but again we need to tell the truth, strive for accuracy, and take responsibility for our words and actions.

11. *The effective conflict manager knows when and how to incorporate negotiation principles and techniques.* Competent conflict managers know that when tangible resources are scarce, conflicts involving them take more than basic interpersonal communication skills to resolve; they require more advanced problem-solving or negotiation techniques. Competent conflict managers know that negotiation works best when the parties trust each other and the situation is one where mutually satisfactory outcomes are possible, even though the parties may not know that at the outset.

Competent conflict managers adhere to the four principles of negotiation. In bargaining situations, people often confuse the problem at hand with the people involved. Keeping these elements of the situation separated helps you to focus on issues rather than on personalities. In addition, you should focus on the interests of the people involved rather than on their articulated positions. By focusing on interests, you may find areas of overlap, which is not likely to happen if you focus just on the people's positions. When looking for areas of overlap, brainstorm many options, some of which may allow both parties to gain from the situation. Many situations that appear initially as win–lose are eventually resolved in a win–win fashion. We recommend that negotiators try to agree ahead of time on objective criteria that may facilitate mutually satisfactory outcomes.

Competent conflict managers can explain how one converts a potentially competitive negotiation into a cooperative one. Options for doing so include:

- seeking commonalities
- talking cooperation
- consulting before acting
- communicating frequently
- controlling the process, not the outcomes
- thinking positively
- considering your BATNA
- engaging in fractionation

12. *The effective conflict manager views conflict as a process.* Competent conflict managers know the five stages of constructive, successful conflict: the prelude to conflict, the triggering event, the initiation phase, the differentiation phase, and the resolution phase. They know that the prelude to conflict sets the stage by identifying the people, place, and time of your conflict; that the triggering event functions as a stimulus often leading to the initiation of your conflict; that the initiation phase is the response to a triggering event; that the differentiation phase is the ongoing interaction pattern; and that the resolution phase is the mutually satisfactory agreement or outcome and requires a follow up.

Competent conflict managers can explain how avoidance, chilling effect, and competition conflict cycles are spin offs at one stage or another of the constructive, successful conflict process. The conflict avoidance cycle is characteristic of a relationship between people whose first impulse is to avoid initiating conflict or to quickly withdraw when conflicts arise. The chilling effect conflict cycle occurs because the offended individual does not initiate the conflict because he or she fears the outcome. The competitive conflict escalation cycle gets mired down in differentiation, instead of progressing to the resolution stage.

The key to effective conflict management is an understanding of both what gives rise to conflict (what we have termed the prelude to conflict) and what occurs at different stages in the process of conflict. The way we view our relationship with the other person, our past successes and failures in enacting conflict with the other, how we identify an issue, how we assign blame, and how we voice our complaint affect the pattern of interaction. Somewhere in the maze of options, including avoidance, chilling, and competitive cycles, is potentially productive conflict behavior. Similarly, in each stage of productive conflict, there are opportunities to spin off into the avoidance, chilling effect, and competitive cycles. As with the destructive cycles, productive conflict behavior stems from attitudes about conflict and from what is assumed true.

When we see conflict as something that is a normal part of relationships, when we are willing to listen and assert ourselves, and when we are realistic about our expectations for the outcome of the conflict, we are less likely to deteriorate into destructive conflict cycles. Becoming aware of behavior and ways of thinking about conflict can help us; the more aware we are of behaviors at each stage of a conflict, the more successful we are in dealing with the conflicts in our lives.

13. *The effective conflict manager strives to create and maintain a favorable communication environment.* Competent conflict managers can explain the role played by the climate in conflict situations. On the one hand, an imbalance of power, distrust, and defensive behavior create a harmful conflict environment, where mutually satisfactory outcomes are unlikely. On the other hand, equity, trust, and supportive behavior create a nurturing conflict environment that is more likely to produce mutually satisfactory outcomes.

Communicators who create nurturing climates are more likely to create mutually satisfying outcomes because they participate in the decisions, agreements, solutions to problems, and resolution of conflicts that affect them. If we feel safe enough to assert our interests, needs, and goals, listen to the expression of others, and cooperate in the process of achieving an understanding, we are more likely to cooperate and collaborate.

14. *The effective conflict manager avoids letting stress and anger gain control over her or his communication behavior in conflict situations.* Competent conflict managers can identify the sources of stress in their lives, and they can deal constructively with them. They remember many of the suggestions from Chapter 11 on how to better manage the stresses in their lives.

Competent conflict managers know when they are starting to feel angry and how to control it by taking a time out, by engaging in relaxation exercises, by engaging in helpful self-talk, and by "finding the fear" that manifests itself as anger. We are going to feel both stress and anger. They are unavoidable. What we do with each, though, is within our control. We can learn to rid ourselves of thoughts that contribute to stress and learn to control anger.

15. *The effective conflict manager knows the role of positive face, autonomous face, and face saving in conflict.* People are motivated to create and maintain favorable impressions of themselves. Not only are people striving to present and save face, this motivation may generate or exacerbate conflict situations because the introduction of face issues into a conflict can escalate the severity of the conflict, making it difficult for people to resolve the original issue. A person's positive face is supported when others appear to value what the person values, express admiration for the person, or show acceptance of the person as a competent individual. Autonomous face is the desire people have for freedom from constraints and impositions. When others respect a person's independence, the person's autonomous face is supported. The desires for positive and autonomous face, under the best of circumstances, can create a dilemma. One may communicate support of another's positive face by expressing admiration for that person, spending time with that person, and so on but, by doing so, one can encroach on the person's autonomy. Supporting a person's positive and autonomous face requires a balance under the best of circumstances.

You can use general and specific techniques to support another's face in conflict situations. In general, people want others to like, respect, encourage, consult, include, appreciate, and reward them. They want others to talk to them, greet them warmly, help them when needed, and make them feel safe. We can also support others in a more specific way. To do this, you need to determine what traits or characteristics the other perceives in himself or herself and point out the ones you have in common or are capable of supporting.

16. *The effective conflict manager knows when and how to forgive and perhaps reconcile.* Forgiveness is a cognitive process that consists of letting go of feelings of revenge and desires to retaliate. Even though you have not forgotten the relational transgression, you can let go of feelings of anger, resentment, and revenge. In many ways, forgiveness is the opposite of revenge. Revenge is based on the notion of "an eye for an eye." One wants to follow evil with more evil. Forgiveness is a process that starts with anger over a transgression and moves toward transforming the meaning of the event. Cognitively, forgiveness is characterized by a reduced focus on the other person and the transgression as a defining event in one's life (in nonforgiveness, one might obsess over the source of hurt), affirmation of the other as an individual, lack of desire for revenge, and a rejection of the role of victim. It is the ability to move beyond victimization or the feeling of being a victim that leads to a state of forgiveness. The affective dimensions of forgiveness include the presence of positive feelings and absence of negative feelings toward the other. Forgiveness is defined behaviorally as movement toward reconciliation rather than avoiding the other or withdrawing and giving up a grudge against the other.

While forgiveness refers to how we manage our negative and positive feelings, reconciliation is a behavior process in which we take actions to restore a relationship or create a new one. Once you have forgiven the other for the relational transgression, you do not have to reconcile unless it is to your advantage to do so. You may wish to forgive at a distance and not communicate your forgiveness to the transgressor, or you may decide that you wish to reestablish a relationship or create a new one, so you chose to reconcile. Through the processes of forgiveness and reconciliation, we can forge new relationships or repair former ones and move forward by letting go of the past. Of all the skills in conflict, the ability to put the conflict into perspective and move forward is one of the most important for our well-being.

Like the ability to analyze conflicts and the ability to effectively communicate feelings and desires, the effective use of forgiveness and reconciliation strategies to cope with difficult conflicts is a skill we can learn. The process of forgiveness and reconciliation works like a self-fulfilling prophecy. We tell each other that the act is forgiven, which allows us to act without reference to the offense; we therefore feel better about our relationship with one another and can talk about our relationship without reference to the offense; so in turn, we tell each other that all is forgiven. We call this a "forgiveness/reconciliation loop."

17. *The effective conflict manager knows how to mediate conflicts as a neutral third party.* A dispute is a conflict that has reached a point where the parties are unable to resolve the issues by themselves (necessitating the intervention of a third party) because there is a breakdown in communication and normal relations are unlikely until the dispute is resolved. Unlike other forms of dispute resolution such as conciliation, ombudsperson, arbitration, and adjudication/litigation, mediation differs in that a neutral third party facilitates communication between the conflicting parties so that they may work out their own agreement.

As facilitators, mediators know how to create a supportive and constructive environment to encourage the disputants to communicate, cooperate, and work out their own mutually satisfying solution. Mediators are neutral and unbiased, have no decision-making power with respect to the outcome of the mediation, must maintain confidentiality, communicate with competence themselves, and encourage cooperation and discourage competition between the parties. Mediators are also communication rule enforcers because they announce and enforce communication rules. Rules are obligations (they tell us what we must say or do, such as "agreeing to confidentiality") and prohibitions (they tell us what we had better not say in certain situations, such as "no name calling").

Once the parties realize that they cannot resolve the dispute without help, the mediation steps are as follows:

1. One or both disputants seek mediation, or mediators talk them into it (the intake process).
2. The mediators bring the disputants together and make an opening statement.
3. Following the mediators' opening statement, they ask each person to take a few minutes to describe the dispute from his or her point of view without interruption.
4. The mediators find common ground on which to build agreement.
5. The mediators write up the final agreement.
6. The mediators end the mediation.

18. *The effective conflict manager knows how to formulate a mutually satisfactory agreement.* When drafting the agreement, the mediators need to employ the following format and say that "X agrees to this . . . Y agrees to that . . ." The mediators attempt to keep the agreement simple. They use clear, specific details (spelling out who, what, where, when, and how). It helps to think of the agreement as a list of behavioral commitments because it enumerates the specific observable actions each party needs to take to fulfill the agreement. In developing the agreement, the mediators should strive for balance or "something for everyone." The agreement also needs to address questions of feasibility and practicality because the parties should find the agreement workable and mutually acceptable. Finally, the culminating step occurs when the mediators ask both parties to sign the agreement.

Think about It

1. Why do you think people have such negative views of conflict? Do you think that as people know more about conflict, they fear it less? Why or why not?
2. What do you think you can do to help the people in your life learn to deal with conflict more effectively?
3. If you had a chance to talk to a student who was planning on taking a class in conflict management, what would you tell that person to expect? What are the benefits of taking such a class? What are the disadvantages?

Work with It

Read the case study and answer the questions that follow it.

I was recently hired as a daycare worker for a preschool. My co-worker worked in this field for a long time, and she has been at this particular center longer than anyone else, but the woman rules with a fist of iron! These kids get told exactly what to do at all minutes of the day. I think little kids are best off just having fun and being taught something along the way. She seems to think that unless kids are forcibly disciplined, they'll walk all over her. I don't know how to bring this up to her, or whether I should talk to my supervisor about it. None of the parents are complaining, but the kids just seem miserable.

After reading the above narrative, how would you answer the following questions?

1. If you were the daycare worker, how would you effectively communicate, confront, or negotiate with the other in this conflict situation and how would you de-escalate conflict?
2. If you were a third colleague who knows the two at the daycare center, how could you effectively intervene in this conflict?

Remember It

Write an essay in which you apply as many of the ideas presented in this book and summarized in this chapter as you can to your life situation. Make sure to address the following:

1. How would you effectively communicate, confront, or negotiate with the other in your conflict situations and how would you de-escalate conflict?
2. How would you effectively intervene in the conflicts of others?

NOTES

1. Paul Brenner, *If Life Is a Game, How Come I'm Not Having Fun?* (Albany, NY: SUNY Press, 2001), p. 87, 89.
2. Ibid., p. 90.
3. Ibid., p. 73.
4. Brian J. Mahan, *Forgetting Ourselves on Purpose: Vocation and the Politics of Ambition* (San Francisco: Jossey-Bass, 2002), p. xx–xxi.
5. David L. Miller, *Gods and Games: Toward a Theology of Play* (New York: Harper Colophon Books, 1973).
6. John Goldingay, *Walk On: Life, Loss, Trust, and Other Realities* (Grand Rapids, MI: Baker, 2002), p. 100.
7. Wanda J. Smith, K. Vernard Harrington, and Christopher P. Neck, "Resolving Conflict with Humor in a Diversity Context," *Journal of Managerial Psychology* 15 (2000), 606–625.
8. Robert E. Neale, *In Praise of Play: Toward a Psychology of Religion* (New York: Harper & Row, 1969), p. 173.
9. Hugo Rahner, *Man at Play* (New York: Herder & Herder, 1972), pp. 7–8.
10. Anthony D. Pellegrini (Ed.), *The Future of Play Theory: A Multidisciplinary Inquiry into the Contributions of Brian Sutton-Smith* (Albany, NY: SUNY Press, 1995).
11. Kenneth Cloke, *Mediating Dangerously* (San Francisco: Jossey-Bass, 2001), pp. 3–4.
12. "How IBM Boss Embraced His Dilemmas," *Strategic Direction* 20 (2004), p. 17.

ANSWERS

Work with It 2.2

1. Tangible
2. Intangible

Work with It 2.3

1. personality
2. behavioral
3. relationship/normative
4. misplaced
5. displaced
6. false
7. mere disagreement
8. real

Work with It 4.2

1. assertive
2. nonassertive
3. passive-aggressive
4. nonassertive
5. aggressive
6. aggressive
7. nonassertive
8. assertive
9. nonassertive

Apply It 7.1

1, 6, 7, 12, 13, and 15 are all conflicts over scarce resources.

Work with It 8.1

1. a
2. a
3. b
4. a
5. b
6. a
7. b
8. b
9. a
10. a
11. b

Work with It 8.2

1. *Attribution theory.* Misattribution is the cause of the conflict. I can overcome such conflicts by being more aware of my biases.
2. *Psychodynamic theory.* Tension, feelings, or anxiety is the cause of the conflict. I can overcome such conflicts by stress reduction therapy.
3. *Social exchange theory.* An imbalance exists in the resources of exchange. My partner needs to restore the balance by helping out more or by paying for her share if we hire a housekeeper.

Work with It 9.2

1. I work in a clothing store and since it is back to school time I have seen a lot of parent–child conflicts.

   - *Prelude phase:* I know that parents and their children are from two different time periods. I also realize that usually the parents are paying for the clothing, so they think that they should have a lot to say about buying it. They have different ideas over what is cool, and what isn't.
   - *Triggering phase:* The boy wanted to wear the big baggy pants.
   - *Initiation phase:* His mother refused to let him buy them.
   - *Differentiation phase:* This disagreement went on for about five minutes. The

whole time the boy constantly argued that this was the way everyone else wears them. Then the mother went into why they were so horrible. She complained mostly about how having the jeans dragging on the floor would bring in all the germs that he walked through. No matter what the boy said his mother would find something to disagree about.

- *Resolution phase:* Finally the boy gave in and his mother got him to buy a pair of jeans that were much shorter.

2. My dad and I went to Subway to eat lunch.

- *Prelude phase:* My dad planned on buying one sub and then getting the next free for me. Subway has this sticker accumulation deal where you receive one sticker for every sub you buy. When you fill up the card you are entitled to a free sub, but they clearly state on the card that you can't redeem the full card for a free sub on the same day you filled it up. Meanwhile, my dad asked me to take a seat and wait while he got a sub. Of course he got a sticker for buying his sub and put it on his card, which filled his card up. He came over to me and left his order and then went back to order another sub.

- *Triggering phase:* I guess he thought he could get away with something. When it came time to pay for the second sub, he turned in his card filled with stickers.

- *Initiation phase:* The owner responded with the fact that he couldn't have the free sub the same day he filled up the card.

- *Differentiation phase:* My dad got angry and said that he was not willing to come back the next day to receive his free sub. The owner proceeded to ring up my sub on the cash register and my dad started yelling and cursing. The owner yelled back, and told my dad to leave the store. I tried to get my dad to calm down and just leave but he wouldn't. They both engaged in a shouting match for another minute. (During this phase, the two got caught up in an escalation conflict cycle.)

- *Resolution phase:* There was no resolution in the sense of an agreement. Instead, the escalation cycle culminated with the father storming out of the store cursing, and the owner telephoning the police.

GLOSSARY

ABC approach is a way of analyzing stressful events by focusing on the activating event or stressor (A), our relevant beliefs (B), and the consequences of the stressor (C).

Accommodating conflict strategy occurs when at least one person smoothes over a conflict, gives in to the other, obliges the other, and doesn't make waves.

Accommodation means smoothing over conflicts, obliging others, and not making waves. Those who simply give in try to maintain the illusion of harmony.

Account is an explanation for behavior when questioned.

Acknowledgment occurs when the offended party evaluates an account and honors or rejects it.

Adjudication is an ADR in which a neutral judge and jury in the legal system hear attorneys who prosecute or defend people and decide a case; either party may later appeal the decision.

ADRs are alternatives to dispute resolution, such as adjudication, arbitration, or mediation.

Adverse effects make people uncomfortable and dissatisfied with the relationship.

Aggressive communication is the ability to force one's will (i.e., wants, needs, or desires) on another person through the use of verbal and/or nonverbal acts done in a way that violates socially acceptable standards and carried out with the intention or the perceived intention of inflicting physical and/or psychological pain, injury, or suffering.

Analysis refers to the study of processes, their ingredients, and the relationships among them.

Anger is a strong feeling of displeasure, a synonym for antagonism and rage.

Anger controllers are those who practice S-TLC. Anger controllers do not let their feelings dictate how they respond in conflict situations.

Anger-ins are people who have a hard time even admitting that they are angry.

Anger-outs are the exact opposite of the anger-ins, because they are people who are quick to express their anger, vocally or physically.

Anxiety, an additional product of frustration and tension, occurs when people think that someone will interfere with their goals, when they fear their own impulses in a situation, or when they disapprove of their own actions.

Apologies are admissions of blameworthiness and regret on the part of the offender.

Arbitration is an ADR in which a neutral third party considers both sides of a dispute and makes a decision that is more binding than that of a judge in the legal system, if both parties have agreed in advance to abide by the decision (no appeal).

Argument is the exchange of claims about some idea.

Aspiration point is a person's preferred negotiation option that would maximize her or his gains.

Assertive communication is defined as the ability to speak up for one's interests, concerns, or rights in a way that does not interfere with the interests or infringe on the rights of others. (See also Personalized communication and I-statements.)

Attribution theory states that people act as they do in conflict situations because of the conclusions they draw about each other.

Autonomous face is the desire people have to be free from constraints and impositions (often referred to in the literature as "negative face").

Avoidance means not addressing a conflict at all. Behaviors indicative of this strategy include choosing to withdraw, leave the scene, avoid discussing issues, or remain silent,

Avoiding conflict strategy occurs in a conflict situation when one or both parties do not address the issue at all.

Bargaining range consists of resistance points and aspiration levels that exist between negotiators.

Basic communication rights are derived from those rights, concerns, or interests common to all communicators, such as the right to be listened to and taken seriously and the right to say no, refuse requests, and turn down invitations without feeling guilty or being accused of selfishness.

BATNA stands for the Best Alternative to a Negotiated Agreement.

Behavioral commitments are concrete observable actions each party needs to take to resolve the conflict and reach agreement.

Behavioral issue conflicts concern observable specific and individual behaviors such as the way we handle money, time, space, and so on.

Brainstorming, which is a means for creating solutions to problems, consists of a process that requires people to list all possible solutions, irrespective of their initial feasibility.

Bridging occurs when a new option is developed that satisfies both parties' most significant needs.

Caucus means that the mediator steps aside with one disputant for a private discussion.

Chilling effect occurs when one person in a relationship withholds grievances from the other, usually due to fear of the other person's reaction.

Collaborating conflict strategy occurs when both parties work together to develop a mutually satisfying outcome or agreement.

Collaboration means using integrative behaviors and developing mutually satisfying agreements to solve the problem once and for all. When people collaborate, they work together toward the same ends in compatible roles.

Common ground is a conflict management technique in which mediators help conflicting parties identify the attitudes, values, behaviors, expectations, and goals they share, which can serve as a basis for an agreement.

Communication, from the authors' point of view, is based on the transactional model of communication as opposed to the linear model for managing conflict situations.

Communication apprehension refers to the level of anxiety a person feels in response to interpersonal, group, or public communication situations.

Communication considerations refer to three aspects of the conflict situation—the occasion, the other person, and your needs—that should guide the way we choose to react to the situation.

Communication rules enforcer means that mediators establish the rules by which participants will interact, such as taking turns to talk without interruptions by the other party, and enforce them.

Communication skill is the successful performance of a communicative behavior and the ability to repeat such a behavior.

Comparison level (CL) is a standard with which people determine how satisfactory or attractive a relationship is based on what they feel they deserve.

Comparison level of alternatives (CL_{alt}) is a standard with which people determine how satisfactory or attractive a relationship is based on what an alternative relationship has to offer.

Compensation occurs when Party A provides something of value (often monetary) to Party B to make up for losses caused by A's behavior or that resulted from A's demands.

Competing conflict strategy occurs when at least one person dominates or tries to force his or her decision on the other.

Competition is a situation in which we have a desire to win by besting the other in an argument, a game, or some kind of larger rivalry.

Competitive conflict escalation cycle means that the conflict bogs down in the differentiation stage when competitive interests lead to divergence rather than integration, and often gets out of hand.

Competitive negotiation is an exchange in which one starts high, concedes slowly, overstates the worth of one's concessions, conceals information, argues forcefully, and outwaits the other.

Compromise means making sure that no one totally wins or loses. As a strategy favoring trade-offs involving "give and take," it is designed as a realistic attempt to seek an acceptable (but not necessarily preferred) solution of gains and losses for everyone involved.

Compromising conflict strategy occurs when no one totally wins or loses, each getting something (perhaps) of what she or he wanted.

Concessions are a type of account in which one grants something of value to the other person without asking anything in return, or when he or she drops a demand on the other.

Conciliation is an ADR in which a neutral third party practices "shuttle diplomacy" by traveling back and forth between conflicting parties who are unable to meet together for any one of a variety of reasons.

Conflict (see Interpersonal conflict).

Conflict climate refers to the psychological atmosphere impacting a conflict including these bi-polar concepts: imbalance of power versus equity, distrust versus trust, and defensive versus supportive behavior.

Conflict communication options consist of assertiveness, nonassertiveness, aggressiveness, and passive-aggressiveness.

Conflict communication process refers to the steps that constructive or destructive conflict goes through.

Conflict games follow a series of steps toward a well-defined payoff (usually a "snare") intended to hurt, embarrass, anger, or offend the other person.

Conflict issues are the focal point of the conflict, the "trigger" that people point to when they are asked what the conflict was about.

Conflict management is the behavior a person employs based on his or her analysis of a conflict situation.

Conflict metaphor happens when one is asked to compare one term (conflict) with something else (struggle, exploding bombs, being on trial).

Conflict phase is a stage in the interaction that is similar across many conflicts.

Conflict resolution refers to only one alternative in a conflict situation in which the parties solve a problem or issue.

Conflict strategy is an overall plan consisting of a "cluster of behaviors" that people use in a specific conflict situation.

Conflict style is a preferred set of behaviors for dealing with conflict situations used whenever possible.

Confrontation is a conflict process in which the parties call attention to problems or issues and express their feelings, beliefs, and wants to one another.

Confrontation avoidance cycle is characteristic of those people whose first impulse is to avoid initiating conflict or to quickly withdraw when conflicts arise.

Confrontation steps consist of the following: (1) preparation: Identify your problem/needs/issues; (2) tell the person: "We need to talk"; (3) interpersonal confrontation: Talk to the other person about your problem; (4) consider your partner's point of view: Listen, empathize, and respond with understanding; (5) resolve the problem: Make a mutually satisfying agreement; (6) follow up on the solution: Set a time limit for reevaluation.

Consequences statement is a description of the consequences the problematic behavior has for you or others (wastes your time, you have to expend effort, you could lose friends, your parents may get angry, etc.). The statement contains the word "because."

Control the process means that the parties create the conditions for a fair and honest problem-solving discussion, but they can't predict the outcome with certainty.

Cooperative negotiation is an integrative form that combines formal bargaining techniques with many skills taught in basic interpersonal communication courses such as effective listening, assertiveness, supportive communication, and collaboration.

Core relational rules define our expectations about the way we should behave toward others as well as the way they should behave toward us.

Corrective facework consists of statements meant to ameliorate the effect of face-threatening messages.

Cost cutting means that one person will reduce the price of an item so that the other is more easily able to accept and live with the solution.

Cycle of behavior exists when people get a sense of repetitiveness in behavior.

Deception is generally defined as the intentional alteration of truthful information to significantly change another's view.

Defensive behaviors consist of evaluation, control, strategy, neutrality, superiority, and certainty.

Defensive coping mechanisms are methods learned through experience that help one to feel less stress, at least in the short run.

Destructive conflict occurs when there is an expansion of the issues, number of people involved, costs to the participants, and intensity of negative feelings.

Differentiation phase or ongoing interaction pattern occurs when the participants work out the problem using constructive or destructive strategies and tactics presenting both sides of the story, moving back and forth, and escalating and de-escalating.

Disclaimers are additions to the message that soften the forcefulness of the message and help to minimize threats to face before they happen.

Displaced conflict occurs when people direct a conflict toward the wrong person, avoiding a confrontation with the appropriate person.

Dispute is defined as a conflict in which communication has broken down and the parties are unable to resolve the issue by themselves.

Distress arises when we don't feel control over a situation, or when the source of stress is unclear.

Emotional residues are lingering emotional responses to the memory of the transgression.

Equifinality means that we cannot necessarily predict how something will turn out based on the way it started, nor can we infer what the beginning stages of a process were based only on our observation of its ending.

Eustress, a good kind of stress, is a short-term stress that encourages us to expend more energy on important activities and take them more seriously.

Excuses are a type of account that admits that the offense occurred but denies responsibility for it, such as "He made me do it."

Exit strategy means leaving the relationship entirely.

Face refers to people's image of themselves.

False conflict occurs when at least one person in an interdependent relationship thinks that there is a conflict but after talking to the other(s) involved, finds there is no conflict.

Feelings statement is a description of your feelings (such as feeling angry, neglected, offended, surprised, depressed/unhappy, etc.).

Forgiveness is a cognitive process that consists of letting go of feelings of revenge and desires to retaliate.

Forgiveness/reconciliation loop consists of three steps: After forgiving one another, we tell each other that the act is forgiven, which allows us to act without reference to the offense; in turn, we feel better about our relationship with one another and can talk about our relationship without reference to the offense; in turn our actions confirm what we said so that our behavior constitutes the reality of our forgiveness.

Fractionation is a conflict management technique that involves breaking down complex issues into smaller, more manageable ones, and then dealing with each piece one at a time.

Framing is where mediators ask neutral or "friendly" questions (that avoid blame or passing judgment) and summarize issues.

Goal statement is a specific description of what you want (one may want the other to appear on time in the future or call if delayed, etc.).

Gunny-sacking is storing up hurts and anger until one can't take it anymore and one erupts, often becomes verbally abusive, and perhaps turns violent.

Harmful conflict climate consists of an imbalance of power, distrust, and defensiveness, which fosters accommodation (chilling effect) or competition (meeting force with force).

Healthy trust, unlike pathological trust or suspicion, consists of flexibility and responsiveness to changing situations (see Trust and Unhealthy trust).

Helping orientation means that we have a favorable attitude toward others and desire to help rather than hurt them.

Hyperstress is a kind of stress that happens when too many tasks and responsibilities pile up on us, and we are unable to adapt to the changes or cope with all that is happening at once.

Hypostress, or underload, happens when we're bored or unchallenged by our situations.

Identity goals concern how bargainers view each other in the situation.

Imagined interaction is a form of intrapersonal communication in which you think about what you might say and another might say in response to you in a particular conversation.

Imbalance of power becomes a conflict issue when one person works to obtain and hold more power than others and is threatening to the less powerful.

Impression management means that people are motivated to create and maintain favorable impressions of themselves; that is, they engage in managing their faces (people's image of themselves) when around other people.

Incompatible means occur when we want to achieve the same goal but differ in how we should do so; for example, we agree on the same car, but not whether to finance it or pay cash.

Incompatible outcomes/goals occur when we are seeking different outcomes; for example, we want to buy two different cars but we can only afford one.

Inevitability of conflict principle means that we should cease our efforts to find perfect people and learn how to manage the conflicts we are sure to have with those closest to us.

Information reception apprehension triggers shortcomings in an individual's ability to receive information from others.

Initiation phase is where at least one person makes known to the other the presence of a felt conflict.

Instrumental goals are those that require the opponent to remove obstacles blocking completion of a task.

Intake, in formal mediation, refers to the preliminary phase in which the parties seek help from a third person, who decides to intervene.

Interdependence occurs when the relationship would be characterized by all involved in it as one that is important and one that is worth the effort to maintain.

Interests are the same as needs that are satisfied by different positions.

Interpersonal conflict is defined as a problematic situation with the following four unique characteristics: the conflicting parties are interdependent; perceive that they seek incompatible goals or outcomes or they favor incompatible means to the same ends; the perceived incompatibility has the potential to adversely affect the relationship if not addressed; there is a sense of urgency about the need to resolve the difference.

I-statements personalize the conflict by owning up to our feelings rather than making them the responsibility of the other person.

Justifications are a type of account in which one acknowledges that an act was committed while claiming that no one was hurt or the other deserved it.

Language of cooperation is *"we-based."*

Legitimate power recognizes that a situation exists in which someone must take control of a situation or the welfare or interests of the group may suffer.

Linear model of communication studies communication by focusing on message senders as the starting point and message receivers as the end point.

Listening is a desire to pay attention to the other person, characterized by openness to the other person's views, willingness to suspend judgment during the discussion, patience to hear the other out, an empathic response to the other person, and a commitment to listen to all that the other person has to say.

Logrolling is a process in which each side grants to the other those issues that the other gives top priority as long as one does not also give them top priority.

Loyalty strategy refers to diminishing the problem's importance in light of the various good things in the relationship.

Mediation is an ADR in which a neutral third party facilitates communication between the conflicting parties so that they may work out their own mutually acceptable agreement.

Mediators are viewed here as unbiased facilitators of communication between the parties in a private setting, who also have no decision-making power with respect to the outcome of the mediation.

Mere disagreements, while real conflicts, may occur over issues that are peripheral to a relationship, as when relational partners hold different political views or find themselves disagreeing over the worth of a movie.

Meta-conflict perspective means that we look on the conflicts we have experienced, analyze what we did well and what we did poorly, and learn from our mistakes.

Mind-mapping is a method for making your ideas visible.

Minimax principle means that people try to minimize their losses and maximize their gains.

Misplaced conflicts occur when people argue about issues other than the ones at the heart of the conflict.

Mixed motive situation occurs when those involved have incentives to both cooperate and compete.

Negative view of conflict sees conflicts as painful occurrences that are personally threatening and best avoided or quickly contained.

Neglect strategy refers to ignoring the problem and its effect on the relationship.

Negotiation, as a type of conflict management, consists of an exchange of proposals and counter-proposals as a way to reach agreement.

Neutral speech occurs when one does not talk down or talk up to the others but talks to them as equals and relies on "objective language."

Nonassertive communication is the failure to speak up for one's interests, concerns, or rights.

Nonverbally aggressive communication occurs when one or both parties physically attack the other.

Nurturing conflict climate consists of openness, assertiveness, and cooperation.

Objective criteria are guidelines we apply across a variety of situations to ensure fairness, such as taking turns, ruling by majority, and tossing a coin or drawing straws.

Offending situations occur when a person believes that the other has acted in an intentionally hurtful way.

Ombudsperson is an ADR where someone cuts through the red tape on behalf of individuals who feel abused by the larger system (often governmental agencies) in which they work, study, or seek support.

Outcomes are the results people are seeking to achieve when they engage in conflict.

Overblown conflict occurs when people exaggerate a conflict, generally using a relatively unimportant issue as a focal point.

Passive-aggressive communication is the ability to impose one's will on others through the use of verbal and/or nonverbal acts that appear to avoid an open conflict or accommodate to the desires of others, but in actuality are carried out with the intention (or perceived intention) of inflicting physical and/or psychological pain, injury, or suffering.

Perception is the process in which we make sense of what we see and hear.

Personality issue conflicts focus on a whole constellation of behaviors such as being dominating, introverted, selfish, lazy, or overachieving.

Personalized communication refers to the use of "I" statements (i.e., I think, I feel) versus "you" or depersonalized statements (i.e., you always, most people think).

Personal stress occurs within a person and refers to wear and tear on one emotionally and physically.

Phase theory assumes that conflicts unfold in fairly predictable ways over a period of time and progress through recognizable stages of interaction.

Physical aggression occurs when one or both parties physically attack the other.

Positions are the same as the final part of an I-statement (the goal part of the statement—what you want).

Positive face is supported when others appear to value what the person values, express admiration for the person, or show acceptance of the person as a competent individual.

Positive view of conflict happens when we see an interpersonal conflict situation as an opportunity to resolve problems and improve our relationships with the people who mean the most to us.

Power is the ability to influence or control events.

Powerful speech refers to verbal and nonverbal messages used to dominate and control others.

Powerless speech is "talking up to others," making requests or asking questions (showing that one is in need or is uninformed), speaking softly, and sounding tentative, uncertain, or unsure of oneself.

Prelude to conflict is known as the frustration or latent stage in the conflict management process.

Preventive facework is an attempt to avoid or minimize threats to face.

Principled negotiation leads to cooperative negotiation and consists of four principles: separating the people from the problem, focusing on interests rather than positions, generating a variety of possibilities before deciding what to do, and insisting on the use of an objective standard on which to base the results.

Prisoner Dilemma (PD) is a game that that highlights the role of trust/distrust and cooperation/competition in a conflict situation (see also Mixed motive situation).

Problematic behavior statement is a description of the offensive, upsetting, incorrect, selfish, problem producing behavior (such as the other saying something insulting, nasty, or sarcastic, leaving clothes all over the room, or forgetting an important date, etc.).

Problematic situations occur when partners perceive that they seek different outcomes or they favor different means to the same ends.

Process is a series of steps, phases, stages, actions, operations, or functions bringing about a result, such as the process of registering for classes or the process of obtaining life insurance.

Process view of conflict recognizes that a conflict is ongoing, dynamic, changeable, moving through steps or phases, and never ending.

Productive conflict occurs when a conflict is kept to the issues, and there is no escalation.

Projection occurs when people attribute what they are feeling to others rather than owning the feeling themselves.

Psychodynamic theory says that people experience conflict because of their intrapersonal states. Misplaced and displaced conflict (where the conflict is acted out with the wrong person or over the wrong issue), overblown conflicts (where the conflict receives more attention than it really deserves), and bickering (where the primary purpose is to hurt the other) are conflicts that are best explained by this theory.

Rationalization occurs when we defend questionable behavior or our reactions to stress with reasons that simply aren't connected to the behavior.

Reaction formation occurs when people do the opposite of their true feelings.

Real conflicts exist in fact, are perceived accurately, and range from minor issues to those that are serious enough to hurt the relationship if they are left unattended.

Reconciliation is a behavioral process in which we take actions to restore a relationship or create a new one following forgiveness.

Reframing is a conflict management technique in which mediators restate negatively loaded, biased, or accusatory statements made by one of the parties in more neutral terminology or restate positions in a way that makes the disputants look at the issues differently.

Relational goals involve attempts to gain power or establish trust.

Relational transgressions are extremely problematic situations in which core rules of a relationship are violated, leaving high emotional residues.

Relationship strategy (see Conflict strategy).

Relationship stress occurs outside the individual and refers to wear and tear on a relationship.

Relationship/normative issue conflicts involve rules, norms, and boundaries that partners have tacitly or overtly agreed on.

Remedy means that an offender takes one of three types of actions to restore a relationship with the offended person: offers an account (through excuses or justifications), makes a concession, offers an apology, or acts in a way that combines any of these.

Repair sequence, which occurs when we realize that we have offended another person, consists of the following: an offending situation (when the other's behavior is seen as intentionally hurtful, whether or not that person did intend it), a reproach (or request for an explanation of an offense from the one offended), a remedy (or an account, concession, or apology supplied by an offender), and an acknowledgment (or evaluation of the account supplied by the one offended).

Repression is when we try not to think about our situation.

Reproach occurs when one calls attention to an offense.

Resistance point is an identifiable amount that negotiators are willing to concede to each other with minimum loss.

Resolution phase is where those involved in a conflict agree to some outcome.

Revenge is based on the notion of "an eye for an eye."

Rules are obligations (they tell us what we must say, what we should say) and prohibitions (they tell us what we better not say in certain situations).

Scarce resources are limited, with not enough for everyone.

Schismogenesis occurs when the behaviors of one person intensify the behaviors of another person. This is experienced as an escalation of the conflict.

Scripts are routinized events that we perform with little deviation each time we do them.

Secondary emotion means that the origin of the anger is in other emotions such as fear, disappointment, hurt, and frustration.

Self-fulfilling prophecy is one in which people act toward us in the way that we expect.

Self-talk, as you can guess, is verbalizing inner messages, either out loud or to ourselves.

Sense of urgency occurs when we approach the point where an issue must receive attention or else.

Skill is a behavior that can be repeated as needed.

Social exchange theory states that people assess their interpersonal relationships in terms of their value, determined by subtracting the costs from the rewards associated with the relationship.

S-TLC, as a way of managing conflicts, is an acronym for Stop, Think, Listen, and Communicate.

Stopping in conflict management is taking a time-out such as exiting temporarily to calm yourself, counting backward from 100, or changing the problematic topic for a while to allow time for the air to clear.

Strategy (see Conflict strategy).

Stress is the tension generated from an event that appears unmanageable.

Stressors are the sources of stress.

Sublimation means that people may put their efforts toward something socially desirable in order to deal with the stress of some event in their life.

Supportive behaviors involve nonjudgmental description, problem orientation, spontaneity, empathy, equality, and provisionalism (tentativeness).

Supportive facework occurs when we reinforce the way the other is presenting himself or herself.

System is a set of interrelated components acting together as a unit.

Systems theory views communication and conflict as systems and takes issue with the idea of equating conflict with breakdowns.

Tactic is a specific observable behavior that moves a conflict in a particular direction in line with a conflict strategy or style.

Theory is a means of explaining how something works by directing attention at causes and effects.

Thinking about changing the other person, situation, or self in conflict management is a way of analyzing a situation.

Threats are statements that link the other person's noncompliance with negative outcomes.

Thromise is a message that sounds like a promise (i.e., if you do x you will receive y) but serves also as a threat because noncompliance will hurt the other or deprive the person of some benefit.

Trained incapacity occurs when a person's abilities and talents actually limit the person's thinking.

Transactional model of communication views communication as an interactive process by which people make or create meaning together.

Transforming the meaning of the event means changing the way we view an event in light of other events in our lives.

Triggering event is a behavior that at least one person in the conflict points to as the "beginning" of the problem.

Trust is the belief that another is benevolent or honest toward the trusting individual, and that the other person's caring transcends any direct benefits the other receives as a result of caring.

Truth bias means that we assume that others tell us the truth until proven otherwise.

Uncertainty in the conflict situation occurs when we have insufficient information to understand another's motives, goals, or behaviors or when we do not understand how another is responding to us.

Undesired repetitive pattern (URP) is an automatic, "knee-jerk" response to one another: Something one says triggers an automatic response in the other, and the episode quickly escalates out of control.

Unforgiveness is an emotional response to a relational transgression, consisting of resentment, bitterness, hatred, hostility, residual anger, and fear.

Unhealthy trust is typically inflexible, rigid, and consistent in actions toward others, without regard for the situation (see Healthy trust and Trust).

Unimportant conflict is not likely to continue to create problems in the future because it is insignificant or a one-time event.

Unreal conflicts either don't exist in reality but are thought to exist in someone's mind, or do exist in reality but are misperceived.

Ventilation approach happens when we express our anger but not to the person who we are blaming for it.

Verbal aggression/abuse consists of verbal insults and name calling, often accompanied with screaming and throwing objects.

Verbally aggressive communication is defined as a person's predisposition to attack the self-concept of another person in order to cause psychological pain for the other.

Victimization refers to the feeling of being a victim.

Voice strategy means talking about the problem.

REFERENCES

Achterberg, Jeanne, Stephanie Matthews, and O. Carl Simonton, "Psychology of the Exceptional Cancer Patient: A Description of Patients Who Outlived Predicted Expectancies," *Psychotherapy: Theory and Research and Practice* 6 (1976), 13–14.

Adler, Ronald B., *Confidence in Communication: A Guide to Assertive and Social Skills* (New York: Holt, Rinehart & Winston, 1977).

Agustí-Panareda, Jordi, "Power Imbalances in Mediation: Questioning Some Common Assumptions," *Dispute Resolution Journal* 59 (2004), 24–31.

Alberti, R. E., and M. L. Emmons, *Your Perfect Right: A Guide to Assertive Behavior* (San Luis Obispo, CA: Impact, 1970).

Alberts, Jess K., and Gillian Driscoll, "Containment vs. Escalation: The Trajectory of Couples' Conversational Complaints," *Western Journal of Communication* 56 (1992), 394–412.

Allen, Mike, and William A. Donohue, "The Mediator as an Arguer," in Joseph W. Wenzel (Ed.), *Argument and Critical Practices* (Annandale, VA: SCA, 1987), p. 280.

Alloway, David L., and Janis F. Anderson, "Individual Differences of the Perceptions of Verbal Aggression," paper presented at the Western Speech Communication Association Convention, San Diego, February. 1988.

American Psychological Association, "The Different Kinds of Stress," retrieved October 26, 2005, from http://apahelpcenter.org/articles/article.php?id=21.

Arendt, Hannah, *The Human Condition* (Chicago: University of Chicago Press, 1956).

Augsburger, David, *Caring Enough to Not Forgive* (Ventura, CA: Regal Books, 1981).

Augsburger, David, *Caring Enough to Hear and Be Heard* (Ventura, CA: Regal Books, 1982).

Avtgis, Theodore A., "Adult-Child Control Expectancies: Effects on Taking Conflict Personally Toward Parents," *Communication Research Reports* 19 (2002), 226–236.

Bach, George R., and Peter Wyden, *The Intimate Enemy: How to Fight Fair in Love and Marriage* (New York: Avon, 1969).

Bach, Gerald R., and Herb Goldberg, *Creative Aggression: The Art of Assertive Living* (New York: Avon Books, 1974).

Baker, William H., "Defensiveness in Communication: Its Causes, Effects and Cures," *Journal of Business Communication* 17 (1980), 33–43.

Baron, Jonathan, "Confusion of Group Interest and Self-Interest in Parochial Cooperation on Behalf of a Group," *Journal of Conflict Resolution* 45 (2001), 283–296.

Bateson, Gregory, *Naven,* 2nd Ed. (Stanford, CA: Stanford University Press, 1958).

Bazerman, Max, "Why Negotiations Go Wrong," *Psychology Today* 20 (June 1986), 54–58.

Beaumont, Sherry L., and Shannon L. Wagner, "Adolescent-Parent Verbal Conflict: The Roles of Conversational Styles and Disgust Emotions," *Journal of Language and Social Psychology* 23 (2004), 338–368.

Bell, Mae Arnold, "A Research Note: The Relationship of Conflict and Linguistic Diversity in Small Groups," *Central States Speech Journal* 34 (1983), 128–133.

Belloc, Hilaire, *The Silence of the Sea,* retrieved May 17, 2005 from www.quoteland.com/topic.asp?CATEGORY_ID=32.

Benoit, William L., and Shirley Drew, "Appropriateness and Effectiveness of Image Repair Strategies," *Communication Reports* 10 (1997), 153–163.

Berne, Eric, *Games People Play* (New York: Ballantine Books, 1964).

Berstene, Thomas, "The Inexorable Link between Conflict and Change," *The Journal for Quality and Participation* 27 (2004), 4–9.

Bingham, Lisa B., "Employment Dispute Resolution: The Case for Mediation," *Conflict Resolution Quarterly* 22 (2004), 145–174.

Bippus, Amy M., "Humor Motives, Qualities, and Reactions in Recalled Conflict Episodes," *Western Journal of Communication* 67 (2003), 413–426.

Bippus, Amy M., and Emma Rollin, "Attachment Style Differences in Relational Maintenance and Conflict Behaviors: Friends' Perceptions," *Communication Reports* 16 (2003), 113.

Bixenstine, V. Edwin, and Jacquelyn Gaebelein, "Strategies of 'Real' Opponents in Eliciting Cooperative Choice in a Prisoner's Dilemma Game," *Journal of Communication Research* 15 (1971), 157–166.

Bixenstine, V. Edwin, and Kellogg V. Wilson, "Effects of Level of Cooperative Choice by the Other Player in a Prisoner's Dilemma Game," *Journal of Abnormal and Social Psychology* 67 (1963), 139–147.

Blake, Robert R., and Jane Srygley Mouton, *The Managerial Grid* (Houston: Gulf, 1964).

Bograd, Michele, "Why We Need Gender to Understand Human Violence," *Journal of Interpersonal Violence* 5 (1990), 133.

Bornstein, Gary, and Zohar Gilula, "Between-Group Communication and Conflict Resolution in Assurance and Chicken Games," *Journal of Conflict Resolution* 47 (2003), 326–339.

Bostrom, Robert N., *Persuasion* (Englewood Cliffs, NJ: Prentice Hall, 1983).

Bowers, John Waite, "Guest Editor's Introduction: Beyond Threats and Promises," *Speech Monographs* 41 (1974), ix–xi.

Braiker, Harriet, and Harold Kelley, "Conflict in the Development of Close Relationships," in Robert L. Burgess and Ted L. Huston (Eds.), *Social Exchange in Developing Relationships* (New York: Academic Press, 1979), 135–168.

Brenner, Paul, *If Life Is a Game, How Come I'm Not Having Fun?* (Albany, NY: SUNY Press, 2001).

Brown, Penelope, and Stephen Levinson, *Politeness: Some Universals in Language Usage* (Cambridge: Cambridge University Press, 1987).

Burke, Kenneth, *Permanence and Change* (Indianapolis: Bobbs Merrill, 1954).

Burrell, Nancy A., and Dudley D. Cahn, "Mediating Peer Conflicts in Educational Contexts: The Maintenance of School Relationships," in Dudley D. Cahn (Ed.), *Conflict in Personal Relationships* (Hillsdale, NJ: Erlbaum, 1994).

Burrell, Nancy A., William A. Donohue, and Mike Allen, "The Impact of Disputants' Expectations on Mediation: Testing an Interventionist Model," *Human Communication Research,* 17 (1990), 104–139.

Buttny, Richard, "Accounts as a Reconstruction of an Event's Context," *Communication Monographs* 52 (1985), 57–77.

Buttny, Richard, "Blame-Account Sequences in Therapy: The Negotiation of Relational Meanings," *Semiotica* 78 (1990), 219–247.

Buysse, Ann, Armand DeClercq, Lesley Verhhofstadt, Else Heene, Herbert Roeyers, and Paulette Van Oost, "Dealing with Relational Conflict: A Picture in Milliseconds," *Journal of Social and Personal Relationships* 17 (2000), 574–597.

Buzan, Tony, *The Mind Map Book* (New York: Penguin, 1991).

Cahn, Dudley D., *Intimates in Conflict* (Hillsdale, NJ: Erlbaum, 1990).

Cahn, Dudley, and Sally Lloyd (Eds.), *Family Violence from a Communication Perspective* (Thousand Oaks, CA: SAGE, 1996).

Cai, Deborah A., and Edward L. Fink, "Conflict Style Differences between Individualists and Collectivists," *Communication Monographs* 69 (2002), 67–87.

Canary, Daniel, E. M. Cunningham, and Michael J. Cody, "Goal Types, Gender, and Locus of Control in Managing Interpersonal Conflict," *Communication Research* 15 (1988), 426–447.

Canary, Daniel J., William R. Cupach, and Richard T. Serpe, "A Competence-Based Approach to Examining Interpersonal Conflict: Test of a Longitudinal Model," *Communication Research* 28 (2001), 79–104.

Carey, Colleen M., and Paul A. Mongeau, "Communication and Violence in Courtship Relationships," in Dudley D. Cahn and Sally A. Lloyd (Eds.), *Family Violence from a Communication Perspective* (Thousand Oaks, CA: Sage Publications, 1996).

Carnevale, Peter J., Dean G. Pruitt, and Steven D. Seilheimer, "Looking and Competing: Accountability and Visual Access in Integrative Bargaining," *Journal of Personality and Social Psychology* 28 (1973), 12–20.

Carter, Candice C., "Conflict Resolution at School: Building Compassionate Communities," *Social Alternatives* 21 (2002), 49–55.

Caughlin, John P., and Rachel S. Malis, "Demand/Withdraw Communication between Parents and Adolescents: Connections with Self-Esteem and Substance Abuse," *Journal of Social and Personal Relationships* 21 (2004), 125–148.

Caughlin, John P., and Anita L. Vangelisti, "An Individual Difference Explanation of Why Married Couples Engage in the Demand/Withdraw Pattern of Conflict," *Journal of Social and Personal Relationships* 17 (2000), 523–551.

Cloke, Kenneth, *Mediating Dangerously* (San Francisco: Jossey-Bass, 2001).

Cloven, Denise H., "Relational Effects of Interpersonal Conflict: The Role of Cognition, Satisfaction, and Anticipated Communication," Master's thesis, Northwestern University, Evanston, IL, 1990.

Cloven, Denise H., and Michael E. Roloff, "Sense-Making Activities and Interpersonal Conflict: Communication Cures for the Mulling Blues," *Western Journal of Speech Communication* 55 (1991), 134–158.

Cole, C., and R. Ackerman, "A Change Model for Resolution of Stress," *Alternative Lifestyles* 4 (1981), 135.

Collier, Mary Jane, "Culture and Gender: Effects on Assertive Behavior and Communication Competence," in Margaret L. McLaughlin (Ed.), *Communication Yearbook 9* (Beverly Hills, CA: Sage, 1986), p. 578.

Conrad, Charles, "Communication in Conflict: Style-Strategy Relationships," *Communication Monographs* 58 (1991), 135–155.

Coogler, O. J., *Structured Mediation in Divorce Settlement* (Lexington, MA: Lexington Books, 1978).

Coombs, Clyde H., and George S. Avrunin, *The Structure of Conflict* (Hillsdale, NJ: Lawrence Erlbaum Associates, 1988).

Coulson, Robert, *Family Mediation: Managing Conflict, Resolving Disputes* (San Francisco: Jossey-Bass, 1996).

Cramer, Duncan, "Linking Conflict Management Behaviors and Relational Satisfaction: The Intervening Role of Conflict Outcome Satisfaction," *Journal of Social and Personal Relationships* 19 (2002), 425–432.

Cramer, Duncan, "Relationship Satisfaction and Conflict over Minor and Major Issues in Romantic Relationships," *Journal of Psychology* 136 (2002), 75–81.

Cronen, Vernon E., W. Barnett Pearce, and Lonna M. Snavely, "A Theory of Rule-Structure and Types of Episodes and a Study of Perceived Enmeshment in Undesired Repetitive Pattern ('URPs')," in Dan Nimmo (Ed.), *Communication Yearbook 3* (New Brunswick, NJ: Transaction Books, 1979), pp. 225–240.

Cross, Gary P., Jean H. Names, and Darrell Beck, *Conflict and Human Interaction* (Dubuque, IA: Kendall Hunt Publishing, 1979).

Cummings, H. Wayland, Larry W. Long, and Michael Lewis, *Managing Communication in Organizations,* 2nd Ed. (Scottsdale, AZ: Gorsuch Scarisbrick Publishers, 1987).

Cupach, William R., and Sandra Metts, "Accounts of Relational Dissolution: A Comparison of Marital and Non-Marital Relationships," paper presented at the International Communication Association Convention, Honolulu, May 1985.

Cupach, William R., and Sandra Metts, "The Effects of Type of Predicament and Embarrassability on Remedial Responses to Embarrassing Situations," *Communication Quarterly* 40 (1992), 149–161.

Cupach, William R., and Sandra Metts, *Facework* (Thousand Oaks: Sage Publications, 1994).

Daniels, Steven E., and Greg B. Walker, *Working through Environmental Conflict: The Collaborative Learning Approach* (Westport, CT: Praeger, 2001).

Danielsson, Claire, "A Holistic Approach to Dispute Resolution at a Community Mediation Center," in Dudley D. Cahn (Ed.), *Conflict in Personal Relationships* (Hillsdale, NJ: Erlbaum, 1994).

Derr, C. Brooklyn, "Managing Organizational Conflict: Collaboration, Bargaining and Power Approaches," *California Management Review* 21 (1978), 76–83.

Dersley, Ian, and Anthony Wootton, "Complaint Sequences within Antagonist Argument," *Research on Language and Social Interaction* 33 (2000), 375–406.

Deutsch, Morton, "Conflicts: Productive or Destructive," *Journal of Social Issues* 25 (1969), 7–41.

Deutsch, Morton, *The Resolution of Conflict* (New Haven, CT: Yale University Press, 1973).

DeVito, Joseph, *The Interpersonal Communication Book,* 6th Ed. (New York: HarperCollins, 1992).

Dickson, Fran C., Patrick C. Hughes, Linda D. Manning, Kandi L. Walker, Tamara Bollis-Pecci, and Scott Gratson, "Conflict in Later-Life, Long-Term Marriages," *Southern Communication Journal* 67 (2002), 110–121.

Diekmann, Andreas, "The Power of Reciprocity: Fairness, Reciprocity, and Stakes in Variants of the Dictator Game," *Journal of Conflict Resolution* 48 (2004), 487–505.

Dobash, R. Emerson, and Russell P. Dobash, "Research as Social Action: The Struggle for Battered Women," in Kersti Yllo and Michele Bograd (Eds.), *Feminist Perspectives on Wife Abuse* (Newbury Park, CA: Sage, 1988), p. 60.

Donnelly, Doris, *Learning to Forgive* (Nashville, TN: Abingdon Press, 1979).

Dorado, Miguel A., Francisco J. Medina, Lourdes Munduate, Immaculada F. J. Cisneros, and Martin Euwema, "Computer Mediated Negotiation of an Escalated Conflict," *Small Group Research* 33 (2002), 509–524.

Drake, Laura E., "The Culture-Negotiation Link: Integrative and Distributive Bargaining through an Intercultural Communication Lens," *Human Communication Research* 27 (2001), 317–349.

Dressler, Joshua, "Hating Criminals: How Can Something That Feels So Good Be Wrong?" *Michigan Law Review* 88 (1990), p. 1454.

Dumlao, Rebecca and Renee A. Botta, "Family Communication Patterns and the Conflict Styles Young Adults Use with Their Fathers," *Communication Quarterly* 48 (2000), 174–189.

Edwards, Renee, and Richard Bello, "Interpretations of Messages: The Influence of Equivocation, Face Concerns, and Ego-Involvement," *Human Communication Research* 27 (2001), 597–631.

Edwards, Renee, James M. Honeycutt, and Kenneth S. Zagacki, "Imagined Interaction as an Element of Social Cognition," *Western Journal of Speech Communication* 52 (1988), 23–45.

Ellis, Albert, "Overview of the Clinical Theory of Rational-Emotive Therapy," in Russell Grieger and John Boyd (Eds.), *Rational-Emotive Therapy: A Skills-Based Approach* (New York: Van Nostrand Reinhold, 1980), pp. 1–31.

Ellis, Albert, and Robert A. Harper, *A New Guide to Rational Living* (North Hollywood, CA: Wilshire Book Co., 1975).

Emerson, James G., *The Dynamics of Forgiveness* (Philadelphia: The Westminster Press, 1964).

Emery, Robert E., David Sbarra, and Tara Grover, "Divorce Mediation: Research and Reflections," *Family Court Review* 43 (2005), 22–37.

Enright, Robert D., and Robert L. Zell, "Problems Encountered When We Forgive One Another," *Journal of Psychology and Christianity* 8 (1989), 52–54

Erbert, Larry A., and Kory Floyd, "Affectionate Expressions as Face-Threatening Acts: Receiver Assessments," *Communication Studies* 55 (2004), 254–270.

Erickson, Stephen K., and Marilyn S. McKnight, *The Practitioner's Guide to Mediation: A Client-Centered Approach* (NY: John Wiley, 2001).

Exline, Julie Juola, and Ray F. Baumeister, "Expressing Forgiveness and Repentance: Benefits and Barriers," in Michael E. McCullough, Kenneth L. Pargament, and Carl E. Thorsen (Eds.), *Forgiveness: Theory, Research, and Practice* (New York: The Guilford Press, 2000), pp. 133–155.

Fairhust, Gail T., Stephen G. Green, and B. Kay Snavely, "Face Support in Controlling Poor Performance," *Human Communication Research* 11 (1984), 272–295.

Faludi, Susan, *Backlash: The Undeclared War Against American Women* (New York: Crown Publishers, 1991).

Feld, Scott L., and Dawn T. Robinson, "Secondary Bystander Effects on Intimate Violence: When Norms of Restraint Reduce Deterrence," *Journal of Social and Personal Relationships* 15 (1998), 277–285.

Feldman, Clyde M., and Carl A. Ridley, "The Role of Conflict-Based Communication Responses and Outcomes in Male Domestic Violence toward Female Partners," *Journal of Social and Personal Relationships* 17 (2000), 552–573.

Fisher, Roger, and William Ury, *Getting to Yes: Negotiating Agreement without Giving In* (Boston: Houghton-Mifflon, 1981).

Fitzgibbons, Richard P., "The Cognitive and Emotional Uses of Forgiveness in the Treatment of Anger," *Psychotherapy* 23 (1986), 629–633.

Foa, Uriel G., and Edna G. Foa, *Societal Structures of the Mind,* (Springfield, IL: Thomas, 1974).

Folger, Joseph, and Marshall Scott Poole, *Working through Conflict* (Glenview, IL: Scott Foresman, 1984).

Folger, Joseph, Marshall Scott Poole, and Randall K. Stutman, *Working through Conflict,* 2nd Ed. (New York: HarperCollins, 1993).

Folger, Joseph, Marshall Scott Poole, and Randall K. Stutman, *Working through Conflict,* 4th Ed. (Boston: Allyn & Bacon, 2001).

Folger, Joseph, Marhsall Scott Poole, and Randall K. Stutman, *Working through Conflict,* 5th Ed. (Boston: Allyn & Bacon, 2005).

Forgas, Joseph P., and Michelle Cromer, "On Being Sad and Evasive: Affective Influences on Verbal Communication Strategies in Conflict Situations," *Journal of Experimental Social Psychology* 40 (2004), 511–518.

Fow, Neil Robert, "An Empirical-Phenomenological Investigation of the Experience of Forgiving Another," Doctoral dissertation, University of Pittsburgh, 1988.

Freeman, Sally A., Stephen W. Littlejohn, and Barnett W. Pearce, "Communication and Moral Conflict," *Western Journal of Communication* 56 (1992), p. 319.

Harden Fritz, Janie M., "Responses to Unpleasant Work Relationships," *Communication Research Reports* 14 (1997), 302–311.

Gamson, William A., "A Theory of Coalition Formation," in Claggett C. Smith (Ed.), *Conflict Resolution: Contributions of the Behavioral Sciences* (Notre Dame, IN: University of Notre Dame Press, 1971), pp. 146–156.

Gayle, Barbara Mae, "Sex Equity in Workplace Conflict Management," *Journal of Applied Communication Research* 19 (1991), 152–169.

Gibb, Jack, "Defensive Communication," *Journal of Communication* 11 (1961), 141–168.

Giunta, Stephen A., and Ellen S. Amatea, "Mediation or Litigation with Abusing or Neglectful Families: Emerging Roles for Mental Health Counselors," *Journal of Mental Health Counseling* 22 (2000), 240–252.

Goffman, Erving, *The Presentation of Self in Everyday Life* (New York: Overlook Press, 1959).

Goffman, Erving, *Interaction Ritual: Essays on Face-to-Face Behavior* (New York: Pantheon Books, 1967).

Goldingay, John, *Walk On: Life, Loss, Trust, and Other Realities* (Grand Rapids, MI: Baker, 2002).

Gottman, John, "Temporal Form: Toward a New Language for Describing Relationships," *Journal of Marriage and the Family,*" 44 (1982), 943–962.

Gottman, John, and R. Krokoff, *Marital Interaction: A Longitudinal View* (Unpublished manuscript, University of Washington, Seattle, WA, 1989).

Gottman, John, Robert Levenson, and Erica Woodin, "Facial Expressions during Marital Conflict," *Journal of Family Communication* 1 (2001), 37–57.

Graham-Berman, Sandra A., Susan E. Cutler, Brian W. Litzenberger, and Wendy E. Schwartz, "Perceived Conflict and Violence in Childhood Sibling Relationships and Later Emotional Adjustment," *Journal of Family Psychology* 8 (1994), 85–97.

Griffin, Em, "Accountability and Forgiveness: Saying the Tough Words in Love," paper presented at the Speech Communication Association Convention, Denver, November 1985.

Gross, Michael A., Laura Guerrero, and Jess K. Alberts, "Perceptions of Conflict Strategies and Communication Competence in Task-Oriented Dyads," *Journal of Applied Communication Research* 32 (2004), 249–270.

Guerrero, Laura K., and Walid A. Afifi, "Some Things are Better Left Unsaid: Topic Avoidance in Family Relationships," *Communication Quarterly,* 43 (1995), 276–296.

Hall, Calvin S., *A Primer of Freudian Psychology,* 2nd Ed. (New York: World, 1979).

Hample, Dale, and Judith M. Dallinger, "A Lewinian Perspective on Taking Conflict Personally: Revision, Refinement, and Validation of the Instrument," *Communication Quarterly* 43 (1995), 297–319.

Hart, Roderick P., and Donald M. Burks, "Rhetorical Sensitivity and Social Interaction," *Speech Monographs* 39 (1972), 75–91.

Hart, Roderick P., Robert E. Carlson, and William F. Eadie, "Attitudes toward Communication and the Assessment of Rhetorical Sensitivity," *Communication Monographs* 47 (1980), 1–22.

Harvey, Thomas R., and Bonita Drolet, *Building Teams, Building People: Expanding the Fifth Resource* (La Verne, CA: University of La Verne, 1992).

Hastings, James, (Ed.), *Encyclopedia of Religion and Ethics* (Edinburgh: T. & T. Clark, 1974).

Hayakawa, S. I., *Language in Thought and Action,* 4th Ed. (NY: Harcourt, Brace, Jovanovich, 1978).

Healey, Jonathan G., and Robert A. Bell, "Assessing Alternate Responses to Conflicts in Friendship," in Dudley D. Cahn (Ed.), *Intimates in Conflict: A Communication Perspective* (Hillsdale, NJ: Erlbaum, 1990), pp. 25–48.

Hebl, John H., "Forgiveness as a Counseling Goal with Elderly Females," Doctoral dissertation, University of Wisconsin, 1990.

Heisel, Marnin J., and Myrian Mongrain, "Facial Expressions and Ambivalence: Looking for Conflict in All the Right Faces," *Journal of Nonverbal Behavior* 28 (2004), 35–52.

Hess, Herbert J., and Charles O. Tucker, *Talking About Relationships,* 2nd Ed. (Prospect Heights, IL: Waveland Press, 1980).

Hewitt, John P., and Randall Stokes, "Disclaimers," *American Sociological Review* 40 (1975), 1–11.

Higgins, Gina O'Connell, *Resilient Adults: Overcoming a Cruel Past* (San Francisco: Jossey-Bass, 1994).

Hobman, Elizabeth V., Prashant Bordia, Bernd Irmer, and Artemis Chang, "The Expression of Conflict in Computer-Mediated and Face-to-Face Groups," *Small Group Research* 33 (2002), 439–465

Hocker, Joyce L., and William W. Wilmot, *Interpersonal Conflict,* 4th Ed. (Dubuque, IA: Wm C. Brown, 1995).

Holmes, John, "The Exchange Process in Close Relationships: Microbehavior and Macromotives," in Melvin J. Lerner and Sally C. Lerner (Eds.), *The Justice Motive in Social Behavior* (New York: Plenum, 1981), pp. 261–284.

Holmes, John G., and John K. Rempel, "Trust in Close Relationships," in Clyde Hendrick (Ed.), *Close Relationships* (Newbury Park, CA: Sage, 1989), pp. 187–220.

Homans, George, *Social Behavior: Its Elementary Forms* (New York: Harcourt Brace Jovanovich, 1961).

Honeycutt, James M., Kenneth S. Zagacki, and Renee Edwards, "Imagined Interaction and Interpersonal Communication," *Communication Reports* 3 (1990), 1–8.

Hope, Donald, "The Healing Paradox of Forgiveness," *Psychotherapy* 24 (1987), 240–244.

"How IBM Boss Embraced His Dilemmas," *Strategic Direction* 20 (2004), p. 17.

Hubbard, Amy S. Ebesu, "Conflict between Relationally Uncertain Romantic Partners: The Influence of Relational Responsiveness and Empathy," *Communication Monographs* 68 (2001), 400–414.

Hunter, R. C. A., "Forgiveness, Retaliation, and Paranoid Reactions," *Canadian Psychiatric Association Journal* 23 (1978), 171.

Infante, Dominic A., Teresa A. Chandler, and Jill E. Rudd, "Test of an Argumentative Skill Deficiency Model of Interspousal Violence," *Communication Monographs* 56 (1989), 163–177.

Infante, Dominic A., and C. J. Wigley, "Verbal Aggressiveness: An Interpersonal Model and Measure," *Communication Monographs* 53 (1986), 61–69.

Isard, Walter, and Christine Smith, *Conflict Analysis and Practical Conflict Management* (Cambridge, MA: Ballinger Publishing, 1982).

Jakubowski, Patricia, and Arthur J. Lange, *The Assertive Option: Your Rights and Responsibilities* (Champaign, IL: Research Press, 1978).

Jia, Wenshan, "Chinese Mediation and Its Cultural Foundation," in Guo-ming M. Chen and Ringo Ma (Eds.), *Chinese Conflict Management and Resolution* (Stamford, CT: Ablex, 2001), pp. 289–295.

Johnson, Amy Janan, "Beliefs about Arguing: A Comparison of Public Issue and Personal Issue Arguments," *Communication Reports* 15 (2002), 99–112.

Johnson, Cathryn, Rebecca Ford, and Joanne Kaufman, "Emotional Reactions to Conflict: Do Dependency and Legitimacy Matter?" *Social Forces,* 79 (2000), 107–137.

Johnson, David W., and Roger T. Johnson, "Implementing the 'Teaching Students to be Peacemakers Program,'" *Theory into Practice* 43 (2004), 68–79.

Julien, Danielle, Mathide Brault, Élise Chartrand, and Jean Bégin, "Immediacy Behaviours and Synchrony in Satisfied and Dissatisfied Couples," *Canadian Journal of Behavioural Science* 32 (2000), 84–90.

Julien, Danielle, Howard J. Markman, Sophie Léveillé, Élise Chartrand, and Jean Bégin, "Networks' Support and Interference with Regard to Marriage: Disclosures of Marital Problems to Confidants," *Journal of Family Psychology,* 8 (1994), 16–31.

Julien, Danielle, Nicole Tremblay, Isabelle Béllanger, Monique Dubé, Jean Bégin, and Donald Bouthillier, "Interaction Structure of Husbands' and Wives' Disclosure of Marital Conflict to their Respective Best Friend," *Journal of Family Psychology* 14 (2000), 286–303.

Kabanoff, Boris, "Predictive Validity of the MODE Conflict Instrument," *Journal of Applied Psychology* 72 (1987), 160–163.

Kahn, Lynn Sandra, *Peacemaking: A Systems Approach to Conflict Management* (Lanham, MD: University Press of America, 1988).

Kauhnan, Gershen, *Shame: The Power of Caring* (Cambridge, MA: Shenkinan Publishing, 1980).

Kepner, James E., *Healing Tasks: Psychotherapy with Adult Survivors of Childhood Abuse* (San Francisco: Jossey Bass, 1995).

Kilmann, Robert, and Kenneth W. Thomas. "Developing a Forced-Choice Measure of Conflict-Handling Behavior: The Mode Instrument," *Educational and Psychological Measurement,* 37 (1977), 309–325.

Kimmel, Melvin J., Dean G. Pruitt, John M. Magenau, E. Konar Goldband, and P. J. D. Carnevale, "Effects of Trust, Aspiration and Gender on Negotiation Tactics," *Journal of Personality and Social Psychology* 38 (1980), 9–22.

King, Andrew, *Power and Communication* (Prospect Heights, IL: Waveland Press, 1987).

Kingsolver, Barbara, *The Poisonwood Bible* (New York: HarperTorch, 1998).

Klein, Renate C. A., and Robert M. Milardo, "The Social Context of Couple Conflict: Support and Criticism from Informal Third Parties," *Journal of Social and Personal Relationships* 17 (2000), 618–637.

Klimoski, Richard, "The Effects of Intragroup Forces on Intergroup Conflict Resolution," *Organizational Behavior and Human Performance* 8 (1972), 363–383.

Knapp, Mark L., and Mark E. Comadena, "Telling It Like It Isn't: A Review of Theory and Research on Deceptive Communications," *Human Communication Research* 5 (1979), p. 271.

Koerner, Ascan F., and Mary Anne Fitzpatrick, "You Never Leave Your Family in a Fight: The Impact of Family of Origin on Conflict-Behavior in Romantic Relationships," *Communication Studies* 53 (2002), 234–252.

Kohut, Heinz, "Narcissism and Narcissistic Rage," *The Psychoanalytic Study of the Child* 27 (1972), 379–392.

Komorita, S. S., and A. R. Brenner, "Bargaining and Concession Making under Bilateral Monopoly," *Journal of Personality and Social Psychology* 9 (1968), 15–20.

Konstam, Varda, Miriam Chernoff, and Sara Deveney, "Toward Forgiveness: The Role of Shame, Guilt, Anger and Empathy," *Counseling and Values* 46 (2001), 26–39.

Kriegsberg, Louis, *The Sociology of Social Conflicts* (Englewood Cliffs, NJ: Prentice Hall, 1973).

Lambert, W. G., *Babylonian Wisdom Literature* (London: Oxford University Press, 1960).

Lamott, Anne, *Traveling Mercies* (New York: Anchor Books, 1999).

Lane, Shelley D., "Empathy and Assertive Communication," paper presented at the Western Speech Communication Association Convention, San Jose, CA, February 1981.

Larzelere, Robert, and Ted L. Huston, "The Dyadic Trust Scale: Toward Understanding Interpersonal Trust in Close Relationships," *Journal of Marriage and the Family* 42 (1980), 595–604.

Lattimore, Paul J., Hugh L. Wagner, and Simon Gowers, "Conflict Avoidance in Anorexia Nervosa: An Observational Study of Mothers and Daughters," *European Eating Disorders Review* 8 (2000), 355–368.

Lax, David A., and James K. Sebenius, *The Manager as Negotiator* (New York: Free Press, 1986).

Likerman, Meira, "The Function of Anger in Human Conflict," *International Review of Psychoanalysis* 14 (1987), p. 152.

Linn, Matthew, and Dennis Linn, *Healing Life's Hurts: Healing Memories through Five Stages of Forgiveness* (New York: Paulist Press, 1978).

Lloyd, Sally, and Beth Emery, "Physically Aggressive Conflict in Romantic Relationships," in Dudley D. Cahn (Ed.), *Conflict in Personal Relationships* (Hillsdale, NJ: Lawrence Erlbaum Associates, 1994), pp. 27–46.

Loving, Timothy J., Kathi L. Hefner, Janice K. Kiecolt-Glaser, Ronald Glaser, and William B. Malarkey, "Stress Hormone Changes and Marital Conflict: Spouses' Relative Power Makes a Difference," *Journal of Marriage and the Family* 66 (2004), 595–612.

Lulofs, Roxane S., "The Social Construction of Forgiveness," *Human Systems* 2 (1992), 183–198.

Lulofs, Roxane S., "Swimming Upstream: Creating Reasons for Unforgiveness in a Culture that Expects Otherwise," paper presented to the Speech Communication Association Convention, San Antonio, TX, November 1995.

Lulofs, Roxane S., and Dudley D. Cahn, *Conflict: From Theory to Action*, 2nd Ed. (Boston: Allyn & Bacon, 2000).

Macaskill, Ann, John Maltby, and Liza Day, "Forgiveness of Self and Others and Emotional Empathy," *The Journal of Social Psychology* 142 (2002), 663–665.

Mack, Raymond W., and Richard C. Snyder, "The Analysis of Social Conflict: Toward an Overview and Synthesis," in Fred E. Jandt (Ed.), *Conflict Resolution through Communication* (New York: Harper and Row, 1973).

Mahan, Brian J., *Forgetting Ourselves on Purpose: Vocation and the Politics of Ambition* (San Francisco: Jossey-Bass, 2002).

Manning, Tony, and Bob Robertson, "Influencing, Negotiating Skills and Conflict Handling: Some Additional Research and Reflections," *Industrial and Commercial Training* 36 (2004), 104–109.

Margolin, Leslie "Beyond Maternal Blame: Physical Child Abuse as a Phenomenon of Gender," *Journal of Family Issues,* 13 (1992), 410–423.

Margulies, Nancy, *Mapping Inner Space: Learning and Teaching Visual Mapping,* 2nd Ed. (Zephyr Press, 2001).

Marshall, Linda L., "Physical and Psychological Abuse," in William R. Cupach and Brian H. Spitzberg (Eds.), *The Dark Side of Interpersonal Communication* (Hillsdale, NJ: Erlbaum, 1994) pp. 281–311.

Marwell, Gerald, David Schmitt, and B. Boyesen, "Pacifist Strategy and Cooperation under Interpersonal Risk," *Journal of Personality and Social Psychology* 28 (1973), 12–20.

McComack, Steven A., and Timothy R. Levine, "When Lies Are Uncovered: Emotion and Relational Outcomes of Discovered Deception," *Communication Monographs* 5 (1990), p. 121.

McComack, Steven A., and Malcolm R. Parks, "Deception Detection and Relationship Development: The Other Side of Trust," in Margaret L. McLaughlin (Ed.), *Communication Yearbook 9* (Beverly Hills: Sage Publications, 1986), pp. 377–389.

McCorkle, Suzanne, and Barbara Mae Gayle, "Conflict Management Metaphors: Assessing Everyday Problem Communication," *The Social Science Journal* 40 (2003), 137–142.

McCorkle, Suzanne, and Janet L. Mills, "Rowboat in a Hurricane: Metaphors of Interpersonal Conflict Management," *Communication Reports* 5 (1992), 57–66.

McCorkle, Suzanne, and Melanie Reese, *Mediation Theory and Practice* (Boston: Allyn & Bacon, 2005).

McCroskey, James C., "Oral Communication Apprehension: A Summary of Recent Theory and Research," *Human Communication Research* 4, (1977), 78–96.

McCullough, Michael E., Kenneth L. Pargament, and Carl E. Thorsen, *Forgiveness: Theory, Research, and Practice* (New York: The Guilford Press, 2000).

McCullough, Michael E., Steven J. Sandage, and Everett L. Worthington, Jr., *To Forgive Is Human* (Downers Grove, IL: InterVarsity Press, 1997).

McKinney, Bruce, William Kimsey, and Rex Fuller, *Mediation: Dispute Resolution through Communication,* 2nd Ed. (Dubuque, IA: Kendall Hunt, 1990).

McKinnon, William, Carol S. Wiesse, C. Patrick Reynolds, Charles A. Bowles, and Andrew Baum, "Chronic Stress, Leukocyte Subpopulations, and Humoral Response to Latent Viruses," *Health Psychology* 8 (1989), 389–402.

Messman, Susan J., and Rebecca L. Mikesell, "Competition and Interpersonal Conflict in Dating Relationships," *Communication Reports* 13 (2000), 21–34.

Metts, Sandra, "Relational Transgressions," in William R. Cupach and Brian H. Spitzberg (Eds.), *The Dark Side of Interpersonal Communication* (Hillsdale, NJ: Lawrence Erlbaum, 1994).

Metts, Sandra, and William R. Cupach, "Situational Influence on the Use of Remedial Strategies in Embarrassing Predicaments," *Communication Monographs* 56 (1989), 151–162.

Meyer, Janet R., "The Effect of Verbal Aggressiveness on the Perceived Importance of Secondary Goals in Messages," *Communication Studies* 55 (2004), 168–185.

Miller, David L., *Gods and Games: Toward a Theology of Play* (New York: Harper Colophon Books, 1973).

Minirth, Frank, Don Hawkins, Paul Meier, and Richard Flournoy, *How to Beat Burnout* (Chicago: Moody, 1986).

Morrill, Calvin, and Cheryl King Thomas, "Organizational Conflict Management as a Disputing Process," *Human Communication Research* 18 (1992), 400–429.

Morris, Debbie, with Gregg Lewis, *Forgiving the Dead Man Walking* (Grand Rapids, MI: Zondervan, 1998).

Murray, Robert J., "Forgiveness as a Therapeutic Option," *Family Journal* 10 (2002), 315–331.

Neale, Robert E., *In Praise of Play: Toward a Psychology of Religion* (New York: Harper & Row, 1969).

Nicotera, Anne, (Ed.), *Conflict and Organizations: Communicative Processes* (Albany: State University of New York Press, 1995).

Norton, Robert, and Barbara Warnick, "Assertiveness as a Communication Construct," *Human Communication Research* 3 (1976), 62–66.

Nye, Robert D., *Conflict among Humans* (New York: Spring Publishing, 1973).

Oates, Joyce Carol, *Because It Is Bitter, and Because It Is My Heart* (New York: Penguin Books, 1990).

O'Connor, Kathleen M., Josh A. Arnold, and Ethan R. Burris, "Negotiators' Bargaining Histories and Their Effects on Future Negotiation Performance," *Journal of Applied Psychology* 90 (2005), 350–362.

Oetzel, John, Stella Ting-Toomey, Martha Idalia Chew-Sanchez, Richard Harris, Richard Wilcox, and Siegfried Stumpf, "Face and Facework in Conflicts with Parents and Siblings: A Cross-Cultural Comparison of Germans, Japanese, Mexicans, and U.S. Americans," *Journal of Family Communication* 3 (2003), 67–93.

Oetzel, John, Stella Ting-Toomey, Tomoko Masumoto, Yukiko Yokochi, Xiaohui Pan, Jiro Takai, and Richard Wilcox, "Face and Facework in Conflict: A Cross-Cultural Comparison of China, Germany, Japan, and the United States," *Communication Monographs* 68 (2001), 235–258.

Olson, Loreen N., "'As Ugly and Painful as It Was, It Was Effective': Individuals' Unique Assessment of Communication Competence during Aggressive Conflict Episodes," *Communication Studies* 53 (2002), 171–188.

Olson, Loreen N., "Compliance Gaining Strategies of Individuals Experiencing 'Common Couple Violence,'" *Qualitative Research Reports in Communication* 3 (2002), 7–14.

Olson, Loreen N., "Exploring 'Common Couple Violence' in Heterosexual Romantic Relationships," *Western Journal of Communication* 66 (2002), p. 104.

Olson, Loreen N., and Dawn O. Braithwaite, "'If You Hit Me Again, I'll Hit You Back': Conflict Management Strategies of Individuals Experiencing Aggression during Conflicts," *Communication Studies* 55 (2004), 271–286.

Olson, Loreen N., and Tamara D. Golish, "Topics of Conflict and Patterns of Aggression in Romantic Relationships," *Southern Communication Journal* 67 (2002), 180–200.

O'Sullivan, Patrick B., "What You Don't Know Won't Hurt Me: Impression Management Functions of Communication Channels in Relationships," *Human Communication Research* 26 (2000), 403–431.

Palmer, David L., "The Communication of Forgiveness," paper presented at the annual meeting of the Speech Communication Association, New Orleans, November 1994.

Pawlowcott, Donna R., A. Meyers, and Kelly A. Rocca, "Relational Messages in Conflict Situations among Siblings," *Communication Research Reports* 3 (2000), 271–277.

Pearce, W. Barnett, "Keynote Address: Communication Theory," *Institute for Faculty Development: Communication Theory and Research* (Hope College, Holland, MI, July 1992).

Pearson, Judy C., *Interpersonal Communication: Clarity, Confidence, Concern* (Glenview, IL: Scott Foresman, 1983).

Pellegrini, Anthony D. (Ed.), *The Future of Play Theory: A Multidisciplinary Inquiry into the Contributions of Brian Sutton-Smith* (Albany: SUNY Press, 1995).

Pike, Gary R., and Alan L. Sillars, "Reciprocity of Marital Communication," *Journal of Social and Personal Relationships* 2 (1985), 303–324.

Pilisuk, Marc, and Paul Skolnick, "Inducing Trust: A Test of the Osgood Proposal," *Journal of Experimental Social Psychology* 11 (1968), 53–63.

Pingleton, Jared P., "The Role and Function of Forgiveness in the Psychotherapeutic Process," *Journal of Psychology and Theology* 17 (1989), 27–35.

Poitras, Jean, "A Study of the Emergence of Cooperation in Mediation," *Negotiation Journal* 21 (2005), 281–300.

Powell, Larry, and Mark Hickson, III, "Power Imbalance and Anticipation of Conflict Resolution: Positive and Negative Attributes of Perceptual Recall," *Communication Research Reports,* 17 (2000), 181–190.

Pruitt, Dean G., *Negotiation Behavior* (New York: Academic Press, 1981).

Pruitt, Dean G., and Melvin J. Kimmel "Twenty Years of Experimental Gaming: Critique, Synthesis, and Suggestions for the Future," *Annual Review of Psychology* 28 (1977) 363–392.

Pruitt, Dean G., and Steven A. Lewis, "Development of Integrative Solutions in Bilateral Negotiation," *Journal of Personality and Social Psychology* 31 (1975), 621–633.

Pruitt, Dean G., and Jeffrey Z. Rubin, *Social Conflict: Escalation, Stalemate, and Settlement* (New York: Random House, 1986).

Putnam, Linda L., "Bargaining as Organizational Communication," in Robert D. McPhee and Phillip K. Tompkins (Eds.), *Organizational Communication: Traditional Themes and New Directions* (Newbury Park: Sage, 1985), p. 129.

Putnam, Linda L., and Trisha S. Jones, "The Role of Communication in Bargaining," *Human Communication Research* 8 (1992), 262–280.

Putnam, Linda L., and M. Scott Poole, "Conflict and Negotiation," in Fred M. Jablin, Linda L. Putnam, Karlene H. Roberts, and Lyman W. Porter (Eds.), *Handbook of Organizational Communication: An Interdisciplinary Approach* (Newbury Park, CA: Sage, 1987), pp. 549–599.

Rahim, M. Afzalur, "A Measure of Styles of Handling Interpersonal Conflict," *Academy of Management Journal* 26 (1983), 368–376.

Rahner, Hugo, *Man at Play* (New York: Herder & Herder, 1972).

Remer, Rory, and Paul de Mesquita, "Teaching and Learning the Skills of Interpersonal Confrontation," in Dudley D. Cahn (Ed.), *Intimates in Conflict: A Communication Perspective* (Hillsdale, NJ: Lawrence Erlbaum Associates, 1990).

Rempel, John K., "Trust and Attributions in Close Relationships," unpublished doctoral dissertation, University of Waterloo, Ontario, 1987.

Rempel, John K., John G. Holmes, and Mark P. Zanna, "Trust in Close Relationships," *Journal of Personality and Social Psychology* 49 (1985), 95–112.

Rettig, Kathryn D., and Margaret D. Bubolz, "Interpersonal Resource Exchanges as Indicators of Quality of Marriage," *Journal of Marriage and the Family,* 45 (1983), 497–509.

Retzinger, Suzanne M., *Violent Emotions: Shame and Rage in Marital Quarrels* (Newbury Park: Sage Publications, 1991).

Richardson, Julia, "Avoidance as an Active Mode of Conflict Resolution," *Team Performance Management* 1 (1995), 19–23.

Rocca, Kelly A., "College Student Attendance: Impact of Instructor Immediacy and Verbal Aggression," *Communication Education* 53 (2004), 185–195.

Rogan, Randall C., and Betty H. La France, "An Examination of the Relationship between Verbal Aggressiveness, Conflict Management Strategies, and Conflict Interaction Goals," *Communication Quarterly* 51 (2003), 458–469.

Rogers, Carl R., *On Becoming a Person* (Cambridge, MA: The Riverside Press, 1961).

Rogers, Carl R., and Rosalind F. Dymond, *Psychotherapy and Personality Change* (IL: University of Chicago Press, 1954).

Roloff, Michael E., "The Catalyst Hypothesis: Conditions under Which Coercive Communication Leads to Physical Aggression," in Dudley D. Cahn and Sally A. Lloyd, *Family Violence from a Communication Perspective* (Thousand Oaks, CA: Sage Publications, 1996), pp. 127–150.

Roloff, Michael E., and Denise H. Cloven, "The Chilling Effect in Interpersonal Relationships: The Reluctance to Speak One's Mind," in Dudley D. Cahn (Ed.), *Inmates in Conflict: A Communication Perspective* (Hillside, NJ: Lawrence Erlbaum Associates, 1990), pp. 49–76.

Roloff, Michael E., and Douglas E. Campion, "On Alleviating the Debilitating Effects of Accountability on Bargaining: Authority and Self-Monitoring," *Communication Monographs* 54 (1987), 145–164.

Roloff, Michael E., and Danette E. Ifert, "Conflict Management through Avoidance: Withholding Complaints, Suppressing Arguments, and Declaring Topics Taboo," in Sandra Petronio (Ed.), *Balancing the Secrets of Private Disclosures* (Mahwah, NJ: Lawrence Erlbaum Associates, Publishers, 2000), pp. 151–163.

Roloff, Michael E., and Danette Ifert Johnson, "Reintroducing Taboo Topics: Antecedents and Consequences of Putting Topics Back on the Table," *Communication Studies* 52 (2001), 37–50.

Roloff, Michael E., Kari P. Soule, and Colleen M. Carey, "Reasons for Remaining in a Relationship and Responses to Relational Transgressions," *Journal of Social and Personal Relationships* 18 (2001), 362–385.

Ronan, George, Laura E. Dreer, Katherine Dollard, and Donna W. Ronan, "Violent Couples: Coping and Communication Skills," *Journal of Family Violence* 19 (2004), 131–137.

Ruben, Brent, "Communication and Conflict: A Systems Perspective," *Quarterly Journal of Speech* 64 (1978), 202–210.

Rummel, R. J., *Understanding Conflict and War: The Conflict Helix,* Vol. 2 (Beverly Hills, CA: Sage Publications, 1976).

Rummel, R. J., "A Catastrophe Theory Model of the Conflict Helix, with Tests," *Behavioral Science* 32 (1987), p. 238.

Rusbult, Caryl E., Dennis J. Johnson, and Gregory D. Morrow, "Determinants and Consequences of Exit, Voice, Loyalty, and Neglect: Responses to Dissatisfaction in Adult Romantic Involvements," *Human Relations* 39 (1986), 45–63.

Rusbult, Caryl E., and Isabella M. Zembrodt. "Responses to Dissatisfaction in Romantic Involvements: A Multidimensional Scaling Analysis" *Journal of Experimental Social Psychology* 19 (1983), 274–293.

Salari, Sonia Miner, and Bret M. Baldwin, "Verbal, Physical, and Injurious Aggression among Intimate Couples over Time," *Journal of Family Issues* 23 (2002), 523–550.

Sander, Frank E. A., and Robert C. Bordone, "Early Intervention: How to Minimize the Cost of Conflict," *Negotiation* 21 (2005), 1–4.

Schlenker, Barry R., *Impression Management* (Monterey, CA: Brooks/Cole, 1980).

Schlenker, Barry R., and Bruce W. Darby, "The Use of Apologies in Social Predicaments," *Social Psychology Quarterly* 44 (1981), 271–278.

Schlenker, Barry R., B. Helm, and James T. Tedeschi, "The Effects of Personality and Situational Variables on Behavioral Trust," *Journal of Personality and Social Psychology* 32 (1973), 664–670.

Schmidt, Mellis I., "Forgiveness as the Focus Theme in Group Counseling," Doctoral dissertation, North Texas State University, 1986.

Schrodt, Paul, and Lawrence R. Wheeless, "Aggressive Communication and Informational Reception Apprehension: The Influence of Listening Anxiety and Intellectual Inflexibility on Trait Argumentativeness and Verbal Aggressiveness," *Communication Quarterly* 49 (2001) 57.

Scott, Lorel, and Robert Martin, "Value Similarity, Relationship Length, and Conflict Interaction in Dating Relationships: An Initial Investigation," paper presented at the annual meeting of the Speech Communication Association, Chicago, November 1986.

Sells, James N., and Leslie King, "A Pilot Study in Marital Group Therapy: Process and Outcome," *Family Journal* 10 (2002), 156–166.

Selye, Hans, *Stress without Distress* (New York: J. B. Lippincott, 1974).

Sereno, Kenneth K., Melinda Welch, and David Braaten, "Interpersonal Conflict: Effects of Variation in Manner of Expressing Anger and Justification for Anger on Perceptions of Appropriateness, Competence, and Satisfaction," *Journal of Applied Communication Research* 15 (1987), 128–143.

Shepherd, Tara L., "Content and Relationship Dimensions of a Conflict Encounter: An Investigation of Their Impact on Perceived Rules," paper presented to the Speech Communication Association Convention, Anaheim, CA, November 1982.

Shockley-Zalabak, Pamela S., and Donald Dean Morley, "An Exploratory Study of Relationships between Preferences for Conflict Styles and Communication Apprehension," *Journal of Language and Social Psychology* 3 (1984), 213–218.

Shotter, John, *Social Accountability and Selfhood* (Oxford, England: Basil Blackwell, 1984).

Siddiqui, Afshan, and Hildy Ross, "Mediation as a Method of Parent Intervention in Children's Disputes," *Journal of Family Psychology* 18 (2004), 147–159.

Sillars, Alan L., Stephen F. Coletti, D. Parry, and Mark A. Rogers, "Coding Verbal Conflict Tactics: Nonverbal and Perceptual Correlates of the 'Avoidance-Distributive-Integrative' Distinction," *Human Communication Research* 9 (1982), 83–95.

Sillars, Alan, Linda J. Roberts, and Kenneth E. Leonard, "Cognition during Marital Conflict: The Relationship of Thought and Talk," *Journal of Social and Personal Relationships* 17 (2000), 479–502.

Simons, Herbert W., "Persuasion in Social Conflicts: A Critique of Prevailing Conceptions and a Framework for Future Research," *Speech Monographs* 39 (1972), 227–247.

Simons, Herbert W., "The Carrot and the Stick as Handmaidens of Persuasion in Conflict Situations," in Gerald R. Miller and Herbert W. Simons (Eds.), *Perspectives in Communication in Social Conflicts* (Englewood Cliffs, NJ: Prentice Hall, 1974), pp. 172–205.

Skuja, Kathy, and W. Kim Halford, "Repeating the Errors of our Parents? Parental Violence in Men's Family of Origin and Conflict Management in Dating Couples," *Journal of Interpersonal Violence* 19 (2004), 623–638.

Smedes, Louis, *Forgive and Forget: Healing the Hurts We Don't Deserve* (San Francisco: Harper & Row, 1984).

Smith, Christine B., Margaret L. McLaughlin, and Kerry K. Osborne, "Conduct Control on Usenet," *Journal of Computer-Mediated Communication* 2 (1997), retrieved on April 7, 2005 from http://jcmc.indiana.edu/vol2/issue4/smith.html.

Smith, Wanda J., K. Vernard Harrington, and Christopher P. Neck, "Resolving Conflict with Humor in a Diversity Context," *Journal of Managerial Psychology* 15 (2000), 606–625.

Solomon, Denise Haunani, Leanne K. Knobloch, and Mary Anne Fitzpatrick, "Relational Power, Marital Schema, and Decisions to Withhold Complaints: An Investigation of the Chilling Effect on Confrontation in Marriage," *Communication Studies* 55 (2004), 146–171.

Solomon, Muriel, *Working with Difficult People* (Englewood Cliffs, NJ: Prentice Hall, 1990).

Spitzberg, Brian H., and Michael L. Hecht, "A Component Model of Relational Competence," *Human Communication Research* 10 (1984), 575–599.

Spring, Janis Abrahms, with Michael Spring, *How Can I Forgive You?* (New York: Harper Collins, 2004).

Stamp, Glen H., "A Qualitatively Constructed Interpersonal Communication Model: A Grounded Theory Analysis," *Human Communication Research,* 25 (1999), 543.

Stamp, Glen H., Anita L. Vengelisti, and John A. Daly, "The Creation of Defensiveness in Social Interaction," *Communication Quarterly* 40 (1992), 177–190.

Sternberg, Robert J., and Lawrence J. Soriano, "Styles of Conflict Resolution," *Journal of Personal and Social Psychology* 47 (1984), 115–126.

Stiff, James B., James Price Dillard, Lilnabeth Somera, Hyun Kim, and Carra Sleight, "Empathy, Communication, and Prosocial Behavior," *Communication Monographs* 55 (1988), 199–213.

Stiff, James B., Hyun J. Kim, and C. N. Ramesh, "Truth-Biases and Aroused Suspicion in Relational Deception," paper presented at the International Communication Association Convention, San Francisco, May 1989.

Strasser, Judith A., "The Relation of General Forgiveness and Forgiveness Type to Reported Health in the Elderly," Doctoral dissertation, Catholic University of America, 1984.

Strauss, Murray A., "A General Systems Theory Approach to a Theory of Violence between Family Members," *Social Science Information* 12 (1973), 103–123.

Subkoviak, Michael J., Robert D. Enright, Ching-Ru Wu, Elizabeth A. Gassin, Suzanne Freedman, Leanne M. Olson, and Issidoros Sarinopolous, "Measuring Interpersonal Forgiveness," paper presented at the American Educational Research Association Convention, San Francisco, April 1992.

Suzuki, Shinobu, and Andrew S. Rancer, "Argumentativeness and Verbal Aggressiveness: Testing for Conceptual and Measurement Equivalence across Four Cultures," *Communication Monographs* 61 (1994), 256–279.

Tavris, Carol, *Anger: The Misunderstood Emotion* (New York: Touchstone through Simon & Schuster, 1989).

Thomas, Kenneth W., "Conflict and Conflict Management," in M. D. Dunnett (Ed.), *The Handbook of Industrial and Organizational Psychology* (Chicago: Rand McNally, 1976).

Thomas, Kenneth W., and Louis R. Pondy, "Toward and 'Intent' Model of Conflict Management among Principle Parties," *Human Relations* 30 (1977), 1089–1102.

Thorsen, Carl E., Alex H. S. Harris, and Frederic Luskin, "Forgiveness and Health: An Unanswered Question," in Michael E. McCullough, Kenneth L. Pargament, and Carl E. Thorsen (Eds.), *Forgiveness: Theory, Research, and Practice* (New York: The Guilford Press, 2000), pp. 254–280.

Ting-Toomey, Stella, "An Analysis of Verbal Communication Patterns in High and Low Marital Adjustment Groups," *Human Communication Research* 9 (1983), 306–319.

Ting-Toomey, Stella, John G. Oetzel, and Kimberlie Yee-Jung, "Self-Construal Types and Conflict Management Styles," *Communication Reports* 14 (2001), 87–104.

Tisak, Marie S., and John Tisak, "Expectations and Judgments Regarding Bystanders' and Victims' Responses to Peer Aggression among Early Adolescents," *Journal of Adolescence* 19 (1996), 383–392.

Tracy, Karen, "The Many Faces of Facework," in Howard Giles and W. Peter Robinson (Eds.), *Handbook of Language and Social Psychology* (New York: John Wiley & Sons, 1990), pp. 209–226.

Tracy, Laura, *The Secret among Us: Competition among Women* (Boston: Little Brown, 1991).

Tracy, Sarah J. "When Questioning Turns to Face Threat: An Interactional Sensitivity in 911 Call Taking," *Western Journal of Communication* 66 (2002), 129–157.

Trainer, Mary F., "Forgiveness: Intrinsic, Role-Expected, Expedient, in the Context of Divorce," Doctoral dissertation, Boston University, 1984.

Trzyna, Thomas, "Forgiveness and Time," *Christian Scholar's Review* 22 (1992), 7, 8.

Tutzauer, Frank, and Michael Roloff, "Communication Processes Leading to Integrative Agreements: Three Paths to Joint Benefits," *Communication Research* 15 (1988), 360–380.

Ury, William, *Getting Past No: Negotiating with Difficult People* (New York: Bantam Books, 1991).

Verdeur, Carolee Rada, "Parental Verbal Aggression: Attachment and Dissociation in Adolescents," *Dissertation Abstracts International:* Section B: The Sciences & Engineering, Vol 63(3-B), Sep 2002, p. 1571.

Viscott, David, *Risking* (New York: Pocket Books, 1977).

Volf, Miroslav, "Forgiveness, Reconciliation, and Justice," in Raymond G. Helmick and Rodney L. Petersen (Eds.), *Forgiveness and Reconciliation* (Radnor, PA: Templeton Foundation Press, 2001), pp. 27–49.

Wade, Susan Helen, "The Development of a Scale to Measure Forgiveness," Doctoral dissertation, Fuller Theological Seminary, 1989.

Walker, Lenore "Psychology and Violence against Women," *American Psychologist* 44 (1989), 695–702.

Walker, Velma, and Lynn Brokaw, *Becoming Aware,* 6th Ed. (Dubuque, IA: Kendall Hunt, 1995).

Wall, James A., *Negotiation: Theory and Practice* (Glenview, IL: Scott Foresman, 1985).

Wall, James A., Jr., John B. Stark, and Rhetta L. Standifier, "Mediation: A Current Review and Theory Development," *Journal of Conflict Resolution* 45 (2001), 370–391.

Walsh, Belinda R., and Emma Clarke, "Post-Trauma Symptoms in Health Workers Following Physical and Verbal Aggression," *Work & Stress* 17 (2003), 170–181.

Walster, Elais H., G. William Walster, and Ellen Berscheid, *Equity Theory and Research* (Boston: Allyn & Bacon, 1978).

Wehr, Paul, *Conflict Regulation* (Boulder, CO: Westview Press, 1979).

Weinstein, Eugene A., "The Development of Interpersonal Competence," in D. A. Goslin (Ed.), *Handbook of Socialization and Theory and Research,* (Chicago: Rand McNally, 1969), pp. 753–775.

Weinstock, Jacqueline S., and Lynne A. Bond, "Conceptions of Conflict in Close Friendships and Ways of Knowing among Young College Women: A Developmental Framework," *Journal of Social and Personal Relationships* 17 (2000), 687–696.

Weisinger, Hendrie, *Anger at Work* (New York: William Morrow & Company, 1995), pp. 161–164.

Wilmot, William W., and Joyce Hocker, *Interpersonal Conflict,* 6th Ed. (New York: McGraw Hill, 2001).

Wilmot, William W., and Joyce Hocker, *Interpersonal Conflict,* 7th Ed. (New York: McGraw Hill, 2007).

Wilson, Steven R., Carlos G. Aleman, and Geoff B. Leatham, "Identity Implications of Influence Goals: A Revised Analysis of Face-Threatening Acts and Application to Seeking Compliance with Same-Sex Friends," *Human Communication Research,* 25 (1998), 64–96.

Wilson, Steven R., and Linda L. Putnam, "Interaction Goals in Negotiation," in James A. Anderson (Ed.), *Communication Yearbook 13* (Newbury Park, CA: Sage, 1990).

Winstead, Barbara A., Valerian J. Derlega, Robin J. Lewis, Janis Sanchez-Hucles, and Eva Clark, "Friendship, Social Interaction, and Coping with Stress," *Communication Research* 19 (1992), 193–211.

Witteman, Hal, "Analyzing Interpersonal Conflict: Nature of Awareness, Type of Initiating Event, Situational Perceptions, and Management Styles," *Western Journal of Communication* 56 (1992), p. 264.

Worthington, Everett L. "Unforgiveness, Forgiveness, and Reconciliation and Their Implications for Societal Interventions," in Raymond G. Helmick and Rodney L. Petersen (Eds.), *Forgiveness and Reconciliation* (Radnor, PA: Templeton Foundation Press, 2001), pp. 171–192.

Wuellner, Flora Slosson, *Forgiveness, the Passionate Journey* (Nashville, TN: Upper Room Books, 2001).

Zietlow, Paul H., and Allan L. Sillars, "Life-Stage Differences in Communication during Marital Conflicts," *Journal of Social and Personal Relationships* 5 (1988), 223–245.

Zornoza, Ana, Pilar Ripoll, and Jose M. Peiro, "Conflict Management in Groups that Work in Two Different Communication Contexts: Face-to-Face and Computer-Mediate Communication," *Small Group Research* 33 (2002), 481–508.

INDEX

ABC approach, 201
Accommodation
  as a communication option, 60
  as a conflict strategy, 81
Accounts, 222
Acknowledgment, 224
Adjudication, 251
Aggressive communication, 61–63
Alternative dispute resolution (ADR), 251
Analyzing conflicts, 42–50
  mind-mapping, 48–50
  specific questions for, 43
Anger
  and anger controllers, 207
  and anger-ins, 205
  and anger-outs, 206
  controlling, 207–208
  responding to, 211
  as secondary emotion, 201
  ventilation approach, 205
Anxiety, 136
Apologies, 223–224
Arbitration, 251
Argument, 30
Aspiration point, 117
Assertive communication, 66–70
Attribution theory, 138–140
Autonomous (negative) face, 217
Avoidance
  as a communication option, 60
  as a conflict cycle, 164–167
  as a conflict strategy, 81

Bargaining range, 117
BATNA, 129
Behavioral commitments, 261
Brainstorming, 123
Bridging, 126

Caucus, 259
Chilling effect, 167–169
Climate
  defensive versus supportive, 188–191
  nurturing versus harmful, 178
Collaboration
  as a conflict strategy, 83–84
  phases of, 87–91
  as a preferred strategy, 83–84
Common ground, 260
Communication
  aggressive, 61–63
  apprehension of, 61
  assertive, 66–67
  choosing best option for, 70–72
  considerations, 70
  defined, 53
  linear, 52
  nonassertive, 60–61
  and nonverbal aggression, 62–64
  options for, 59
  passive-aggressive, 65
  rights, 67
  skills, 97, 134
  transactional, 53
  and verbal aggression, 63
Communication rules enforcers, 255
Comparison level, 144
Compensation, 125
Competition, as a conflict strategy, 82
Competitive conflict escalation cycle, 169–171
Competitive negotiation pattern, 118
  escalation factors, 170
Compromise, as a conflict strategy, 82
Concessions
  in bargaining, 119
  in impression management, 223
Conciliation, 251

Conflict
climate, 178
cycle (*see* Cycles of conflict)
defined, 3
destructive, 15
as a fact of life, 9
management versus resolution, 12
metaphors, 7
phase, 153
process view, 13
productive, 15–16
theory (*see* Theories of conflict)
types (*see* Types of conflicts)
viewed negatively, 7
viewed positively, 9
Conflict avoidance cycle, 164–167
Conflict issues
behavioral, 34
defined, 32
intangible, 34
normative/relational, 34
about personality, 34
tangible, 32
Conflict management, defined, 3
Conflict messages
consequences statements, 108
feeling/needs statements, 108
goal statements, 108
I-statements, 106
personalized communication, 106
problematic behavior statements, 108
responsibility, 106–107
Conflict process
differentiation, 159–161
initiation, 159
prelude, 155–159
resolution, 161–162
triggering event, 158
Conflict proneness, 268
Confrontation
defined, 96
steps in, 97
Confrontation avoidance cycle, 164–167
Consequences statement, 108
Cooperative negotiation pattern, 119

Core relational rules, 230
Corrective facework, 221–224
Cost-cutting, 124
Cycles of conflict
confrontation avoidance cycle, 164–167
chilling effect, 167–169
competitive conflict escalation cycle, 169–171
defined, 153
schismogenesis, 164
undesired repetitive pattern (URP), 164

Deception, 230
Defensive coping mechanisms, 199–200
Defensiveness, versus supportiveness, 189–191
Describing the dispute, 259
Destructive conflict, 14–16
Differentiation phase, 159–161
Disagreements, versus interpersonal
conflicts, 23
Disclaimers, 214
Displaced conflict, 25, 200
Dispute, 251
Distress, 198

Ego, 136
Emotional residues, 231
Equifinality, 14
Eustress, 198
Evaluative ability, 47
Excuses, 223
Exit strategy, 85

Face
autonomous (negative) face, 217
corrective facework, 221–224
defined, 216–217
positive face, 217
preventing threats to, 218–220
responding to others, 224–225
supportive facework, 220–221
False conflict, 23
Feeling/needs statements, 108
Forgiveness
advantages of, 235–237
defined, 232

and forgiveness/reconciliation loop, 244
  and moving beyond victimization, 237–239
Fractionation, 129
Framing, 260

Games, 31
Goal-centeredness, 46
Goals, 46
Goal-statement, 108
Gunny-sacking, 69

Harmful conflict climate, 178
Healthy trust, 186
Helping orientation, 230
Hyperstress, 198
Hypostress, 198

Id, 136
Ideal conflict manager, 271
Identity goals, 46
Imagined interactions, 98
Impression management, 215
Incompatible goals, versus means, 5
Inevitability of conflict, 14
Information reception apprehension, 103
Initiation phase, 159
Instrumental goals, 46
Intake, 256
Intangible issues, 34
Interdependence, 4–5
Interests, versus positions, 122
Interpersonal conflicts, 2
  versus mere disagreements, 23
Interpersonal violence, 11
Issues (see Conflict issues)
I-statements, 106

Justifications, 223

Language of cooperation, 128
Latent conflict (see Prelude to conflict)
Lies, 230
Linear model of communication, 52–53
Listening, 50–52

Log-rolling, 125
Loyalty strategy, 85

Mediation, 251
  common ground, 260
  defined, 251
  describing the dispute, 259
  ending the mediation, 263
  final agreement, 261
  formal versus informal, 252–253
  intake, 256
  opening statement, 257
Mediators
  communication rules enforcer, 255–256
  role, 253–255
Meta-conflict perspective, 13
Metaphors, for conflict, 7
Mind-mapping, 48
Minimax principle, 117
Misplaced conflict, 25
Mixed motives, 187

Negative face (see Autonomous face)
Negative view of conflict, 7
Neglect strategy, 85
Negotiation, 117
Neutral speech, 182
Nonassertive communication, 60–61
Nonverbal aggression, 63–64
Nurturing conflict climate, 178

Objective criteria in negotiation, 127
Objective standards as trained incapacity, 48
Offending situation, 222
Ombudsperson, 251
Opening statement, 257
Outcomes, 16

Passive-aggressive communication, 65
Pathological trust, 186
Patterns and cycles in conflict (see Cycles of conflict)
Perception, 5
Personalized communication, 106
Personal stress, 84

Phases of conflict (*see* Conflict process)
Phase theory, 153–154
Physical aggression, 63–64
Playful spirit, 270–271
Positions, versus interests, 122
Positive face, 217
Positive view of conflict, 9
Power
   defined, 178
   imbalance, 179
Powerful, versus powerless speech, 182
Prelude to conflict
   defined, 155
   elements of, 155–158
Principled negotiation, 121
Prisoner's Dilemma (PD), 187–188
Preventive facework, 218
Problematic behavior statement, 108
Problematic situations, 3
Process, 154
Process view of conflict, 13
Productive conflict, 14–16
Psychodynamic theory, 135–137

Rationalization, 200
Reaction formation, 200
Real conflicts, 26
Reconciliation
   defined, 232
   as self-fulfilling prophecy, 242
   steps toward, 239
Redefinition, 47
Reframing, 260
Relational goals, 46
Relational stress, 84
Relational transgressions, 230
Remedy, 222
Repair rituals, 222–224
Repression, 200
Reproach, 222
Resistance point, 117
Resolution phase, 161–162
Responding to impression management, 224–225
Responsibility for behavior, 106–107
Revenge, 232

Rights, 67
Rules, 255

Scarce resources, 117
Schismogenesis, 164
Secondary emotion, 210
Self-fulfilling prophecy, 242
Self-talk
   defined, 98
   effect on stress, 201–203
Sense of urgency, 6
Skill, 134
Social exchange theory, 143–144
S-TLC, 40
   communicating, 53–55
   listening, 50–53
   stopping, 42
   thinking, 43–44
Strategies and tactics
   accommodation, 81
   avoidance, 81
   collaborative, 82
   competitive, 82
   compromise, 82
   defined, 78, 80
   exit, 85
   loyalty, 85
   neglect, 85
   voice, 85
Stress
   ABC approach, 201
   defined, 197
   impact on conflict, 203–204
   personal, 84
   relational, 84
   self-talk and, 201–203
   stressors, 199
   types of, 198
Styles of conflict, versus strategies, 78–80
Sublimation, 200
Superego, 136
Supportive facework, 220
Supportiveness, versus defensiveness, 189–191
Systems theory, 147–148

Tactics (*see* Strategies and tactics)
Tangible issues, 32
Theories of conflict
   attribution, 138–140
   phase, 153–154
   psychodynamic, 135–137
   social exchange, 143–147
   systems, 147–148
   uncertainty, 141–143
Theory, 134
Third-party intervention (*see* Mediation)
Threats and promises, 120
Thromise, 120
Trained incapacities, 46–47
Transactional model of communication, 53–54
Transforming meaning, 232
Triggering events, 158–159
Trust, 184–188
Truth bias, 230
Types of conflicts
   argument, 30
   competition, 29
   conflict game, 31
   false conflict, 23
   mere disagreements, 23
   misplaced conflict, 25
   overblown conflict, 27
   physical aggression, 31
   real conflict, 26
   unimportant conflict, 28
   unreal conflict, 23
   verbal aggression, 31

Uncertainty, 164
Undesired repetitive pattern (URP), 164
Unhealthy trust, 186
Unforgiveness, 232

Victimization, 238
Violence, 63–64
Voice strategy, 85